Angel Capital

Angel Capital

How to Raise Early-Stage
Private Equity Financing

GERALD BENJAMIN, M.S.
JOEL MARGULIS

WITHDRAWN

WILEY
John Wiley & Sons, Inc.

For general information about our other products and services, please contact our Customer Care Department within the United States at (800) 762-2974, outside the United States at (317) 572-3993 or fax (317) 572-4002.

Wiley also publishes its books in a variety of electronic formats. Some content that appears in print may not be available in electronic books. For more information about Wiley products, visit our web site at *www.wiley.com*.

Library of Congress Cataloging-in-Publication Data:

Benjamin, Gerald.
  Angel Capital : how to raise early-stage private equity financing / Gerald Benjamin, Joel Margulis.
    p. cm.
  Includes index.
  ISBN 0-471-69063-5 (cloth)
  1. Angels (Investors). 2. Venture capital. I. Margulis, Joel, 1937– . II. Title.
  HG4751.B458 2005
  658.15'224—dc22

2004019938

Printed in the United States of America

10 9 8 7 6 5 4 3 2 1

To Carol,
For your patience,
support,
encouragement,
and
love

—Gerald Benjamin

To Juliette and Lester Rosenblatt,
who have the right thoughts
and
do the right things

—Joel Margulis

Contents

PART THREE

RESOURCES FOR ENTREPRENEURS RAISING CAPITAL

CHAPTER 8
Alternative Funding Resources in Accessing Angel Capital   **183**

CHAPTER 9
Directory of Alternative Funding Resources   **203**

CHAPTER 10
Building Your Own Database of Angel Investors   **213**

PART FOUR

UNDERSTANDING THE ANGEL INVESTMENT PROCESS

Preface

The number one concern of start-up entrepreneurs and growing small business owners and managers is how to finance their venture. When the personal financial resources of the entrepreneur are exhausted, when the tradition of going to family and friends for "cradle equity" has been thoroughly "worked," and when incurring personal debt from a bank for a loan is no longer a viable option, then raising private capital can be one of the toughest challenges for many entrepreneurs. Whether you have an as-yet-unproven, visionary start-up or already own a small, established company hungry for expansion capital, access to capital on the right terms is critical to your success.

Available for financing are an array of alternative capital resources, but the problems center on which are most appropriate for you and where do you find them. While economic conditions during the previous four years have had an impact on capital availability and increased competition among entrepreneurs for that capital, alternative, nontraditional capital resources are out there.

For some companies—those possessing the right mix of attributes—money will be available; yet for many, understanding where to look, how to present, and how much money is needed comprise just a few of the questions for which business owners are ill-prepared to answer. How do you uncover the dozens of alternative ways to finance your company and prepare for raising capital?

How to identify qualified, hard-to-find private investors who prize their privacy is a case in point. Also, how do you motivate them to read your business plan, to meet with you, and how do you interest them in your venture and your deal? Sometimes asking the less obvious questions is most useful (e.g., when should you not seek angel capital?). Are your current money sources structured most advantageously for you? Have you overpaid? Has your company grown and have you recognized the changing needs of your business? Are you prepared for your company's capital requirements in the next phase of growth?

Capital is the single most important ingredient in getting a venture off the ground. But finding it can be a challenge—particularly if you are running out of funding options. Suppose your venture is too small for institutional players. What do you do once you've exhausted your personal financial resources? Where do you go after the banks, the leasing companies, the venture capital firms have turned you down? Which financing sources are worth exploring and which are not (e.g., conventional lenders, institutional venture capitalists, or business angels?).

The fledgling entrepreneur has long turned to a wealthy uncle or well-heeled friends to provide that cradle equity for the early growth of a promising business. However, it's always been hard for companies to know where to turn to find unrelated investors, and similarly difficult for willing risk takers to find new ventures in which to invest. As a primary source of capital for early-stage and growing companies, the angel capital segment of the investor market is a vital source for today's entrepreneur. But much like the capital they provide, these private equity and debt investors remain true to their name—private. Yet, what we are seeing is the majority of venture capitalists evolving out of early-stage and investing in later-stage, larger deals, thus creating a huge vacuum that business angels have moved in to fill.

Private investors, or business angels, are a primary source of financing for many early-stage deals. However, most small business people have limited knowledge about the angel equity market, business angels, the private equity investment process, and how deals get done. Also, few formal mechanisms exist for bringing angel investors and entrepreneurs together. The strict regulations imposed on offerings, together with the incomplete understanding by entrepreneurs of the complexities of the equity financing process, create the need for the groundbreaking research on what works in *Angel Capital*.

Also, what type of information do investors expect, and how do you effectively present that information? What are private, not institutional, investors looking for? What documentation is needed, and how do you craft your presentation to investors? International Capital Resources' proprietary research in building the largest database of business angel investors in the United States provides valuable insights into the motivations, preferences, and expectations of the selective private equity investor.

Angel Capital is about the manner in which successful entrepreneurs must go about the business of raising capital, the efficient manner of knowing where they are, where they are going, what they are doing, and how they are doing it.

This book describes a model of the funding process uniquely suited to the private placement transaction. A model of this process is the only way to consciously manage the increasingly demanding, exhausting process of efficiently and effectively raising money.

Angel Capital is about the careful planning entrepreneurs must do in order to ensure the success of the capitalization and financial transaction process. This book offers the expertise of the people who have created the largest network of private investors in the country and by the firm that is recognized as the leading expert on accessing and cultivating relationships with angel investors.

In addition, the book is about the secretive, highly specialized segment of the investor market that is a major source of funding for entrepreneurial ventures. It provides intelligence on a segment of high-net-worth investors specially interested in financing earlier-stage, developmental-stage, and expansion-stage ventures.

Angel Capital covers a lot of ground. Part 1, "The Challenge and the Solutions," focuses on how entrepreneurs are creatively addressing the challenge of practicing capitalism in the face of a significant capital gap. We suggest how they should structure their search for capital as they confront an "inefficient" market, and provide a proven strategy for taking control of the capital-raising program.

Part 2, "Understanding the Angel Investor," explores angel investors— who they are and where they can be found. In addition, we present an overview of alternative sources of capital. A comparison is made between angel investors and the institutional investor community, correcting the misconception that the institutional community is the primary source of funding for early-stage deals. Then, from scores of presentations and interviews, we turn to what private investors look for in a deal—their criteria and their expectations. We explain who the private investors are and how they relate to others in the capital market.

In addition, we present the results from a major new study of 60 angel investors designed and conducted by the authors for this text. This study will further clarify, in the investors' own words, what they seek in early-stage private equity transactions. This information will help entrepreneurs work more effectively with investors in selling illiquid "story" securities. Investors also share their wisdom in candid insights regarding the venture process and, in particular, about valuation and due diligence. These are critical topics for entrepreneurs as they try to understand the more cynical view of investors following the "dot-bomb" fiasco, as well as the public equity stock market meltdown, resulting in losses in their portfolios.

We also reproduce here our pioneering typology on the primary angel investor "types," acknowledged by many researchers and educators to be the major contribution to the angel investor literature. And we show how entrepreneurs can use this information to better position themselves with investor prospects in presenting and selling their deals.

Part 3, "Resources for Entrepreneurs Raising Capital," deals with a set of tools entrepreneurs will find invaluable in the search for investors. We provide a comprehensive historical introduction to alternative funding resources, particularly those related to angel investors, notorious for prizing their privacy. These resources and tools—past and present—will help entrepreneurs deal with the formidable tasks they face. We share our own resources and that of others on new directions emerging as sources of investors and capital. Next, we have assembled one of the most current and comprehensive directories of alternative capital resources in the United States. Using our unique classification system, you, the entrepreneur, will be able to locate the full range of directories, software, incubators, finance conferences, investor meetings, venture forums, venture capital clubs, offline and online networks, and financial intermediaries. As you proceed thorough the financing process—from planning and developing documentation through presentation, investor introductions, and professional counsel—you may need to keep track of all the investors and others who can help you, a daunting task in itself, especially because the funding venture never ends. It just changes form from one type of financing to another. For this reason, we discuss setting up your own investor database.

Part 4, "Understanding the Angel Investment Process," describes the new capital-raising reality facing entrepreneurs now and for the foreseeable future. Investors have altered their investment approach, responding to losses they incurred, placing new emphasis on risk assessment, hedging, and co-investment strategies. Also, we will help entrepreneurs to appreciate the investors' "return to basics," as well as their renewed vigor in attending to the aspects of the early-stage venture investment process—a marked change from their lackadaisical approach that characterized the late 1990s. In this part of the book, we pay special attention to sensitizing you to your preparation for more intense interaction on comprehensive due diligence, aggressive valuation negotiations, stricter investor-oriented deal terms, and discussions about potential exit strategies because of reduced initial public offering market activity.

Finally, in the Appendices, we have assembled some stand-alone tools. The entrepreneur will find a comprehensive How-To Workbook on drafting and presenting an investor-oriented business plan, assembled by one of Silicon Valley's most respected business planning consultants. Also included is a legal primer on securities laws issues for nonlawyers pertaining to private placements, and a comprehensive glossary relevant to entrepreneurial finance and venture capital investment banking. Last, the authors have gathered from their own libraries a comprehensive suggested reading list for those who wish to expand their understanding of the angel capital topic.

THE ENTREPRENEUR

Entrepreneurs in need of capital need this book. This book is about initiating the process of raising capital for companies at earlier stages of development and for whom traditional financing resources are not available. For the entrepreneur who has failed at these traditional sources of financing, *Angel Capital* offers a step-by-step formula for reaching the highly secretive and selective market of the private investor, a segment of the investor market that has become a major source of funding for entrepreneurial ventures.

Entrepreneurs include those people raising capital on their own, CEOs of ongoing businesses looking for nontraditional financing, and owners of small businesses failing to qualify for loans from traditional sources and seeking expansion capital to grow their businesses. This category also includes owners of financially troubled companies who seek capital to reorganize and inventors who desire capital to commercialize their technologies. Furthermore, the entrepreneurial group encompasses people who have acquired technologies through various research centers and defense conversion centers that look for financing to commercialize those technologies. Finally, this group includes company employees who dream about starting their own business.

We present guidelines not only for making a deal financeable, enabling entrepreneurs to evaluate the workability of their transaction, but also for developing a capitalization strategy for the funding process uniquely suited to the angel-driven, private placement transaction. Entrepreneurs must learn to efficiently and conscientiously manage the increasingly demanding, exhausting process of raising money. We have tried to define the problem and offer nontraditional resources for those companies that merit funding. If entrepreneurs don't know where they're going in trying to raise alternative forms of capital for their venture and have no clear road map to point the way, they will likely end up in a place they did not expect to be and do not recognize. *Angel Capital* provides a road map to financing on a path that otherwise would remain tortuous.

Angel Capital is not a dry compendium of alternative forms of financing or a public domain directory of out-of-date funding sources available in any library. It is, instead, a set of tools that enables entrepreneurs to (1) determine whether private investors are a workable and appropriate source of capital for their deal, (2) increase their awareness of the private investor perspective so they can frame an investment proposal with the greatest chance for success, and (3) develop a winning strategy to locate, contact, and establish relationships with angel investors.

Few entrepreneurs relish raising capital. Not having been academically or experientially trained for the task, they view it as an onerous activity. Still, it is an activity inextricably woven into their job description and inextricably woven into their chances for success. The troublesome task of raising capital is simply inescapable. *Angel Capital* analyzes the problem, then presents strategies for addressing it. But more important, the book provides entrepreneurs with tools for articulating their vision, enabling them to move forward in the private market, furnishing contacts with which to begin their search for capital. However, too often the entrepreneurs are ill-prepared, not having built their management team, prepared for valuation and due diligence, or written their business plan. In a word, they have not developed a capitalization strategy. This book presents a workable capitalization strategy.

For entrepreneurs, *Angel Capital* also provides protocol on how to cost-effectively begin developing their own proprietary info-base of high-net-worth individuals. The book contains a directory to the major resources that have resulted in substantial investments, plus a complete state-of-the-art syllabus on writing and presenting your business plan. In addition, the book contains exhibits that entrepreneurs can use in educating the rest of the players in their company.

Entrepreneurs must understand how different the process is for approaching the private investor. They must know where they are in the sales process—whether prospecting or screening investors, getting ready for a first presentation, or doing due diligence on the investors' ability to invest. They must know where they are in the transaction process—whether going through the negotiation process and structuring the transaction, completing the transaction with attorneys and accountants and other financial and legal advisers, or managing the relationship with investors after they have invested money. In the maze of emotion, complexity, and hard work, they can get lost.

Finally, this book will help the entrepreneur become a more informed consumer of financial intermediary services. Once entrepreneurs have exhausted their personal network, reaching out to the private market can be time consuming and expensive. People starting ventures haven't the luxury of time, especially when they are without intellectual property protection or significant market lead. Nor do they usually possess the requisite collateral, cash flow, or assets to sustain an open-ended funding program.

Finding private investors is all about building relationships with self-made millionaires, 90 percent of whom are worth between $1 million and $10 million, people who may have owned their own businesses, and are successful because they know what to invest in and wish to broaden their investments. This book provides resources and contact information so people can get started in the process of financing their ventures on their own more efficiently, bestowing on them some of the most powerful tools they will need, while saving them thousands of dollars in costly mistakes and unnecessary fees.

Because private investors prize their privacy and because they do not *have* to invest—as do professional investors, fund managers, and bankers—the traditional models and methods of searching for financing simply will not work in penetrating this market. Books presently flooding the mass market and business literature advocate models for accessing professional venture capitalists, venture leasing, or Small Business Association loans, but these approaches will not help in accessing the private investor. So the entrepreneur has to understand the private financing process, a process completely different from that of applying for a loan, or seeking out professional venture capital or funds from professional money managers, who are paid a fee to manage the institutional money. *Angel Capital* gives valuable insight into the investor's motivation, preferences, and expectations. In their own words, these investors provide a set of guidelines on how to approach them in ways that won't run afoul of what is legitimate and appropriate.

This personal testimony by the investors themselves regarding what the active private investor looks for in a deal allows the entrepreneur to know—without wasting time pursuing the wrong investors—whether his or her venture meets crucial investment criteria. If the venture does meet the criteria of particular investors, this book becomes a valuable resource as the entrepreneur proceeds to search for them, stimulate their interest, and establish contact and build relationships with them.

The capital-raising process cannot be successfully navigated in ignorance. This book offers the entrepreneur an efficient means for tapping into capital and doing so quickly. There is the need for tools—understandable, realistic tools—that will help the entrepreneur, particularly in early-stage ventures, to embark on fund-raising, capital-finding tasks. The defining factor of the entrepreneur is the ability to raise money. When entrepreneurs can raise money, they become credible.

UNDERSTANDING THE PRIVATE INVESTOR

This book is also about investors and the process they go through in higher-risk transactions, a form of investing that allows the investor to influence the outcome of the investment. This highly selective segment of the investor market that *Angel Capital* addresses has become a major source of capital for these particular types of transactions.

However, this is not a market tracked by economists or written about in the *Wall Street Journal, Fortune,* or *Forbes.* It is, nonetheless, a huge market by any standard.

This private investor market is, in fact, a principal source of capital, contributing to the financial stability of smaller companies that make up a sizable source of the tax base, jobs, and technological innovations in the United States. Successful investors deliver insight directly into the process of high-risk, high-return investing. Through them, we have captured what constitutes effective ways of reaching out to these types of investors. A sizable percentage of the 2.5 million U.S. households comprising this market are prospective targets for early-stage deals seeking financing.

Included in the private investor category are, first, the high-net-worth private investors who choose a target of interest in companies operating at particular stages of development and in industries with which they are familiar. There are also the fund managers and managers of venture capital funds who must screen thousands of deals a year to identify those that the firm will invest in. Fund-raisers raising their own funds or trying to put together a pool of money to invest would also fall within the category of private investor.

As we have said, little information exists on direct investing, an esoteric, idiosyncratic arena in which high-net-worth private investors choose a target of interest in companies operating at the stages of development and in industries with which they are familiar. Moreover, as we have likewise mentioned, private investors prize their privacy—a major reason for their interest in this arena in the first place. Through the research we have provided here, entrepreneurs can learn to appreciate the private investors' perspective.

Private investors, after all, are just that—private; by design they are difficult to reach. They safeguard their privacy, expressly avoiding any form of solicitation. Moreover, these private investors do not have to invest. They invest with caution because they are risk-averse. But they also invest with a broader range of criteria beyond internal rate of return and the return on investment normally associated with the institutional or professional investor. These are distinguishing characteristics. Furthermore, investors are, in the words of one of them, "very smart" and appreciate those who deal with them honestly and straightforwardly, and who understand what they are going through.

No other resource currently available comprehensively covers what these particular investors look for, nor does any other resource contain critical information dispensed by the investors themselves on what they are looking for in an investment and just how they prefer to be approached.

Neither the challenge nor the problem is new. But the formulation of our strategy is. This so-called inefficient private placement market seems unorganized. International Capital Resources (ICR) and the authors have penetrated this huge but hidden, misunderstood market. The authors have placed on the reader's plate a meaty analysis of angel investors as alternative sources of capital—what they look like and what they look for in a deal. But most important in looking at the private investor is the typology, a review of the different types of private investors. Nothing like it has ever been compiled before.

Angel Capital is about our experience in creating and qualifying one of the largest private investor networks in the country and about what works and doesn't work. This book is about our experience in working with more than 500 entrepreneurs a year. It's about our experience in building a proprietary database of private investors, engaging them in conversations, and in arranging their presentations at forums over the past few years and conducting research on their criteria, expectations, experience, and preferences. It's about bringing to bear our experience in penetrating this highly lucrative market for entrepreneurs seeking capital.

Finally, *Angel Capital* is important for macroeconomic reasons: Larger companies are reducing their workforces, not creating jobs. But successful early-stage companies hold the promise of technological advancement and the increasing competitiveness of American industry. Such companies also possess the potential for jobs in our recessionary and recovering economy, both nationally and, particularly, regionally. Where do these companies go when banks have turned them away? Where do these companies go when they don't have collateral and cash flow? The Small Business Administration's lending practices are restrictive, and the venture capital industry has moved out of early-stage investing for economic and demographic reasons.

Private investors have stepped into the breach, attempting to fill the void. Thus, *Angel Capital* debunks the misconception that the venture capital industry is the primary source of capital for these early-stage deals. Because of a shakeout in the industry, large funds have resulted. Large funds must make large investments in order to put their money to work. Moreover, the compensation structure in the venture capital industry is such that the funds are rewarded for the money under management: One to three percent of the money under management is paid to the general partners. So not a lot of economic incentive exists to raise a small fund, nor is there a lot of time to do so. From the venture capital industry's point of view, it seems better to work with a couple of institutional investors with a couple of large deals than it is to work with scores of smaller investors or scores of much riskier entrepreneurial ventures requiring nurturing to develop the business.

Angel Capital is not a dry textbook sporting different financing methods that have no applicability. It offers an inside look at the emergence and making of a capital market that holds the prospect for the financing of people's dreams. This book is not designed as an encyclopedic, shelf-bound dust collector but rather a useful manual, crafted solely to benefit entrepreneurs in planning, managing, organizing, executing, and monitoring the effectiveness of what they are doing and how they are doing it, where they are and whither they are tending, as they attempt to penetrate one of America's largest capital markets.

The entire process of private transactions is covered, from investors' developing the initial deal flow through the harvesting of returns. As Warren Buffett has declared, what counts is not the size of a motor but its degree of efficiency. This is a book that efficient entrepreneurs will want nearby in this new millennium.

Acknowledgments

We are deeply grateful to the very best of literary agents, John Willig, Literary Services, Inc. of Barnegat, New Jersey, who connected us to the people at John Wiley & Sons. We thank Bill Falloon at Wiley for his support and cooperation. We also wish to acknowledge the superb contribution made by William D. Evers, Esq., Attorney at Law, San Francisco, California, for his "Legal Primer on Securities Law Issues for Nonlawyers." Also, we recognize the excellent "Manual for Drafting and Presenting an Investor-Oriented Business Plan" prepared by consultant Charles Roedel of Roedel and Company, San Jose, California.

Introduction

It is a part of probability that many improbable things will happen.

—Aristotle, *Poetics*

In writing this book, we intend to make probable many of the improbables that every entrepreneur faces in raising capital for his or her venture.

In spite of a recessionary economy, slow economic recovery, and a persistent bear stock market since the tech meltdown over three years ago, a number of trends suggest that the fundamentals of the private equity market prevail. These trends include the continued fervor of individuals to start businesses in America, a pool of investors investing a portion of their portfolio in private equities to offset poor public equity returns, improved portfolio performance and recovery of their wealth, improved survival rates for start-ups, and reduced costs of starting up a business.

According to the Panel Study of Entrepreneurial Dynamics sponsored by the Kaufman Foundation, entrepreneurship remains strong in the United States. About 6 in every 100 adults are engaged in trying to start new firms. That means approximately 10 million adults are attempting to begin start-up companies. New business creation is a fundamental indicator of entrepreneurial activity in the U.S. economy, according to the study authors. These 10 million adults represent more than 10 percent of all nonagricultural workers in the country, estimates the Small Business Administration (SBA).

Regardless of recessionary times, investors face no shortage of deals for investors to review. In 2001, 3.5 million businesses were started in the United States. Only 950,000 of these were purchased or inherited. The rest were new start-up companies.

What we see here is a major trend in our society toward entrepreneurial behavior. Instead of having a resume handy, many seem to have a business plan in his or her top desk drawer, creating a diverse array of investment possibilities. Little wonder that one in three American households includes someone who has started, tried to start, or helped fund a small business. Entrepreneurial behavior is a major trend in our society.

Along with this growth trend in dreaming, potential dream makers are growing in numbers and shifting their investment orientation as well. Despite the volatile markets (a stock market loss in 2001 of $1.3 trillion) and economic downturn, the combined wealth of high-net-worth Americans increased 3 percent last year to $26.2 trillion. These are individuals with financial assets of at least $1 million, excluding real estate. Substantial wealth exists and is available for investment regardless of public stock market losses. In addition, in 2002, 3.3 million U.S. households with a net worth of $1 million to $10 million—excluding real estate and representing those households most likely to provide early-stage angel investment—have invested approximately 83 percent of their investable assets in equity-related transactions, rather than putting them into mortgages or equivalents. One billion dollars per week was being invested into equity by the first quarter of 2004. While there are five times more offerings than investment, the equity market remains strong. According to the IRS, 1 taxpayer in 15 now has a six-figure income. In 2000, 8.3 million households met this criterion, up 15 percent over the previous year. There is no shortage of risk capital.

Where are they coming from? Whether it's the transfer of wealth from the old to the young, technology entrepreneurs, loyal employees who have cashed out tradable stock, or middle-aged casualties of corporate downsizing with large severance payments, a significant number of individuals with the requisite financial capability do engage in direct investing. While the number of qualifying households may seem large, correcting the number to identify those willing to assume the risks associated with venture investing results in approximately one million households having the discretionary net worth to invest directly in early-stage deals. Many of these investors have already realized significant profits from other early-stage, private equity investments—and need no prodding! What we must not forget is that 90 percent of all U.S. millionaires are self-made, not inheritors of wealth; therefore, they know innately that they can derive profits and returns from successful start-up ventures.

Sophisticated investors understand that to ensure adequate returns for retirement or other objectives, a diversified portfolio is necessary, incorporating alternative asset classes in addition to public stocks, bonds, and cash investments. Furthermore, investors plotting a recovery strategy to get their portfolios back on track understand that they will benefit from the historically strong performance in private equities to offset disappointing returns in public equities. They are aware of a well-documented low correlation between venture capital and large public stocks. It has not escaped these investors that companies such as General Electric, Ford, Hewlett-Packard, Intel, and Microsoft were all founded during recessionary or depressed economic times, as reported in *USA Today*.

Entrepreneurs might believe that a litany of reasons is responsible for high-net-worth individuals to be disillusioned and perhaps ignore this reality: September 11, the "dot-bomb" fiasco and tech stock bubble burst, stock market volatility, low interest rates, a stagnant initial public offering (IPO) market, the return to government deficit spending, overpaid CEOs running public corporations like casinos, electronic speculators, predatory hedge funds, fraudulent public stock values and financial statements, deceptive investment bank shenanigans, faithless analysts, collusive accountants and financing of the securities market through brokers, and creation of speculative vehicles to securitize loans and income streams. While your suspicion of financial and regulatory integrity is clearly justified, these events didn't just happen overnight and are not likely to quickly fade away. There is, however, a more positive side.

The impact of innovative technology on our lives is axiomatic. Our lives will remain intertwined by technological developments in education, computer hardware and software, telecommunications, medical science, and media entertainment. The U.S. economy remains larger than the combined economies of Japan, Germany, Britain, France, and Italy, and the U.S. continues to develop and export technology and knowledge in support of these major industrialized economies. Sixty-six percent of all technological innovation comes from small, private companies, start-ups not spin-offs, 99 percent of which are financed by founders, family and friends, and, of course, angel investors. Angels are early- and expansion-stage private equity investors who invest their own money directly into sustainable ventures in industries they know and understand to earn capital appreciation for their loss of use of capital.

As cited in the Kauffman Foundation study, "The National Commission on Entrepreneurship documented the entrepreneurial beginnings of 197 of the Fortune 200 corporations and found the formation of new industries and the development of most new technologies highly dependent on the creation of new firms." Private investors, particularly angels, understand the potential in this finding.

Another factor influencing the creation of investment opportunities is the tremendous improvement in survival rates among small companies in the United States. Major studies support the statistic that approximately 65 percent of all start-ups initiated over the past five years will survive six to ten years. Given that the mean hold time for angel investments range from five to eight years (depending on the particular industry), the chances of investors getting their investment back and seeing a return on investment has, compared with ten years ago, significantly improved.

Another study of those companies that have grown to $5 million to $10 million in annual sales indicates that 30 percent grew from start-ups, not from companies that were purchased or inherited, or through ownership transfer. In addition, of those companies that closed or discontinued, only 47 percent closed because they were losing money. Fifty-two percent of those companies that closed or discontinued did so while breaking even or showing a profit and were closed for other economic reasons.

The last economic trend influencing entrepreneurialism is that the cost of starting a company is decreasing. In a recent study of *Inc.*'s 500 fastest-growing companies, 78 percent surveyed reported that the seed capital to launch their venture was $100,000 or less. Only 22 percent required more than that to get off the ground. ICR research discloses that to start a company that successfully grows to $2 million to $5 million a year in sales will require an angel round after cradle equity from family, friends, and founders of only $500,000. To start a company that will grow to $5 million to $10 million in sales, the preinstitutional Series A rounds are averaging $700,000.

In spite of burgeoning entrepreneurship and ample numbers of promising ventures, an available pool of capital, and a relatively high probability of venture success, there still exists a capital gap. A number of surveys of start-up and small businesses confirm that financing the venture is a major challenge and that many are struggling to meet their growth capital needs.

Entrepreneurs may be confused by the different studies published that estimate the number of angel investors in the United States. But we have to remember that all studies are estimates and extrapolations from available data pried from a group that prizes its privacy, a group that is not legally required to publicly disclose its activity. Still, research from Off-Road Capital in 2001 reveals that more than a quarter of a million high-net-worth individuals invested an estimated $65 billion into at least 30,000 private companies, a number that hugely eclipsed the venture capital firms' investment in the same year, both in terms of quantity of capital and number of investments.

A study published by Josh Friedman estimated the number of active angels in 2002 at 300,000. Jeffrey Sohl of the Center for Venture Research has estimated angel investing to be $10 billion to $20 billion per year in as many as 30,000 deals. We estimate the number of sophisticated active angel investors at more than 400,000 in the United States, plus many more who take on a passive role. Active investors are those who have acquired the proper tools and skills through training and experience to develop deal flow, manage due diligence, negotiate and structure deals, value early-stage companies, oversee and advise companies postinvestment, and harvest returns by guiding their investee companies to liquidity. Of course, passive investors participate in more formal structures, such as investment clubs or funds, but still others are present as lead investors ready to take on a more active role.

An angel is a private, nonrelated investor, investing their own money, typically $25,000 to $ 250,000 per investment, alone or in syndication with other private investors. These investors focus on young, early-stage ventures with significant potential for growth. They invest primarily through equity transactions and seek substantial capital appreciation, as we have noted, over a five- to eight-year hold time for their risk and loss of use of that capital. Angel money is not cradle equity from family and friends, founder's capital, or bootstrap capital. Angel money is not loans from banks or investment from institutional or professional money management investment firms. Angels do not form a monolithic group. Angels maintain their uniqueness while participating in a mutual dynamic. This reminds us of the philosophical question John Paul Sartre wrestled with in much of his writing and tried to answer with his concept of the "group in fusion," a convention in which we invest meaning to a number of people (in our case, angel investors) collectively while knowing full well that no label can adequately identify the individuals in that group. In our own research, we have identified at least ten types of angel investors: the socially responsible investor, the partner investor, the deep-pocket investor, the barter investor, the manager investor, and others.

Active angels invest in industries they know and understand through their direct experience. They focus on fast-growing companies. Angels also trade knowledge and experience for equity, or get more actively involved in a venture, even if they are not the lead investors but can take on a variety of roles in this capacity. Angels manage risk in early-stage investing through unique hedging strategies, and have keen knowledge in all phases of the private equity investment process. Angels may be proactive or passive investors and, if proactive, also invest time and energy in such roles as director, advisory board member, consultant, adviser, counselor, and may perform a functional role on a temporary or interim basis, for example, as CFO or CEO. Angels, unlike many institutional counterparts, focus on building successful sustainable companies, not just creating wealth through successful exit.

Angel investment is the cornerstone of the economic strength of our nation. There can be no capitalism without capital. The tremendous economic benefits that we have accrued over the past fifteen years have been largely due to the infusion of angel capital into early-stage companies and the fostering of entrepreneurial, small business. The statistics speak for themselves: Small companies represent 47 percent of all sales, 51 percent of the private gross domestic product, 52 percent of all business net worth, and 99 percent of all U.S. companies. In 2001, small firms contributed approximately 60 percent of the jobs created in our country. In addition, based on recent studies, 55 percent of all innovations comes through these small companies, helping to keep the United States globally competitive—a product innovation level twice the number of innovations per employee as that of large public companies.

So if the entrepreneurs are present, and the investors are available and able to understand the present opportunity, and if funding is not overly capital intense and potential for venture survival is high, why—the entrepreneur is left to ask—is it so difficult to raise money for the venture? The primary reason for the capital gap is the inefficient marketplace for illiquid securities.

We remain continually amazed that in spite of the scope of detrimental factors, angel investing optimistically continues to flourish. Here's a rundown of some of those barriers: inadequate capital gains tax incentives—particularly inadequate compared to similar incentives in other industrialized countries; a scarcity of legitimate, well-organized investment networks to facilitate bringing together investors and ventures; downsized lending by banks as a result of stricter enforcement of banking regulations; and educational institutions that have failed to provide investors and entrepreneurs with an understanding of private equity finance transactions. Additional failures lie in the lack of effort to spread the knowledge about what is involved in planning for capitalization and investment; and a climate of legal and regulatory constraints literally strangling the free flow of information between ethical, well-intentioned entrepreneurs and sophisticated self-made, affluent private investors possessing the experience, analytical skills, and understanding of the risks involved when they make their own informed investment decisions.

Furthermore, in this inhospitable environment, a highly inefficient marketplace exists for early-stage company stock. This inefficient marketplace is characterized by a lack of analysts, severely limited market information, and tremendous cost and inconvenience for both buyers and sellers. Assistance from professionals is extremely expensive for this market because of a lack of standardization of transaction types. Investors know the myth of short-term liquidity. Efforts by groups like the Pacific Stock Exchange to create exchange modes have all been failures, and in the midst of all of this, the investor must try to infer valuation solely from "blue sky" forecasts and projections. And the search for evaluation of and completion of transactions requires considerable time, energy, and money.

Last, many securities industry professionals believe that the companies involved in these transactions are not investable because they lack standard and consistent deal structures, circumstances that raise transaction costs, and create high liability exposure per transaction for brokers. In sum, elements of the market wherein the entrepreneur has chosen to raise capital are characterized by subjectivity, lack of formalized structures, and those "blue sky" financials—each and all of which represent weighty challenges to thorough due diligence. When you combine these circumstances with visceral investor cynicism—emanating and reinforced in large measure from their portfolio losses in the dot-com and telecom fiascos—entrepreneurs, able to "walk a mile" in the investors' shoes, begin to get a feel for the challenges investors face.

While this book is about raising private equity, we admit to a bias: that angel capital—despite the geopolitical and economic situation—remains the primary source of funding for entrepreneurs seeking early-stage financing, after family, friends, and the founders themselves. Five other trends provide justification for seriously considering alternative capital resources, resources that reemphasize that angels ought to remain the entrepreneurs' first capital consideration.

These trends reflect important new developments in professional venture capital, corporate venture capital, institutional venture capital, valuations of private companies, and the state of the IPO market. For companies needing large sums of capital, in the appropriate industries, with seasoned management, and with believable financial projections suggesting very high revenue potential, the professional venture capitalist is an option. But venture capital fund-raising, investment distribution, and returns have been adversely effected by the economic downturn in the past three years. As smaller, less successful funds have succumbed, estimates are that 50 percent of venture capital firms will disappear within the next five years, while venture capital fund size among survivors will continue to increase in response.

Venture capitalists also are continuing the trend of increasing fund size because of changes in the law, changes that permit investment of retirement funds into venture capital transactions, increase money management services for larger institutional investors, promise of lucrative fees associated with managing larger funds, and to cover rising overhead transaction and research costs. These ingredients are also contributing to a corresponding increase in the size of the mean investment in early-stage deals.

Commonly, we see a $500 million fund that must focus on larger, later-stage deals and other late-stage situations, for example, leveraged buyouts, companies trading at a discount to asset value, large private investments into public companies, recaps, and roll-ups. This trend is supported by statistics of the number of Series A deals by the venture capital industry. In the first two quarters of 2003, the entire industry completed a total of only 291 transactions. By 2003, Series A rounds had declined to 21.3 percent of total venture capital investment, compared to 45.6 percent in 1999. Also, an implication of larger fund size is a corresponding change in mean deal size. The mean deal size in 2001 was $8.5 million, and the median deal in the same year reached $12.2 million. These transaction sizes involved much more capital than do the launching of most early-stage ventures. To the entrepreneur, this means that the average amount of capital per partner has swelled to such levels that partners can each work on only two to four deals per year.

So the state of affairs surrounding venture capital has changed drastically. Prior to recent developments, we were all aware of increasing fund sizes, a circumstance that influences both the size of mean investment and the stage of development of companies attractive to the industry. We are also aware that many venture capital firms are nursing troubled investee companies, and reinvesting time and money in their own portfolio companies; and they have a penchant for specific industries, such as wireless, infrastructure, semiconductor, enterprise software, life science, and so forth. Larger investments translate to fewer deals, carrying with them salient legal and economic incentives. For example, it takes just as much time for a venture capital firm to transact a small deal as it takes for a large deal: a small deal typically is not standardized, is more costly, and perhaps inherently carries increased legal liabilities. Recent research by a number of respected industry associations demonstrates that because of larger amounts of capital under management per partner in each fund, partners have less time available for investment start-ups. Making the early-stage, higher-risk, smaller investments less attractive to the venture capital industry are the rising costs of smaller deals and the fee structure of those firms that derive a small percentage administration fee to be deducted from the money under management.

As a result, venture capital fund raising has taken a nosedive. In 2001, 331 funds raised $40 billion, but in 2000, 653 funds garnered $107 billion. In 2002, 108 venture funds raised $6.9 billion, but because 26 firms returned $5 billion in uninvested money to their limited partners, the net amount of new capital raised was just $1.9 billion—a drop of 95 percent from the previous year! Today, while unprecedented, more funds are releasing limited partners from their commitments, bowing to pressure from investors to scale back the billion-dollar-plus megafunds raised during the tech boom.

Venture capital investment is declining from its high three years ago. Full-year 2002 venture capital spending totaled about $21 billion, the lowest full-year sum since 1997's $15 billion, and early-stage investing was effected more than later-stage investing. The 756 Series A deals in 2002 fell below 1995 levels, and most of these Series A rounds went to serial entrepreneurs from venture capital firms they knew and had previously made money for, explains PricewaterhouseCoopers/Thompson Venture Economics/National Venture Capital Association Money Tree Survey. By comparison, total venture capital investments in 2000 were $89.8 billion.

Although starting to show signs of gains, venture capital returns have been down. As reported by Thompson Venture Economics U.S. Private Equity Performance Index, which measures cash flows and returns for more than 1,700 U.S. venture capital and private equity partnerships, the 20-year return for all private equity has slipped to 15.5 percent. Venture capital fund returns plunged by an average of 28 percent in 2001, marking the first calendar year loss since venture capital firms began tracking fund returns in 1980. The good news is that venture funds posted positive annual returns in 2003 for the first time in three years, returning 8.1 percent for one year, likewise reported by Thompson Venture Economics and the National Venture Capital Association. Funds closed in 1998, during the bubble peak, have returned just 55 percent of investor capital, whereas funds closed in 1996 had returned 361 percent in the same period. For the three years ending December 2003, venture funds suffered an average loss of 19 percent. There are significant implications for funds' survival and the ability to raise further funds as a result of these return statistics.

Corporate venture capital backing of start-ups has tumbled. Corporations with venture capital investment divisions invested only $143 million in them during the first quarter of 2001, that figure down 81 percent from the $2 billion invested in the first quarter of 2000. In 2000, corporate investors accounted for 17 percent of all venture capital investment. By June 2001, 45 percent of corporate venture capital arms had shut their doors.

Institutional venture capital activity is decreasing as well. Institutional venture capital divisions—in other words, banks that have venture capital portfolios—have written off millions and had to lay off staff. In the late 1990s after short-term interest reached record highs on the New York Stock Exchange and Nasdaq, and bank cash as a percentage of portfolio hit a two-year high, a number of banks felt impelled to enter the venture capital market, especially on the heel of changes in Securities Exchange Commission Prudent Man Legal Rules. This was done without an honest and full appreciation of all the risks and skills necessarily involved in this type of investing.

Valuations by venture capital firms of early-stage companies are plummeting. Venture capital firms face a level of reasonable expectations regarding valuation. PricewaterhouseCoopers' Money Tree Report calculates that valuations are down from three years ago, at levels as low as one-to-three times revenues. Median premoney valuations dropped from $37 million in 2000 to $12 million in 2003; and for seed stage from $6 million in 2001 to $3 million in the same time period. For first round, the valuations on done deals dropped from $14 million to $9 million. Because private companies are priced only when they seek new rounds of funding, the private sector lags behind public valuation trends by roughly 6 to 18 months. So valuation statistics on done deals can be expected to decline further over the next year or two.

Finally, the IPO market has tanked. Venture capital firms have felt the impact of an IPO market that has dried up and is in full retreat. And, as a result, the liquidity doesn't exist in the immediate future to absorb venture-backed companies at the rate of investment in 2000 and 2002. IPO.com of New York cites that in 1998, 230 IPOs raised $29 billion. IPO activity then skyrocketed to 526 IPOs, raising $99 billion in 1999. In 2000, it skidded to

427 IPOs, raising $102 billion. Then, activity dropped precipitously—79 percent, in fact, to 89 IPOs, raising a mere $41 billion in 2001. Could it have gotten worse? Yes. The IPO count in 2002 was 57, raising only $20 million, only 12 of which venture-backed companies. And as bad as these statistics read, it got even worse: in 2003, just 12 IPOs for the entire year, many of which are now trading below their offering price.

It is true that less than five percent of venture capital deals provide liquidity to limited partners through IPOs; however, it's important to note that IPOs generate very high returns, and that 63 companies withdrew IPOs in 2001. With the worst IPO market in the past 20 years, we are indeed enmeshed in an IPO "nuclear winter," due, in our opinion, to dismal after-market performances of an immature crop of companies, particularly dot-coms, foisted onto a greedy and blindly enthusiastic public. Brokerages and fund managers are now paying the price in reputation of unloading the risks of these unsustainable private investments onto an unsuspecting, gullible, trusting public market.

Traditional venture capital firms currently hold $80 billion in uninvested capital, and, along with corporate and institutional venture capital firms and IPOs, remain sources of capital. But the astute entrepreneur, struggling to bring his or her vision to reality, cannot rely solely on these sources of capital. As some entrepreneurs cope with this shortfall in capital availability, they will turn to bootstrapping—or customer financing if the company is operating. For some, these strategies might work. But for those with more immediate and intensive capital needs, their only option is outside financing. True, they can reduce burn rates to postpone the inevitable, but sooner or later, that hungry capital gorilla will begin pounding the door. Unfortunately, some will be denied financing, having wasted five to seven years of their life working for a salary, without ever having realized it.

Although important, these alternative sources of private equity capital can provide only a fraction of the capital needed to fuel the growth of this rapidly expanding sector of our economy during a time when society is shifting from a manufacturing, labor-based economy to an entrepreneurial, knowledge-based, technology-driven economy, outsourcing off-shore of such jobs not withstanding. Also, this capital for the most part does not help to reduce the capital shortfall for very early-stage companies that lack cash flows and that require relatively smaller financing amounts.

The fact is that the majority of all small businesses, start-ups, and expansion ventures in North America and a significant portion in Europe continue to be financed initially by the founders, their families, and their friends. After this initial funding, in the United States 90 percent of all rounds of financing under $1 million and 80 percent of all dollars invested in early-stage companies will continue to be provided by about 250,000 to 400,000 active business angel investors each year.

Business angel investors have been referred to as the invisible or hidden market. However, for early-stage private companies experiencing sales under $5 million, serving nonglobal markets, seeking smaller rounds (typically $250,000 to $1,500,000), lacking patented technologies, and resting among industries not currently the rage of Wall Street, Sand Hill Road, and Route 128, angel investors remain the primary source of funding for early- and expansion-stage capital.

Amazingly, all this investing occurs regardless of (1) inadequate capital gains tax incentives, particularly inadequate when compared to similar incentives in other countries; (2) a scarcity of legitimate, well-organized investment networks to facilitate matching of investors and ventures; (3) the downsized lending of banks as a result of stricter enforcement of banking regulations; (4) educational institutions that have failed to provide investors and entrepreneurs with a full understanding of this unique type of investment transaction and what is involved in planning for the capitalization and investment process; and (5) a climate of legal and regulatory constraints that is strangling the free flow of information between ethical, well-intentioned entrepreneurs and sophisticated, self-made, affluent private investors possessing the experience, analytical skills, and understanding of the risks involved when they make their own informed investment decisions.

Entrepreneurs can appreciate that investors understand that these new companies are the cornerstone of our economic success, having created, according to the SBA, 67 percent of all jobs, and offering significant investment opportunities. Start-up businesses specifically create 27 percent of new jobs (according to David Birch at MIT) and 91 percent of new jobs in California (according to the Census Bureau). Small companies represent 47 percent of all sales, 51 percent of the private gross domestic product, 52 percent of business net worth, and 99 percent of all companies in the United States. More specifically, venture capital–backed companies created 6,000 new jobs from 2001 to 2003 compared to a 2.3 percent payroll decline in the United States. The Bureau of Labor Statistics forecasts that by 2005, small firms will be contributing 60 percent of new jobs. When you combine these contributions to the expectation that 55 percent of all technical innovation comes through these small companies, you begin to appreciate why funding new ventures is critical to our economy and country. It is the small companies, after all, that can boast twice the number of product innovations per employee as large companies, helping to keep the United States globally competitive.

In the words of the SBA, "Interest in owning or starting a small business has never been greater." And it is clearer than ever before that small firms are the struts of our economic stability and growth; that is why these small companies need the capital to keep charging the battery of the nation's economic vitality.

The importance and significance of the angel investor contribution is now recognized: Angels are mainstream!

The central problem entrepreneurs face is the absence of an efficient private venture investor market leading to under investment, because no organized capital provider system targets entrepreneurial companies. Information about sources of funds or venture opportunities is not readily available. No secondary market currently provides small company investors with an exit strategy; restrictive securities regulations limit the flow of information; and many securities industry professionals believe these companies are not investable because of a lack of standard, consistent deal structures, structures that raise transaction costs and create high liability costs per transaction.

Capital shortage is fatal for small, growing businesses. The future success of those that survive start-up is dependent on the availability of additional growth capital as well as the entrepreneur's ability to develop the skills and attitudes to be successful at the money-raising game. Today venture capital firms, lenders, government programs, and other traditional financing sources are willing to take the risk to a small extent, and this is important and appreciated; unfortunately, when they do, it is with unacceptable valuation concessions and cost to the entrepreneur. On the other hand, early-stage ventures have the best chance for funding, survival, retention of a larger share of venture ownership and control, and long-term success by developing an efficient capitalization strategy to find and approach angel investors.

Contrary to the belief of those exhausted by the fund-raising process, there is no shortage of pre-IPO risk capital. Based on studies by International Capital Resources (ICR), approximately 2 million U.S. investors today have the demographic profile and the financial resources—more specifically, the discretionary net worth—to eliminate the capital gap. However, interestingly enough—and for reasons we will discuss in the ensuing chapters—only about 250,000 to 400,000 of this group are active. And the great challenge for intermediaries and entrepreneurial finance services and introduction networks is to make this market more efficient, allowing more of the qualified 2 million to become active in the market. This, then, is the challenge we address in the book, the challenge of facing the inefficiencies blocking the other million-plus from getting actively involved. So the issue centers not only on entrepreneurs who are uneducated about the process of raising capital, but also on the millionaires—90 percent of whom, we remind you, are self-made—and the newly affluent, who know how to grow a company and are now more likely to consider active angel investing.

Thus, the gap is not the problem but a symptom of the failure of our society and elected representatives to change antiquated securities laws, laws that effectively strangle the free flow of communication between ethical entrepreneurs and sophisticated, well-informed capitalists. This chasm in what we call the pre-IPO market will continue to exist only as long as we fail to muster the courage and take responsibility for bridging the gap with pragmatic solutions based on rigorous research.

Do you truly believe that significant differences exist between entrepreneurs and business angel investors? Risking their life savings, homes, and children's education to make their dream a reality, entrepreneurs face a 25 percent failure rate for start-ups. Risking hard-won capital, high-net-worth, self-made entrepreneurial investors face a complete loss of capital 33 percent of the time. These groups of individuals are indeed two sides of the same coin!

The similarities between these two groups of risk takers far outweigh their differences. But for entrepreneurs to recognize and build on these similarities in their quest for capital, they must do four things:

1. Overcome their insecurities about raising capital and asking for money, and educate themselves to investors and the investment process.
2. Reassess their values/attitudes toward asking for money and develop the skills to make money-raising part of their job description.
3. Take time to appreciate the art of successful private investing from experienced veterans who have made the most and financially survived to tell their stories, and to increase empathy for the entrepreneur's ideal "customer."
4. Determine if they have or know how to get the skills to be effective at the money-raising game, and to learn when to ask for help, and how to find it.

This last challenge is most critical, since, in our opinion, the defining factor of successful entrepreneurs is not whether they have created a better mousetrap but whether they can raise the money to bring the better mousetrap to market.

PART ONE

The Challenge and the Solutions

CHAPTER 1

The Challenge

INTRODUCTION

The grand impresario Florenz Ziegfeld had a backer—an angel, in Broadway parlance—named Jim Donahue who at the time of the 1929 stock market crash was disastrously affected financially. Deeply despondent over his losses, Donahue took his own life by throwing himself out of his office window. When Ziegfeld heard the news, he immediately penned a note to Donahue's widow that read, "Just before your husband 'fell,' he promised me $20,000." Needless to say, three days later the money arrived. And that's the kind of chutzpah it took then—and takes now—to raise capital for high-risk deals.

THE CHALLENGE

Make no mistake: Raising funds for an early-stage venture or a small, but rapidly growing business is an arduous task.

Where do you turn once you have exhausted the founders' financial resources and those of family and friends, but are not yet able to access venture capital? What if you're worn out from simultaneously running your company while struggling with venture capital firms, banks, factors, leasing companies, and the like? What if you lack the ability to bootstrap and to fund growth from cash flow or retained earnings? What if you have not yet achieved financial strength and public reputation sufficient to support a small corporate offering registration (SCOR) or a direct public offering? What if your venture is not defined by the venture capital community as a "darling" industry? What if your deal is too small for institutional players, say, less than $3 million?

During the formative years of a start-up, entrepreneurs assume the responsibility for, and risk associated with, making their dream become a reality. Typically, a substantial portion of their net worth is committed to the venture. But by the first major round of funding, entrepreneurs often have exhausted their own financial resources and those of family, friends, associates, and business contacts. So entrepreneurs face a daunting challenge. Although it is correct that cradle-equity from family and friends is a form of angel investing, it is neither the primary nor the only funding source for start-ups or for most small companies.

This challenge so often faced by entrepreneurs reveals only part of the task involved in early-stage capital formation. Even though these entrepreneurs create benefits—jobs, advancement of technology, capital expenditures, asset growth, and contribution to tax revenues—the supply of needed capital for early-stage ventures recently has contracted, and entrepreneurs face a much more difficult environment, as some sources of capital have been reduced or eliminated. There are three reasons for this: (1) start-ups need more money than in past years; (2) traditional capital and financing have diminished; and (3) more competition exists for start-up capital. There are a few reasons for this: first, a reduction of newly affluent angel investors in the market; second, traditional capital sources failing to keep pace with the level of entrepreneurial activity in the United States; and third, more competition—direct and indirect—for start-up capital sources.

Many of the young entrepreneurs successful in the 1970s, 1980s, and 1990s have, in their industries, morphed into the active investors of today. But the dot-com bubble bust has clipped the wings of many of those newly affluent investors who before the shakeout seemed to possess insatiable appetites for promising venture opportunities in high tech. Many entrepreneurs without extensive knowledge of alternative capital resources may have inferred that all angels had disappeared for a while. It is true that some angels have had their net worth shrunk by public market losses estimated for the U.S. at more than $7 trillion over the past three years, and, as a result, lost their accredited legal status or lost discretional net worth liquidity for higher-risk private deals. Still, solid angel players merely regrouped and assumed more realistic and cautious approaches to finding and making new investments, sticking particularly "closer to the knitting," that is, investing in areas they fully understand.

More accurately, angels are available, but those remaining in the game, as we have pointed out, are making fewer investments, investing fewer dollars per deal, and providing reserves to shore up their positions later, should it be necessary, and are perhaps taking longer to make investment decisions because of the increased time frames for due diligence. Due diligence, after all, has become much more rigorous. We commonly find entrepreneurs taking six to nine months to raise rounds less than $1 million. Other implications for entrepreneurs are more intense demands for documentation (e.g., business plans) and more intensive negotiations about deal terms and valuation, which have become more beneficial to investors. In a word, the days of raising high-risk capital with an executive summary and a PowerPoint presentation are long gone!

Second, traditional sources of capital, for example, banks that offer corporate lending, have failed to keep pace with demand from entrepreneurs for financing. The last statistics available show that Small Business Administration estimates of start-ups fall well below actual numbers of business start-ups in this country. In the early 1990s there were only five million small businesses. Today, if you count home-based businesses, almost five million businesses are begun each year. So demand far exceeds the financing possible from traditional sources, especially those sources requiring cash flow, assets, collateral, or other financing criteria normally associated with more developed operating companies.

The third reason why it is more challenging today to raise capital from among those with impressive personal wealth—especially those interested in investing in higher-risk deals—is that they are the target of everyone from charitable fund-raisers to the most successful money managers. In a word, there is simply more competition for the money that is out there than there was 10 years ago. These investors are also completing more than 700,000 investment transactions each year, which benefit as many as 500,000 start-up and small companies. These numbers remain constant, though locating investors since the dot-com bust has become more challenging.

In addition, the high-net-worth, affluent market is the target of multiple solicitations, not just from entrepreneurs offering private equity deals. According to Giving U.S.A., charitable donations in 2003 totaled $240 billion, the majority of which came from individuals. This amount is a 2.8 percent increase over 2002, and 2.2 percent of the nation's gross domestic product (GDP). This money was raised largely by professional fund-raisers, a major competitor with entrepreneurs for discretionary net worth dollars! Such donations also offer significant tax breaks as well.

Ten years ago everyone had a resume tucked neatly away in the desk drawer; today more than 10 million visionaries have an idea or plan for a new business. And with the people, regardless of economic conditions, currently intent on starting their own businesses, regions such as Silicon Valley, New England, Southeast Texas, New York Metro, and Orange County, California, have become zones of entrepreneurial fervor. A proven way to wealth can involve coming up with an idea, then raising the money to fund it into a reality. Today, as much as in the late 1990s, highly successful individuals are attempting to achieve their own success and enhance their personal wealth through entrepreneurial ventures.

Raising money today is much harder than it was five years ago, primarily because finding investors has become an "in" thing. Entrepreneurs have not discarded their dreams, but those with impressive personal wealth—especially those inclined toward investing in high-risk/high-return deals—have become the target of everyone, from charitable fund-raisers, to purveyors of luxury consumer products, to the world's most successful money managers.

Understandably, new money managers, foreign money managers, and other advisers seeking to manage funds aggressively target higher-net-worth individuals. In fact, with the failure of and disappearance through acquisition of so many investment banks, brokerage and money management firms, a survival mentality has gripped those who remain and compete with professional money managers for private capital. Besides, as the flow of deals remains steady, private investors become more sophisticated in evaluating what constitutes an attractive high-risk/high-reward opportunity. In short, there is simply more competition for the same amount of money than there was five years ago.

International Capital Resources of San Francisco (ICR) surveyed more than 480 entrepreneurial ventures seeking capital. The entrepreneurs cited an expanding array of financing methods they were relying on to accomplish their financing goals. However, the majority identified one alternative financing resource as a practicable and preferred option: private equity investors.

Exhibit 1.1 presents the primary funding methods mentioned during those interviews (no percentage is given for methods receiving only minimal recognition).

ICR discovered that 61 percent of entrepreneurs who came to its firm in their search for capital were relying on the direct participatory investment, casting an eye primarily toward informal, high-risk venture investors as their means of raising capital. Eighteen percent anticipated relying on their personal financial resources and those of family, friends, and business contacts. Only 9 percent of these primarily earlier-stage and developmental-stage companies were capable of relying on profits and working capital in order to fund their growth plans. Only 7 percent turned to banks for debt financing, and 3 percent chose joint ventures and alliances. Finally, only 2 percent of the 480 companies queried showed interest in approaching professional venture capital firms to fund their venture.

These findings have been supported by a 2001 study that found that the percentage of INC 500 CEOs who have raised start-up capital did so 88 percent from personal assets, 39 percent of personal assets from other cofounders, 30 percent from family and friends, and 3 percent from venture capital. Seed capital for the same group in 2001 came from co-founders 39 percent of the time, family and friends 30 percent of the time, and strategic partners and customers 11 percent of the time.

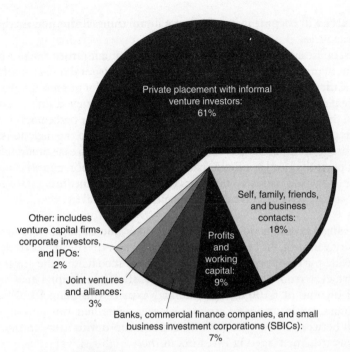

Private placement with informal
venture investors:
61%

Self, family, friends,
and business
contacts:
18%

Other: includes
venture capital firms,
corporate investors,
and IPOs:
2%

Profits
and
working
capital:
9%

Joint ventures
and alliances:
3%

Banks, commercial finance companies, and small
business investment corporations (SBICs):
7%

Exhibit 1.1   Primary Targeted Funding Sources

THE ANGEL INVESTOR

Although the concept designated by the term *angel* dates back to the Golden
Age of Greece, its modern coinage dates only as far back as the Broadway in-
siders to describe the well-heeled backers of Broadway shows who made
risky investments in order to produce shows. Angels frequently invested in
these shows for the privilege of rubbing shoulders with theater personalities
they admired as much as to earn a return on investment (ROI). As a review
of the biographies of the great impresarios attests, money for those shows
was raised as much by attitude, good preparation, and luck as by the quality
of the offerings.

Angels today—numbering about 400,000 active investors according
to *Forbes*—are in many ways the same: wealthy individuals and families
willing to invest in high-risk deals offered by people they admire and
with whom they seek to be associated. Angels are also financially sophisticated private investors willing to provide seed and start-up capital for
higher-risk ventures. In essence, angels are private informal venture capitalists, although as we will discuss, as the angel market develops, more for-

mal structures will become inevitable to facilitate transactions and increase market efficiencies.

Public equities are traditionally a long-term play, and investors appreciate this. But many have come to realize that recovery from the Bear market, as has been the case in the past, can take a long time. For example, following the Great Depression, the Dow Jones Industrial Average didn't recover its 1929 highs until 1954—25 years later! By investing a percentage (e.g., one to five percent) of their equity portfolios into private transactions in order to offset public equity performance, the investors increase predictability in their portfolios and maximize chances for performance, and so can accelerate recovery. Sophisticated investors recognize that venture capital as an alternative asset class is an investment vehicle instrumental in accomplishing this goal.

Active angel investors possess the discretionary income needed to invest in such risky ventures. In fact, a portion of their private equity portfolio is often set aside for this purpose. This discretionary income sets the angel investor apart, even from the merely affluent. An affluent individual may have an annual income of $100,000 but annual expenses totaling $150,000. Large incomes, we know, can carry even larger debts. For this reason, we distinguish between those who are affluent and those who are wealthy. In setting standards for targeting investors in these high-risk ventures, many entrepreneurs mistakenly judge investors solely on their income; income alone has little to do with what counts in these types of ventures. They do this primarily because data on income of individuals is more readily available, whereas finding out an individual's net worth involves asking them the level of their net worth. What counts are the discretionary funds for early-stage, high-risk transactions, funds possessed only by wealthy angel investors, not necessarily by the affluent, whose debts can exceed their considerable annual incomes.

The reader ought not forget, however, that although they represent a potentially limitless source of funding for entrepreneurs and small business ventures, private investors are unfortunately just that—hard to reach, intensely selective, and usually immune to cold, "over-the-transom" investment solicitations.

STRUCTURE OF THE PRIVATE INVESTOR MARKET

Angel investors also possess a healthy appetite for self-arranged private deals. Such direct investment serves to maintain the self-confidence of these high-net-worth investors and demonstrates their continuing ability to make money. These investors have amassed wealth precisely because they know how to invest. Furthermore, it is reasonable to assume that they will remain active investors. Many want to enjoy the small percentage of their capital allocated for private equity. After all, even the most conservative investment adviser will leave a client some money to play with. It is this "play money" that ought to become the target of entrepreneurs seeking funding for high-risk, relatively illiquid, direct investment securities. These deals, in turn, offer the possibility of exceptional capital appreciation.

Investing to earn the potentially extraordinary returns of a new business is extremely risky. The angel has the opportunity to earn above-average returns and enjoy the challenge of helping younger visionaries grow a business, but even after meticulous due diligence, investors lose their investment capital 33 percent of the time. However, these risks do not frighten away sophisticated angel investors. These investors love the action, manage the risk, and search for the "big hit" in pitting their skills against the market. And, at the same time, they continue to contribute to an economic system that has done well by them and that they are devoted to.

Angel investors include such high-net-worth individuals as the retired, wealthy officers of corporations and private companies with $1 million to $5 million in pension assets to invest; the recipients of the estimated $20 billion in windfall transfers in the late 1990s; the high-net-worth casualties of corporate downsizing; and the thirty-something and forty-something chief executive officers (CEOs) of small capital companies that made their fortunes through stock offerings, or sale of their companies in the 1990s. These investors have saved money, are financially astute, and possess engaging, challenging intellects.

Furthermore, these angel investors are concerned with after-tax returns and return after expenses—the expenses, for example, of due diligence. They represent "patient" money, remaining comfortable with a long-term, buy-hold strategy, money not designed, as the Atlanta, Georgia, G&W *Premium Finance Gazette* puts it, "for high current income," but instead money that "often won't be available for some time." (The *Gazette* cites some examples: $25,000 invested in 1956 in Warren Buffett's Berkshire Hathaway has a 1995 estimated value of $90,000,000; the same amount invested in 1989 in Home Depot reached an estimated value of $3,500,000.) Last, angel investors define risk idiosyncratically, for example, the nature of potential loss (irrecoverable or affordable), the need for liquidity, and the need for control.

Less dramatic examples abound, such as the New York pediatrician who invested $50,000 in a medical instrument start-up. Five years later, after an initial public offering (IPO), the doctor cashed out for $2 million. Or take the six New Jersey physicians who, along with several other private investors, each put up $13,000 to start a facility to treat kidney stones. In ten years, they earned seven times their investment, and the venture remains profitable and pays investors impressive gains, demonstrating that sustainable companies need not be sold or taken public to provide return *of* investment and return *on* investment.

Angel investors are different from their venture capitalist counterparts, who are more conservative, collect substantially more dollars from pension funds and the like, and put the bulk of the capital to work in later-stage deals. The angels have more time to spend with fledgling companies, helping them to build sustainable companies rather than ventures solely for exit. This hands-on guidance is invaluable to entrepreneurs who are the recipients of more than capital but wisdom, knowledge, experience, and expertise of previously successful entrepreneurs in the investors.

MAKING SENSE OF THE HIGH-NET-WORTH MARKET

The classification model for targeting the most appropriate financial demographic segments of the high-net-worth market—so entrepreneurs have the best possibility of locating angel investors—has not varied since our first book (1996) and is not subject to changes, changes that *have* occurred in economic conditions. The structure of the high-net-worth private investor market (see Exhibit 1.2) can be segmented into four categories: first, investors with a net worth of a minimum of $500,000, comprising a little more than 1.7 million U.S. households; second, a group of investors with a net worth of $1 million to $5 million (about 672,000 households); a third group worth $5 million to $10 million (about 158,000 households); and last, a segment with a net worth of more than $10 million (roughly 9,000 households).

This market includes the target group that offers the entrepreneur or inventor maximum possibility for finding investors. Growing at an annual rate of 14 to 20 percent, this high-net-worth market compares favorably, for example, with the current 8 percent growth rate in pension funds. Furthermore, each of these segments is adding about 1,000 households a year.

While we de-emphasize the use of income as a primary demographic in targeting the high-net-worth group, Exhibit 1.2 shows a similarity between the structure of affluence, or income, and net worth. Notwithstanding our earlier distinction between income and net worth, some correlation naturally exists between net worth and income. But do not be swayed by the numbers.

We see that there are about 672,000 households with a net worth of $1 million to $5 million and 158,000 households worth between $5 million and $10 million. Also note that 0.7 percent have a net worth of $1 million to $5 million. Less than 0.2 percent have a net worth of $5 million to $10 million.

EXHIBIT 1.2   Structure of the High-Net-Worth Private Investor Market

Structure of Net Worth	
Net Worth	U.S. Households
$500,000	1,773,593 (1 .9%)
$1,000,000	672,098 (0.72%)
$5,000,000	158,690 (0.17%)
$10,000,000+	9,334 (0.01%)
$9.8 trillion market	2,613,715
Structure of Affluence (Income)	
Adjusted Gross Income*	No. of Returns†
$100,000–200,000	2,597,908 (2.26%)
$200,000–500,000	676,038 (0.5%)
$500,000–1,000,000	118,350 (0.1%)
$1,000,000 or greater	52,019 (0.045%)
	3,444,315 (2.905%)

*Total number of returns = 114,700,000.
†Includes salary, interest, dividends, stock sales, capital gains. Could be individual, joint return, single, or unmarried filing separately.
Source: Internal Revenue Service

So the percentages of households correlate closely to those percentages of returns. Those with incomes of $200,000 to $500,000 equal 0.5 percent of returns; those with incomes of $500,000 to $1 million filed 0.1 percent of the returns. Thus, the numerical similarities point to a similarity between the structure of income and net worth. Still, the fact remains: discretionary net worth forms the true measure of our target market.

The majority of investors represented in the categories of net worth ranging from $1 million to $10 million are self-made. Most rich Americans have earned their money; theirs is not inherited money, reveals the 1995 Rand study by the Santa Monica nonprofit research group. These individuals have built and own their own companies and have generated their personal fortunes through hard work and through understanding an industry or a business.

However, while these numbers seem large—a $9.8 trillion market and approximately 2.6 million U.S. households that might be appropriately targeted—the market for higher-risk, developmental, or expansion deals is substantially less than that. A portion of these investors is not composed of accumulators, or people investing in growth investments with possible capital appreciation; instead, they represent savers and those looking for income from their investments—circumstances incompatible with earlier-stage investments.

Other circumstances also lessen the pool of investment dollars. The dollars diminish when you correct statistics for geographic locale and proximity of the company seeking the direct investment, and age of the prospective investor. The dollars also diminish when you scan such items as net worth (exclusive of house and car), previous investment history, current holdings, status and role in the business community, and interests in specific industries.

Considering the circumstances, our own calculations indicate that for higher-risk, early-stage, manufacturing-related deals, the true market contracts to about 400,000 investors. This range exists because investors who engage in direct investing in early-stage deals typically surface only a few times a year, and only when seeking new investments that follow a liquidation or windfall event, or simply when they are in the mood for a change.

INVESTOR ACTIVITY IN EARLY-STAGE DEALS

Although it is true that private investors prize their privacy and that obtaining information about private transactions in this highly secretive market is difficult, ICR's proprietary research in building its national database of angel investors, plus other important studies, can help us understand the extent of the activity of the high-net-worth investor's direct investment in early-stage deals.

Angels are financially sophisticated private investors of means willing to provide seed, research and development (R&D), start-up, and expansion capital to investors and young or less-experienced entrepreneurs for high-risk ventures. For many entrepreneurs, the process of finding angels proves to be inefficient, and for many, frustrating and disappointing. You could make hundreds of presentations, spend countless hours and untold dollars searching for the hard-to-find private investors—unless you use proven strategies to identify them and, thereby, establish contact. This is why segmenting the high-net-worth market into target categories most appropriate for your particular venture remains even more critical in today's challenging capital-raising market.

In his landmark study funded by the Small Business Administration, Dr. Robert J. Gaston suggested that approximately $55 to $56 billion a year was being placed into as many as 720,000 companies. Dr. William Wetzel, Jr., at the University of New Hampshire Whittemore School of Business has suggested that approximately $15 billion of this $55 to $56 billion was being placed into approximately 60,000 very-high-risk, early-stage, seed,

R&D, or start-ups per year. Meanwhile, the Small Business Development Center at the University of California, Irvine, has suggested that in California alone approximately $30 billion is being invested in about 240,000 transactions per year.

The debate on the size of this "invisible" market still rages. Josh Friedman wrote recently in the *Los Angeles Times* that angels invest in 50 times the number of deals as venture capitalists do, although in smaller amounts. In the United States, his research posits, approximately 300,000 angels invested $30 billion, although this was sown from 2001 levels. Longer-term estimates by Jeffrey Sohl made in 1999 in *Venture Capital Journal* indicate that angels invest about $20 billion per year in 30,000 deals. The National Venture Capital Association estimated the angel investment at $100 billion in 1998.

As Osnabrugge and Robinson observe in *Angel Investing*, "obtaining accurate numbers for the size of this market is difficult." We agree that the best market size estimates are, at best, extrapolations, attempts to quantify what the academic and business literature—and even the popular press—know is essentially a secret capital market.

Although these estimates vary, the amount of capital and number of transactions involved signal a vast market. In contrast, the venture capital industry invested a full year total of $21 billion in 2002 into 3,011 deals, of which only $303 million went into seed and start-up transactions. This represents significantly less total investment when compared with $106 billion invested in 2000 and $41 billion invested in 2001 by the professional venture capital industry.

Simply put, private investors, or business angel investors, are a primary, if not *the* primary, source of capital for early-stage and growing companies.

ANGELS: A GOLDEN CAPITAL SOURCE

It is no longer a question of whether angels are a viable capital resource for early-stage ventures. Angels are a source—in fact, the primary source—of capital, worth the entrepreneur's time, energy, and financial resources to seek and access; they should be considered before other alternative, nontraditional capital resources. One entrepreneur we worked with felt motivated to turn first to an angel instead of an institutional investor because of the willingness of angels to commit large stakes in individual companies based on the understanding that angels, in turn, want a voice in management. Speaking to the *San Francisco Business Times,* he put it this way: "The typical venture capital firm wants to get involved only when you are further along—and for more money than you need. The primary advantage of going with individuals is that it is much quicker and you can tailor the details of the deal to the individual investor."

If you have a successful track record as an entrepreneur, the institutional venture community is more inclined to look at your next deal. But what of the other 99.9 percent of entrepreneurs seeking start-up capital. Without the lengthy record, where can they turn?

We estimate that more than two million high-net-worth individuals with the financial capital, when combined with the lowest interest rates in 45 years and poor stock market performance, offer the potential for investment into higher-risk, higher-return ventures. More than ever, there are organizations, research groups, networks and academics studying about and publishing in the angel capital market. Angel capital has gone mainstream! These veterans offer money and added value to those entrepreneurs who can figure out a strategy to reach them and present their vision and their deals in a persuasive and compelling manner.

When you want to bring in a funding partner early, and you want active involvement and access to their brainpower and perspective based on start-up experience, the angel investor is hard to beat. Research shows that venture capital gets involved when entrepreneurs are further along with their companies. Dealing directly with angels can be quicker, even in today's more cautious investment environment, and entrepreneurs can tailor the details of their deals to the individual investor. Especially when seeking to raise less than $3 million, and searching for investors who bring expertise that can complement the management team, angels offer an edge. Furthermore, when entrepreneurs don't want to give up significant control too early, active angels offer the best game in town.

INVESTORS WORTH ACCESSING

So, as many entrepreneurs in our experience have discovered, these investors are worth accessing.

Still, there exists the old problem of meeting these investors. In his book *Giant in the West,* Julian Dara writes that Joseph Strauss attempted to get funding to build the Golden Gate Bridge for 19 years before he found A.P. Giannini, who ultimately financed the $6 million necessary for construction. Although contemporary entrepreneurs have been creative in identifying and accessing alternative sources of capital for their growing ventures, we have to be realistic: How many of us have the patience of a Joseph Strauss?

For many entrepreneurs, finding, attracting, building relationships with, and closing with private business angel investors remains inefficient. The reason is simple: Angels prize their privacy. These individuals are hard to find; moreover, a fair review of the literature will indicate that there is little formal guidance in identifying their whereabouts. Currently, most angel investors are located primarily by word-of-mouth contacts from other investors or by reliance on professional intermediaries with a book of investors in related fields.

Angels are hard to locate for the simple reason that they are not legally bound to disclose their activities and are secretive about their investment interests, since once "outed" everyone eagerly solicits them to access their wealth. Is it any wonder they cling to their privacy? Because of these circumstances, you could make hundreds of presentations, spend countless hours, and waste thousands of dollars searching for private investors; largely, labor lost. Lost, that is, unless you learn to use proven strategies that make the search more efficient. This means not only identifying these people but also establishing contact and managing relationships with them throughout the funding process.

The challenge, then, lies in efficiently accessing these investors. How do you find them? Chapter 3 will tell you how. But before tracing a strategy that works, you need the information in Chapter 2 on direct, private investment to determine whether your deal—and you—are financeable.

The Solution:
The Private Placement

Giving half the business away to make it four times bigger makes the entrepreneur twice better off.

—an Angel Investor

THE PRIVATE PLACEMENT

Sixty percent of transactions concluded at the seed, R&D, and start-up stages have fairly fixed financing structures. It is no accident that the transaction structure most commonly used by angels is the private placement. The formal definition of a private placement is the issuance of treasury securities of a company to a small number of private investors in the form of senior debt, subordinated debt, convertible debt, common stock, preferred stock, warrants, or various combinations of these securities. Although the vast majority of these investments by institutional investors involves debt securities, exempt offerings are common, involving direct, equity, and/or debt investing by private investors.

The informal, more practical, realistic definition of the private placement is any deal that the entrepreneur can legally negotiate and an attorney can write up. In essence, the private placement in angel transactions becomes a written record of the agreement and deal struck between the entrepreneur and the angel investor, which is precisely why we do not advocate indulging prematurely in overly structured transactions. Peddling highly structured transactions in the current angel market precludes the angel's propensity to negotiate. More constructive for the entrepreneur is an open-minded, negotiation-oriented approach. This more flexible posture, when supported by a strong business plan, is the constructive strategy to open the negotiation door with prospective investors. In fact, our experience tells us that angels are more inclined to circle wagons around less-structured deals, leaving them free to assemble legal, accounting, investment banking, and other expertise to structure an agreement acceptable to all the parties, and based on the particular attributes of the deal.

With private placement investments, private investors often require direct participation in a venture in order to limit the downside risk associated with relatively illiquid investments. These direct participatory investments begin with transactions for a smaller amount and generally are more quickly arranged than public offerings. Besides, because of the lack of Securities and Exchange Commission (SEC) requirements, these more flexible transactions let the company circumvent onerous public offering requirements and access the nonaffiliated market without full regulatory compliance. Thus, these investments prove much less expensive to all concerned.

The relaxation of SEC requirements is possible under private placement exemption offered by Section 4(2) of the Securities Act of 1933. More recently, Regulation D offers entrepreneurs a safe harbor; in other words, by complying with Regulations D's relatively easy-to-follow exemptions, entrepreneurs can offer shares of stock in their company directly to a limited number of individual or organizational investors, for example, to angels. It is true that these exemptions apply only at the federal level; therefore, it remains incumbent on the entrepreneur to be cognizant of complying with state "Blue Sky" laws, or the state statutes enacted to protect investors from insubstantial securities offerings. For early-stage deals, the Regulation D exemption offers an ideal approach, especially for those offers of less than $1 million, since they are least mired in legal provisions and requirements. For example, Rule 504 allows companies a way to raise up to $1 million in a 12-month period without having to be subject to federal requirements, although the company is still obligated to notify the SEC of its offering.

In private placements, business owners receive cash for equity, and they can choose from a menu of financing options. In some cases, debt and equity can be mixed to create a funding solution. Furthermore, the private placement can include all kinds of financing not publicly sold:

> *Senior debt.* Lowest cost financing from banks or insurance companies, generally a loan on a first priority status secured by company assets.
> *Subordinated debt.* Higher interest rate than senior debt in exchange for higher risk (paid after senior debt is paid), sometimes packaged with warrants ("sweeteners").
> *Subscription warrant.* A security that can be converted into or exchanged for a company's stock.
> *Preferred stock.* Pays a dividend to the holder and usually includes more

rights than common stock (in bankruptcy, considered junior to debt) and can be converted into common stock.
Common stock of the company.

While all these financing options are feasible, after the dot-com debacle, we see angel investors inclined toward preferred stock. Why preferred stock? Here are some reasons: (1) Preferred stock is senior to common stock, providing leverage to influence management when things "go south"; (2) it requires the entrepreneur to remain in contact with the investor; (3) it provides warning mechanisms permitting the investor to make changes in the management or act to protect the investment; (4) it can provide for income on the investment in the form of dividends; (5) it is redeemable by the corporation, for example, through a sinking fund with compulsory repayment; and (6) it offers the investor convertibility to common stock so that the investor can share in growth.

Private placement investments, in fact, consist of anything that is not a public offering. Such leeway lets money-raisers exercise the limits of their creativity and negotiating skills. Herein lies the strength of the private placement, and the main difference between an institutional private placement investment and direct, participatory investment by an angel. The former is primarily debt; the latter is not. A private placement usually means a subordinated debt transaction in the institutional market, but for angels it usually means an equity transaction between an individual and the company, a transaction that brings with it several advantages and responsibilities.

A private placement investment has the advantages of confidentiality and lower cost. First, with their less stringent disclosure requirements, direct investments enable private investors—who keenly prize their privacy—to maintain confidentiality in their financial transactions. Second, reduced cost figures prominently in choosing direct investment, especially in comparison with public offerings. For instance, the cost of a private placement investment (i.e., a capitalization transaction handled directly by the company) is markedly less than the cost of a public offering, or even a SCOR.

Also, with most early-stage investing, private placement deal structures tend to be equity or equity-related, including the ability to accommodate subordinated debt. Even when subordinated debt or convertible debt is involved, these structures offer convertibility into equity so that the investor can share in the upside possibilities should the venture become successful.

The private placement offers flexibility during negotiations between the private investor and the entrepreneur, a flexibility unavailable when purchasing stocks of public companies. Don't forget, in the case of early-stage ventures, that the company, its management, and strategy, even its technology, are unproven. From the investors perspective, the seed or start-up investment is the riskiest investment in the private equity alternative asset class. Undeveloped and underdeveloped technology, unproven management, and unpenetrated or undeveloped markets all spell risk. It is precisely for these reasons that investors seek to manage risk early on by negotiating through the private placement terms that make such risk more palatable, if not entirely manageable.

Finally, other benefits also derived by the entrepreneur from use of the private placement include (1) a more rapid time frame for concluding the financing when compared with direct public offerings and other alternative offering structures; (2) more than just the capital invested in the form of the knowledge, experience, and contacts brought to the table by angel investors in the deal; and (3) the proven fact that private placements have historically accommodated smaller transactions, the size of the transactions in which most early-stage entrepreneurs are involved.

The private placement is many times primarily perceived by entrepreneurs in its legal aspects. This myopic view misses the marketing aspects inherent in offers to private investors on an individual basis. The private placement is more limited than its public offering cousins, and by virtue of this is less formal and more targeted. The range of resources available to guide the entrepreneur on the legal aspects of private placement is wide, and we mention a few in Appendix B. We emphasize the market aspects of exempt offerings based on our experience raising early-stage capital. And our bias, albeit cynical, is rooted in experience: keep lawyers out of the process as long as you can but never close a deal without their counsel. As you will see in the next section, savvy entrepreneurs will be those prepared to identify multiple avenues for raising the capital that they seek, including angels and other nontraditional capital resources.

SELECTING THE RIGHT CAPITAL SOURCE

As an inventor, entrepreneur, or owner of a small but rapidly growing business hungry for capital, you must ask if nontraditional resources will suit your deal. For ventures at the preseed, seed, R&D, start-up, or expansion stages, a vast array of financing methods are available. After tapping one's own finances, and that of family, friends, and other founders, and perhaps having exhausted the bootstrap financing option, what alternative sources remain? Even a partial list can seem confusing: academic institution research financing, community loan development funds, technology licensing, venture leasing, transaction purchase order, corporate investment by strategic partners, incubator-based financing, and of course angels and venture capital.

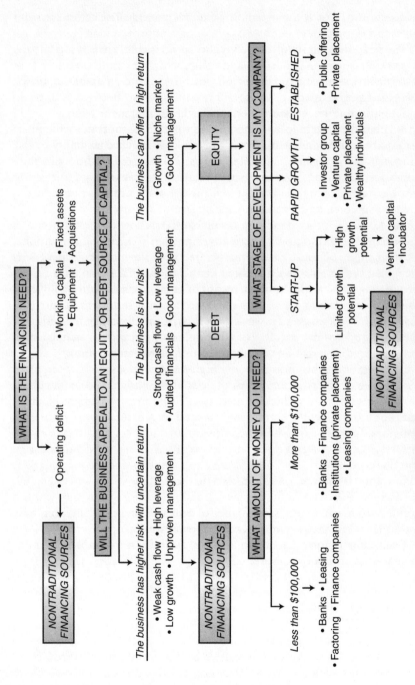

Exhibit 2.1 Selecting the Right Capital Source

The question is, which is most appropriate for your deal? Exhibit 2.1 helps answer this question.

The first decision involves clarifying the financing need. If a company has working capital, fixed assets, and equipment, then more traditional equity or debt sources of capital are in order. However, if an operating deficit exists, or if the company possesses no revenues, only alternatives to traditional financial sources seem reasonable, as illustrated in the chart.

Another decision involves determining whether the business will appeal to an equity or debt source of capital, a decision determined primarily by risk and return. If the business can offer a high return, more traditional equity sources seem feasible. This alternative requires the presence of a large, or rapidly growing, established market for the company's product or service, a clear niche market, and seasoned management with a strong track record of success. If, on the other hand, the business offers a low risk, debt becomes appropriate, using traditional sources of financing. To qualify for traditional debt financing, you must have demonstrated cash flow to service debt, low leverage on the balance sheet, audited financials by a CPA firm, and experienced management with a positive record of good credit histories. However, if the business offers high risk with uncertain returns—as do many entrepreneurial ventures because of a weak cash flow, a high leverage in terms of a large amount of debt, a low growth rate, or an unproven management team—nontraditional financing resources remain the only option.

If, however, the business can offer high return and low risk, it can focus on what type of equity or what type of debt to establish. If the debt transaction involves less than $100,000, perhaps private investors might be interested. But most likely the entrepreneur would turn first to banks or finance companies. In more cases, however, private investors get involved in equity transactions. But an established company, or a company demonstrating rapid financial growth, will be attractive to the institutional equity markets and/or public market, making appropriate the traditional sources of capital. But for a start-up with limited growth possibility (i.e., a company without the ability to reach annual sales figures of $50 million to $60 million) only nontraditional financial resources seem appropriate.

Examining Exhibit 2.1 should help you establish the suitability of a private placement for your venture.

IS YOUR DEAL FINANCEABLE?

In later chapters, we report results of our study in which private investors describe what they look for in a deal. Investors' decisions may seem idiosyncratic, their motivations diverse. They are. But this diversity merely reflects their characteristic individuality. Do not overlook their underlying concurrence: They share far more than may seem apparent. You will also see that what we advise here fits with what investors say they look for in a venture. What follows, then, are things to think about in making your deal financeable (Exhibit 2.2).

Management team experience is crucial. An astute investor has said, "If the critical element in a successful real estate transaction is 'location, location, location,' the critical element in a successful business endeavor is 'management, management, management.'" In determining if your deal is financeable, consider the quality of the managers, their references, the extent to which the team is complete, whether they have worked together as a team, their past success in the venture's industry, and the relevance of their backgrounds to the entrepreneurial task at hand. Especially in an early-stage venture, experience in the industry far exceeds the importance of functional expertise. The venture needs a CEO who understands the industry, its market, and the application of its underlying technology more than it needs a financial expert, operations officer, or advertising maven.

EXHIBIT 2.2 Is Your Deal Financeable?

Management team . . . . ✓
—Requisite skills, driven, worked together, chemistry, experience in industry, pride
   in enterprise
Large market size (qualified buyers and unique market niche) . . . . ✓
Market readiness + need + product appeal . . . . ✓
—Is missionary selling required?
Competition understood . . . . ✓
—Current—future (3–7 years)
—Barriers (beyond price)
Established or emerging industry . . . . ✓
Protected proprietary technology . . . . ✓
—A real solution
Does it work? . . . . ✓
Production can be currently performed . . . . ✓
Channel economics . . . . ✓
—Demonstrate understanding of cost to bring product/service to market
High margins (at least 15%, pretax) . . . . ✓
Above average profit potential . . . . ✓
Capital intensity . . . .✓
Reasonable projections . . . . ✓
Valuation . . . . ✓
Clear and believable exit plan . . . . ✓

Source: International Capital Resources

Market size must be calculated. Assess the size of the market, specifically whether the total number of potential customers in the target market share is substantial enough to generate the revenues stipulated in the marketing plan. Consider whether there are there enough qualified buyers to provide revenues and subsequent return to investors? This calculation needs to be not only accurate but demonstrable. Entrepreneurs need to demonstrate that they understand exactly who their customers will be and describe knowledge and understanding of these customers. Investors also have an inclination toward rapidly growing markets and markets that will continue to grow.

Market readiness should be considered as well. Will the technology or product require missionary selling, the kind that convinces people they need it? Missionary selling, of course, will increase the cost and expand the time needed to bring the product to market.

Competition must not be underestimated. Although many entrepreneurs will insist that none exists, every compelling venture has a direct or indirect competitor. More to the point, however, is not the immediate competition but the competition that will surely emerge within three to five years. The discerning entrepreneur anticipates the inevitable competition and the resources those competitors may bring to bear on the market, and also contemplates the barriers that the entrepreneur can erect to the competitor's entry into the market. A clear understanding of the competitive marketplace is paramount in order to be taken seriously by an investor. Poor analysis can kill your deal! Although competitive analysis is far from an exact science, entrepreneurs must demonstrate a deep appreciation for present competitors and future barriers to inspire investor confidence that they have a plan to respond to inevitable challenges.

Typically, investors are interested in reducing the risk associated with the investment by identifying investments involved in *established* or *emerging industries*. The ability to analyze financial projections is much easier for an existing industry because data are readily available in order to test the hypotheses and other assumptions associated with the pro forma. However, investors "swinging for the fence" are inclined toward growing markets or markets that are growing at high rates. For early-stage deals, a fast-growing market can be more forgiving if not more fruitful. The high profit margin potential even if described in pro forma financials can be very compelling to the angel investor looking for high returns.

Proprietary technology is important in reducing the investor's perceived risk in a venture. If you have developed a technology advantage, investors will want assurance that you have protected it. From the investor's point of view, properly protected technology reduces risk in the venture. Intellectual property protection in the form of patents, copyrights, or trade secrets do represent legal advantages. However, because the deepest pocket often wins in legal proceedings, most investors are aware of the shortcomings in patent protection; of course, the investor's appraisal can be influenced by advantages in access to resources or customers, or from being able to exploit a "first-in-the-market" positioning, or being first to enter the targeted market.

Does the product or service work? Has the designed service or product demonstrated its function? Is there a working prototype, or are you still operating at the conceptual stage of development? Obviously, the more useful a service or product is, the more financeable it becomes. Also, is the venture just a one-product company, or has management developed a plan to expand, and offer follow-on products to customers?

Another consideration regarding the financeability of your deal is whether *production* can currently be performed. In other words, will it be necessary to create not only a prototype and a product, but also the machinery necessary to construct a prototype or product? Risk is significantly increased—as are capital requirements—when the production facilities do not exist to manufacture the product.

Channel economics demonstrates that the entrepreneur possesses an understanding of the cost of bringing a product or service to market. The key word here is *demonstrates.* How will management distribute the product or service? In detail, how will the company connect the product or service it offers with the customers it is targeting? This question goes to the heart of how management plans to sell and devise a detailed strategy and cost structure for accomplishing its goals. The question asked by investors is how will distribution be managed. Early-stage company entrepreneurs with their minimal financial resources sometimes can lose sight of how important it is to clarify distribution and cost of distribution to achieve the "hockey stick" projections in their financial forecasts!

High margins are always desirable to investors. They understand that it will take longer than anticipated to bring a product or service to market, that it will take more money, and that it will take longer to realize revenues. Higher margins offset such adversity, offering a sorely needed cushion. We estimate that 90 percent of all the ventures we review in our practice will end up needing more money than has been presumed by entrepreneurs in their business plans. This is precisely why sophisticated investors always discount projections, or give "haircuts" to forecasts from entrepreneurs. Without an understanding of the role that Murphy's law plays in the development and growth of a company, entrepreneurs are doomed by presenting unrealistic milestones to skeptical investors, subjecting themselves to negative consequences of missed deadlines, loss of investor confidence, even the role in and share of ownership in the enterprise.

Post-Bubble risk profiles associated with financial attributes of the venture must possess reasonable targets. Concerning above-average *profit potential,* within 18 to 24 months, the company in its pro formas must demonstrate with confidence the ability to generate revenue streams, if not profits, that will position the investors to get not only a return *of* their investment but a return *on* their investment. There is a wide range of acceptable levels of profit potential in deals that have been completed in the angel market. But typically investors are looking for a real opportunity to realize a 20 to 50 percent ROI per year compounded annually over the term of the hold of the investment. In our experience 15 percent of an investor's private portfolio accounts for 85 percent of returns, a slight variation on the Pareto Principle, but noteworthy regardless. On an eight-year hold, investors aim higher, but will be attracted by 35 percent per year returns, even when swinging for the fence. The central point for entrepreneurs to understand is that they must make clear, compelling cases that their venture will make money. Investors must understand that your early-stage venture is not making money now, but it is your job to convince them that you will make money and be profitable within a reasonable time. This requires clarifying what will drive revenues and costs, and thus margins. It is precisely the size of these margins that create insurance for the venture to absorb unforeseen problems, mistakes, and unexpected costs or slow-downs in revenue generation.

Capital intensity reflects the investment needed to prove to investors that a product or service will work. In biotechnology, for example, companies may spend years and invest millions of dollars before receiving Food and Drug Administration (FDA) approval to market a product. Significant financial risk before proof of concept is available reflects high levels of capital intensity less attractive to angel investors. Research, development, and good manufacturing process (GMP) of a growth hormone, for example, can take up to seven years before permission is granted to test in humans—seven years of preclinical testing to figure out if it works, if it is toxic, and if the correct dose is being administered. Add a few more years of separate phases of clinical trials to determine safety and efficacy. Then file a product license application (PLA) and wait a couple of years for the FDA's approval. Finally, the company arrives 12 years later, having spent $200 million—the estimated average cost of bringing one protein to market. Such is the burden and risk that create capital intensity, and this example goes a long way toward explaining why highly capital intensive biotechnology ventures are less often funded in the current angel market.

On the other hand, being able to develop and bring a product or service to market quickly reflects a less capital-intensive circumstance. Investment will come more easily once the concept has been proven, permitting money to be used to move the product or service into the marketplace. Quick movement to the marketplace spawns a less capital-intensive situation.

Valuation is necessary to assess the financeability of your venture. Based on the most current compilation of data available at the time of writing, median premoney valuations of seed rounds of completed venture deals have diminished to a range of $3 to $6 billion. First Round Series A median premoney valuations are also down to a range of $9 million to $14 million. Read any overview of market trends, and the entrepreneur will discover that the aggregate dollar amount of investments has declined and the number of "down rounds" is increasing. Entrepreneurs need to have reasonable expectations when it comes to valuations from investors, and to avoid overshopping their deal to attain unreasonably high valuation expectations. As you consider your valuation, compare it with these statistics and others that you can locate that are consistent and comparable with your venture.

As ventures progress in the evolutionary life cycle to later stages of development, obviously the valuation will increase significantly. To raise money during the early stages of a company, when its valuation is lowest, more will have to be ceded to investors. This circumstance illuminates two things that influence the financeability of a deal: The investor must feel that the valuation is credible (in other words, it has to fall in line with valuations occurring elsewhere in the market); and from the entrepreneur's point of view, valuation should be based on achieving milestones so that more money than is presently needed is not being raised. This prevents giving away more of the company than is necessary when it is at a low valuation.

A clear and believable exit plan must be part of the picture. Investors who invest in companies directly, in most cases, will not be able to harvest their investment (especially in equity investments) until those equity investments are liquidated. And although a number of workable liquidation options exist, the plan for liquidation must be explicit. The investor must know whether liquidation will occur through a "claw back"—a sale back to the entrepreneur—or through the merger or acquisition by a public company and the trading of that illiquid stock for publicly traded securities. Liquidation may also occur through the sale of the company to other entrepreneurs, or through an IPO.

Simply declaring that one of these days the company will go public falls well short of an investor's expectation because most investors realize that few companies go public. You need a realistic plan for liquidating the investment, paying it off, and/or providing for ROI to the investor. In the venture capital industry's portfolios, more than 6,000 companies owned by venture capital funds await IPO's, merger, acquisition, or sale. Imagine how long this "overhang" will take to liquidate if it is not written off. The downdraft on exit in the venture capital industry is estimated to last a minimum of five years! The IPO market remains moribund, with the lightest new offering market in 10 years. According to Thompson Financial, there were 510 IPOs in 1999, 373 in 2000, 108 in 2001, 97 in 2002, and 88 in 2003. If you compare these statistics to the more than 5,000 IPOs in the 1990s, you will appreciate why investors roll their eyes when the entrepreneur says he will return their investment with an IPO.

The second exit factor to consider is the implication of the amount at which companies go public or are purchased or sold, and the implications such amounts have for investors' targeted multiples of return at liquidation. For example, although the number of IPOs may be larger, only 264 companies went public with a deal size close to $300 million. Remember that investors make big profits and achieve high-level interest rates of return for their portfolios only when a company they have invested in goes public or is purchased by a public company at a significant premium. Ask yourself about the implications for premoney valuations and investor requirements for shares of stock of the company in exchange for their capital when most companies that do sell are selling for only $100 million to $300 million in the current merger-and-acquisition market. How much of the stock in your company will the investor require to achieve targeted multiples over the term of the hold to compensate the investor for loss of use of capital?

The astute entrepreneur needs to think about all these things in determining whether your deal is financeable and whether—given its time-intensive and resource-intensive nature—the *Sturm und Drang* of raising private capital is merited.

From our experience in working with more than 4,000 companies since 1987, we know that added points need to be raised. Do not risk overshopping your deal by introducing your venture to investors before it is ready. Most companies, before meeting with investors or retaining placement counsel, determine that their product or service solves a problem for their customers. Some obtain orders or at least conduct research with customers or potential customers. Many develop a backlog of orders. Also, packaging, or the packaging idea, is developed, a prototype completed, and data from test runs are ready. Finally, progress has been made in developing pro forma financial statements that meet reasonable economic preconditions.

We have already discussed the need for the presence of a growth industry and the need for strong management in crafting a deal attractive to investors. With management, however, we need to address some less obvious features. Investors need to know that management has made a capital commitment to the venture. This is not to suggest that a reasonable investor would require someone to put up a house as security; even so, the members of the management team should be willing to pledge a substantial portion of their net worth to the venture. In addition, the team must also acknowledge its responsibility in raising the necessary funds for the venture. Although this feat often takes months to accomplish, the task belongs to the team, not to others. Also, team members must be willing to travel to meet with investors. Our experience has taught us that money cannot be raised by proxy or through impersonal contact or through presentations on the Internet. Raising money is accomplished only by meeting face to face with potential investors.

You must be realistic about raising capital. Give yourself reasonable time to complete the financing; do not allow *desperation* to hover over a deal. Remember this well: In the eyes of an investor, desperation is a deal killer.

Finally, determining the financeability of your deal should form the basis of your *situational awareness,* a term that jet fighter pilots use to establish the position of their aircraft, especially in relation to the ground. At such sizzling speed, their lives depend on knowing precisely where they are, even when flying upside-down. Although not as breath-taking or life-threatening, your situational awareness—the management team, market, competition, industry, proprietary technology, production, channel economics, high margins, profit potential, capital intensity, projections, valuation, and exit plan—depends on sensing where you are in relation to your "ground."

ARE YOU FINANCEABLE?

It is one thing to think about whether your deal is financeable, quite another to ponder whether you yourself are capable of being funded. One of the facts of life in private placement investment is that plans do not get funded, people get funded. Yes, it is important that your deal is financeable, but more important is whether you can inspire the confidence in an investor to write a check.

Do you have the traits that will assure an investor that you can accomplish your goal and make good on the proposed ROI? What it takes is outlined in Exhibit 2.3.

One of the most important traits of a successful fund-raiser is having the vision to create, conceptualize, and communicate a workable solution to a problem. Sometimes the visionary starts with a blank sheet of paper and develops something new because he or she understands the market or the technology. Other times, he or she diagnoses a unique combination of existing technologies. For example, a recent client has effectively combined CD-ROM technology with developments in biochip technology, creating a capability for conducting basic laboratory testing with the same elements in CD-ROMs that are used in personal computers. And on other occasions the creative visionary anticipates what customers want in the future. But as we have mentioned, it is not the vision, but the skill to communicate and act successfully on that vision which also matters.

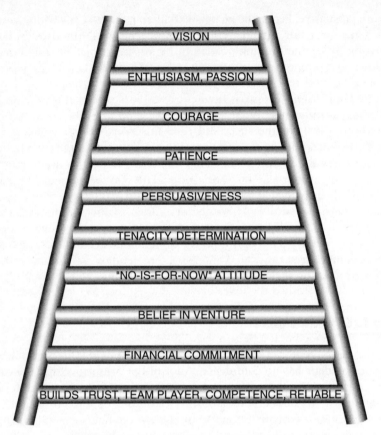

VISION

ENTHUSIASM, PASSION

COURAGE

PATIENCE

PERSUASIVENESS

TENACITY, DETERMINATION

"NO-IS-FOR-NOW" ATTITUDE

BELIEF IN VENTURE

FINANCIAL COMMITMENT

BUILDS TRUST, TEAM PLAYER, COMPETENCE, RELIABLE

Exhibit 2.3　Traits of a Successful Fund-Raiser
Source: International Capital Resources

Enthusiasm, courage, patience, persuasiveness, and tenacity are also among the traits of a successful fund-raiser. Enthusiasm reflects the entrepreneur's drive to see his or her vision become a reality. Enthusiasm will enable the entrepreneur to hang in over the long haul, through hours, days, weeks, and years of work to build a sustainable company. It is this enthusiasm that will generate an investor's zeal for being associated with the venture. Nor is courage any less imperative, since asking people for money is hardly the favorite pastime of even the most gregarious and bold among us. Courage means stepping up and being willing to take the necessary risks to grow a start-up. Only the most confident entrepreneur with passion and intestinal fortitude receives the monetary vote of the angel investor.

Also indispensable are the patience to endure setbacks and the ability to remain persuasive. Persuading a person that an enterprise is worthwhile and will generate a fair rate of return demands tenacity, the dogged determination to see the funding process through. Invariably there will be setbacks that entrepreneurs must endure; however, these roadblocks and detours cannot deter or dissuade entrepreneurs from pressing forward in executing their vision. Investors fund entrepreneurs who will prevail despite temporary derailments.

Another trait of the successful fund-raiser involves adopting a "no-is-for-now" attitude, particularly regarding selling their offerings. In other words, deal with rejection in a positive light. Refuse to take "no" for an answer. Deflect it. After all, "no" often means "No, I'm not interested now" or "No, I'm not interested in the deal as it is presently structured." Probe. Make suggestions: "What if I were to involve another investor? Might you be interested then?" Or, "If I were to restructure the venture, would you be more inclined to invest?" Plumb your present target for the names of investors likely to think about the deal. Above all, remember not to take "no" personally. Take "no" to mean "No, not at this time." Take it to mean that you have not yet furnished the investor with enough reasons for saying "yes." Above all, do not let a "no" alienate you to the extent that you alienate your potential investor.

We mentioned that a person seeking funding for a venture must radiate confidence. No one can expect an investor to believe in a venture in which the entrepreneur has no confidence. A lot of the confidence that the entrepreneur displays in the venture can be demonstrated by the percentage of personal net worth the entrepreneur is willing to stake in the venture. Therefore, the entrepreneur needs to commit more than "sweat equity"; that is, forego a salary, perhaps until the investors receive their money. In this way, the entrepreneur demonstrates financial commitment, a commitment vital to the success of the venture, and crucial to installing in the mind of the investor that the entrepreneur truly believes in the venture.

Finally, there is the matter of building trust, without which no venture is likely to get launched, much less sail smoothly. Just as you build an investor database one name at a time, you build financing one relationship at a time. People become involved only in relationships that improve their self-image. Thirteen-year-old George Washington listed among his 110 "Rules of Civility": "Associate yourself with men of good quality if you esteem your own reputation." Whether young George was capable of such mature thinking at so early an age or simply copying Roman maxims in his notebook, the point remains the same: People are not likely to get involved in relationships that may lower their self-esteem.

Build trust with others by being honest and by responding candidly to all issues. Things can get sticky; make them less so by confronting possible problems at the start. If you have had a problem with alcohol or other drugs, do not wait until the other party's private investigator uncovers the information. Confess—as personal and painful as it may be. A confession can turn a negative into a positive. Be able to look someone in the eye and explain your situation as no one else can.

IS YOUR RISK FINANCEABLE?

Before embarking on the path to raising capital, the entrepreneur asks three important questions: Is the deal financeable? Am I personally financeable? Is the risk in the deal financeable?

To assess the risk of your financeability, our research has identified six areas that investors focus on in their assessment of an investment (Exhibit 2.4). In our experience, if three or more of these risks arise, a red flag halts the investor.

The first of these is management risk: Will the management team stick together? We've termed this risk "team risk." Do the members of the management team get along with one another? In giving birth to the company, will the team be able to work through the highs and lows of the entrepreneurial experience?

The second risk involves market change and the team's ability to accept the impact. This risk relates to business strategy and how well the management team has thought through its business strategy and done its homework relative to what's happening in the market and, moreover, the implications this could have for the plan they have outlined in its documentation.

The third area of the risk in your deal focuses on whether growth still lies ahead. Is a visionary leading the early stages in the development of the product or the market, or is someone riding in the tail wind of the lead racing car? Do we really have someone putting the technology together, someone with the courage to be a leader?

Fourth in assessing the risk in your deal stresses the sensitivity of the en-

EXHIBIT 2.4   Is Your Risk Financeable?

1. Will management stick together? (Team Risk)
2. Could market change and impact acceptance? (Business Strategy Risk)
3. Is there still growth ahead? (Product/Technology Risk)
4. Anything brewing in market that could affect your company? (Market Risk)
5. Will manufacturing/R&D work as planned? (Operations Risk)
6. Financial performance of venture to date (Financial Risk)

Source: International Capital Resources

trepreneur's ear to the vibrations of the marketplace. What out there might affect the company? Sometimes entrepreneurs get so close to their own technology, so close to the features of their own deal, so close to developing the business plan, to putting the management team together, to raising the money, that they overlook the pulse of the market. Entrepreneurs must not ignore market information. They do so at their own peril. Entrepreneurs can ill afford a business plan that lacks a sense of the market within the past 6 to 12 months—a time period after which market circumstances practically guarantee a shift in technology.

Operations risk has to do with the extent to which the manufacturing plan can be worked out, and whether the research and development by the company lead to investor confidence. Will the prototype and product that issue from the manufacturing process meet the time frames and cost projections?

Last comes the critical financial risk, a risk that takes different forms: How much money has been invested into the company to date? Has the company raised any money, or will the company need to approach investors beyond family and friends? How much financing needs to occur before there emerges proof of the concept? (This assessment relates to capital intensity discussed earlier.) Another assessment risk concerns the company's ability to generate revenues and/or profits within a reasonable period of time, typically 12 to 18 months. And what was the financial performance of companies that the principals of the management team have been involved with previously? All of this, as well as the actual financial stability of the managers themselves, will be considered as part of the financial performance of today's venture.

Companies seeking funding must remember that sophisticated investors will take all these types of risk into consideration not only in considering whether to invest, but also in their developing the deal terms and conditions of agreement under which they would be willing to invest.

THE BENEFITS AND DISADVANTAGES OF EQUITY

Each week in the United States, $5 billion in new equity and secured transactions are offered. Only $1 billion a week are subscribed to by individual and organizational investors, effective June 2004. In effect, companies making equity offerings in the public market have only a 20 percent chance of raising the capital they require—and only after significant financial, time, and emotional commitment. With this level of success, why go through the challenge posed by the equity financing process—public or private?

Since private placement investments are primarily equity, it is best to know equity's advantages and disadvantages (Exhibit 2.5).

EXHIBIT 2.5 Advantages/Disadvantages of Equity

Advantages	Disadvantages
• Capital	• Dilutes ownership
• Permanent capital that increases company's net worth, borrowing capacity, and overall financial strength	• More expensive than debt when successful
• Enhance credibility	• No means of reversing the transaction
• No scheduled repayment	• Give up control/flexibility
• No personal liability	• Difficulty finding investors
• Help	
• Accountability	

Source: International Capital Resources

In studies we have performed periodically since 1994, on average 61 percent of entrepreneurs who have contacted us about their search for capital report using the private placement with informal venture investors as their primary targeted funding source. They chose the private placement of equity resoundingly over further soliciting family, friends, business contacts, the small business investment companies (SBICs), joint ventures, corporate investors, and professional venture capital firms.

First, the advantages. Benefits accrue to the private equity alternative. The private placement is a source of permanent capital without the expensive burden on early-stage cash flows normally associated with debt servicing. This creates cash flow generating capability. Permanent capital increases the company's net worth, creating financial flexibility. The company can then take advantage of overall financial strength and increased borrowing capacity to use credit sources for funding other opportunities. The creative deal structuring possible with the private placement permits access to capital at earlier stages in development than would be the case in more traditional financing situations. Having raised capital from astute investors through the private placement, the company benefits from enhanced credibility in the eyes of the business community, especially other unused capital resources. And foremost among the advantages is the added value brought by the investors who bring more than capital to the deal. As we will explain, in most cases active angel investors have broader agendas than just ROI. They look for deeper involvement—other types of return beyond the financial. Many entrepreneurs have for most of their careers been "Lone Rangers," answering to no one but their own visions and personal ethics; but from this new level of accountability emerges a new experience of responsibility and professionalism, brought on by having investors, a board of directors, or advisory board, and having to report to investors who closely monitor their investment. Entrepreneurs learn how to accept help and guidance from those who have been successful in what they have sought to accomplish.

At the same time, however, equity carries its burden of disadvantages. Private equity is expensive, requiring an internal rate of return of at least 30 percent to be attractive. There is a range of front-end and back-end fees, and various expenses associated with successful equity fund-raising companies. It also provides potential for significant dilution of current shareholders. In a word, equity diminishes ownership. Unanticipated rounds of financing or down rounds at lower valuation can strain relationships with early investors in the deal or lead to litigation with early shareholders. And just as investors bring added value to the company, they often want governance—perhaps a seat on the board or an important managerial post. This situation brings to the surface for the entrepreneur the underlying emotional issue of control of the company. Furthermore, an equity transaction can stretch itself out. We are now seeing $1 million rounds taking six months to one year to complete. With an equity investment, investors will require a clearly articulated three- to five-year strategy. This creates a burden of planning and documentation development that can create stress for the entrepreneur already wearing multiple hats.

Equity will become more expensive than debt if the company is successful. In effect, then, an equity investment offers no means of transaction reversal; that is, you marry your investment partner—unless he or she wants to divorce you. As one investor warned, "For all intents and purposes, many private investments are permanent investments!" Finally, to reiterate what may be the greatest barrier to persons embarking on a successful private placement: Private investors, prizing their privacy, are extremely difficult to locate.

So problems with the private equity alternative do exist. But before reaching this stage of the venture, there comes the disadvantage preceding all the others: the difficulty of finding high-net-worth angel investors, the individuals involved in private placement investment.

MAKING YOUR SEARCH FOR INVESTORS MORE EFFICIENT

The difficulty in locating the high-net-worth angel investor generates a critical question: How is the high-net-worth private or business angel investor different from bankers, professional money managers, venture capitalists, and institutional investors? The difference is that the private investor *does not have to invest*. For this reason, the private investor has a different take on things. So the procedures used to sew up a Small Business Administration loan, to secure subordinated debt financing from an institution, or to approach conventional venture capitalists are not appropriate for accessing the private investor.

Therefore, the conventional wisdom and underlying assumptions that drive the search for funds need to be reexamined. ICR finds that many people approach private investors using the same models and same behavior used to obtain a loan or stir the interest of venture capitalists. But the principles that guide success in finding money among these other markets simply fail with the private investor.

Why? One reason has already been discussed: These investors protect their privacy. Here is another reason, also briefly mentioned earlier: The private investor's reasons for investing are not always exclusively economic. Therefore, the entrepreneur faces difficulty in judging which approach to adopt in trying to locate, attract, and build a relationship with angel investors.

THE PROBLEMS WITH CONVENTIONAL WISDOM

In locating an angel who can work financial miracles, many entrepreneurs employ conventional wisdom. Its precepts are predicated on the procedures applied to financing from banks, professional venture capitalists, and brokerage of public securities. Such a strategy is handicapped. What are these precepts and why don't they work?

In their advice for accessing capital, many popular business books suggest networking for your venture in the hope of securing promising referrals by talking to your accountant, attorney, doctor, dentist, or some other adviser. *Networking* is a term widely used, yet it refers to a concept often misunderstood. Networking is overworked; more important, networking works indirectly. Instead of approaching the investor directly, networking lodges faith in the hands of someone else, hoping that he or she will be able to help, for example, doing initial prospecting and qualifying of the "potential" investor.

Another tenet of conventional wisdom proposes that you concentrate largely on people who understand your industry, in the belief that staying abreast of it will link you to people familiar with your type of company. This presumably qualifies them as investors for your venture. But industry specialization is only one consideration in an investment decision; many other things can influence a private investor's preference. Remember, we said that the private investor's agenda can be significantly more diverse than merely considering internal rate of return or industry experience and specialization. For example, investors may show more interest in investing in a business geographically close to home. Or they may be interested in a new, emerging industry that has been an avocation for many years while they were working in another industry. Or they may be looking for something exciting and fun, perhaps a change from what has long since become drudgery. This type of investor may be looking for something new and different. Thus, over-reliance on industry sources narrows rather than widens the pool of prospective investors.

Conventional wisdom also advises that you advertise. Just peruse the Mart section in the Thursday afternoon edition of the *Wall Street Journal*, and you will discover numerous solicitations for investors advertised there, thinly disguised as business opportunities. These types of classified advertisements supposedly provide another vehicle that entrepreneurs can rely on in order to generate investor contacts. But be warned: In many places, advertising a private placement investment is illegal. This restriction has been eased in some states, for example, in California. The California Corporate Code's 25102(n) statute permits small business entrepreneurs to advertise for wealthy angel investors. But restrictions have not been eased everywhere. Even where it is legal, the entrepreneur must be cautious. An advertisement for a private placement investment that reaches inappropriate or unqualified investors could instigate legal problems about the way these investors were solicited. By definition, a private placement investment is the limited offering of securities to a small group of private investors with whom the entrepreneur has an established relationship and whom the entrepreneur believes are appropriate and qualified for that investment opportunity. So be careful with advertising, regardless of the extent to which others may engage in it.

Last, conventional wisdom advises entrepreneurs to turn finally to family and friends, people who know them, have the money to invest, and retain a genuine interest in supporting the entrepreneur. Family and friends should be the first—not the final—source you entreat after you have personally invested a substantial portion of your own net worth. Many people eventually appeal to family and friends after networking, canvassing industry, and ferreting out investment bankers. Family and friends and one's own resources should be the initial sources of capital at the earlier stages of financing a venture.

On close examination, then, conventional wisdom may be conventional, but it hardly qualifies as wisdom. In Chapter 3, our strategy offers a better way, a plan that works.

The Solution: A Strategy That Works

Anyone can sell cold drinks to thirsty people. Marketing is the art of finding or inventing ways to make people thirsty.
—Herman Holtz, Consultant

Can I give my whole philosophy? Two phases with every brand. Getting there. Staying there. As difficult as getting there can be under today's conditions, staying there is even more difficult.
—Steve Meisner, Marketing Director, Ferrari-Carano

AN "INEFFICIENT" MARKET DEFINED

Early on, the investment banking business tagged the private capital market as "inefficient." When investment bankers or venture capitalists portray the private placement or angel market in this way, precisely what do they mean? Why inefficient?

Inefficiency in the private equity market is important for entrepreneurs to understand because it is a problem that leads to underinvestment. This, in turn, contributes to the capital gap we mentioned earlier. The absence of an organized capital provider system creates hardships for the entrepreneurial earlier-stage companies regardless of whether seed, R&D, start-up, or an expanding small business. Systems and the critical information for entrepreneurs and investors to make fast, informed decisions are simply not readily available.

First, no professional analysts are available to tout the private equity offerings or issue research reports, activities characteristic of major investment houses in their effort to increase interest in public stock offerings. Publishing efforts to create periodicals and research journals regarding this market have not been financially successful, and are not widely endorsed.

Largely, however, market information on private offerings is severely limited, both on the micro level (i.e., at individual companies) and on the macro level (i.e., at technical fundamentals underlying the capital market's dynamics). As a result, it becomes difficult for private investors to perform comparative analyses on their deals against baselines of compiled statistics on groups of other deals. Entrepreneurs need to appreciate that investors are forced to operate blindly, without information on valuations, deal structures, terms, return rates, and liquidity multiples or alternatives. Absence of this baseline information slows the investors' evaluation of deal risk/reward potential, leaving subjective nature and personal experience as the tools to rely on in determining if a venture is promising.

Also, no Securities and Exchange Commission (SEC) requirement forces disclosure of such offerings, a notable dispensation for private investors who, above all else, prize their privacy. Moreover, by the very nature of the transactions, the market is inefficient and inconvenient for buyers as well as for issuers and sellers. Were you choosing to sell a publicly traded stock, for instance, you could pick up the phone, call your broker, get a bid on your stock, and sell it—none of which is an option with a private placement investment. You possess, instead, an illiquid commodity. Finding an investor whose idiosyncratic investment criteria match your deal becomes problematic. Moreover, the search for deals worthy of consideration requires considerable time by the investor too.

The search is also extremely inconvenient for the entrepreneur seller because of the angel penchant for privacy. Angels make themselves scarce and difficult to find. The difficulty in locating high-net-worth investors with the qualifications and inclination to do high-risk investing creates barriers and bottlenecks in the capitalization process.

So entering the direct investment market becomes expensive, often prohibitively so. Professional assistance and advisory counsel is expensive. Costs inevitably add up for the entrepreneur: a financial intermediary to help generate investor prospects for the deal; legal counsel to keep you within the requirements of an exempt, private offering (e.g., restrictions on public advertising); investment banking counsel on structuring of the transaction or calculation of valuation; and management consulting support in developing business plan documentation. Furthermore, in private placements, no real-time liquidity exists. From the investor's point of view, unloading your stock may rush you headlong into restrictions: You may be bound by terms and conditions requiring you to hold the stock, or you may confront tax implications of dumping stock too early, thus having to pay excessive taxes on capital appreciation or capital gains.

Based on our proprietary research, the average hold time before liquidity is eight years among ICR's investor network. It is this loss-of-use capital that characterizes the risk in the entrepreneur's early-stage deal. The difficulty posed by the investor's inability to get out of the venture is one of the great inefficiencies of the angel market, with significant implications for entrepreneurs seeking investment capital.

Also, the conditions of the exchange itself remain fuzzy and undefined. How do you transfer a privately owned stock from one private investor to another? Transferring privately owned stock activates a different type of transaction from that of holding stock in a public offering. Also, investors may find themselves having to go back to the company in order to transfer documents to another party. Moreover, the company often has no history, leaving all financial information about the venture resting on "blue sky," that is, exclusively on projections. This circumstance leaves the investor unable to accomplish a fixed analysis, even through due diligence. Therefore, the time dedicated to due diligence remains unspecified, relinquished entirely to the subjective values of this type of analysis. Finally, novice entrepreneurs who bring attorneys into their transactions too early tend to draw out these transactions more than investors do, making them more expensive, complicated, and time consuming.

A STRATEGY THAT WORKS

Therefore, in this inefficient market, the problem arises of how to maneuver it more proficiently. In accessing the affluent, hard-to-find private investor, ICR advocates a strategy different from the conventional suggestions masquerading as wisdom. In contrast, our answer to proficiently searching for investors is shown in Exhibit 3.1.

Build a Capitalization Strategy

We have found from our informal research with successful entrepreneurs—those who have completed their financing rounds and raised the needed capital—that successful money raisers have been those who have understood that the responsibility for that task rests squarely with them, that it is a critical feature of their job description. The task of raising money never goes away from seed, start-up, and early growth through to the establishment of the company in equity markets. The money-raising responsibility changes only in form. During early stages, the task is to convince fellow founders, friends, and family to trust in your vision and integrity. Next, entrepreneurs turn with their deal to nonrelated angels. If they can grow, venture capitalists may get involved, again for equity Series A rounds. If the company survives and prospers, commercial banks provide corporate debt. And, if the venture becomes sustainable, if it grows to meet stock exchange require-

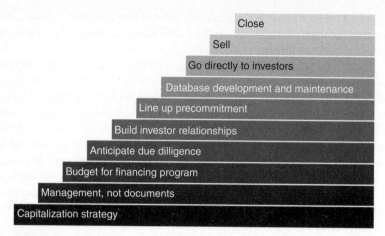

Exhibit 3.1 How to Increase Efficiency in the Private Placement Process
Source: International Capital Resources

ments, the company might be traded on the quoted equity markets. Savvy entrepreneurs embrace the challenge of raising capital as a defining characteristic of their chosen roles, and incorporate development of winning strategies into their professional skill development.

Many companies fail in their capitalization strategy because their initial capital is insufficient to support operations through to the next milestone. A major tenet of capitalization strategy is to raise only enough funding to accomplish that next step in the venture's development, and to add to this an amount to cover the costs anticipated to raise the next round of required financing. This strategy will save the company from surrendering too much equity when its valuation is lowest. Many companies raise too much money too early, while not spending enough time to understand their financial requirements. This understanding requires analysis and forecasting of cash flow and timing the offerings so that achievement of the next milestone represents a significant step down in the investor's perceived risk in the venture.

Reducing the perceived risk associated with the venture improves the valuation in the following rounds, letting the company raise more money while ceding less of it. For example, one entrepreneur confided to us that he had taken his company public, raising $23 million. However, by the end of the process he owned less than five percent of it, a perfect example of failing to develop a sound capitalization strategy. To his deep regret, he had surrendered too much of the company too early, that is, when its valuation was low.

As you develop your capitalization strategy and establish clear milestones, you need to understand the correlation of stage of development with private capital sources and the amount of capital required at critical stages in the development of the venture. A classic study by one of the five largest accounting firms of the time found that 328 manufacturing and service companies had successfully achieved sales of $1 million to $50 million in the period between 1989 and 1994. They found that it took an average of 28 months for successful companies to pass from seed and start-up through survival on to the initial market growth stage.

One of the interesting findings is the correlation between the amount of capital needed at each of those stages and the source of the private capital (Exhibit 3.2). During the seed and start-up stages, these companies successfully raised on average between $75,000 and $150,000 from those investors who had an affinity for the entrepreneur and the founders. Typically, these individuals included family, friends, neighbors, acquaintances, business associates, professional colleagues, and providers of professional services to the entrepreneurs, who often were also investors.

During the survival stages, generally these ventures successfully raised $200,000 to $210,000 from individuals and investors, a group that typically includes suppliers and distributors, future suppliers and distributors, employees, potential employees, and customers—all people with an affinity for the technology or product. Add to this gathering those other individuals, such as manager-investors, who invested in the venture and took an operational management position. These are the people who form the backbone of individual participatory investment.

Last, during the initial market growth stage of their development and fi-

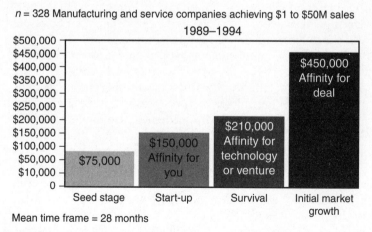

n = 328 Manufacturing and service companies achieving $1 to $50M sales 1989–1994

Mean time frame = 28 months

Exhibit 3.2 Correlation of Stage of Development with Private Capital Source
Source: International Capital Resources

nancing, these companies typically raised $450,000 to $500,000 from non-related individuals and investors and groups with an affinity for the deal. These likely were private placement investments or direct public offerings, institutional venture capital investments, or bank loans and credit lines arranged by the principals.

The chart in Exhibit 3.2 on the correlation of stage of development with the private capital source provides a road map, complete with stopping-off points along the way. You should avoid trying to tap family members and friends at a stage of development requiring an amount they cannot contribute, say $500,000. Likewise, why approach manager-investors for an amount in this range when they typically invest only $100,000? The idea is to gain a sense of the best source for capital at each stage of the development of your venture. As you develop a capitalization strategy, keep in mind the amounts of capital typically being raised at these pivotal points in a developmental-stage company.

Focus on Management, Not Documents

Although development of the professionally prepared business plan and presentation (see Appendix A) is important to funding, only implementation of the ideas contained in the plan bear value. We emphasize the importance of the Investment Opportunity Profile over the business plan as a marketing tool during the initial stages of investor development and as a way to inspire, as well as assess, investors' interest in the venture. And while we affirm that investors invest in people, not documents, this does not render business plans and summaries unimportant. In the beginning, you want to focus on management, but eventually you will need documentation to enunciate your vision. Documents may not be crucial in the early going, but be assured their time will come. Never minimize their importance.

But before preparing documents, you should create a number of company boards, particularly a board of directors or an advisory board. A respected board of directors is one of the most important credentials that a private company seeking funding can possess, and it is central to potential investors being able to distinguish the "pedigrees" from the "mutts."

Getting the most from your board means selecting individuals who add value, not merely serve in an honorary capacity. Look at the legal debacles we read about daily in the business press. An entrepreneur's best insurance against future litigation lies in his or her careful selection and scrutiny of the board of directors. Many entrepreneurs believe boards are just a check against their Lone Ranger tendencies. Not so. Independent boards serve in an important advisory capacity, providing help, counsel, and insight in carrying out your business plan. We will discuss later how the Sarbanes-Oxley

Act has established new standards for all business entities, whether public or private companies.

So an independent board is important in attracting new investors, investors who must know these people will stay on if and when things get bad. In this highly litigious age, as the entrepreneur adds more investors while the company develops, he or she correspondingly becomes vulnerable to lawsuits. PricewaterhouseCoopers, in their *Growing Your Business* booklet, suggests the following tips for getting the most from your compnay's board in the current environment: Establish an independent nominating committee rather than have a CEO unilaterally identifying board members; ensure that the board as a whole has the necessary skills and experience; exclude those who are not independent, for example, those who happen to be close to the CEO but who themselves lack the knowledge, judgment, skills, and experience; provide an in-depth industry orientation to all board members; foster trust with your board by being open, and seek their counsel on major issues; and, finally, create a safe environment for asking questions by using meetings to communicate, not just to present facts.

Entrepreneurs should remember that poor decisions about investors and board members "let in" to the transaction can make your deal less attractive to needed investors, venture capital, or corporate lenders when you seek future rounds.

Even if entrepreneurs need to provide director and officer insurance—which on a $5 million round might cost $100,000—the availability of such insurance and coverage can make attracting prospective board members easier, especially if they have concerns about financial vulnerability. Does such director and officer insurance protect you? Yes, it does, but fraud and misrepresentation will preclude policy coverage. Still, carefully read a potential policy and familiarize yourself with all its exclusions. Failure to do so could lead to your paying twice the price for half the coverage.

If you have trouble developing a board of directors because of issues relative to the liability exposure of directors and officers, an advisory board is an alternative that will allow you to bring people into the organization, provide counsel, and gain the benefit of the board relationship while lessening their legal exposure.

Next, identify respected technical advisers and establish professional advisory relationships; they are indispensable to a winning team. Assembling a credible fund-raising team and establishing constructive and cooperative relationships among its members should also be a high priority. The team will include not only the entrepreneur, founders, managers, and board of directors, but also the attorney, accountant, CPA, advisory board members, technical advisers, investment bankers, and any financial intermediary or finder assisting in introducing investor prospects for the transaction. Even more important—and this is reiterated by private investors—you must assemble a credible management team instead of placing faith in the capability of documents alone to generate investor interest (Exhibit 3.3).

It's also important to develop a complete set of references you can use with your investors to prepare for the due diligence process. To clarify, sometimes you need technical advisory support. Technical advisers possess different proficiencies. For example, some advisers can provide support in developing the business plan, or in completing a competitive analysis for the marketing section, or in assisting in obtaining patent protection.

Next, though perhaps less recognized as part of the team but in our experience absolutely critical, is your including any lead investors or investors initially interested in the deal among your resources and reference list. This kind of thinking helps you use all the resources available in building the most effective team with which to move forward. Once you've exhausted your own resources and that of family, friends, and referrals, consider a financial intermediary or other resource to supplement your pool of investor prospects. A *competent* financial intermediary will help you with your private placement in a number of ways: provide introductions to qualified, accredited investors interested in your type of deal, help you raise funds by helping to place the security, provide knowledge about the private market, share extensive private capital sources they can tap on your behalf, bring experience of the private placement process, guide the company to help you to legally attract qualified investors, share their aptitude for fund-raising with your team, and identify sources you may have missed or were unaware of as appropriate for your deal.

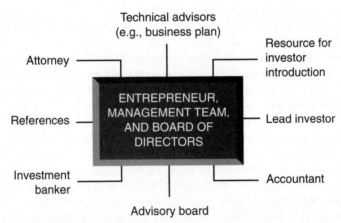

Exhibit 3.3 A Winning team for the Private Placement
Source: International Capital Resources

Finally, it will pay to remember that venture documents are like milk: They spoil with time. An experienced entrepreneur carrying only a "B" plan will always be financed over a novice with an "A" plan or product. Remember what we have stressed about funding: Business plans do not get funded; people get funded.

Budget for the Financing Program

Ironies abound in the money-raising game; for example, only companies that "look like" they don't need capital are successful at raising money from high-net-worth investors. Another irony is that it takes money to raise money. This means building a budget to raise money. While every exuberant entrepreneur believes that skilled professionals will line up to work on commission for the privilege of being associated with his or her venture, good help willing to work "on the come" (i.e., on commission) is hard to find. Worse, you'll get what you pay for—nothing. We have often advised entrepreneurs to start early, assign an individual to be solely responsible for and focused on fund-raising, premarket the deal vigorously before beginning the capital raising, and never stop fund-raising by making it part of your job description and daily task list.

Regardless of these suggestions, many entrepreneurs exhaust their resources developing their product and spending money on attorneys and consultants in pursuit of venture documents. But money needs to be set aside to raise capital. Entrepreneurs commit a common error in using all their money for product development and for documentation, leaving no money to raise money.

Another risk unfolds here: Working on the come creates dependency on the commission for remuneration. In many cases an intermediary will operate outside your direct control during fund-raising. The concern is that since intermediaries work on commission, pressure will mount to persuade investors to close. The intermediaries may make inappropriate promises to investors, misrepresent the opportunity, or, in their exuberance, fail to disclose risk. This last circumstance especially adds to the hazard of employing people who work solely on commission.

In Exhibit 3.4 we outline expense items typically associated with raising capital, which include a number of different expenses usually paid up front as well as fees that follow the completion of the transaction.

Estimates indicate that $10 million is required to get 0.5 percent of the mind of the U.S. market. Similarly, you will need financial resources to gain consciousness of the affluent, high-risk investors' market. So develop a budget, detailing the anticipated up-front costs of raising money and a realistic schedule allowing 6 to 12 months to close the transaction. Remember to

EXHIBIT 3.4   Expense Items in Raising Capital (6%–25% of capital raised)

Up—Front Expenses	Back —End Fees
• Development of a financing strategy	• Investment banking
• Business plan, financing proposal, profiles	• Finders' fees
• Financial projections (accountant or CPA)	• Brokerage fees (e.g., sales commissions, underwriting fees, due diligence, processing costs, red—tape fees)
• Legal security documents (disclosure documents, terms sheet, investment agreement, stock purchase agreement)	• Legal fees • Offering fees —State and federal
• Printing	

• Capital search
  —Profile
  —Travel
  —"Advertising"
  —Presentation materials
  —Telephone
  —Seminars
  —Postage
  —Printing	

—Other	

Source: International Capital Resources

calculate these costs into your forecasts. Running out of money before raising capital or setting up unreasonable, overly optimistic funding schedules will create an atmosphere of desperation that will accompany you like a shadow in your discussions with investors and finally work against your financing goal.

For the entrepreneur new to raising capital, costs can be shocking. Although raising private capital is less expensive than going to the public marketplace, costs still loom. However, no direct correlation exists between money spent and money raised. In our experience, a "rule of thumb" for total fees and expenses of fund-raising range from 10 to 25 percent of the money raised. Some entrepreneurs may spend $100,000 to raise $1 million, while others will need to spend $100,000 to raise $400,000.

To be sure of covering start-up costs, budget a minimum of 10 percent of the amount to be raised in your capitalization program, figuring that during the first few months costs will outstrip investment capital raised. This budget can be used in paying up-front fees associated with documentation development, accounting and legal counsel, printing of marketing materials, and providing a budget for a range of investor development expenses. Then budget an additional 5 to 10 percent to cover the back-end fees. Investment banking fees for a professional placement agent, finders fees for a financial intermediary, and other residual legal and offering fees can all add up. As any seasoned capital development professional knows, it costs money to raise money. It is "pound foolish" to operate on a tattered shoestring when a small investment can help you achieve your capitalization goal.

Anticipate Due Diligence

Anticipation is a wonderful thing. It works wonders in all aspects of life. In tennis, for instance, being able to anticipate where your opponent's shot will land enables you to get in position to control the game. But tennis is not the only activity in which anticipation works to your advantage. You can increase the efficiency in the financing process by, for example, anticipating due diligence that puts you in a position to accomplish your goal faster. Due diligence is the analysis you can be sure will be conducted by the investors and their advisers in order to determine your venture's strengths, weaknesses, future profitability, competitive position, and identifiable and possible risks.

Typically, the investor and/or agents such as attorneys, accountants, or private investigators perform due diligence in these cases. These are typically sophisticated and experienced businesspeople who will evaluate not only the venture but also you and your business and personal background.

Entrepreneurs can expect due diligence to take two weeks to six months! Due diligence is no more than the caution any prudent person would exercise with their own money. Sophisticated investors recognize that nothing takes the place of a full-venture audit, an in-depth assessment of the founder and entrepreneurs, and close scrutiny of the deal elements themselves to judge the viability of a prospective early-stage investment; moreover, the investor will require numerous face-to-face meetings with the entrepreneur, thorough review of the business plan and strategy, and interviews with customers, suppliers, and competitors; and he may seek counsel from relevant industry or technical experts.

The entrepreneur can expect—following the losses investors suffered as a result of lax due diligence during the dot-com debacle—that investors will investigate the principals, including comprehensive background and reference checks, as well as possibly conducting interviews with former superiors, peers, subordinates, and business associates. To the entrepreneur, this due diligence may seem elaborate, but we caution them to expect it and to be prepared in advance of it. For more cautious and skeptical investors, nothing will replace legal and financial audits, a keen assessment of market potential, and the investors yearning to know potential risks in the venture and realistic future profit and return potential. By nature, entrepreneurs are optimistic and may understate risk factors, weaknesses in technology, and potential delays in penetrating their market. Such an attitude not only is legally suspect, but irresponsible, as the entrepreneur enters a much more critical investment climate.

An example of a due diligence case illustrates the point. A company was offered at a $1.6 million acquisition price, then was subjected to due diligence by one of ICR's partners. The principals of the venture stated that there was a net worth of approximately $1 million, plus off-balance-sheet assets of $600,000. The CPA conducting the due diligence requested the company's financial statements and tax returns. Subsequent analysis by the accountant showed operating losses of more than $800,000 for the previous 18 months, fraudulently prepared tax returns, and a $400,000 tax liability. Due diligence revealed the real value of the venture to be only $500,000.

The lesson for you is crucial: Know your own company thoroughly and hire competent personal advisers to assist you in preparing for due diligence.

Due diligence typically is best approached with full disclosure by admitting to yourself in advance those areas of the venture that reflect the strengths but that also unmask weaknesses and expose risks. Only by this procedure can you anticipate the questions that are sure to come and be able to address them honestly. So prepare in advance of meetings with investors all information necessary to support your answers. This becomes imperative, because during due diligence nothing less than your credibility is at stake.

Too often, we have seen greed overtake the entrepreneur's ethics, even those with the best of intentions. Examples of ethical lapses were featured in a 1999 article in *Fortune Magazine*:

- Companies investing in other companies that turn around and buy services from the investor company to inflate their services.
- Companies recognizing revenues prematurely.
- Companies reporting barter transactions as revenues.
- Companies recording sales at full value, not the actual price paid when using coupons or discounts.

Although it may be difficult to remain above the fray, especially when others raising money seem to be awash in deceit, the ethical entrepreneur anticipating today's thorough due diligence will not lose his or her ability to say "no."

As Exhibit 3.5 indicates, many factors go into investor due diligence, the preinvestment research that will verify your proposal's viability for receiving financing. This preinvestment research will scrutinize the skills and background of your management team, check references, examine the appropriate industry sector, interview customers and suppliers, assess product realization, study the potential of growth in the market and potential competitors, consult with technical advisers and other investors before investing, establish a premoney valuation for the venture, explore financial projections and other business attributes, and test the ability to match the deal with personal investment criteria.

Beware that preinvestment audit can involve questions about a number of areas of concern to investors, including management, products or services, industry, market, sales and distribution, competition, human resources, suppliers, production, and R&D. In addition, financial projections will be analyzed, particularly if the case is made that management can reach the objectives they have forecasted. Also scrutinized will be the company's expected financial needs and capital requirements, valuation calculations, balance sheet, liabilities, shareholders' equity, income statements, cash flow analyses, use of proceeds, and all supporting financial assumptions underlying projections. Lastly, investors might request a closer review of a range of miscellaneous documents.

While we have focused on the entrepreneur anticipating and preparing for due diligence by the investor, we advise entrepreneurs not to be shy in conducting the same procedure on investors that investors conduct on them. Be assertive in your due diligence of investors. Do not hesitate to inquire about the investors' investment objectives and their track record of investments with companies of similar size and within the same industry. Ask questions about other investments in the industry that could present a conflict of

---

EXHIBIT 3.5 Due Diligence, Preinvestment Research to Verify Proposal Viability

- Management team skills and background
- Reference check
- Industry sector research
- Customer/supplier interviews
- Product realization
- Market growth potential and competitors
- Consultation with others before investment
- Valuation
- Financial projections in investment proposal
- Other business attributes
- Fit/match with investor's personal criteria

Source: International Capital Resources

interest. And clearly define what ongoing role the investor may want to play in the venture.

In further conducting due diligence, you should obtain references of the investors and follow up on what the paperwork reveals. Also be clear about the financial terms of the investment before signing an agreement. Use professional advisers whose experience in anticipating problems can keep a bad situation from becoming worse. Use advisers who understand that you want to do the deal. (Avoid deal breakers.)

Build Relationships with Prospective Investors

Angels do not invest in business plans; they invest in people. The relationship between the angel and entrepreneur is the most significant factor in moving forward the sale of the illiquid investment security. When the chemistry between dreamer and dream-maker merge, other factors, such as business plans and private placement memoranda with risk-disclosure statements, become secondary. The relationship is everything. Astute entrepreneurs will appreciate that people are motivated to acquire relationships that improve their self-image. Investors have different motivations for investing, just as they have different motivations for declining the opportunity. Still, people invest in people. This seems to be the sense of it: "I'm investing in you. If the association uplifts me, you have a better chance of gaining my contribution to the venture." By the same token, a transaction they think will lower their self-perception will keep them on the sidelines.

So in raising capital, you need to move outside meetings and toward building successful relationships with investors and their advisers; proceed beyond the one-dimensional professional level. The gimme-your-money-and-get-lost syndrome will no longer suffice—if, in fact, it ever has. *You always get the capitalist along with the capital.* To cultivate a relationship with investors, you must add value through the relationship. Properly managed, even investors who initially turn you down can end up providing feedback on your offering as well as guidance on your development and presentation. They can simultaneously provide you with a cost-effective way to cultivate investor referral. Again, those who refuse early may well become investors at a later, less risky stage of the venture's development.

In raising capital, also get to know prospective investors who inquire about your venture before you have contacted them. Last year, more than $200 billion was donated to philanthropic causes, most of it by individuals, a substantial portion of which was raised by professional fund-raisers. As any successful fund-raiser will tell you, the key to getting a check is matching the donor with the cause. You see, there is such a thing as a $250,000 lunch!

To raise funds, gather information on prospective investors before any contact so that you can determine whether a match exists between them and your investment. Good research takes time, so if you cannot handle this yourself, private investigators with access to online databases can be an inexpensive and efficient resource for gathering and packaging the necessary information preceding your meeting with prospective investors. Remember this quote from John D. Rockefeller, one of the most generous philanthropists in U.S. history: "The more you know about the person you are asking for a gift, the better your chances of getting it."

So just as you build a database of investors one name at a time, you build funding one relationship at a time. Take the time to understand the personalities of these investor contacts; find out what they expect out of their relationship with you. Accelerate this process by getting comfortable with their advisers. Take the time to understand their concerns: for example, the intergenerational transfer of wealth. Learn about their favorite charities and pastimes. Expand your relationship within the investor's family. As we have pointed out, spouses are increasingly involved in investment decision making. You and your firm may even be able to speed the investment education of the children of these middle-aged private investors, children who have reached an age when investments may have begun to pique their interest.

Assembling profiles of possible investors becomes another way of building relationships. Three types of profiles exist: demographics, psychographics, and—our choice—*biographics*. Demography categorizes information by gender, race, age, geographic locale, and so on. Psychographics measures such things as values and attitudes: "How do you feel about the job the president is doing? Excellent? Good? Fair? Poor? No opinion?" Or "What's your opinion of the NRA? Favorable? Unfavorable? No opinion?" Psychographics aims at the individual's thoughts and feelings, opinions often extrapolated for a look at their broader implications.

The third type of profile originates from the new field of biographics. It is based on the research techniques of case studies and content analyses that assess the personal history and lifestyle of the individual. A biographical profile gathers not only names and addresses—where people live can tell you a great deal about them—but also professions, positions, memberships, family histories, personal histories, financial positions, and investment histories. In Chapter 5 we illustrate this kind of information in our pioneering new study of 60 investors from ICR's network of angel investors. Our advice is simple: Stay close to the gold. Don't just look at investors as deep pockets; instead, cultivate a relationship with them; treat them as peers, if not as mentors.

Remember too, if properly managed, even investors who turn you down at first can provide invaluable feedback about your offering, guidance on offering development, and valuation and pricing, while simultaneously providing you a cost-effective way to develop the venture and cultivate additional investor referrals. Commonly, investors who reject you at very early stages become investors later, once the venture is more fully developed.

Line Up Precommitment

The entrepreneur can increase efficiency in finding investors by lining up a commitment from them before spending time and money on preparing documents. Private placement investments involve two types of documents: (1) the business plan and (2) the private placement investment memorandum or risk disclosure document. Basically, the business plan proposes reasons *for* investing, while the risk disclosure document suggests reasons *against* investing.

Ironically, many entrepreneurs incur $10,000 to $25,000 in legal fees to prepare a risk disclosure document—even before building interest in the venture—which presents investors with reasons why they should not invest. Before the dot-com bubble, a significant percentage of investors were willing to invest without a complete business plan; that is not the case today. In its newest study of 1,300 investors in its proprietary investor database, 95 percent of those who responded required a full business plan and financials for review before seriously considering the deal. This important new finding suggests a reduction in the difference in rigor associated with supporting documentation between informal, private investors and their institutional counterparts in the venture capital community, which insists on complete documentation. A better use of resources is to prepare a business plan and stellar executive summary rather than prematurely expending scarce resources on legal risk disclosure documentation too early in the fund-raising process and before sensing the extent of private investor interest in the deal.

At ICR we have found the investment opportunity profile (IOP) to be the treasured tool in stimulating investor interest prior to doling out money on documents. The IOP, an investor-oriented executive summary, supplies the investor with enough information to decide whether to look at a complete package of documents. After submitting an IOP to a number of prequalified investors, the entrepreneur will feel confident about spending time and money on more documentation.

In a published survey, The Capital Network made a dramatic finding about investors in a network: Unsolicited plans rarely receive funding. The IOP helps improve this low funding rate. An excellent summary tool, the IOP was developed in close cooperation with investors in the ICR network and includes the information investors say they need. The IOP, then, speeds up qualifying the investors while it assists in developing confidence about precommitment.

The IOP summary should highlight the most important points of your business, those that will convince potential investors that your venture will succeed. The criteria were developed by surveying sophisticated investors from around the country in ICR's proprietary database, and indicates what investors want to see in your executive summary:

The Company's Business

- Define business purpose and strategic mission.
- Provide summary of your company's history and current status.
- State overall corporate strategy and objectives.

The Products or Services

- Describe important features and benefits—relate to market needs and to the competition.
- Describe existing products and status of new products.
- Discuss pricing and margins for both your products and your competitor's products.
- Explain proprietary position.
- Articulate any relevant regulatory or environmental issues.

The Market

- Market analysis.
- Market strategy—How are you going to reach the market?
- Competitive advantage—What makes you different?
- Competition.
- Discuss the issues or circumstances that "drive" or create the market.

The Management Team

- Give brief backgrounds of key individuals—specifically, why they add value to the company, their past successes and achievements, and so forth.
- History of working together as a team, roles, and responsibilities.
- Board composition.

The Financial Summary and Deal

- Provide revenues, income, and expenses projected over three to five years.
- Key financial assumptions.
- Define funding requirements to achieve break-even and profitability.

■ Anticipated valuation and deal structure overview.
■ Use of proceeds.
■ Exit strategy.

But what precisely do we mean by "line up precommitment"? What is its operational meaning? How do you accomplish "precommitment"? You do so by making certain that you are talking to real investors. Again, the IOP becomes strategic. The IOP helps in developing confidence about precommitment and at the same time speeds up the qualifying of investors.

Developing confidence about precommitment leads us directly to the business of qualifying investors. And how is that best accomplished? Based on our experience, the way to get frank answers is by asking frank questions of the investors themselves. Who better to answer them? Exhibit 3.6 outlines a sampling of such questions: Has the investor previously invested in deals that address this market? What is the dollar amount he or she has invested within the past three years in this type of deal? How typical is that amount? What degree of familiarity has he or she with this particular industry? What motivation is involved? What does the investor feel he or she needs to know about this particular investment opportunity? How much capital is available to him or her? Will he or she co-invest? Do the criteria match the deal? How long will the investor's due diligence take? What most successful investment would the investor like to make again? What security or deal structure is preferred? How much time is expected to reach liquidation? Is the investor willing to meet in person with the entrepreneur? Has the investor read the business plan?

Are these questions easy to ask? No. Must they be asked? Absolutely. These are the questions that must be asked if the deal has any chance of moving forward. We advise having a preoffering commitment or serious level of interest equivalent to three to four times the money you need before spending serious money on legal documentation. Using the IOP can help you ascertain whether sophisticated investors are interested in your deal.

Aggressively Manage Database Development

The cost of developing and maintaining your company's investor database goes beyond those expense items listed in Exhibit 3.4.

As an example, ICR has invested more than $350,000 in development and periodic update of its 1,357 high-net-worth, early-stage investor database since 1989. In addition, there are monthly expenses associated with keeping contact information on investors current and accurate; updating changes in their status, such as liquidity; investment size; preferred stage of development; industries of interest; level of preferred involvement; results

EXHIBIT 3.6   Key Questions for Qualifying Angel Investors

- Has investor invested in deals that address this market?
- Dollar amount of investment of this type made in last year? Typical investment size? How many per year?
- Familiarity with industry?
- Motivation to invest?
- What does investor need to know about the opportunity?
- How much capital is available?
- Does investor co-invest with others?
- Do investor's criteria match parameters of your deal?
- How long does investor's due diligence process take?
- All-time greatest investment investor would like to make again?
- Preferred security or deal structure?
- Time until liquidation?
- Is investor willing to meet in person?
- Has investor read the plan?

Source: International Capital Resources

from past investments; and current level of investment activity, for example, the number of investments made per year. These expenses come on top of database development programs used to expand the database with new investors; for example, web site, book research and publishing, seminars, conferences, newsletter and quarterly mailings to inform investors about developments in the private equity market.

Aggressive database development and maintenance practices begin with using multiple sources to build your proprietary high-net-worth listing. Database development involves gathering pertinent information quickly and thoroughly on investors who have been located through investor contacts. Most important, your database, when you maintain it properly, is your best record to legally defend your private placement exemption. By keeping accurate and updated records with supporting notes on how the investor came to you, by documenting the careful development of the relationship, by chronologically logging the documents sent to them at their request, and by keeping track of all communications, the entrepreneur can defend his or her strategy for raising capital just in case such defense becomes necessary.

Also, aggressive database development means qualifying the investors whose names you permit to be listed on your proprietary database. In our experience, the best way to qualify individual investors is by examining individual wealth data and characteristics—as opposed to relying on more generic statistical categories, such as what you might find in census data.

Many times an in-person interview or subscription questionnaire is the only way to obtain sensitive information, such as previous investment behavior, financial holdings and portfolio (especially that segment of the portfolios placed into private equity), current status in a profession or industry (whether they are entrepreneurs building a company or have previously done so), and, finally, net worth excluding home and automobile in order to meet accredited status. For example, ICR sends a questionnaire to every investor in its database periodically to ensure that the data on those investors are as current and complete as investor disclosure will allow.

Some entrepreneurs rely on simple databases or sales databases to keep track of their investor contact information. Although these tools are adequate when only a small number of investors are included, they quickly become inadequate as the financing campaign develops; for example, past prospects who might be interested at later stages of development, current investors, current investor prospects being worked out and at different stages in the sales pipeline, and referral sources used in different ways to generate new prospects. All investor databases being used to raise money eventually should be converted to a relational database platform, using software to assist in database management. Individuals building the database must be persistent in their contact with the investors on the list. Many entrepreneurs establish regularly written and electronic communications updates as a way of facilitating staying in touch with the investors whom they have identified and with whom they hope to be working in the future.

Later we will have more to say about the technical nuts and bolts of building and maintaining an investor relational database.

Go Directly to Qualified Investors

The search for direct, private investors can be speedily accomplished in a number of ways. Trying to keep the securities instruments as simple as possible is one commonsense approach. Anticipating the due diligence questions—especially those coming early in your interaction with investors—is another. Be clear about your deal structure, that is, whether you are seeking equity or debt, and what valuation you place on your venture in anticipation of negotiations.

The cornerstone of any strategy—the goal of which is to increase the efficiency of the private placement process—invariably involves the challenges of finding and going directly to investors capable of investing in early-stage, higher-risk ventures. To implement such a strategy requires that entrepreneurs break down their fund-raising program into campaigns directed toward the key components of the angel capital market. These targets include potential individual investors to whom the entrepreneur is related, involved with socially, or is closely associated with professionally; individual, nonrelated, high-net-worth investors interested in high-risk/high-return transactions; venture forums; angel groups, formal and informal; financial intermediaries with proprietary databases of investors available for referral; and direct private offerings under protection of new government legislation. All these sources can lead to investor prospects to expand your potential pool of capital suitable for your venture.

We mentioned earlier the conservative approach of lining up three or four times the money you need before spending financial resources on documentation. How do you begin to do this?

You start by going directly to prospective investors with whom you are closely related, who know you, and who trust in your integrity and might wish to support your vision. This includes family, more distant relatives, friends, neighbors, acquaintances, fellow school alumni, business associates, professional colleagues, and perhaps fellow members of any clubs or organizations. In our many years of working with entrepreneurs, many turn to much more difficult capital sources before working with this source of "cradle equity." It is true that these sources may not subject you to the same level of due diligence as more sophisticated, nonrelated investors, but a small success in the beginning of the fund-raising process can be a real morale booster.

Next, continue working this resource by turning to the professional service providers in your personal database. These direct sources include your doctor, lawyer, accountant, banker, tax adviser, and insurance and securities broker. When you approach this group, also solicit referrals to others they may know, others who just might be interested in your deal.

The last group you go to after working with those who have an affinity for you personally are potential investors who would stand to benefit financially if your venture became a sustainable company. Included among the investor prospect group that has a natural affinity for the venture are suppliers, distributors, customers, and potential employees or managers. Included in this group is anyone who may be enamored with your technology and would support a company commercializing the technology. The tremendous success by Red Tail Ale in raising capital from loyal beer drinking customers illustrates the point.

In short, the first pass involves dealing directly with the people who have money to invest. The strategy of going directly to people with an affinity for you, your venture, and the technology is much more constructive than turning to a directory, cold mailing lists, or public advertisements.

The second approach suggests building your own database or prospective investor leads. Sophisticated private investors who prize their privacy and do not get involved in angel groups are difficult to locate and establish relationships with. Lacking the elements of more formal networks, these investors, based on our research, find their deals by referrals from family, friends, co-workers, and colleagues, and through professional intermediary referrals. Rarely can you reach them by contacting them directly or by sending information over the transom.

However, it is true that many lone angels are dissatisfied with these existing channels of communication for generating deal flow. Based on research by Harrison & Mason, as many as 43 percent suggest they are open to other means to find promising deals. And herein lies the opportunity for entrepreneurs to build their investor bases. By understanding how self-sufficient investors generate their deal flow, astute entrepreneurs can find openings to spawn leads for their own deal and identify potential investors with whom to develop relationships.

While most solo angels do have a deal flow development strategy beyond family and friends referral, most have developed it intuitively, not having taken the time to make it explicit. Individual investors who remain unaffiliated with angel groups do use a number of channels to get the word out regarding their investment interests and to augment their deal flow. These channels include listing under a business address in upscale directories and software databases, membership in regional venture capital associations, joining highly protective offline investor networks and online matching services, speaking at local venture-related seminars and conferences, volunteering to participate in incubator advisory boards, publishing articles or being interviewed and quoted in books and articles for the business and investment press, and joining preferred industry associations. ICR, the angel investment company founded by one of the authors, has used all these sources to successfully locate and surface qualified investors since 1989.

The third technique for going directly to investors is correctly using venture forums. Each year more than 60 major venture forums, conferences, and investment meetings in the United States bring together entrepreneurs and investors.

In these forums, conferences, and meetings, individuals meet directly with investors, receive valuable feedback on their ventures and offerings, discover investor interest in the entrepreneurs' transactions, and obtain the critical contact information needed to follow up on prospective investors after the event.

In our directory in Chapter 9, we list a number of the most prominent venture forums still active across the country. Venture forums are fairly consistent in their structure. Typically there will be a keynote speaker, and a limited number of prescreened and member-sponsored entrepreneurs will present their submitted business plans. Presentations with visual support usually last 10 to 30 minutes. The presenters may be augmented by other companies seeking financing who set up booths or tables and exhibits. There may be a luncheon, dinner, or after-presentation social hour, during which entrepreneurs can network with the attendees. Although many in the audience will be service providers and consultants, a number of lone angels do attend these events. Breakout sessions or private meetings immediately after the event between entrepreneurs and potential investors are also common.

The key to mining the most out of time and money spent on the venture forum strategy is to be prepared by doing your marketing planning before the event, and to hit a home run with a standout road show presentation. We discuss a mix of essential elements in preparing for a successful venture forum presentation in Appendix A. Do your market research by knowing as much as you can about the investors who will be present, and which of those investors will most likely be interested in your deal. Which investors invest at your minimum size of investment at your stage of development, around your geographic area, and in your industry? Answering these questions is a good starting point.

Position yourself vis-à-vis the other presenting companies. Find out a bit about the other firms competing for the investors' attention, especially those presenters immediately before and after you. Make sure to emphasize your strengths over competitors at the event.

Before presenting, make sure the size of your deal and size of the minimum investment is consistent with investments by investors at past venture forums offered by the sponsoring organization. Usually this information is available to prescreened companies who the forum wants to feature at the event, and are provided when requested.

Make sure that you are organized. Have readily available business plans professionally duplicated and bound. Also, have copies of any electronic material, for example, video or CD, web site address updated, reference list, and a color copy of the slides from your presentation. Take careful notes following any discussions with investors, collect contact information, and put it into your database as soon as possible after the event.

Last, remember to follow up with investors after the event in a timely way, and to provide promptly any further information they may have requested. Angel groups take a number of different manifestations, from the informal to the formal.

Informal groups include angel or venture capital clubs, and informal networks and associations. Informal groups are loosely tied affiliations of angels sharing the responsibility of deal flow development and due diligence. By banding together, the individuals leverage their capital by pooling it, allowing not only risk sharing, but opening the door to participating in larger deals than would have been possible as a solo investor. The mix of investors ranges across all types of investors, and we refer the reader to Chapter 7 on "Angel Investor Types" for more details. The informal group gives the more independent investor the benefit of shared resources without the burden of more constricting rules of participation associated with larger more formal organizations.

More formal angel enterprises have developed for numerous reasons. A major study by the Kauffman Foundation in 2002 suggests that business angel investing groups are growing in North America, and that angel groups are formalizing in response to increasing demands and complexities in the private equity market. Today, according to the Center for Venture Research, more than 170 such organizations dot the United States and Canada.

More formal angel organizations have well-defined legal structures; part- or full-time management; standardized investment processes; and public relations components, for example, a web site, and so forth. They may also have a structured angel investment fund.

The forces driving more formalization in angel groups are numerous and include a desire to attract higher-quality deals and generate better returns to get more investors involved; increased awareness of the long-term returns from venture investing stimulating newly affluent and less-experienced investor involvement; the need for pools of capital to fill the gap in the private market created by institutional venture capitalists moving to larger, later-stage transactions; the legal complexity of private deal structures; the large numbers of high-net-worth investors and visionary entrepreneurs looking for ways to more efficiently bridge the capital gap; and the desire for increased interaction among investors who can become isolated in their investment activity.

More formal angel investor groups may involve pledge funds or limited partnerships. Manager-led limited liability companies (LLCs) are common to aggregate individual angel funds into pools of capital to co-invest. Voting might be used, and a majority of members can direct where funds are invested. Structure can vary significantly, from nonprofits and management companies, to independent LLCs, to the formal venture capital partnership with the angel group as the general partner.

The size of groups ranges from about 20 to the largest at 80 investors. All investors are accredited, and may pay dues to help the group cover administrative costs and operation expenses. More formal groups have investment requirements, and members are expected to invest a minimum amount each year, $25,000 to $100,000 in each deal, for example, or they may be subject to investing a fixed amount over some period of time.

Most important to the entrepreneur in raising capital is that these groups have regularly scheduled meetings. Presenting companies are usually sponsored by a group member, and the company's documentation is subject to prescreening before its presentation. The entrepreneurs give their road show, followed by a question-and-answer period with the angel group members.

Angel groups have led investors who scout out deals at venture forums, incubator and research organizations, university entrepreneurship programs, and through their own and other angel group members' networks of contacts. In addition, most have web sites describing how to apply to get your deal considered by the group. Then, a screening committee usually makes decisions about deals that fit the group's criteria. Investment into a company is sometimes done by the angel group as an organization, at other times directly by individual members. The key for the entrepreneur is to have a sponsor respected by the members of the angel group.

As a case study, one angel group in Northern California started by an individual angel investor obtained sponsors, a law firm, a CPA firm, and a commercial bank to fund start-up operations. In its first year, the angel group attracted 50 members, each of whom paid $300 a year and $60 per dinner meeting. They held six events with 12 companies presenting. Four companies were funded fully and four received partial funding, totalling approximately $2 million in investment. The group's most successful investment was $750,000, which led to a successful venture capital round. The company was recently merged into a publicly traded corporation for $300 million. The group is now setting up a $30 to $50 million venture fund.

The fifth strategy we discuss is the use of financial intermediaries to assist you in developing leads for financing your venture.

Whether described as intermediaries, finders, placement agents, investment bankers, or brokers, most entrepreneurs understand their role. A good financial intermediary can be as challenging to find as an angel investor. In general, attractive intermediaries are experienced in the private equity process; known by legal, accounting, and investment banking players in their region; respected for their records; published authors and educators on raising capital; and recognized as one with a reputation for having built a database of real and active investors.

A financial intermediary helps you to raise the capital you need. This can be accomplished by prospecting his or her database and referring leads; or, in the case of licensed placement agents, actually placing the securities with a private or organizational investor. The intermediary is an expert in the private market and is an invaluable guide, and, when authentic, can significantly increase your chances for financing success. A skilled intermediary can also assist you in getting organized, planning your capitalization program to avoid giving up more equity than necessary, and helping in drafting investor-oriented, compelling documentation and presentations.

Intermediaries typically work for a retainer and also receive a success fee when their efforts result in the entrepreneur raising capital. A retainer is an up-front fee to secure their services exclusively for a time, and defrays expenses while working on your campaign. The success fee is a percentage of the money raised and can vary from 2 to 10 percent. Sometimes intermediaries will take equity in the venture or warrants to buy company stock at a set price. If equity is taken, it is usually at a set percentage of equity raised at a predetermined, negotiated price. Experienced intermediaries will have references and be willing to undertake due diligence to confirm their business development statements.

The landscape in the financial intermediary community has changed dramatically, with many firms closing and going out of business because of a loss of investors, or from having been swallowed up because of mergers, acquisitions, and other consolidations. The new directions involve these entities doing more research, publishing, avoiding conflicts of interest, and expending more on due diligence in order to identify fundable and sustainable ventures for their investor contacts. All these activities will facilitate finding trustworthy intermediaries.

Government is also getting the message about the efficiency of going directly to the investor. For instance, California's Commissioner of Corporations and others who appreciate the challenge of raising capital have helped enact laws that offer opportunities for private placement investment. A concerted effort by the SEC and the State Department of Corporations (SDC) in California has struck a balance between the need to protect investors and the need to offer emerging growth companies flexibility in their capital-raising activities.

Although we have cautioned you about advertising, be aware that new laws are coming onto the books. The California legislature has taken the lead in the United States with its innovative new program, enacting section 25102(n) of the California Corporate Code, mentioned earlier. This section allows entrepreneurs to advertise for angel investors following a simple, inexpensive procedure. [Section 25102(n) also grants an easing on dollar amount and number of purchasers, an action that may reverberate nationally.] Some believe that regulation is unfair to small companies, that there is no empirical evidence that small offerings are any more fraudulent than large offerings, and that, in general, compliance is strangling capital formation. However, this law opens the way for angels to use their own judgment in assessing the risks and rewards of an offering, just as the multi-million-dollar institutional investor does.

Sell

You must invest time in the investor if you want the investor to invest money in you. The high-risk investment represents nothing less than a sale. Make no mistake: The private placement investment is a sale, and a sale involves obtaining a decision. High-risk, early-stage private equity illiquid story securities with potential for high return are not bought. They are sold! Attracting a group of affluent, sophisticated co-investors to write checks for high-risk ventures—in some cases far below investment-grade securities—relies on your ability to cultivate relationships. So stay close to the gold. Don't just view investors as deep pockets. A respectful attitude is crucial. Cultivate a relationship with investors by treating them as peers or mentors.

However, mailing out business plans cold and following up with telephone calls do not constitute a sales strategy. Selling has changed since the 1990s. Documents are like milk, spoiling with time. Business plans don't get funded; people get funded! Entrepreneurs need to focus on selling, and during early investor screening and interest development, they don't need to develop elaborate venture documentation. They will find, instead, that an IOP is adequate to generate investor interest in meeting with them and moving the deal forward.

Selling early-stage deals has changed over the past five years. Many entrepreneurs cling to the notion that selling is beneath them, that it is too manipulative, but such thinking hinders their soliciting the high-net-worth private investor market. It behooves entrepreneurs to enlist their best efforts in this part of the strategy.

We have suggested that selling is different from times past because of the buyers, the regulations, the investment decision-making procedures, the presentations and promotions, and the packaging of investments. All are different.

First, high-net-worth investors today are sophisticated, educated, and experienced. New laws, licensing regulations, and consumer- and investor-protection statutes and practices stifle old-fashioned exuberance. Worse, during the late 1990s, a number of brokers, investment bankers, money managers, and their representatives were accused and convicted of duping clients. Considering the publicity that accompanies criminal wrongdoing in the sale of limited partnerships, closed-end funds, and other types of high-risk investments, investors who have remained in the market and not exited alternative asset class investing have become justifiably cautious when they approach high-risk/high-return venture investments.

Investment decision making today belongs in many cases to committees. And at least as significant in private transactions is the influence of a spouse. In fact, ICR concluded from our own research that one of the major reasons for nixing investments is a spouse who does not feel comfortable with the deal or the entrepreneur.

Technological innovations have also transformed investment presentations. Developments include multimedia, laptop and wireless computers, visual graphics, DVD visual and CD audio programs to support the PowerPoint graphs and charts, Internet web sites with passwords for investors to join online presentations about the deal, telephone and video conferencing to discuss deal questions, and fax and e-mail communications to support marketing material duplication and dissemination.

Among entrepreneurs enamored of the new technology is a tendency to package their deals but to disengage themselves from the selling process, particularly replacing crucial early face-to-face meetings with electronics gadgetry. Moreover, the geopolitical situation, making air travel more difficult and time consuming, may also be contributing to this trend.

With technology spewing out such extensive documentation, due diligence can be carried on long before person-to-person meetings and presentations take place. And although no one asking for money should ever be farther than a handshake away, this modern communication technology may let prospective investors draw their own conclusions before the entrepreneur's personal closing sales presentation.

Today, the sale in these types of investments is not made by an investor-development person or salesperson, but becomes the final step in a meticulously orchestrated public relations marketing and venture advertising strategy. However, these circumstances do not make the basics of selling obsolete. The principals still need to know their venture and be able to explain their financing proposal. They must use sales, promotion, and packaging techniques, and must learn the art of asking questions to get the answers they want. Like it or not, they must cultivate the ability to manipulate.

As Exhibit 3.7 illustrates, selling is a process. So here is the checklist you need to manage. First, make sure your presentations are face-to-face. Maintain a positive mind-set. If someone rejects you, don't be thin-skinned; realize that rejection may be because the risk is too great now. Enter the investors in your database for later consideration. Be closely informed about investors and be prepared for the questions investors are likely to ask. In Chapter 12, "Preparing for Due Diligence," we have compiled many of the questions that entrepreneurs can expect to encounter during the venture audit with angel investors. We refer the entrepreneur to this extensive list to prepare themselves for questions likely to arise.

Remember to pick the best person (not necessarily the CEO) to present your case. Also remember to preview and practice the presentation before soliciting the investors. Two heads are always better than one; three are better than two; so present as a team, and during the presentation maintain eye contact and positive body language, and be selective about word choice. Of like importance is the clarity of your vision, of what you're trying to accomplish with your charts and graphics, and of the connection between your presentation and the investor's values. Don't ask for the money too quickly, but remember to ask for it. Don't underestimate the courtesy of a follow-up note. And don't forget to update your database.

EXHIBIT 3.7   Selling Process

- Face-to-face
- Mind-set (attitude about money, rejection)
- Informed (venture, investor)
- Be prepared for questions/objections
- Select "best" person to present
- Preview before soliciting
- Present as a team
- Eye contact, body language, and word choice
- Content: clear vision/value connection
- Timing: do not ask too quickly
- Ask for the money
- Send a thank you note or give a follow-up call
- Update database

Source: International Capital Resources

Furthermore, selling remains an activity; therefore, if there is no activity being managed, the result is no sale. Fundamental to the sale is understanding the funnel and the pipeline. The funnel represents the need to have a large number of targeted prospects interested in the deal, affluent enough to afford it, located reasonably close to you so that you can follow up, and savvy enough to understand your message when contacting them.

The funnel works like this: You need about 100 contacts in order to identify 10 interested parties. You need those 10 in order to get into 5 meetings with prospective investors. Those 5 meetings will lead to 3 presentations, from which you can initiate negotiations and finally close 1 investor. Then you will need the next 100 contacts so you can start over again. And, as we warned earlier, successfully raising capital involves being able to deal with rejection while persisting in your objective.

Once you have identified a qualified, interested prospect, the pipeline comes into play. You must begin to manage the prospect, moving the deal forward daily, if not hourly. Critical in managing the pipeline is fulfilling investor inquiries, getting documents to interested investors in a timely fashion, and getting the right documents to them based on their requests. Inherent in this step is listening closely to what the investor is asking for, as opposed to what you think the investor must need, then identifying and convincingly responding to objections and moving the prospective investor forward to a decision.

You must understand and manage the funnel and the pipeline in order to position yourself for the close.

Since sooner or later the handshake will occur, Exhibit 3.8 delineates what the principles are behind the close. Basically, closing simply involves asking for the decision. For most people, trying to close a deal becomes a specter on the horizon. But in order to get into the position to ask for a decision, you're going to have to invest some time in the investors and listen closely to what they have to say. Remember, you can't rush things without coming off as desperate. Remember, too, that the key differences between private investors and traditional investors is that private investors don't have to invest. Therefore, doesn't it make sense to focus on *their* interests, on *their* criteria? And don't forget that what you're selling here is a high-risk, illiquid "story" security. So keep in mind that high-risk, illiquid story securities are not bought; they are sold. And what is selling? Successfully closing and asking for the decision.

Manage the Close

In order to manage the close of your transaction, you must understand the sales process. Selling involves a minimum of eight activities: (1) prospecting, (2) qualifying, (3) building rapport, (4) making the presentation, (5) overcoming objections, (6) using trial closes, (7) closing the sale, and (8) following up.

The close is only one link in the chain, but as the penultimate step, it depends on your having successfully managed the previous steps. To successfully manage the close, you must understand its single purpose: getting a decision.

EXHIBIT 3.8   The Principles Behind the Close

- Ask for the decision.
- Invest time in the investor. Listen!
- Do not rush the close. By doing so, you come off as desperate.
- Private investors do not have to invest. Focus on their interests, criteria.
- High-risk illiquid story securities are not bought, they are sold!
- Understand the sales "funnel": generate leads and manage the "pipeline" (selling process).
- Always know where you are in the sales process.
- No sales activity = no close.
- Prepare exhaustively for every investor interview.
- Do telephone follow-up with investor after all meetings.
- Participate actively in negotiation.
- Put any offer in correct legal form.

Source: International Capital Resources

Important in the relationship between the sales process and closing is knowing how near you are to a close. Therefore, you need to understand the steps in the sales process to close at the right time. Not surprisingly, if you do not know where you are in the sales process, you will not get to the place you want to be—closing the investor. Closing is the result of moving the investor to a decision. Therefore, if there are no sales, you have not positioned yourself to obtain a close. An indicator of whether you are positioning yourself for a close will come from monitoring your selling activity.

It is important to have a clear vision about the venture—its present and its future. Ask yourself what the value of the investment is to this investor. Fund-raisers understand the values of the people they contact. They understand, as should you, that different investors have different values. Approach each accordingly. Be able to explain the connection between your venture and the personal values of the investor.

Once a qualified, interested investor has been identified, you should request an appointment, normally by phone, to describe the investment directly to the investor. After setting the appointment, confirm it with a letter.

If you are inexperienced and alone in your venture, bring along to the closing meeting your investment banker, other advisers, and other investors involved in the deal, if possible. Do not go in alone. Always present as a team; the power of a team effort works. Always practice and preview the close with your associates before you meet with the investor. Get a sense of exactly how the team will move to the close. Your team should review the business plan, other venture documents, and data on the investment. Principal authors of the material should attend the meeting with the investor to answer questions. In other words, prepare exhaustively for every investor interview and closing as if these were your only opportunities. If you do not, they will be.

Select the best salesperson to effect the close; do not close simply because you have the time or because you are the CEO. When the team meets with the investor—preferably at the company's location—members should express their appreciation for the investor's time and trouble but move quickly to the business at hand. Explain how the investor's investment will be used and how much money is needed. Review the proposal page by page, answering any questions.

Exhibit 3.9 lists the elements of a successful presentation to investors. As we indicated, essential to any close is having the guts to ask the tough questions. These critical questions should include the following: Are you an accredited investor? Is this deal of interest to you? Do you have the liquidity to make this investment? What portion of your portfolio are you putting into high-risk ventures? What is your minimum investment? When can you invest? What might be your financial capability to participate in the next

EXHIBIT 3.9 Preparing for the Investor Presentation

1. Qualify investors.
2. Present investment opportunity in bite-size pieces, and explain how these pieces fit together.
3. Focus on return on investment.
4. Present your story logically:
   - Overview
   - Your moneymaking track record
   - Basics: what, when, how, how much
   - Describe the market opportunity
   - Demonstration
   - Close with emphasis on your unique position in the market.
5. Use multimedia in your presentation.
6. Present realistic, defensible pro forma financial statements and assumptions. Present an accurate, realistic profit-making scenario.
7. Q&A—Be sincere, enthusiastic, professional, and listen to investor's comments, questions, and pay attention to nonverbal clues.
8. Practice over and over, every chance you get.

round? Has our documentation made clear what the administrative steps are in putting your money into the transaction? These are the difficult questions. But they must be asked.

What qualities make a private investor a true prospect? The list is brief: investing capacity, interest in your deal, congruity between his or her preferred level of activity and the level of activity comfortable for you. In addition, the true prospect will have a tolerance for risk, a willingness to spend time on due diligence, an openness to developing a relationship, and an interpersonal response to the entrepreneurial team.

Near the end of the meeting, ask if you can call on the investor again to answer any questions and to learn of a decision. Set a date and time for a return visit. Thank the investor once again. Here are some things to keep in mind: Ask for the money face to face. Do not ask for it in a letter or over the telephone. Asking for money also demands that you justify your request, but accept a rejection gracefully, using it as an opportunity to clarify the investor's inevitable objections and concerns. Again, prepare for those objections and concerns by knowing your venture. Remember that the private investor does not have to invest.

The essence of the close is asking for the money. So be certain the investor understands the procedure for investing money in the venture. Do not, however, rush the close. Rushing the close, that is, attempting to close before completing all the other steps in the selling process, will result in your being perceived as desperate and, as we have warned, desperation can quickly quash a deal. Timing the close well means not asking too early, but this does not mean that you should avoid an early close if one is in the offing.

Initiate return calls to the investor and any follow-up meetings only by mutual agreement. Keep communicating until you receive that final decision. But regardless of the outcome of the meeting, always send a thank you note. This will keep the door open for future contact. Once the investor has been closed, acknowledge him or her by expressing your appreciation in person and in writing. Reaffirm directly to the investor that the investment will make a difference in the venture.

Finally, update your database with the information you have drawn from the meeting.

Another principle behind the close—and we've mentioned this before—involves investing time in the investor and time in developing a relationship if you want the investor to invest money in you. Private investors do not invest unless asked. In the investment process, they expect gratitude, respect, appreciation, dignified treatment, thoughtful use of their time, sincere interest in them as people, homework done on their background, some involvement in the venture, and a focus on their interests. In short, they expect planning, time, and attention. Attending to these details will bring investors into a meaningful relationship with the principals and increase the chances of an investment in the venture. Significant angel investments rarely come from strangers. Whether old or new, these investors have become friends.

DREAMERS AND DREAM MAKERS

As we declared at the outset, funding is an arduous task. But a lesson we have learned along the way may encourage you in your search for angels. Investors and entrepreneurs are people on opposite sides of a transaction, although they have more in common than might be obvious. For what is the real difference between founders with the dream of commercializing their idea into a $100-million-a-year company and the dream maker who anticipates a return 20 times over an initial investment?

Using the documented statistics on performance of the venture capital industry, let us try to demonstrate this point. Based on the Thomson Venture Economic U.S. Private Equity Index, early/seed fund types returned a negative 18.3 percent for one year, and negative 26.3 percent for three years before providing positive returns of 54.1 percent for five years with an investment horizon of 2003. The Private Equity Performance Index is based on analysis of cash flows and returns for more than 1,600 U.S. venture capital and private equity partnerships. According to Forbes's Richard Karlgaard, 75 percent of venture capital firms will be gone in five years, and it is estimated that 27 percent of venture capital firms formed during the past six years will not be able to raise a second fund. Clearly, early-stage investing has been affected more than later-stage and public-equity markets by economic conditions and other factors.

Small Business Association (SBA) studies have shown that just 50 percent of all start-ups survive their first year, and only 10 percent survive a decade. The statistics for investment failure in the venture capital industry run higher than the failures made by private investors.

The primary reason for such statistics rests on the obligation of professional venture capitalists to invest the money under their management. In this sense, venture capitalists are much like bankers who must lend money deposited with the bank to make margin profits, and, because of such pressure, make "bad" loans. Fund managers must invest, causing them to become entangled in bad investments as they stretch for a clear winner. Private investors, on the other hand, do not have to invest. From this fact arises another: Experienced, prudent, private investors concentrate on avoiding a bad choice instead of trying to strike gold on the two, three, or four investments they have made. Another factor is the venture capitalists' focus on the exit, "swinging for the fence," and commensurate high rates of return associated with exit, while angels focus on building sustainable companies. Angels understand that as long as a sustainable company prevails, they are assured of getting their money out, as well as earning a return over time either from cash flows or ultimate sale, or merger or acquisition.

But regardless of the number of investments, regardless of whether the investor is a self-made millionaire or an inheritor of wealth, each, like you, is a gambler and a dreamer. You share dreams and common ground on which to build a relationship.

It is difficult to reach high-net-worth, private investors. The competition for the attention of those with impressive personal wealth is brisk. The key, as with any marketing program, is to target qualified prospects and to use a mix of sources and resources to find them.

After diligent targeting and sourcing, meeting high-net-worth, direct investors amounts to plain hard work, persistence, and attention to detail. Moreover, your approach must entertain as well as incite interest. Consistent application of the principles set forth in this chapter will serve to develop investor awareness of entrepreneurs and those ventures that merit such attention. Sooner or later the persistent entrepreneur will capture the interest and investment of these high-risk investors when they are seeking new investments following a liquidation, or simply when, for whatever reason, they have decided to diversify or add to their portfolio.

In conclusion, deals are the dependent—not the independent—variable. That is why the product must fit the customer and why the dreamer must be matched with the right dream maker. Investors come to a situation with a portfolio, an asset allocation strategy, and an idiosyncratic tolerance level for risk. Except in some cases—following a windfall, an inheritance, a transfer of retirement pension assets, or a sale of a business or stocks—the investor will deal only within the context of that investment strategy. Take a lesson from this chapter: Focus on the customer, keeping in mind that in today's competitive fund-raising market, the customer is the investor.

PART TWO

Understanding the Angel Investor

CHAPTER 4

Alternative Sources of Capital

THE IMPACT OF ECONOMIC TRENDS ON THE ACCESSIBILITY OF CAPITAL

A number of macroeconomic trends are having significant impact on the entrepreneur's ability to find investors and to raise capital. These trends include a better understanding of undercapitalization's effect on building sustainable companies; declining interest rates and the desirability of traditional debt and credit; government intervention through tax incentives; contraction of the institutional venture capital market and negative impact on the desirability of the alternative asset class; and a moribund IPO market.

Capital is the coal that stokes the fires of entrepreneurship in the United States. No capital, no start-up. No capital, no expansion. This everyone knows. Particularly for start-ups and small businesses, finance-related issues appear to be the number one cause of failure, according to Festervand & Forrest's extensive research prepared for the SBA. Eighty percent of new businesses fail because of undercapitalization. Major culprits include an inability to secure adequate long-term financing, the high cost of financing, highly leveraged financing, excessive debt, and cash flow problems. Also, in their 1998 study of business bankruptcy, Sullivan, Warren, and Westbrook reported that 28 percent of business owners who ended up in bankruptcy court identified financing difficulties as the major reason for their failure. Even though interest rates have declined steadily for the previous four years for corporate borrowing, traditional debt has become a less workable alternative for raising capital. Moreover, despite all the lending programs within the SBA, not enough is being done to bolster financing availability in our capitalistic society and make funding more accessible for start-ups.

For the SBA program, for example, applicants must display more than just good character and management skills; they must demonstrate a history of earnings and a cash flow record. Moreover, without collateral, and generally without a one-third capital contribution to the total cost of the project, applicants simply will not get the loan. The White House Conference on Small Business put it succinctly: "Small companies still face complicated state and federal requirements." What we have, then, is capitalism without the capital.

Even as the government has increased appropriations for SBA loans with the Small Business Guaranteed Credit Enhancement Act of 1993, even as it has permitted a capital gains exclusion for certain small business stock investments with the Omnibus Budget Reconciliation Act of 1993 and the 2003 Tax Act, and even as it has eased the burden of financial institutions lending to small business with the Capital Availability Program, capital continues to shrink. Adding to this shrinkage has been the increased investment of financial institutions in government securities.

However, some economic trends will influence the future attractiveness of higher-risk, early-stage investments. The government's tax incentive bill, for example, contains provisions that can stimulate investment growth. As the top marginal income tax increased to 39.6 percent, the ceiling on the capital gains rate on all asset classes was retained at 28 percent, and the 2003 Tax Act reduced long-term capital gains to just 15 percent through 2008.

As we can see in Soja and Reyes Investment Benchmark research, the American government has historically recognized that it needs to nurture young companies. The strategy it has used to stimulate investment has been to create tax incentives and to reduce restrictions on investment managers: for example, the 1978 Revenue Act that has provided capital gains incentives for equity investment; the 1979 Employee Retirement Income Security Act's (ERISA's) "Prudent Man" rule that crested new guidelines allowing pension investment into venture capital; the 1980 Small Business Investment Incentive Act that stimulated growth of small business development companies; the 1980 ERISA's "Safe Harbor" regulations that broadened discretion of venture fund mangers; the 1981 Economic Recovery Act that lowered the capital gains rate; the 1986 Tax Reform Act that reduced tax on long-term capital gains; and the 2003 Tax Act that provided dividend and capital gain relief.

Provisions in the Omnibus Budget Reconciliation Act of 1993 serve as a case in point. This law placed a capital gains tax ceiling on investments in risky start-ups when money is left for longer than five years. With the average "hold time" of eight years, this incentive offers tangible potential benefit for investors. The Act, having squeaked by the House by only two votes—and having needed the Vice President's vote to break a 50-50 tie in the Senate—drops the tax on capital gains from 28 percent to 14 percent upon liquidating stock in small business holdings or selling the company. This decrease applies to stock issued after the date of the bill's enactment, August 10, 1993.

More recently, federal law encourages the financing of new businesses in the form of the tax rollover opportunity created in 1997. Created by Congress to channel capital into "qualified small businesses," the investor can roll over a capital gain from the sale of qualified stock held for more than six months if the investor buys the stock of a different "qualified small business" within a 60-day period beginning on the date of the original sale. The law provides for an indefinite tax deferral, so that, in effect, for those who act within 60 days of making a profit on the sale of a prior venture investment can roll over that profit—tax free—into new ventures again and again. Favorable tax treatment is an economic trend that has repeatedly stimulated small business.

Our position is clear: reduced interest rates for borrowing has not made debt a solution for financing earlier-stage ventures. And even with substantive tax incentives, we are not seeing a major shift in capital to the higher-risk, alternative asset market. Why? Government intervention, while responsive to the problem of the capital gap and capital availability, and laudable, has been largely ineffective at helping you raise money. This is so because it is the capital market that drives public policy—not public policy that continuously drives the capital market.

In fact, a more plausible explanation of the reason why entrepreneurs face such a daunting challenge in raising capital is better provided by close examination of the 1,700 venture capital firms. Perhaps, it may be said that as goes the venture capitalists, to some extent, so goes the angel capital market.

According to the PricewaterhouseCoopers/Thomson Venture Economics /NVCA Money Tree Survey, total investment in the venture capital industry has declined from $105.9 billion in 2000 to $18.2 billion in 2003. The number of deals declined from 8,082 in 2000 to 2,715 in 2003. This retraction following the dot-com bust suggests that the flood of venture capital is over. Corporate venture capital investment has declined from $16.9 billion in 2000 to $1.1 billion in 2003. Although the percentage of investment into medical devices and equipment, biotechnology, and life sciences has increased, interest in software, telecom, and networking equipment has declined. Most important to entrepreneurs is that early-stage investing was affected most. For example, start-up and seed financing fell to $303 million (148 deals) in 2002 and to $354 million (166) deals in 2003. The amount invested into start-up and seed deals in 2002 represented a reduction of 62 percent from 2001. In this contracting economic situation, entrepreneurs must remember that thousands of venture-funded companies that previously had received early-stage funding are now seeking second rounds. It is estimated that fewer than 10 percent will be successful at further fund-raising. Furthermore, as venture capital investment has pulled back, and capital overhang is estimated at more than $50 billion, internal rates of return are continuing to slide and further act to drive away capital investment into venture capital funds.

Another economic trend that has an impact on the availability of capital is the moribund IPO market. As Bill Davidow has said, "When everyone is running for the door, the only measure of success becomes how wide you can build the door." Investors are facing the lightest new offering market in years. Since venture capital returns are closely a function of IPO exit, entrepreneurs can appreciate that absence of this high-return exit can dampen enthusiasm for high-risk, long-term investments.

According to the research firm Equidesk, 5,000 companies went public during the 1990s at IPOs of typically between $25 million and $35 million. The number of IPOs has declined steadily since 1999 to the lowest level in many years. There were 510 IPOs in 1999, 373 in 2000, 108 in 2001, 97 in 2002, and only 88 in 2003, according to Bloomberg Financial Markets. Although recently there seems to be a burst of investor interest in IPOs, the average deal size has ballooned to close to $340 million. Also, as more than 6,000 companies owned by venture capital portfolios await exit, it could be a very long time to liquidate so many companies. Some experts are estimating both an IPO and merger and acquisition downdraft for up to five years, with merger and acquisition eight times more likely for deals in the range of $100 million to $300 million.

ALTERNATIVE SOURCES OF CAPITAL AND HOW THEY AFFECT EARLY-STAGE INVESTMENT

As Exhibit 4.1 illustrates, the array of alternative sources of financing offers many choices to the inventor, start-up entrepreneur, and fast-growing small business owner. In this section, we provide a comprehensive overview of these alternative sources of capital.

Corporate Investment and Strategic Alliances

These methods involve entering into a contract to do business with a much stronger and better-known business partner. The shared prestige can boost the start-up's credibility. When properly structured, this strategic relationship benefits suppliers, customers, vendors, and distribution sources. It is a venture with complementary customers or technology. Corporate alliances involve long-term relationships, synergy with an existing product line, related products to feed into distribution, shared risk, and industry contacts— all aspects encompassing resources beyond the funding itself. Moreover, corporate investment is more affordable than venture or institutional capi-

EXHIBIT 4.1   Main, Alternative, and New Early-Stage Financial Sources

- Business angels—private placements
- Academic institutional research financing
- Venture capital (industry specific)
- Bootstrap financing
- Self-finance: savings, loans, credit cards
- Licensing technology
- Royalty
- Joint venture
- Venture leasing
- Family, friends, colleagues, and associates
- Barter investment
- Transaction financing
- Strategic alliances
- Corporate investments (one new fund/week)
- Private equity funds
- Direct investing by financial institutions
- International financing—immigration investment
- Direct private offering
- Incubator-based financing
- Community loan development funds
- Economic development programs

Source: International Capital Resources

tal, resulting in a higher valuation and more equity than what comes from traditional or early-stage funding. Corporate investors, however, may not accommodate an exit strategy. U.S. companies are completing approximately 5,960 joint ventures or strategic alliances per year with foreign and other U.S. companies; the majority of these transactions involve only two companies and are joint ventures. Strategic alliances, however, take a long time to formulate.

Lease Financing

Lease financing possesses an inherent edge in raising funds because you use the equipment you lease as collateral. Advantages to leasing include avoiding a down payment. Leasing is an installment purchase that, at the expiration date, offers a few options: The lease may be extended; the leased items may be bought at par to their market value; or the lease ends.

Licensing

This method of financing involves entering into a contract to provide technology or a product or some other commodity to the licensee. The licensee, in turn, will provide a fee and/or a royalty based on revenues for specific benefits (e.g., rights to distribute within a defined territory for a specified time). The second party is granted the right by the owner of a product to manufacture, sell, or use it in some way.

Franchising

Similar to licensing, franchising requires the franchisee to pay for the right to sell the service or product of a franchiser in exchange for a fee and portion of the income from sales or profits. The franchiser may supply expertise, as in the case of McDonald University. Franchises involve virtually every kind of business. The franchiser may sell a single franchise or franchise a geographical territory. This alternative capital resource requires no debt service or loss of equity in the company. One start-up company sold 10 franchises for $25,000 each, raising $250,000 to fund further growth. Also, the franchisees assume all costs for opening, staffing, and running new outlets as well as assuming all contingent liability. Franchises are responsible for 50 percent of U.S. retail sales, although overcrowding has recently slowed the franchising movement.

Research and Development Arrangements

Like other alternatives in this list, R&D arrangements offer variations. Basically, however, an R&D limited partnership grants R&D funding to a company perfecting a technology. The limited partners stand to gain through tax benefits and substantial royalties. Depending on the details of the agreement, the company responsible for developing the technology also has options: to eventually buy the technology, to develop and market the technology, or to join with the limited partners to form a new company. R&D is an effective way to get promising technology off the ground, especially when a strong entrepreneurial management is not available.

Venture Capital Firms

These sources are professional investors and independent middlemen who chiefly manage and invest other people's money. The limited partners in funds tend to be institutions, including pension funds, insurance companies, universities, and corporations. Although most wealthy private investors have abandoned professional funds, a number of family endowments still invest. (As pointed out earlier, professional venture capital firms are not the best source of funding for small companies or start-ups.) Professional fund managers seek bigger companies that may develop into $50 million to $100 million businesses within three to five years. To generate returns to investors, these funds must work with fewer, larger deals, those with "superstar" possibilities that can cover the losses from the high percentage of failures inherent in investments. These funds try to outperform the venture capital industry, and rarely get involved in deals with a deal size less than $7 million.

Cash Management and Tax Strategies

Cash management activates immediate cash flow, involving techniques detailed elsewhere in this list, such as bartering and factoring. Cash management techniques often enlist tax strategies to create cash, such as taking tax deductions for depreciation of fixed assets (computers, perhaps, or other equipment and furniture).

Private Placement (Exempt Offerings)

The private placement is the issuance of treasury securities of a company to a small number of private investors. A private placement is an offering of senior debt, subordinated debt, convertible debt, common stock, preferred stock, warrants, or various combinations of these securities.

Government Financing (Loans and Grants)

Small business is big business in the United States, responsible for a whopping 51 percent of the gross national product (GNP), 60 percent of all new jobs created, and 47 percent of all domestic sales. Begun in 1953, the SBA—an independent agency of the federal government—has become the largest long-term source of financing in the country. Through 7(a), the SBA's General Loan Program, loans are made by private lenders with the government guaranteeing 70 to 90 percent of the loan up to $750,000. The 7(a) Loan Program accounts for 90 percent of the SBA's loan business. (The SBA generally defines "small" as having under 100 employees if a company is engaged in manufacturing or wholesale; if in retail or service, a company's annual sales must not exceed $3.5 million. These definitions qualify 99 percent of all businesses in the United States.)

The SBA array of programs includes the 502 Local Development Company Program, directed in rural areas to long-term, fixed-asset financing, and the 504 Certified Development Company Program, directed to long-term, fixed-asset financing through nonprofit certified development companies (CDCs). CDCs are companies sponsored either by private interests or by the local or state government. Other SBA programs operating under 7(a) include the GreenLine Program, the Vietnam-Era and Disabled Veterans Program, the Handicapped Assistance Loans, the Women's Pre-qualification Loan Program, and the Low Doc Loan Program for loans under $100,000 to companies with less than $5 million in annual sales and fewer than 100 employees.

Also operating under the aegis of the SBA is the SBIC Program. There are fewer than 100 active SBICs operating in the United States. This program is the only entity under U.S. banking legislation that can lend money *and* own equity in small businesses. SBICs borrow the capital that they, in turn, must lend only to small businesses that operate on a thin margin. However, SBICs like to see assets that can be liquidated if the business fails, and they require entrepreneurs to invest a substantial portion of their net worth and/or postpone salary. SBICs will engage in some subordinated debt.

SBA loans can cover inventory, machinery, working capital, and acquisition of commercial property. In applying for a loan, the small business owner must meet the requirements of both the SBA and the lender, having to supply among other documents a current profit and loss statement, a balance sheet, a schedule of business debt, a current personal financial statement, a business plan, and collateral. The government rarely lends money directly to the entrepreneur, and the SBA provides no grant money for business start-up or expansion. Most lenders opt out on anything less than $50,000.

Bartering

Bartering, the trading of products or services without the use of money or its substitute, is another alternative business practice to financing your company. Bartering involves the exchange and subsequent good use between two companies of each other's slow-moving or "dead" inventory or services. What accrues to each company is a commodity that may generate added capital. More important, bartering conserves cash. Although bartering is not for every business—such as those not needing additional customers—those that engage in it find new barter partners through barter newsletters and member directories.

Commercial Finance Companies

These firms handle riskier lending transactions and are open to higher leverage than banks. Most have an asset focus, for example, receivables, inventories, and fixed assets. Commercial credit companies typically charge interest rates of three to five points over prime, and all require substantial collateral and/or personal guarantees.

Banks

Traditional banks are creditors, specifically short-term lenders, granting 30- to 90-day loans. They also may lend over longer periods (more than five years), but banks are not investors. Banks generally require excellent credit ratings and a perceived ability to repay the borrowed money. Depending on the circumstances, they may also require a large percentage of self-financing. However, currently, corporate lending interest rates are at their lowest in 45 years, having been lowered repeatedly for four straight years by the Federal Reserve.

Initial Public Offerings

IPOs are generated when a privately held, usually emerging, company complies with requirements and regulations, then registers with the SEC, makes disclosures to the public, and issues shares for the first time. Investors receive a share of company profits through the issuance of dividends but permit the company to retain control—unless that control gets transferred to the shareholders. As a public company listed on an exchange, the company must comply with relevant federal and state laws.

International Sources of Capital

No longer the exclusive purview of large corporations, international trade has flowed increasingly into the ken of small businesses. International sources of capital have blossomed as a result, running the gamut from local commercial banks to the federally, state, and locally funded Center for International Trade Development. In addition, the SBA's Export Working Capital Program, like the SBA's other programs, guarantees 90 percent of a private sector loan up to $750,000. Although not exclusively for international funding, the Department of Commerce's Minority Business Development Agency (MBDA) funds Business Development Centers across the country. The Department of Commerce also supplies nonfinancial aid through its National Trade Data Bank (NTDB), which contains international information valuable to exporters. What we have mentioned here hardly scrapes the top layer of options open to the international businessperson who, unfortunately, faces daunting regulations and requirements.

Employee Stock Ownership Plans

Employee stock ownership plans (ESOPs) involve an internal buyout of a company in which the employees buy shares and thus buy ownership.

Hence, equity capital is raised fairly inexpensively by a knowledgeable and dedicated workforce as it operates in its new capacity as company stockholders. Each employee's share of stock thus becomes the company's contribution to the employee's retirement fund.

Management Buyout

This involves another type of internal buyout of a company in which the management buys shares and thus buys ownership. Such a buyout may have been generated by the management's concern for remaining in control of the company's future instead of having it bought by outsiders. Like employees who buy ownership, managers know the intimate workings of the company, putting them in position to leverage up the company.

Incubator-Based Financing

Incubators provide support within a close geographical locale for seed, start-up, and other early-stage companies looking to expand. Such support can come not only in funding but also in the form of a physical plant, office management, and marketing services. Corporate or university based, incubators help companies raise capital, offer technical assistance, and perform valuation. A fully functioning incubator could house a number of growing companies sharing a common business, for instance, in software. They also might share space and equipment and even professional guidance. The stage of development of incubators varies widely from state to state.

As the *New York Times* reported in January 1999, the number of incubators operating in the United States reached 550 in 1998; of these, 30 offered services but no physical space ("incubators without walls"). Forty-five percent were located in urban areas, 36 percent in rural areas, and 19 percent in suburbs. Forty-five percent had no particular focus, but one quarter of the incubators focused on technology. Ten percent were dedicated to general manufacturing, 9 percent to other specific industries, 6 percent to services, and 5 percent to minority-owned businesses. That a few incubators merely sustain "failed" entrepreneurs, as investor and author Geoffrey Moore *(Crossing the Chasm* and *Inside the Tornado)* has pointed out, good incubators, he reassures us, "attract . . . key resources—advisers, partners, investors, and visionary customers." Incubators, he has explained, "give a structure to the bottom levels of basic needs so that entrepreneurs can focus on the higher levels." Incubators have continued to spread, and in 2004, according to the National Business Incubator Association, 950 incubators are operating in the United States.

Asset-Based Loans and Factoring

Asset-based loans are virtually self-explanatory: loans granted on the basis of a company's assets, chiefly the company's accounts receivable. The accounts receivable become collateral. A lender provides funds as products are shipped, expecting to receive a percentage of the value of those accounts. The accounts themselves will continue paying as they normally do: to the company; not, however, to the lender. The company uses a predetermined portion of the actual payments by the accounts to repay the debt. In this way, the owner of an early-stage company is allowed to sell a portion of the revenue stream rather than hurrying to give equity in the company or burden the balance sheet with debt.

In factoring—a type of financing based on accounts receivable—the factor (lender) accepts direct responsibility for the company's accounts, taking responsibility for the credit risks and collection of the receivables. Factoring is more expensive than accounts receivable financing, although both require extensive bookkeeping and neither comes cheap.

Self-Finance

Self-financing often supplements institutional financing and may be required by a funding institution to assure a dedication to and interest in the company, invention, or venture. Self-financing may include the use of credit cards, whose interest rates vary widely. According to a 1997 study implemented by Arthur Andersen's Enterprise Group and National Small Business United, approximately 34 percent of respondents indicated the use of credit cards for initial financing of the start-up. A good personal credit record will determine how much money a credit card company is willing to offer. Credit cards do offer one of the quickest and easiest means of obtaining credit. Entrepreneurs have been known to apply for ten credit cards in one day, creating a $100,000 line of credit overnight.

Community Development Corporations

Nonprofit organizations staffed by civic and business leaders and sponsored by individual citizens, church groups, and even bankers may submit applications to become CDCs. These community loan development funds, established to improve community life, even have begun equity investing. Eligible CDCs must have established 501(c)(3) tax-exempt status. The CDC must describe its proposed collaborative partnership with neighborhood residents, local businesses, and financial institutions. A government agency then designates which groups qualify, granting their contributors yearly tax credits of five percent for 10 years. The designated CDC launches employment and business opportunities within a geographical area for low- and moderate-income individuals. The CDCs require scheduled progress reports. Established CDCs use past performance as a criterion for a venture's receiving more funding.

Small Corporate Offering Registration

As William D. Evers makes clear in his "Primer on Securities Law Issues for Non-Lawyers," SCOR offerings "represent an abdication by the SEC . . . to the states of jurisdiction over public or private offerings of $1 million or less." Forty-eight states have SCOR statutes for public offerings. The 50-question Form U-7 is the required disclosure document. In many states, financials must be audited. Connected to SCOR is the federal rule known as Reg. A, which is expensive. Because of "SEC review and the required precision of offering detail for 'full disclosure,'" Evers explains, "legal fees [reach from] $25,000 to $60,000." Furthermore, these figures do not include filing fees and "Blue Sky clearing." (For a discussion of securities law issues with an emphasis on small business, see Appendix B.)

Thus, with all the nourishment that small businesses bring to the economic dinner table, it is no wonder that the government understands the need for supplying some coal of its own to stoke the economic fire. Despite the government's best efforts and good intentions, however, its very nature precludes it from playing the role of venture capitalist. Venture capital involves more than capital; venture capital involves adding value to the money invested.

Rather than just throwing money at a company as the government does, investors help a company by knowing about growth and having extensive contacts in the business community. Angel investors add much more than just capital: they provide alliances with corporate partners; assist with equity offerings and with joint ventures and acquisitions; provide industry contacts with customers and vendors; assist in strategy development and recruitment; and bring knowledge-based experience to help grow and guide development of a sustainable company. Venture capital means having extensive research resources with which to analyze the market as well as having financial resources to analyze projections and evaluate valuations. So, unable to influence early-stage ventures because its premises are flawed, the government is not designed to be a venture capitalist. Government programs are designed only to throw money at businesses, not furnish critical added value.

Nor are the venture capitalists themselves likely to offer the necessary degree of added value. As David M. Flynn observes in "The Critical Relationship Between Venture Capitalists and Entrepreneurs: Planning, Decision-

Making, and Control" (in *Small Business Economics,* 1991), "Venture capitalists (VCs) are less involved with their affiliated new venture organization than may be necessary for long-term survival." Entrepreneurs may properly dominate the early stages of a venture, explains Flynn, but in the venture's ongoing development, the venture capitalist might add expertise that the entrepreneur lacks. For example, technical skills may concede to administrative skills so the enterprise can survive. Thus, Flynn urges a higher level of involvement in ventures on the part of the venture capitalists. But the question remains: Will venture capitalists be willing?

In addition, the person trying to raise capital has a dual burden: compliance with federal SEC regulations as well as compliance with the regulations of the state Department of Corporations and Commissions. Even when the SEC has tried to reduce the cost and complexity associated with raising capital in private transactions, the states have chosen to take a more aggressive stance on their statutes. State regulations prevail, causing the nagging bottlenecks that have blocked capital in early-stage investment.

In conclusion, the entrepreneur will find angels involved in a range of alternative early-stage financial sources: private placements, licensing, venture leasing, cradle equity, SCOR offerings, private equity funds, direct offerings, incubators, private lending, and even barter investments.

BUSINESS ANGELS AS THE BEST SOURCES OF CAPITAL, ESPECIALLY FOR EARLY-STAGE INVESTMENT

We know that professional venture capital performs an excellent service, placing billions of dollars in American companies, creating jobs, expanding the tax base, and even putting hundreds of millions of dollars into very early-stage deals. But for the early-stage venture, venture capitalists impose rigid criteria, leaving numerous companies unable to qualify. Thus, as venture capital is the real contributor to later-stage deals, angel capital has become the indubitable contributor to early-stage deals, the resource for the majority of companies. The primary source of capital is the direct, private investor—even though these angel investors possess an inimitable advantage: They do not have to invest.

A problem arises for many people who think that finding a securities firm to underwrite their efforts on a "best-efforts" basis is a guarantee that money will be raised. The problem is that once a firm commits, it has to convince its brokers to sell that offering to their customers. The entrepreneur who chooses a direct public offering by enlisting a securities broker has managed to entail only front-end fees to create documents in line with a public offering. But the transaction still requires that somebody else sell the offering. So the entrepreneur's faith lies in brokers who must convince their customers to buy it.

In the January 1995 issue of *Entrepreneur,* David Evenson sends this sobering message to those hoping for an IPO: "Getting an underwriter to say it will take you public can be a hollow promise unless there's broad-based support within the financial community." Obviously, brokers should have been integrated early enough to harvest their feedback, enthusiasm, and commitment. Broad support must come from those who will analyze the opportunity and provide written reports.

THE APPROPRIATENESS OF YOUR VENTURE FOR A DIRECT, PRIVATE PLACEMENT

As we have explained, the private placement is the issuance of treasury securities of a company to a small number of private investors. This investment is an offering of debt, stock, warrants, or various combinations of these securities. Although the greater number of private placement investments to institutional investors involve debt securities, exempt offerings of direct, equity, and/or debt investing by private investors are common. These private investors often become involved in a venture in order to limit the downside risk associated with illiquid investments. These participatory investors also begin with transactions requiring less money. Moreover, these transactions move quickly compared with a public offering, are more flexible due to the lack of SEC requirements, and are much less expensive.

A more practical and useful definition of the private placement, however, is any deal you legally can put together, then write up and reach agreement on. As Exhibit 4.2 shows, legal definitions for the private placement do exist: cash for equity; all types of offerings not publicly sold; issuance of treasury securities to a small number of sophisticated, private or institutional ventures; and the circumvention of onerous public offering requirements and access to a nonaffiliated market without full registration compliance. But because this is a highly illiquid security that is not bought, it must be sold. So be warned: The expectation is unrealistic that investors—high-net-worth, sophisticated investors—will beat down your door to buy a highly illiquid, "story" security in the current climate of fear and cynicism that pervades the public stock market. Therefore, rather than overly structuring the security and the transaction prematurely, have a more open mind, and take a more negotiable, flexible posture. Then gather a circle of investors and bring in the assistance you need—legal, accounting, and so on—to structure an agreement acceptable to all the parties involved.

Let us clarify a highly illiquid story security. Selling a story security is a

EXHIBIT 4.2   Private Placement, Legal Definition

- Cash for equity
- All types of offerings not publicly sold
- Issuance of treasury securities to a small number of sophisticated private or institutional investors
- Allows company to circumvent onerous public offering requirements and access nonaffiliated market without full registration compliance

Source: International Capital Resources

concept that you are selling blue sky. That is, what you are selling is a story, a compelling, believable story. Your task is to find people who believe the story. Once you accomplish that, you can reach a legal agreement on the financing of the story.

Is your venture suitable for an individual participatory investment? Think about two things: first, the kind of financing typically appropriate to your venture's stage of development; and second, the sources of such financing.

That you are accurate in the assessment of your company's development is an underlying assumption. But without some understanding of how these stages are defined, it will be difficult to define your stage of development.

STAGES OF DEVELOPMENT DEFINED

Seed. A venture in the idea stage or in the process of being organized.

Research & Development. Financing of product development for early-stage or more developed companies.

Start-up. A venture that is completing product development and initial marketing and has been in business less than two years.

First Stage. A venture with a working prototype that has gone through beta testing and is beginning commercialization.

Expansion Stage. A venture that is in the early stage of expanding commercialization and is in need of growth capital.

Mezzanine. A venture that has increasing sales volume and is breaking even or is profitable. Additional funds are to be used for further expansion, marketing, or working capital.

Bridge. A venture that requires short-term capital to reach a clearly defined and stable position.

*Acquisition/Merger.*A venture that is in need of capital to finance an acquisition or merger.

Turnaround. A venture that is in need of capital to effect a change from unprofitability to profitability.

When entrepreneurs are asked their company's stage of development, confusion often reigns. Without knowing how to define the stages, entrepreneurs will waste time targeting the wrong investors. This is especially true in the earlier stages of development, because the earlier the stage, the higher the risk.

For example, a seed company is looking for a small amount of capital (between $50,000 and $250,000), and needs to think through its concept and develop a prototype. Market research has begun but is not yet finished. The business plan is in development and the management team is being formed. Compare a start-up. The start-up is a year-old company, legally structured but already in business. It may be test marketing its product or service and may even be bringing in revenue although not yet making a profit. Management has been assembled and is starting to form a team. The business plan has been completed, and the company is prepared for manufacturing and sales. It lacks only capital.

The differences in stages of development are substantial, and investors' tolerances for risk vary widely. It pays to differentiate your stage of development to target those investors interested in one or another stage of development. This is true because to varying degrees all investors are risk averse. But it is no accident that the primary transaction structure used by angels is the private placement investment. The benefits of this investment are shown in Exhibit 4.3.

First, since angels prize their privacy, confidentiality is an attractive feature of the private placement. Second, from a legal point of view, there are fewer and less onerous disclosure requirements, which is good because complying with state and federal disclosure requirements raises the ante. The benefit for the entrepreneur in incurring less cost spills over to benefit the investor. Thus, in the private placement or exempt offering, privacy is protected and money is preserved.

EXHIBIT 4.3   Benefits of a Private Placement

- Confidential
- Flexible
- Less costly
- More than capital
- Rapid time frame
- Accommodates smaller transactions

Source: International Capital Resources

Flexibility is also demonstrated in transactions with an institution: an insurance company, a pension fund, or an independent third party such as a later-stage venture capital firm. In these transactions, the private placement will accommodate subordinated debt. This is attractive to entrepreneurs because senior debt capability is left unencumbered. This means that if the company proceeds apace, it can obtain long-term bank debt. Subordinated debt provides the cash, is essentially less secured, and has a subordinate position to senior debt, but does not close off acquiring long-term debt as the company increases its cash flow and develops assets. From the entrepreneur's point of view, the accommodation of subordinated debt becomes another attractive feature of a private placement.

Likewise, from the investor's point of view, subordinated debt commonly has convertibility when the terms and conditions are negotiated; convertible subordinated debt, or convertible debenture, offers some protection on the downside of a failed company. For example, if a proprietary technology in the venture is resalable at a later date, or if the company folds and the technology is liquidated, once senior note holders are taken care of, the subordinated note holders will be able to recover some of their money. This provides insurance on the downside.

And convertibility, combined with a subordinated debt, permits sharing on the upside if the company is successful.

If the company is successful, investors convert the principal of the note into stock. Even the interest becomes convertible—if it has not been paid over time or has been held in abeyance. With success, investors will be able to convert to stock and share in the capital appreciation by having previously negotiated a purchase price. Since the company is successful, the price of the stock is higher. The investors will be able to purchase the stock at a lower price and in time liquidate it for appreciation and a return on the investment. If the company is not highly successful (e.g., does not go public or is not acquired but experiences a reasonable degree of success), the investors' debt can be repaid from cash flow. Hence, they will get their principal and their coupon or return on interest. If the company fails, the investors are in line to get some of their money back when the company's assets are liquidated.

All this provides flexibility. Debt can be used in several ways: subordinated debt, convertible subordinated debt, equity, debt and equity, or even royalty financing. In royalty financing, individuals do not take an equity position, nor do they get a note for their money. Instead, they develop an agreement in which portions of the revenues of the company over time will be paid back until a multiple return is reached, perhaps two or three times the original investment. These kinds of transactions are common in the restaurant business, for example, so that the owner will have no partners or note to pay off. Without thus burdening the balance sheet, the valuation of the venture from the bank's point of view expedites a loan. In effect, a portion of the cash proceeds from the business will divert to the investors until they secure a predetermined return on their investment. Gradually they slide from the picture. Flexibility appeals to entrepreneurs and investors alike.

Seed is a riskier investment than a start-up venture but holds the promise of a greater return. In a classic study of 200 companies and 500 financings by venture capitalists from 1978 to 1988, 41 percent of start-ups provided returns to investors compared with 35 percent of seed investments. However, successful seed deals provided an average of 19.4 times the money invested, compared with 9.7 times the money invested in start-ups. Besides, the hold time was not significantly different: 7.2 years for seed deals to provide returns, compared with 6.4 years hold time before harvesting returns from start-ups. Ten-year returns for early-stage/seed investments by venture capital firms with 2003 as the investment horizon performance date have held steady at 35.7 percent.

Another benefit of the private placement is that it is less costly than other types of offerings, for example, a public offering. The private placement is less costly in time and money. The entrepreneurial team can expect to spend in a public offering 900 hours of its time in completing an IPO, whereas the private placement can be completed much more quickly, allowing the principals more time for running the business. In addition, significant variations occur in the cost associated with private placement: front-end fees and back-end fees.

To avoid surprises, the cost for a private placement when handled by the entrepreneurs and the principals of the venture themselves (e.g., preparing and duplicating documents, binding, mailing, phone calls, follow-up meetings) can be anywhere from 3 to 5 percent of the amount raised to a high of 12 to 25 percent depending on whether intermediaries (licensed broker-dealers, investment bankers, and the like) are involved. So although a private placement is less costly than a public offering and other types of offerings, there are costs.

But the great advantage of a private placement comes with what the investor offers the entrepreneur beyond capital. Private investors bring much more than money to the deal; whereas in the venture capital industry, many of the venture capitalists have become money managers and are not spending much time with the companies in which they have invested because those companies are in later stages of development. Early-stage companies need a lot of hand holding, and angel investors are motivated to nurture new ventures as part of their hedging strategy to manage the downside risk in the deal. Thus, it becomes incumbent on the entrepreneur to take advantage of what angels bring to the enterprise.

Still another advantage of the private placements is its quick implementation. Based on our experience, the time frame for private placements is, for the shortest, 3 weeks, and for the longest, 12 months. The range of the time frame is wide. But if a management team is ready to raise capital, has committed itself to the venture, has put aside some financial resources, and is willing to commit the necessary time to the venture, things can happen quickly. And if the venture meets the criteria we have outlined, has developed the capitalization strategy, has been properly managed using the advice and counsel we have provided—particularly with regard to efficiency in the private placement process—a private placement can be concluded in a relatively short period, reasonably in about nine months.

Finally, a significant difference between angel investors and institutional investors is that institutional investors—because of the larger size of the funds under management—are gravitating to later-stage deals, which means they are gravitating toward larger deals. Meanwhile, individual angel investors are typically investing smaller amounts, and investing in smaller rounds. This way an individual investing $25,000, $50,000, or $100,000 becomes a significant player in the transaction. In this way, the private placement accommodates the smaller transactions, which, in fact, are the hardest transactions right now to get financed in the venture capital industry.

In a study of 1,200 investors in its database, ICR found that 20 percent invested less than $25,000 per deal; 40 percent invested $25,000 to $99,999; and 25 percent invested $100,000 to $250,000. Angel investors by their preferred size of investment per deal will tend toward smaller transactions overall. Ninety percent of the time they participate in deals of less than $1 million, with a mean investment size of approximately $50,000.

PROFESSIONAL VENTURE CAPITAL AS A FUNDING RESOURCE FOR EARLY-STAGE COMPANIES

The reasonable question for the entrepreneur to ask is this: "Are professional venture capitalists a realistic option for me to pursue to finance my deal?" It may be fair to say that these could be the worst of times for the venture capital industry. As the Money Tree Survey claims, valuations are down 50 percent, often as low as one to three times revenues; the venture-backed IPO market is soft, averaging eight venture capital–backed IPOs per quarter for the past three years; 50 percent of venture capital firms are predicted to be gone in five years, and 27 percent of venture capital firms formed in the past six years will not raise a second fund; litigation with limited partners is increasing; major write-downs are still to come in many venture capital portfolios; syndication is in vogue to reduce or share risk, making a round more complex; early-stage investing has been effected more than has later-stage; fund managers are refocusing on a few industry sectors; and hundreds of firms are "walking dead" and will go away. The implications for entrepreneurs seem clear: don't rely on venture capital funding; bootstrap while keeping your burn rate low. For example, a win for a CEO may be $2 million to $5 million in a venture capital–funded deal and "You may be working for a salary—but you just don't know it!"

However, if you meet the industry's criteria, the fact is that professional venture capitalists are financing companies. While the majority of venture capital firms focus primarily on expansion capital for venture in rapid growth phases and with a high probability of exit through sale of the company or an initial public offering, a minority are willing to consider early-stage investments.

The PricewaterhouseCoopers/Thomson Venture Economics/NVCA Money Tree Survey reports that venture capitalists invested a total of $40.6 billion in 2001, $21.4 billion in 2002, and $18.2 billion in 2003. These investments went to 4,600, 3,035, and 2,715 companies, respectively. While not a huge number of companies, it is an important contribution to address the capital gap. While Silicon Valley, New England, New York metro, Texas, the Southeast, and Los Angeles/Orange county account for a significant amount of the investment, the fact is that the investments are spread out, albeit to a lesser degree across the country. It is also true that biotechnology, software, medical devices and equipment, telecommunications, networking equipment, and semiconductors also account for the majority of investments by venture capital funds, that is, 66 percent in 2003.

The bottom line for entrepreneurs seeking capital is that if they don't fall into these geographic areas or industries, they're most likely out of luck. And if they do, the competition (especially with companies previously funded by or with management known to the venture capital firms) will be stiff indeed.

According to the Money Tree Survey, in 2003, the entire venture capital industry invested $354 million into 166 start-ups and seed-stage deals. First-round financings were higher at $3.3 billion into 716 deals. Remember, that's $354 million into start-ups out of a total investment of $18.2 billion invested in 2003. As you can see, chances of funding an early-stage deal (in which early-stage is defined as seed/start-up) is slim to slight.

Another way to understand if your deal is appropriate for venture capital is to realistically ask yourself how much capital you need to raise at this time (and at this valuation)! Then consider the typical deal size of venture capital financings. The mean deal size for venture capital firms in 2001 was $9.4 million; $7.4 million in 2002; and $7.1 million in 2003. Now ask yourself, "Do I actually need that much capital, especially at my current premoney valuation?" This is important for entrepreneurs who seek to have something to show for their efforts at the end of their venture's journey, that is, at exit. Especially so since we have seen median premoney valuations plummet in early-stage round classes to $3 million for seed and $9 million for start-up/first round. At these premoney valuations, entrepreneurs would have to be willing to "give away the farm" to attract venture capital dollars.

Another interesting dynamic at work in the venture capital industry is the large funding goals, reflective of and largely because of the increasing funding size of later-stage transactions. Yes, the industry is investing, but mostly in larger, later-stage deals. This is a symptom of the penchant of fund managers to reduce risk by focusing on more developed ventures, and to use more capital per transaction, a function of the larger funds under management. This situation occurs because of the shakeout in the industry, the failure of less successful funds, and the gravitation of limited partners' capital to more successful funds, thus engendering larger pools of capital under management. So although the statistics suggest that the industry is active, the vitality is undercut by the small number of deals actually being made. And the implication of smaller numbers of deals does not bode well for ventures that do not fit the venture capital profile perfectly. A cynical entrepreneur shared this concern when he said, "You'd have better luck getting the capital you need playing lotto than trying to raise it from the venture capital industry."

In 2003, 94 percent of institutional venture capital money went to companies in stages of development beyond seed and start-up. It is no wonder, then, that entrepreneurs are looking away from venture capital until later stages of their developing companies. As an NVCA publication declares, "Most of the venture capital funds invested across the country were received by companies already through at least one round of financing." It boils down to this: Angel investment runs the critical first leg of the relay race, passing the baton to venture capital only after a company has begun to find its stride. As the numbers presented reveal, venture capitalists focus on expansion and later stages of development, when their contribution is most effective. In this way venture capital investment complements rather than conflicts with angel investment.

COMPARISON OF ANGEL INVESTORS WITH PROFESSIONAL VENTURE CAPITALISTS

Entrepreneurs should realize that early-stage investing by professional venture capital will form only a small part of their investment strategy. Arthur Rock, a founder of Intel, said in *Fortune* that venture capitalists are now portfolio managers, "more interested in creating wealth than in creating companies." Another Silicon Valley veteran has dubbed *venture capital* an oxymoron. Still another CEO warned entrepreneurs not to look on investment bankers as their friends, calling them "gatekeepers" as they screen out what to them is just another deal. For entrepreneurs to rely too heavily on that particular resource is a mistake, when, in fact, there remains a larger resource willing to assume a greater risk. The angel investor—patient and interested in adding value to smaller, higher-risk transactions—stands ready to nurture a company through the early leg of the relay. Then the professional venture capital community becomes a more suitable contributor by virtue of its fiduciary responsibility to those institutional investors who have entrusted their money to money managers.

But examining the people who constitute the private investment market is difficult because of their penchant for privacy, the lack of sophisticated measures for accumulating data, the lack of disclosure requirements by the government about private placement investment, and the costly nature of doing qualitative research. Even the job of compiling information through interviews and surveys and then analyzing their content is work. Because of these difficulties, discrepancies appear in estimates of the size and capability of the angel market.

Any estimation of the size of the angel market must inevitably begin with some understanding of the extent of wealth in the United States. According to data obtained by the Environmental Research Foundation, the richest 0.5 percent of Americans, that is, one out of every 200 families, owned more than 45 percent of the nation's privately held net worth. This wealth was composed of 47 percent stock, 62 percent bonds, and 77 percent of all trusts in the United States. Also, the top 10 percent of families owned 83 percent of all income-producing wealth. In Lisa Keister's book *Wealth in America*, she used stocks, bonds, bank accounts, and real estate holdings rather than income in her national survey to conclude that Baby Boomers have accumulated more wealth than their parents, and that their net worth is continuing to increase. It is the Boomers who are at the prime age for angel investment.

In Arthur Kennick's study, "A Rolling Tide: Changes in Distribution of Wealth in the U.S. 1989–2001," he estimates total net worth in the United States at $42.3 trillion. And he reports in "United for a Fair Economy 2001," a 2001 study on the "Distribution of Wealth Ownership," that although the top 1 percent of U.S. households hold 32.7 percent of the nation's wealth, the next 9 percent hold 37 percent of the wealth; the next 40 percent hold 27.4 percent, while the bottom 50 percent hold 2.8 percent of the wealth.

Edmund Wolff's research supports Kennick's findings. In his "Recent Trends in Wealth Ownership 1983–98," sponsored by the Levy Institute, Wolff found that the top 1 percent held 42.2 percent of U.S. net worth; the next 9 percent held 42.2 percent; the next 30 percent held 44.4 percent; the middle 20 percent held 10 percent of the wealth, and the bottom 40 percent held negative net worth.

If we look at investment holdings of stocks, bonds, mutual funds, and Individual Retirement Accounts, the top 1 percent holds 42.1 percent; the next 9 percent hold 36.6 percent; and the bottom 90 percent hold 21.3 percent. Wolff's findings are invaluable to those of us interested in identifying which segments of the high-net-worth market to approach with our venture investment opportunities.

Finally, the Survey of Consumer Finances claims that households in the top 20 percent in the United States saw their net worths rise between 1983 and 1995. Why are these macroeconomic statistics and trends important? Simply because it is historically confirmed that those households with net worths of $1 million to $10 million comprise the group most likely to take on an angel role in investing. These studies confirm that substantial numbers of U.S. households—approximately 2,000,000—meet the net worth criteria for investing in early-stage transactions.

Studies of the business angel market confirm that a source of capital for higher-risk financing for early-stage entrepreneurial ventures not only exists but flourishes. While obtaining accuracy and agreement on the size of the active component of the market is difficult, that this market is huge is beyond dispute. Just keep in mind that all studies are in effect estimates, estimates that all attempt to get at the actual size. Early studies by Gaston, Wetzel, the MIT Venture Capital Network, and UC-Irvine suggested that 250,000 active angels invest at least once a year. Studies by Wetzel and Freer (1994) suggested the number was 300,000 angels investing $10 billion to $30 billion annually. The NVCA has suggested that angels contribute upwards of $100 billion annually. More recently, studies by Friedman estimate that 300,000 angels invested $30 billion per year in 2003. More conservative are 1999 studies by Sohl that $10 billion to $20 billion per year was sunk into 30,000 deals. With three to five million businesses being started each year, and the extent of net worth available (how much of net worth being liquid essentially is the question), the estimates reported above are not only believable but most likely conservative and understated.

Based on ICR's estimates, upward of 400,000 to 500,000 companies are attempting aggressively to raise capital at any given time, and ultimately about $3.5 to $4 billion of the angel market is going into seed, R&D, and start-up stage transactions, the riskiest stages. Approximately 30,000 to 40,000 very early-stage transactions are being concluded in this market at minimum per year. Ninety percent of those transactions are typically for less than $1 million, with a mean investment per investor of $30,000 to $50,000 and a mean investment share in the first round of the financing of approximately 20 percent of the equity.

Venture capital firms, since they are listed publicly in directories, on software, and in online databases, are inundated with requests for capital. To private investors, however, public listings are anathema. If they list anywhere, they list with confidential private networks; for example, one of the 170 formal and informal organizations located throughout leading technology and business regions of the United States, including investment clubs, informal networks, associations, pledge funds, limited partnership and incubators.

Thus, angel investors receive less deal flow. This gives them more time to peruse the deals that do come in, and since they do not have to invest, they become more selective. Private investors, after all, seek a profit on every investment. Professional venture capitalists, on the other hand, accept that a percentage of their deals will fail, some unable to recover even bank account returns. The reason? The professional venture capitalist *has* to invest. For example, in one study of venture capital returns, the fund experienced a total loss 11.5 percent of the time, partial loss 23 percent of the time, and break even 30 percent of the time, and generated multiples of two to ten times investment or more 35.5 percent of the time. In effect, "swinging for the fence" and "taking strike outs" in the process.

By ICR's definition of preseed, seed, and start-up, early-stage represents the riskiest investment; often it means investing in no more than an idea. Some may insist that we overrepresent the activity of angels in this market, but a look at the above numbers should settle the matter. Seed and start-up investments in the angel market amount to tens of thousands of transactions. By comparison, the entire venture capital industry invested in 166 early-stage transactions in 2003. Entrepreneurs will tally more for their time, trouble, and money from an angel investor than from the professional venture capitalist, who better serves as a near-distant, instead of initial, funding source.

Having addressed some of the quantitative differences between angels and venture capitalists, Exhibit 4.4 presents an overview of some of the main qualitative differences between business angels and venture capitalists. When we cross-compare business angels with venture capitalists, business angels seem to be concerned more with a firm's success and creation of a sustainable company, while venture capitalists seem to be more concerned with an exit strategy and concomitant internal rate of return. Business angels are using their own money; venture capitalists are using other people's money. If we consider private investors, the mean number of investments they make a year totals four. The number of investments made by the most active venture capital firm in 2003 was 73, with second and third most active venture investors coming in at 52 deals and 50 deals per year, respectively.

EXHIBIT 4.4 Main Differences Between Business Angels and Venture Capitalists

Business Angels	Venture Capitalists
• Concern with firm success	• Concern with exit strategy
• Own money	• Other people's money
• Smaller equity share	• Larger equity share
• Mean # investments = 4	• Mean # investments = 23
• Small business experience	• Academic credentials
• 80% started a company	• 38% started a company
• Part-time investor	• Full-time investor
• Entrepreneurial manager	• Financial manager
• Value-adding, active investor	• Strategic investor, not hands-on
• Focus on entrepreneur	• Focus on concept and rapid growth potential
• Location important (80%)	• Location important (60%)
• No experience in venture's industry 59%	• No experience in venture's 29%
• ROI objective minimum 30%	• ROI objective minimum 40%
• Generalist	• Specialist
• Short due diligence and negotiation cycle	• Long due diligence and negotiation cycle

Source: International Capital Resources

Thus, angel investors are part-time—although active and value-added—investors, whereas institutional people—almost strictly hands off—are full-time. Angels, 80 percent of whom have started a business, value small business experience; venture capitalists, only 20 percent of whom have started a business, value academic credentials. The business angel focuses on the entrepreneur, while the venture capitalist focuses on revolutionary concepts with rapid growth potential. In huge markets, management can be replaced!

Other differences abound. To 80 percent of the angels, location is important, especially given the cost, time, and frustration associated with air travel in the current geopolitical environment, while location matters to 60 percent of the venture capitalists reimbursed for their travel. Business angels will invest in a company when the angel has no business experience in that company's industry 59 percent of the time, whereas venture capitalists will invest only about 29 percent of the time in industries where they have no direct experience. Thus, you have a better chance in the angel market because about twice as many business angels invest in industries they do not have direct experience in. So you can have a larger number of people to go to because they may not be familiar with your technology, but they do appreciate the market potential.

The angel investor, a generalist who anticipates a minimum ROI of 30 percent, contrasts sharply with the venture capitalist, a specialist, who presumes a minimum ROI of 40 percent. Finally, the business angel requires a short due diligence and negotiation cycle; the venture capitalist favors a long due diligence and negotiation cycle.

PROFESSIONAL VENTURE CAPITAL: HELP OR HINDRANCE TO YOUR FUNDING SUCCESS?

In their 1990 article in the *California Management Review*, "Does Venture Capital Foster the Most Promising Entrepreneurial Firms?" Raphael Amit, Lawrence Glosten, and Eitar Muller suggest that start-ups backed by venture capital have a much higher failure rate than those financed by individual investors. Venture capital is spread thin, say the authors, and venture capitalists negotiate tough deals that drive away the ablest entrepreneurs, those who know the value of their projects. Hence, they conclude, we can expect higher failure rates among firms seeking venture capital than among the total population of new firms.

One reason for the double digit of investment failures among venture capital investments may be that some more inferior deals gravitate toward venture capitalists because of their more aggressive valuation stance. In other words, entrepreneurs with less confidence in their venture may be willing to take less money for equity in their current round of financing. Compare the entrepreneur or inventor who, encouraged by the venture, would rarely sacrifice so much.

For example, suppose a venture capitalist offers an entrepreneur an investment of $1,000,000 but wants 50 percent of the company. The venture capitalist is thus declaring that the venture is worth $2,000,000. The entrepreneur with less confidence in the venture, with less belief in the venture's viability in three to five years, will accept the valuation. If, however, the entrepreneur does have confidence in the sustainability of the venture, why would he or she surrender what may be worth millions within a comparable time frame? As the article's authors surmise, "The most able entrepreneurs will not find the prices offered by the venture capitalists sufficiently attractive." Since, as we have presented, angel capital is accessible for promising deals, the confident entrepreneur need not compromise.

Confident entrepreneurs should confer less on the venture capitalist because they believe in their venture's future value. Venture capitalists are aggressive in their valuation because it serves them to manage the downside risk and increases the possibility of achieving their targeted internal rate of return, especially after having been burned in the dot-com bust of the late 1990s. If the venture capitalist can persuade the entrepreneur to relinquish 50 percent of the venture, for example, the venture capitalist can afford a less successful transaction than either would like, but still provide a reasonable return for the venture capital fund's investors. The venture capitalist will suffer far less than the entrepreneur. At this rate of valuation, chances are the venture capitalist will get back the original investment, particularly if the company is sold or merged.

Amit, Glosten, and Muller put it bluntly: "The most promising entrepreneurs will not seek venture capital financing." That the entrepreneur is better off in the early-stage deal with the direct, private investor than with the venture capitalist seems axiomatic.

In sum, a wide range of financing possibilities awaits; each has its strengths and weaknesses. Some options apply to certain companies, while others would not be suitable. The difference lies in stage of development. Once you are clear about your stage of development, you can evaluate what will work for you. Still, for people lost in the capital gap, only one resource seems workable: the direct, private placement made with the angel investor.

CHAPTER 5

Angel Capital in America: A Study

INTRODUCTION

We conducted a study that examined angel and venture capital available through one investor network. The study profiled early-stage, higher-risk private and institutional investors actively involved in direct, private investment into entrepreneurial ventures, and we sought to clarify investment criteria and describe aspects unique to these investors. Our purpose is to help entrepreneurs seeking capital to better understand angel and venture capital expectations in the private placement, fund-raising process.

The study was sponsored by ICR, a San Francisco–based angel network. One of the authors is the Senior Managing Partner of the firm. ICR is recognized by government agencies, entrepreneurial organizations, academic institutions, entrepreneurs, and institutional and angel investors as having built one of the largest databases of qualified investors interested in early-stage investing in the United States.

The challenge for any angel study is, of course, to identify and locate investors to participate because of their preference for privacy, as we have discussed. We will explain how these investors were attracted to the database and network later. In this chapter, we present an analysis and summary of results of the survey.

METHODOLOGY

The first objective was to identify qualified investors, and then to administer a questionnaire designed to define investment criteria and preferences, as well as characteristics of the investors themselves. Confidentiality was assured to all who participated, and the questionnaire was designed to be nonintrusive in order to facilitate the response rate while providing as much useful and quantifiable data as possible.

The major source of names was developed from ICR's proprietary database of investors built over the previous 15 years. We used a range of techniques to attract investors to the database and, consequently, got them involved in the network. The techniques used included investors who had invested into client ventures, direct mailings to high-net-worth investor lists; radio interview shows followed up with audio tape sales on angel investing, newspaper advertising, and investment seminars; referrals from investors in the network solicited with incentive programs, business periodical advertising, publishing and distributing an angel investment newsletter, investment conference promotion and speaking engagements, publishing and promoting a book on angel investing, and creating a high-traffic web site (*www.icrnet.com*). Obviously, this is not a statistically valid sample. But these techniques provided a cross-sampling of investors from across the United States.

Data were collected by randomly selecting 100 investors from ICR's database of 1,359 investors. Each was sent a letter introducing the study, assuring confidentiality, explaining that results would be published and available publicly. The questionnaire was designed to be easy to complete and return, and was enclosed with the letter. Because an existing relationship was in place between one of the authors of the study and the investors, data collection was made significantly easier than having to build a list of investors to mail to, and to persuade them to participate.

In all, 100 packages were distributed. Sixty completed survey questionnaires were returned.

RESULTS OF THE STUDY

Profiles of the investors who responded conform to expectations consistent with a national network. Fifty percent were from California, 13 percent from Massachusetts, and a sprinkling from across the country, including New York, Illinois, New Jersey, Maryland, Connecticut, Pennsylvania, Ohio, New Hampshire, Minnesota, Florida, Georgia, Colorado, Texas, Utah, and Washington. Given the higher levels of entrepreneurial activity in California and Massachusetts, higher rates of response from those regions were predicted.

Fifty-seven of the respondents were male; three female. In addition, the respondents were well educated. Fifty-seven percent held post-graduate degrees, many from Ivy League universities. Eighteen percent had been president, CEO, or other senior executives in established corporations. Thirteen percent held medical, law, accounting, or engineering degrees and were still practicing.

We asked about their start-up management experience by inquiring if they had founded their own companies. Forty-eight percent had been involved in starting up their own ventures.

We assessed the respondents' investment history and experience. Eighty-three percent reported prior experience investing capital in various businesses for their own account. One hundred percent confirmed that they met accredited investor status. Eighty percent answered that they relied on legal, accounting, or tax advisers when they considered particular investments, and would continue to rely on such advice in the future.

Three quarters of respondents (77 percent) stated that they were individual investors acting for their own account and investment purposes—and not with a view to distribute or resell. One third responded that they were either a professional venture capitalist or employed by a venture capital firm. Twenty-five percent represented a corporate investor. The overlap may be explained by the fact that some venture capitalists, when there is no conflict of interest, can invest privately for their own account. Also, some angels invest through the corporations that they own or run.

To understand the frequency of past investments, we asked respondents to indicate how many entrepreneurial ventures they invested into during the previous five years. Their responses are summarized below:

During the past five years, in how many entrepreneurial ventures have you invested?

Number of Responses	Category
0	None
10	One
10	Two
4	Three
5	Four
2	Five
20	Six or more

Thirty-three percent made only two investments or fewer in five years! Eighteen percent invested three to five times in five years. However, one-third reported six or more investments in this time period.

We also asked respondents to report the size of their past venture investments:

Number of Responses	Category
1	Under $10,000
4	$10,000 to $25,000

Number of Responses	Category
7	$25,000 to $50,000
10	$50,000 to $100,000
5	$100,000 to $250, 000
7	$250, 000 to $500,000
2	$500,000 to $1,000,000
10	More than $1,000,000

We double-queried respondents on investment size by cross-checking on the maximum investment they would consider placing into one venture, and there was no significant deviation in size from their reports of actual investments.

Seven percent of investments were $10,000 to $25,000. Twelve percent ranged from $25,000 to $50,000. Seventeen percent ranged from $50,000 to $100,000 per transaction. Eight percent invested $100,000 to $250,000. Twelve percent of the respondents averaged $250,000 to $500,000 per deal. Only three percent invested $500,000 to $1,000,000. And 17 percent invested more than $1,000,000 per transaction.

We correlated the frequency and size of investment data, and an analysis of actual transactions completed affirms a total of $91,815,000 in private placement investments by just these 60 investors in the previous five years. Furthermore, we asked respondents if they were willing to participate with other investors in investment opportunities that exceed their preferred maximum personal investment. Fifty-two investors, or 87 percent, stated they were willing to pool their capital with other investors. So their inclination to participate with co-investors enhances the total capital financing capability to entrepreneurs beyond the already substantial $91,815,000.

One of the objectives of this study was to attempt to gain a better understanding of angel and early-stage investor preferences. We asked respondents about the age distribution or preferred stage of development of investments that held their interest. The range of categories offered is below:

Number of Responses	Category
16	*Seed.* A venture in the idea stage or in the process of being organized.
14	*R&D.* Financing of product development for early-stage or more.
38	*Start-up.* A venture that is completing product development and initial marketing and has been in business less than two years.

44	*First Stage.* A venture with a working prototype that has gone through beta testing and is beginning commercialization.
41	*Expansion Stage.* A venture that is in the early stage of expanding commercialization and is in need of growth capital.
5	*Mezzanine.* A venture that has increasing sales volume and is breaking even or is profitable. Additional funds are to be used for further expansion, marketing, or working capital.
10	*Bridge.* A venture that requires short-term capital to reach a clearly defined and stable position.
4	*Acquisition/Merger.* A venture that is in need of capital to finance an acquisition or merger.
7	*Turnaround.* A venture that is in need of capital to effect a change from unprofitability to profitability.

Respondents could select as many categories as they wanted, that is, they were not limited to just one category.

If we define early-stage investing as encompassing the categories of seed, R&D, start-up, and first-stage only, then of the 179 respondent selections made, 63 percent preferred investment in early-stage. Growth capital to finance expansion of a business comprised 23 percent of responses, while 15 percent of selections were later-stage (larger transactions). This last group in the study sample were overwhelmingly undertaken by the professional venture capitalists.

Investors in our study show diversity in industry preference. Investors were not restricted, selecting as many industry categories as they were interested in.

Which business or industry category interests you?

Number of Responses	Category
5	Agriculture/Fishing/Forestry
15	Biotech/Pharmaceutical/Life Sciences
31	Communications/Publishing
37	Computer Software
12	Education/Training
14	Energy/Natural Resources
16	Environmental
22	Financial Services/Banking Insurance

Number of Responses	Category
4	Information Technology
7	Internet
26	Manufacturing—High Tech Products
23	Manufacturing—Industrial/Commercial
22	Manufacturing—Consumer Products
2	Material and Chemicals
33	Medical/Health Care
4	Optical
5	Real Estate/Construction
13	Recreation/Tourism
11	Retail Trade
22	Service—Technology Related
10	Service—Other
6	Transportation
6	Telecommunications/Wireless
11	Wholesale Trade

While respondents registered interest in all 24 industry categories offered, investors displayed a preference for Software, Medical/Healthcare, and Manufacturing. Financial Services and Technology-Related Services also rated high. To a lesser extent, Biotech/Pharmaceutical and Life Sciences, Environmental, and Recreation were next highest in preferred industries. The interest in very high tech is driven by venture capital firms and corporate investors. Reduced interest in the more esoteric technologies by angels may be because of losses incurred after the dot-com bust, and reflect their refocusing on industries with which they are directly familiar. We asked investors what the nature of the relationship would be with ventures after they made an investment. We wanted to better understand monitoring techniques investors might use to keep track of investee company performance, how they envisioned adding value, and to what extent they saw themselves becoming involved should problems arise.

To what extent do you normally expect to become involved with a company in your risk portfolio?

Number of Responses	Category
14	No involvement other than reviewing periodic reports and attending stockholder meetings.
34	Representation on the firm's board of directors.

32	Provide consulting help as needed and requested.
14	Work part-time with the firm.
11	Work full-time with the firm.
10	Founders team.
0	Other

Investors could select more than one category. While 14 investors (23 percent) were passive investors, the majority sought more active involvement as necessary. Fifty-seven percent wanted representation on the board of directors, a measure of "control" not unexpected given public and private market results during the past five years. More than half (53 percent) would provide consulting help as needed. Forty-two percent would be willing to work in an interim capacity if needed, and 17 percent would consider involvement directly as a part of the founder team.

Further about the extent of involvement, we asked investors in what functional areas they were qualified and willing to provide management assistance to investee companies.

Are you qualified and willing to provide management assistance in any of the following areas?

Number of Responses	Category
29	Marketing
17	Production
8	R&D
2	Engineering
14	Personnel
38	General Management
9	Finance
1	System Development

Sixty-three percent believed they were qualified to provide general management assistance and would be willing to do so. Among the respondents, all skill areas for venture start-up and development were present and—outside of very technical areas—significant percentages of respondents would make themselves available.

Respondents with proximate geographic preferences in relation to the venture's location (on average, within 300 miles of where they live) amounted to 23 percent. Sixty-five percent reported a preference for investments located within their home state. Twelve percent were willing to invest anywhere in the United States. Follow-up interviews with investors in the study suggest that some of them with a "state of residence" preference would invest out of state if there were a lead investor in the network who lived close to the company, someone able to monitor the deal, someone they knew, respected, and trusted.

We also asked if the investors would consider making an investment when the entrepreneur's proposal was not supported by a complete business plan. Overwhelmingly, investors clearly required a complete business plan before investing, but early in their decision-making process, a comprehensive executive summary would suffice to garner their attention.

We were interested in examining how large of a growth potential would be required to attract venture investors' interest. We asked respondents to consider projected sales, five years out, and received the following results:

Please indicate a venture's *minimum* annual sales projected five years after financing that you would consider of interest. Check ONE only.

Number of Responses	Category
0	$100,000
1	$500,000
11	$1 million
4	$2 million
10	$5 million
9	$10 million
7	$20 million
2	$40 million
3	More than $50 million

Only 20 percent of the investors required the venture to have the potential to grow to $20 million in annual sales or more. Thirty-two percent would be willing to invest if sales in five years ranged from $5 million to $10 million. Most important, a quarter of the investors (27 percent) would still invest if the potential for minimum annual sales was $2 million or less. It is crucial for entrepreneurs to appreciate the significance of these findings. While it is true that to attract professional venture capital and corporate investment, the potential for huge minimum annual sales is mandatory. Such is not the case with angels. Angels who believe they will get investment returns that meet their targeted multiples and personal expectations may still be willing to invest, even when liquidity options are limited as a result of gross revenues, or when payback may come over time from building a sustainable company.

CONCLUDING REMARKS

While the reader needs to be circumspect in making generalizations of these findings to the entire angel market, the fact that the 60-investor sample is representative of a sophisticated angel and active early-stage investor network cannot be denied. The random sample of 60 (4.4%) of ICR's 1,359 investors provides real insight into one investor network, its investor characteristics, investment preferences, investment habits, actual investments placed, investors' expectations for entrepreneurs, documentation, and returns. By using data-based research strategies, entrepreneurs can better use pools of investor resources, increase efficiency by better targeting the investment to appropriate investors, and increase their chances for fund-raising success.

CHAPTER 6

What Do Private Investors Look for in a Deal?

THE HIGH-NET-WORTH INVESTOR MARKET

Positioning your venture for success in fund-raising mandates an appreciation for early-stage investors, particularly understanding angels, what they look for in a deal, their investment criteria, their motivations, and their outcome expectations. These are the critical elements entrepreneurs must understand as they target their deals to the appropriate investors. Targeting the private investor means having the information to answer such questions as these: Who would be interested? Who can afford it? Where are they located? What is the best way to reach them? What message should I emphasize?

As we have demonstrated, private venture investors no longer represent an invisible segment of the venture capital market. These investors form a diverse and diffuse population of individuals of means, many of whom have created their own successful ventures. By providing early-stage financing for start-up firms and growth equity for expanding businesses, these investors fill a void in the institutional venture capital market. They look for products and services in markets with significant growth potential while requiring rewards equal to the risks they incur. They will insist on clarity about when and how they may cash in their investment. And they surely look for competent management, a point we cannot emphasize too much.

Another point we come to is how dependent this market is on individuals with high net worth, the "wealthy," those who possess something beyond high incomes. A person with a high income may be affluent but not wealthy. Only high net worth determines wealth. Earlier, we discussed how some entrepreneurs mistakenly judge investors solely on their income, forgetting that income alone has little to do with the investment potential that counts in these early-stage, high-risk transactions. By focusing on income, the uninitiated can forget how quickly it can become outstripped by expenses.

Income alone, then, does not signal a potential investor. Entrepreneurs should not rely on brokers' lists of investors for two reasons: Brokers' lists are based on income, not wealth; and, in many cases, these lists are based on information publicly available. These lists will not lead entrepreneurs to the investors who make high-risk investments, however much entrepreneurs and their brokers wish it were so.

However, an investor's net worth is much more difficult to plumb than income, particularly net worth exclusive of house and car. A person's net worth is attainable only through interviews, which accounts for the reason that research-based databases become so valuable. By combining net worth with income data, a helpful database, such as the one operated by ICR, turns up those individuals who meet the standards for such transactions. Private discretionary capital of high-net-worth individuals accounts for a sizable resource for investment. As we have mentioned in our e-book, written with Bill Bradley, as high-net-worth individuals, angels have not been an easy target for entrepreneurs. Successful angels are known for their ability to remain "plugged in," while comfortably holding their ground behind the scenes. The popularity of angel investing has made angels more accessible than ever to the entrepreneurial public.

In the days before venture forums, angel clubs, or venture networks, angels were much more difficult to locate. Angel investors have typically been viewed as individuals capable of not only financial contribution to an emerging venture, but perhaps as important is their managerial and strategic contribution. The popularity of angel investing in the greater media has led to a significant increase in the number of high-net-worth individuals seeking private market investment opportunities. As such, a new group of inexperienced angel investors has emerged.

In many cases, today's inexperienced new angel seeks the upside associated with traditional angel investing, but often has little desire to contribute to the development of the venture beyond the original capital contribution. Enter the "passive" angel investor. While the general purpose remains the same—to seed emerging companies—the risk increases to both the entrepreneur and investor as the passive angel contributes little beyond money to the success of the venture.

The angel marketplace is being forced to evolve as more and more diverse high-net-worth individuals participate. The structure of the market is changing to adapt to both the new passive nature of inexperienced angels, as well as to the increased demand of the more seasoned investor. Nonetheless, the angel investor remains a staple in the emergence of start-up companies.

We have noted that only a specific segment of the high-net-worth market is worth targeting for high-risk deals, a market composed of a diverse pool of investors. The principal group for investing in high-risk deals has a net worth of $1 million to $10 million. Net worth of less than $1 million or greater than $10 million will not be a target for high-risk investments. People with a net worth of less than $1 million do not meet the legal qualifications for being involved in this type of investment and can trigger litigation. Such investments are simply too risky for them. Even if the prospective investor meets mandated income levels for accredited status, the investor may not be able to absorb losses that can occur with higher-risk, early-stage investments. This could lead to legal action, particularly with less experienced angels. For those with a net worth of more than $10 million—the approximately 0.5 percent or one out of every 200 U.S. families who own more than 45 percent of the nation's privately held net wealth in stocks, bonds, and trusts—investing is most often accomplished through family offices that bear fiduciary responsibility, the representatives of which are less inclined toward these types of high-risk investments. However, there are exceptions! As any experienced money manager will tell you, "always leave a little high-risk play money" for the client to place on his or her own. So entrepreneurs can target this group if they can reach them directly.

Total U.S. net worth in 2001 was measured by Arthur Kennick in his study "A Rolling Tide: Changes in Wealth in the U.S. 1989–2001" at $42.3 trillion. The top 10 percent of households held 69 percent of the wealth. The bottom 90 percent held about 30 percent. The top tiers are where you will find nonrelated angels for your deal.

Accredited investors make up the group of incomes ranging between $100,000 and $300,000 or more per year. This is the group typically considered affluent. Again, they are affluent, but they are not wealthy. Someone with an income of $100,000 might have no net worth or discretionary net worth available. However, if only income data are available, entrepreneurs should look for those with a gross income of $200,000 to $1 million. This income level offers far better prospects of those having the necessary discretionary funds to make these types of investments.

There are affluent market segments that provide unique asset garnering. The inheritance boom and the unprecedented assets of a mature market combine to make the most tantalizing accumulation of wealth in the history of the world. According to the 1995 Affluent Market Consumer Survey, affluent market segments exist that provide unique asset-garnering opportunities for individuals seeking to raise capital. The thing to realize is that the high-net-worth market is highly segmented; it is not a monolithic market, just as the angel market is not monolithic, but rather a series of types.

In studying this affluent or high-net-worth market, we discover the following segments: the young affluent and low-end affluent (people with a net worth of $100,000, excluding their primary residence); the retired affluent and career affluent (those with a net worth of more than $500,000); established wealth and senior corporate executives (those with a net worth of $1.4 million to $5 million); business owners (whose net worth ranges across other segments, from a low of $500,000 to a high of $5 million); and active wealth (those whose net worth tops $5 million).

Obviously, segments of this market are more inclined than others to early-stage investing. Because of their age, need for income and security, and time remaining to garner capital appreciation, early-stage investing—with its longer-term horizons, lack of dividends, and higher risk—are much less attractive to the retired affluent than to other affluent market segments. Clearly, then, the retired affluent are less of a target for early-stage investing. The young affluent are in the earlier stages of acquiring homes and material things and therefore probably are less inclined to engage in early-stage investing. In addition, the young affluent, more concerned with the time investment of family and career, become much less available to provide the time-intensive dimension of added value that these early-stage companies require. Nor are the young affluent readily available to devote the necessary time to hedge the downside risk associated with this type of investment. So an economic element and a time element make it less appealing. The low-end affluent will not yet have the discretionary net worth. So the entrepreneur's camera lens naturally narrows on established wealth (those looking for socially responsible deals) and on active wealth (those actively placing money back into the economy). Likewise, senior corporate executives are investing in their industries because they understand the opportunity, just as business owners are looking to invest and diversify and grow beyond their businesses. Finally, the career affluent are seeking to broaden their retirement portfolio through capital accumulation over time. Obviously, it is these latter segments that deserve the early-stage entrepreneur's store of energy.

In examining statistics quantifying the optimal market segments of the high-net-worth individuals to target, we have concluded that there are approximately 2,000,000 U.S. households that meet the minimum net worth requirements for direct, private investment. These segments constitute the underlying structure of what is called "the angel market"; that is, the pre-IPO market, providing money to young, rapidly growing companies that hold the potential to develop into significant and sustainable contributors to the country's economy. This capital is the main source of financing for start-ups and fast-growing small businesses, and supplements cradle equity provided by family, friends, and founders. This capital also serves as the precursor to more traditional and institutional capital from venture capitalists and banks.

THE INFORMAL, HIGH-RISK INVESTOR PROFILE

Just who are these investors? What profile fits the hard-to-find, affluent, private, early-stage investor? In Chapter 7 we profile specific types of angel investors. In Exhibit 6.1, using the results of survey questionnaires and follow-up interviews, we sketch the generic informal, high-risk investor from ICR's early study of more than 600 private investors.

These individuals are typically males around 46 to 65 years of age. Age, in fact, influences investment. We see in the age range of 46 to 55 an inclination to redeploy some of their income, particularly toward growth potential. In the 56 to 65 bracket, we see a much more active portfolio management, in which these investors trust their own judgment, not that of brokers, particularly in investments into private business ventures.

Returning to our profile in Exhibit 6.1, these investors typically have postgraduate professional degrees and extensive management experience. In fact, they have been executives in established companies or owned and sold their own companies. And because they can aggressively negotiate strong discounts in valuation, they are interested in earlier-stage deals. Having had to raise money for their own businesses, they are experienced in dealing with investors and understand the potential in these transactions for high returns through capital appreciation.

Based on five-year investment patterns, we showed in our study reported in Chapter 5 the size of investment per transaction, transactions that ranged from less than $25,000 to more than $1,000,000 per transaction: Seven per-

EXHIBIT 6.1 Informal, High Net Worth Investor Profile

- 46–65 years of age, male
- Postgraduate degree, often technical
- Previous management experience; started up, operates, or sold a successful business
- Invests between $25,000 and $1,000,000 per transaction
- Prefers participation with other financially sophisticated individuals
- Strong preference for transactions that match with technical expertise
- 23% prefer to invest "close to home"
- Maintains an "active" professional relationship with portfolio investments
- Invests in 1–4 transactions per year
- Diversification and tax shelter income are not the most important objectives; however, ROI is rarely the only objective
- Term for holding investment is 8 years
- Looks for rates of return from 22.5% to 50%; minimum portfolio return 20%
- Learns of investment opportunities primarily from friends and trusted associates; however, majority would like to look at more investment opportunities than present informal referral system permits
- Income is $100,000/year minimum
- Self-made millionaire

Source: International Capital Resources

cent invested up to $25,000; 12 percent invested $25,000 to $50,000; 17 percent invested $50,000 to $100,000; 8 percent invested $100,000 to $250,000; 12 percent invested $250,000 to $500,000; only 3 percent invested $500,000 to $1,000,000; and 17 percent invested $1,000,000 or more per deal. We concluded that professional venture capital and corporate investors made up the majority of funds invested, investing $1,000,000 or more, but some angels were also identified in this segment. In summary, the majority of individual investments in ICR's investor network are most likely under $500,000 (56 percent). Also, as we reported, these investors are typically willing to pool their money, or they invest with a syndicate of co-investors who ponder hedging strategies and managing risk.

These investors possess preferences for an eclectic mix of industries, with interest in communications, software, education, energy, financial services, manufacturing, medical and health care, recreation, retail, services, wholesale trade, transportation, biotech and life sciences, and high technology, including information technology, optical, telecom/wireless, and Internet ventures.

In addition, entrepreneurs must expand their search for investors geographically. While it is true that 23 percent prefer to invest close to home, 65 percent will invest statewide and 12 percent will invest nationwide. Many of those who will invest statewide are willing to entertain deals out of state if a trusted co-investor is geographically proximate to monitor the deal.

We will see in the composite sketches of types of private investors featured in the next chapter that despite their diversity, much unites them. Investors are like DNA molecules: Although everyone's DNA is assembled from the same nucleotides, everyone's DNA is different. Individual investors, too, are different, reflecting a market of splintered segments composed of distinct individuals. Therefore, no monolithic overture to them will suffice. Entrepreneurs must approach investors individually, in terms not only of personal demography, but also of idiosyncrasy. Thus, a careful measure—something beyond an array of mere market statistics—illuminates the informal, high-net-worth investor as both individual and member of a select group.

In conclusion, angel investors are private, high-net-worth individuals who invest their own money. They focus on fast growth, early-stage ventures for the potential returns these ventures offer. They seek equity with the goal of capital appreciation. They are long-term investors with an average hold time of eight years to liquidity. They are not part of a monolithic group. They invest in a range of industries, but individually stay close to what they know. They can be actively involved or passive, but most of all, they are interested in building sustainable companies as the best hedge against risks of this asset class.

ADVANTAGES AND DISADVANTAGES OF DIRECT VENTURE INVESTING

For entrepreneurs planning to court high-net-worth investors for their venture, it is worthwhile to take a moment, step back from the search, and acknowledge both the advantages of early-stage investing that attracts investors and the disadvantages that create barriers to and bottlenecks for investor involvement.

So the question arises: Why do sophisticated investors get involved in the alternative asset market in the first place, especially with the reported up to 33 percent chance of loss of capital? (See Exhibit 6.2.)

They get involved because this type of investing—direct, early-stage, private equity investing—offers them some unique advantages. One of the advantages is no middleman. This type of transaction is based on their own due diligence, their own assessment, their own intuition, and their own intelligence and analytical skills to identify a winner. One very attractive advantage is the possibility of hitting a home run in this arena.

And because you can hit a home run, the upside potential through capital appreciation on these investments is unlimited. It's not like a loan that will return your capital plus a little percentage in interest. Even in today's down IPO market conditions, companies that are sold or merged at values between $100 million and $300 million are providing substantial multiples to investors involved in the venture early. So beneath the surface bubbles the incentive to hit it big. Another aspect involves many executives late in their career who are bored with the businesses they own or are no longer challenged by their career. For them, direct investing can satisfy by once again

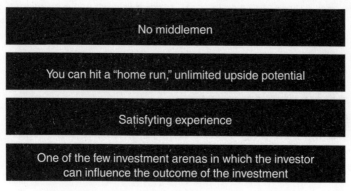

Exhibit 6.2   Advantages of Direct Venture Investing
Source: International Capital Resources

being in the early stages of a company's birth and development, development that can require the investor to wear many hats, become involved in a number of different activities, and confront a number of challenges missing in the larger, more structured, bureaucratic organization. And last, and perhaps most important, by getting deeply involved, direct venture investing is one of the only investment arenas in which the investor experiences the satisfaction of knowing he or she has personally influenced the outcome of the investment.

If, as we have estimated, 2,000,000 households have the net worth potential for early-stage investing, why is it so difficult to find an angel? Part of the reluctance of many high-net-worth investors to enter the direct, private equity market derives from a host of disadvantages: illiquidity, high mortality rates, the anxiety factor during long-term hold, the lack of diversity many times associated with an early-stage portfolio, and the time-consuming nature of active investing. Although the many success stories of astronomical returns are ballyhooed all over the media, the more astute investors remain cognizant of an underlying process inherent in direct investing, a process that drains time, energy, and money: developing deal flow, prescreening deals, conducting due diligence research, investigating, analyzing financials and valuation, negotiating legal terms and conditions, structuring deals, and monitoring and mentoring investments for years to liquidity and returns. Not all investors are suited to long-term, active investment. They may lack the discipline, vigilance, patience, or perhaps recognize that they lack the necessary skills required to attract co-investors, and intervene in and add value to a deal on an ongoing basis.

For every one of those news stories of sky-high returns, investors have heard many horror stories that read like a book of Murphy's Law: investors who fail to return targeted multiples, unmet financial projections, revenue projections sooner and greater than actual, expense projections later and less than actual, the need for more capital than expected and sooner than anticipated, and more rounds of financing needed than planned for by the founders.

THE PRIVATE INVESTOR'S CRITERIA

Understanding investors' criteria means appreciating some of the common sense rules that apply to early-stage, private equity investing.

Generally, most angels agree that when they get involved with direct investing, they have to know something about the business, or at least the underlying technology and market, to conduct their proper due diligence on the people, the market, and the technology. They need to plan on having sufficient reserves for future rounds so that they are not hindered by dilution; in addition, they must make every effort to avoid drowning in deals with unrealistically high valuations and an unclear path to liquidity.

Whether in technology or nontechnology, the private investor in this select group has investment criteria. As Exhibit 6.3 suggests, he or she is steeped in the excitement of this type of investing. To the investor, these feelings figure as prominently as ROI. Remember that a part of this excitement comes from the infectious enthusiasm of the entrepreneurs themselves.

These private investors search for investments that include a proprietary advantage, that is, a unique technology, making a leap in innovation, a significant competitive advantage that can act as a barrier to competition. And private investors look for other qualities in their investments, such as a cost advantage. They also want to understand the industry, or at least understand

EXHIBIT 6.3   Private Investor Criteria

- Exciting, fun (it is also fun to make $$)
- Proprietary advantage or unique technology
- New features recognized competitors don't have that result in significant barriers to competition
- Cost advantage
- Something investors can understand (not too complex)
- The possibility of new markets
- Potential for fast growth and share of the market
- Potential for ROI, 5-10 times investment with solid financials, BS, IS, CFS, and assumptions spelled out
- History of profitability, if applicable, or a borrowed track record
- Not just an invention, but a plan for profit
- A management team with the following attributes:
  —Perseverance
  —Decency
  —Competence
  —Track record
  —Personal financial commitment of their own net worth
  —Burning desire to succeed
- Comfortable with level of active/passive involvement required
- In their price range (affordable loss)
- Geographically close (within 300 miles)
- Allows for incremental funding based on performance
- Allows for due diligence
- Must have a clear exit strategy

Source: International Capital Resources

the underlying technology. They will be acutely conscious of whether the venture—its product or service—is something they can identify with and become excited about.

In addition, their investment decisions often hang on a salable product or service entering a receptive market, satisfying a real market need. Private investors will scrutinize the possibility of new markets—behind which must exist a driving force—and a potential for fast growth, leading to a significant share of the market. Products that require "missionary selling" are not as desirable. This clearly defined market for the company must be without large players already firmly entrenched. Management can be changed; the market cannot. Who the competition is must be clear in the business plan.

Private investors also look for solid financial forecasts with sufficiently supported assumptions as they seek a return of 5 to 10 times their original investment. With credible projections and supporting assumptions, the investor aims for a minimum return of 30 percent ROI. They also want to see a history of profitability in operating companies, that is, a track record that demonstrates financial success. The venture needs to be able to show its potential to deliver the size of returns that investors are targeting.

These private investors want to invest in businesses, not ideas; they want to separate business plans from strategy, have a differentiation strategy based on some element beyond cost, for example, creative product engineering, or proprietary technological leadership. In the wake of the dot-com debacle, a strong business plan is mandatory.

As our study findings support, angels see business plans as a necessity. The business plan demonstrates in writing management's hypothesis about those elements in the business over which it claims control. The logic, strategy, and support provided for the plan reflect management's assumption that there exists some cause-and-effect relationship: If management does X, Y is likely to occur. Without a business plan, however, due diligence to determine the feasibility of management's assumptions becomes even more subjective than it is. For example, assessment of the market potential, which drives all cash flow forecasting, becomes sheer speculation. The caveat is this: Everything that works is simple; but achieving simple is difficult. The business plan is essential because it assesses the true workability of an early-stage venture.

Because experienced, sophisticated investors find risk distasteful, they minimize it in every way possible. Nothing minimizes risk more than the business plan. But the business plan also works to the advantage of the entrepreneur, enabling him or her to achieve two critical goals: recruiting talent and raising capital. The business plan achieves these two goals because nothing better explains the entrepreneur's concept and vision. It helps capture the attention of the investor, defines the argument, and forces the entrepreneur to define the opportunity, strategy, resource requirements, and risks of the venture.

The business plan acts as a resume for the venture. In the entrepreneur's absence, it sends a host of messages to the private venture investor, messages about the management team's grasp of reality, its ability to assess opportunity and risk, its clarity of thinking and communication, and its overall effectiveness. The business plan helps the entrepreneur define goals and strategies, while it helps the investor evaluate the company's potential.

A clear, professional, realistic, and comprehensive business plan is indispensable to entrepreneurs for raising capital, generating investor excitement, and getting their foot in the door for meetings with prospective investors. We refer the reader to Appendix A on how to draft an investor-oriented business plan and how to deliver an investor-oriented presentation.

The quality of the management team—its perseverance, possession of requisite skills and good judgment, decency, competence, track record, personal financial commitment, and desire to succeed—rewinds itself in the minds of private investors as few things do. As we pointed out in our fund-raising strategy, hardly anything is more important. Also indispensable to the team members from the investor's viewpoint is their burning desire to succeed. The spark must glow; else the entire venture soon dims. Extraordinary management who listen and who can work constructively and collaboratively with investors, who exude enthusiasm, who are trustworthy, and who can weather a due diligence background investigation are important to getting financed. The investor, at bottom, has to like you personally, for people have always sought relationships with those who improve our image of ourselves. This is what we mean when we call an entrepreneur "acceptable."

In addition, investors need to feel comfortable with a particular level of active/passive involvement. They look for something in their price range, that is, a venture carrying not only affordable losses but a venture affordable in current and later rounds without undue dilution. For some investors a venture needs to be geographically proximate (within 300 miles). The criteria of private investors must also allow for incremental funding based on performance. A subset of this criteria is that the deal not be subject to high levels of capital intensity, meaning that the requirement that large amounts of capital be invested before proof of the concept and customer acceptance. Another requirement involves reciprocal due diligence on the part of both investor and entrepreneur.

These investors are interested in early-stage ventures with the potential to develop into significant entities that will ultimately be attractive to either the public marketplace or acquisition by or merger with an operating company. These investors are also interested in sustainable companies that can pay back investors from cash flows and retained earnings over time.

COMMON REASONS WHY ANGELS REJECT AN INVESTMENT

Just as investors ardently scan a venture hoping they find certain features, they assiduously avoid others. These investors have shared their reasons with us, reasons that span the range of weaknesses inherent in this type of investing. For one thing, avoiding a mistake in this type of investing is more important to the private investor than picking a runaway winner. Since these investors make only about one to four investments a year, a single poor investment can collapse heavily on the investor. Unlike a venture capital firm, which makes perhaps 15 investments in a year and can absorb a hit, the direct, private investor must take great care with each investment. Therefore, the philosophy of the venture capital firm does not apply to our private investor.

Obviously, investors want a return on their investments, with a minimum return in today's market of 30 percent. If a venture does not show enough potential, if the margins simply are not there, the risk/return ratio is not adequate to attract investors. In some instances, as we indicated earlier, people get funded, not business plans. Therefore, if chemistry or mutual respect is lacking in the management team, if credentials seem weak, if no track record exists, an investor's rejection is almost sure to follow.

Remember that these people want to enjoy making money, so they are looking for something different, not boring. If they do not understand the business; if, for them, the venture is too technical; if they cannot embrace the technology, wrap their arms around it—these too are reasons for not investing. The venture has to strike their fancy. Although not all investors feel the need to have a deep familiarity with the industry, many do wish to invest in areas they know and understand, be it in the technology itself, the application of the technology, or the market the technology is aimed at. Their unfamiliarity with the business technology or the technology market can be a reason for rejecting a venture. And some investors, especially the socially responsible (described among the types of investors in the next chapter), may not see any value to the venture.

Private investors also reject possible investments because entrepreneurs often overvalue their venture. In a VentureOne study of median premoney valuations by round class, analysts found that valuations have diminished across all financing stages. By 2002, seed round valuations had declined to $3 million, and first round financings were down to $9 million premoney. These valuations were on completed deals.

Today it is unrealistic for entrepreneurs to have expectations of inflated valuations, given losses investors suffered from investments made in the late 1990s at inflated valuations. Such unrealistic valuation can lead to a disagreement between the entrepreneur and the investor on the price of the transaction. Some entrepreneurs, aided by the omnipresent spreadsheet program, develop cash flow projections on which they forecast exorbitant returns on investment. Such forecasts are driven by wishful thinking. These poorly developed assumptions, used to drive discounted cash flow estimates of value, are a major reason why private investors reject financial proposals—and the accompanying ventures.

Private investors reject investment opportunities for additional reasons, referred to in connection with investor criteria. Entrepreneurs who lack the fire characteristic of people who believe in their venture will face disappointment. These investors want to see a spark waxing, not waning. Also, for some investors, the proximity of the venture to their home or business figures prominently in accepting or rejecting an investment. The need for missionary selling can be a reason why investors reject investments. Lastly, these investors must believe there is a market that will support the growth of the venture, that will provide a worthwhile rate of return within a reasonable time.

Less well understood is the role assessed risk plays in rejecting a deal, and that investors evaluate risk along a number of different dimensions. One is the team risk and whether the management team will stick together. Another is the business strategy risk. Could the market change and have an impact on the acceptance of the service or product? Is there still growth ahead for the company through its product and technology? Is there anything brewing in the market that could affect the company, creating market risk? Will the manufacturing and R&D work as planned or is there operations risk? And, importantly, what is the financial performance of the venture to date and how have the managers financially performed in other ventures with which they have been involved? These are the risk characteristics in the deal that investors sometimes use to reject an offering.

Finally, rarely will entrepreneurs find investors willing to make direct, private investments to provide exorbitant salaries or back salaries, or to pay off loans or other debts incurred by the venture. Investors are interested in building mountains, not throwing money into a hole that has already been dug.

VARIATIONS IN PREFERRED LEVEL OF INVOLVEMENT AFTER INVESTMENT

Different types of direct participatory investors prefer different levels of involvement in their portfolio companies. These levels of involvement fall along a spectrum ranging from less active involvement to more active (Exhibit 6.4). The private venture investor helps to build value. Most direct

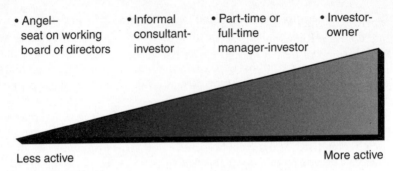

- Angel—
  seat on working
  board of directors

- Informal
  consultant-
  investor

- Part-time or
  full-time
  manager-investor

- Investor-
  owner

Less active   More active

Figure 6.4   Levels of Involvement in Direct, Private Investments
Source: International Capital Resources

investments require additional work beyond the money invested. This additional work often translates into being involved in some aspect of growing the enterprise.

Also, the level of involvement can change dramatically—in either direction—depending on management's performance and the risk to the investor's investment. Passive angels may settle for a seat on a working board of directors, or they may require detailed financial reports prepared periodically. These persons are not looking for operating management responsibility. Meanwhile, consultant-investors may provide consulting help on a temporary basis as it is needed and requested.

Manager-investors, a new breed of investor discussed in the next chapter, provide support and industry knowledge, long-term commitment, and deep pockets. As long as the chemistry is satisfactory, well-connected manager-investors investing within a close geographical area typically expect an operational role in the venture. Investor-owners, for their part, are buyers concerned with control. While involvement may be a knee-jerk reaction to the illiquidity of this type of investing, in most cases it may simply create value through the use of the investors' knowledge and contacts, or reflect a sizable financial commitment. As Andrew Carnegie said, "If I'm going to put all my eggs in one basket, I'm going to closely watch that basket."

It is incumbent on entrepreneurs to ask themselves how much involvement they are willing to accept from investors offering capital. Entrepreneurs need to clarify in advance for themselves the degree of involvement they believe is palatable and so proactively seek investors for their venture whose preferred level of involvement to monitor their portfolios conforms with the entrepreneurs' expectations. Your eagerness for the investors' capital should not blind you to all the things investors can bring to not only monitor the deal but also add value. By using discretion in your choice of investors and communicating clearly expectations on both sides about the level of involvement before taking the investment, the entrepreneur goes a long way in precluding conflict. Remember, it is the quality of the investors that the entrepreneur permits to play a part in his or her venture now—along with the relationship that subsequently develops with them—that will be scrutinized by the investors whom the entrepreneur seeks to bring in on future financing rounds. Involving investors now who can add value can make easier the task of bringing on board additional significant investors later.

HOW ANGEL INVESTORS CAN HELP BEYOND CAPITAL

While more passive investments expect profit derived solely from the efforts of others (e.g., in mutual funds), direct investing in private, early-stage ventures can entail significant involvement, contributing the investor's added value. In several ways, investors can help beyond their infusion of capital (Exhibit 6.5).

Early-stage, active investors can help entrepreneurs of the companies in which they invest, in a number of ways. First, the entrepreneur must recognize that all direct investors offer the potential to provide more than money. To seek only the capital and forget the capitalist is to miss the point. We look at investor contributions as value-added, over and above their capital investment. Investors can help with identifying and facilitating alliances and strategic relationships with more established corporations, using such vehicles as technology transfer, joint venture, or original equipment manufacturers agreements.

Investors can assist with the equity offering by bringing in other investors or by supporting your presentations or discussions with new, prospective investors. They can help with arranging other financing. Through their extensive industry contact network, they can provide introductions with potential customers, suppliers, or distributors. With their general man-

EXHIBIT 6.5   How Investors Add Value Beyond Capital

Alliances with larger corporate partners through technology exchange, original equipment manufacturers, or other agreements
Assist with equity offerings, financing, joint venture, and acquisitions
Provide industry contacts with potential customers, vendors, and financing institutions
Assist in strategy, financing, and recruiting issues
Bring right knowledge and functional experience to help you grow your business
Offer a multidisciplined external contact network

Source: International Capital Resources

agement and technical experience in multifunctional areas, they can assist in strategy development, business planning, and recruitment of key talent for the management team to help grow the business. But most of all, having already "been there" and successfully having done what the entrepreneurs are trying to do, they will bring patience, calmness, and fortitude in the face of the start-ups' emotional "roller-coaster ride," and be a sounding board for ideas on how to cope with unexpected events.

PRIVATE INVESTOR MOTIVATION

Because private investor motivation is a driving force behind their investment criteria, it will pay entrepreneurs to attend to what prompts investors to make their investment decisions.

One motivation in private investment is, of course, ROI, but it is only one factor of many in the decision-making process. The decision of the private investor to invest always turns on this fact: The private investor does not have to invest. Therefore, unlike the institutional investor and the money manager, the private investor market cannot be approached as some monolithic block. Even Stonehenge is not a single giant slab of rock. Like Stonehenge, the private market—despite all its shared elements—is composed of separate entities, exhibiting a complex set of motivations that we need to appreciate.

As Exhibit 6.6 indicates, one significant shared element ironically serves to separate investors: Ninety percent of the millionaires worth between $1 million and $10 million are self-made. Having made it on their own accounts in part for their idiosyncratic natures.

One way they can recapture their successful experience—typically in their forties and fifties, after they have already "made it"—is by investing in new companies, making investments based on the acuteness of their analysis and intuition. Scoring once again reinforces their self-image. Their judgment, once again proven correct, sustains recognition in the investment and entrepreneurial communities in which they live. This serves as an important motivation.

As mentioned earlier, angels come in many different forms; they are anything but monolithic. So no single motivation or set of motivations can describe and sufficiently explain the different types of investors. Through our interview research, we have identified a range of investor motivations, including improvement of self-image and self-esteem through recognition of involvement in the company and by selecting winning companies. Another is alleviating concerns by helping others; for example, the investor who left a career in commodities trading set up a cancer-related medical research fund

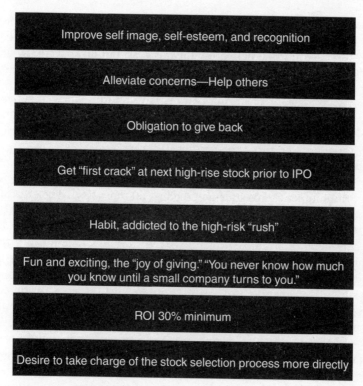

Improve self image, self-esteem, and recognition

Alleviate concerns—Help others

Obligation to give back

Get "first crack" at next high-rise stock prior to IPO

Habit, addicted to the high-risk "rush"

Fun and exciting, the "joy of giving." "You never know how much you know until a small company turns to you."

ROI 30% minimum

Desire to take charge of the stock selection process more directly

Exhibit 6.6   Investor Motivation
Source: International Capital Resources

after the death of his wife to breast cancer. This praiseworthy feeling of obligation, this urge to give back, characterizes many investors who inherit their wealth. Getting a first crack at the next high-risk stock before IPO reflects the angel's understanding that the big money is made before the IPO. Some investors, much like gamblers, develop a habit for this type of investing and become addicted to the high-risk rush. This type of investing can be enjoyable and exciting, and the joy of giving is best characterized by what one investor confided: "You never know how much you know until a small company turns to you for help." Obviously, return of investment and ROI are important motivators, and so is the desire to take charge of the stock selection process more directly.

In their book *Angel Investing*, Osnabrugge and Robinson suggest that business angels' primary motivation for investment encompass (1) expecting a high financial reward, (2) playing a role in the entrepreneurial process, (3) feelings of fun and satisfaction in being involved in an entrepreneurial firm,

(4) creating a job for oneself, and possibly some income, and (5) gaining a sense of social responsibility. To some extent we agree, but we have a different research-based model of the set of forces at work that influence angel investment behavior. One study of returns on investment for angels showed 39 percent of investors reported a total loss of investment, partial loss, or only a write-off or tax benefit as a result of a negative return. Nineteen percent of angels in this survey reported break-even or nominal returns lower than had been projected. Thirty percent reported returns of 50 percent or more, and 12 percent reported returns greater than 100 percent.

Internal rates of return were compounded annually over the term of the hold; returns were cash on cash plus capital gains. A number of the investors did report multiples of investment exceeding 20 times ROI. The greatest returns occurred when the investments were in ventures at the seed, R&D, and start-up stages of development. It is true that ROI is indeed important. But a major consideration in calculating rate of return is how long the investment is held before liquidating. For example, three times the investment over three years yields a 44 percent return, whereas three times the investment over five years yields a 38 percent return. As venture capitalist Lucien Ruby observes, "Venture capital investors do not have to get their desired returns. In fact, they usually do not. But they want to see the desired return as a possibility." So since financial returns are many times just a mirage or goal, what are the nonfinancial returns that motivate investors to get involved in these higher-risk deals?

A particularly fascinating component in the investor's motivation may involve the desire to alleviate misfortune. If the investor's spouse or a child has died from a disease, the investor may hope to be an instrument in research for a cure. In fact, there are a plethora of nonfinancial returns sought by high-net-worth investors who turn to high-risk/high-return private placements. These include creating jobs in geographic areas of high unemployment, developing socially useful technology in medicine or energy, contributing to urban revitalization, encouraging ventures founded by women or minority entrepreneurs, or the more esoteric personal satisfaction derived from assisting entrepreneurs to build successful ventures in a free enterprise economy.

Some investors are motivated by the passionate commitment of the entrepreneur. People committed to a venture can be persuasive; they have enthusiasm and solid entrepreneurial vision, especially when the venture is close to their heart. Entrepreneurs with an ingratiating style, with the investor's concern at heart, and with a passion in their plea, become difficult to shake. The only way to get rid of them, in fact, is to make a token investment or refer them to another investor who more likely will invest in the venture.

Motivation also emanates from the feeling of obligation—noblesse oblige—perhaps born of guilt about how a particular fortune was made in the first place. David Rockefeller outdid his father's campaign of giving away dimes, begun in the first place to improve his deeply tarnished image. The compulsion arises to outdo the previous generation, to give back what may have been gained darkly—and then give still more.

What we mean by getting the first crack is being a part of the first round of financing at what investors hope will be the next high-rise, private stock leading to an IPO. Many people are familiar with the IPO market. Another way of looking at the angel capital market is to see it as the pre-IPO market. By the time a deal reaches the IPO stage, the big money has been soaked up by the early players. The people attracted to this type of investing, those willing to leave themselves subject to high risk, are those who want to play at that level because this is when the return comes in, not when the stock hits the street and is already being managed by a securities broker and the syndication broker dealers.

There is also a habit associated with this kind of investing, not unlike a gambling obsession: the exhilaration experienced just before the check is written. This is another compulsion not to be underestimated.

Another motivation involves the sheer joy of high-risk investments. Possibly adding to a fledgling company's success has returns well beyond ROI. Investors participate in the joy of giving by working closely with entrepreneurs who appreciate their accomplishments, experience, knowledge, and the added value they bring to the dynamic early-stage, creative environment venture. Being part of a start-up, giving birth to a venture, being instrumental in transforming a dream into reality are not experiences to be undervalued.

As Osnabrugge and Robinson state, playing a role in the entrepreneurial process is an "influential motivation." Doing something the investor has already accomplished, and something he or she wishes to do again, can be pleasurable, creating in the investor a sense of satisfaction beyond the money returns involved. For successful entrepreneurs who have the potential to be angels, being shunted aside is a much less desirable alternative in life.

Last, but important, however, is the motivating power of ROI. One investor offers in Exhibit 6.7 the rules of thumb in alerting entrepreneurs to the levels generally regarded by investors as acceptable rates on return by venture stage. At the seed/start-up stage, for example, an investor is looking for a compounded, annualized rate of return of 60 to 100 percent, while at the bridge-to-cash-out stage, the expected rate of return is measured at only 20 percent.

Compare these "rules of thumb" return expectation levels with actual returns of one professional venture fund over 10 years: total loss, 11.5 percent; partial loss, 23 percent; break even, 30 percent; two to five times in-

EXHIBIT 6.7   Stages of Venture Capital

Rule-of-Thumb Required Return Description Internal Rate of Return* Stage of Development	Anticipated Rates of Return
Seed/start-up	60%–100%
Development + mgt. team	50%–60%
Revenues/expansion	40%–50%
Profitable/cash-poor	30%–40%
Rapid growth	25%–35%
Bridge to cash out	20%+

*Before applying subjective factors.

vestment returned, 19.8 percent; five to ten times investment returned, 8.9 percent; ten times or more investment returned, 6.8 percent. These returns are cash on cash plus capital gains. It's fun to make money!

Given the level of returns, and potential for loss, it is easy to understand how prospective investors may not share the entrepreneur's level of optimism for the venture's success. Successful, sophisticated venture investors are risk-averse, quick to discount projections in reviewing proposals. Also, as we have suggested, investors also find that management teams of early-stage enterprises rarely forecast cash requirements accurately. Investors realize that unforeseen follow-on financing is lurking about.

The motivation to take charge of the stock selection process has to do with a trend in the brokerage industry to avoid or circumvent retail brokers and personally assume a more active role by using the information available through various resources, for example, the Internet, trade papers, and magazines. The idea is to take more control in managing one's portfolio. This type of investing allows for ways to diversify based on past experience, a way to control the placement of a percentage of one's portfolio, or a way to steer a portfolio percentage into other equity areas, perhaps increasing the rate of return. People today are taking on the responsibility of managing their retirement, of choosing mutual funds and other asset classes for their various retirement accounts. The desire for increased control, using technology and available information, fuels this type of investing, which gets the investor more deeply involved in the selection process and more directly involved in the deal.

THE ALLOCATION DECISION

Since the founding of ICR in 1989, one of the authors has interacted with more than 4,000 entrepreneurs. A review of the results of the fund-raising efforts of these past clients and contacts suggests that the most accurate predictor of an entrepreneur's success at raising capital is having successfully raised capital in the past. Based on an informal review of 4,000 records, 65 percent of those entrepreneurs who went on to successfully raise capital in their current rounds had raised capital previously from family, friends, cofounders, and angels and/or professional venture capitalists. If you are among the 35 percent who have not yet raised capital from family and friends, who have not been subjected to thorough due diligence, or perhaps who have raised capital but did so before the dot-com bubble burst, stock market meltdown, and recession, just what do these findings mean to you? We contend that by understanding what goes into the investor's decision making, entrepreneurs will be better able to position their ventures, documentation, offerings, and fund-raising presentations, and so increase the probability of a successful financing outcome. How investors have decided to allocate their financial resources will influence whether a private deal will be appropriate for their serious consideration.

An investor's allocation decision is, of course, intrinsically tied to portfolio management. The private investor is not investing an entire life's savings in a single venture. We have never met a sophisticated investor who had not developed an investment plan. Such planning encompasses such elements as (1) defining the industries, markets, and technologies they understand; (2) specifying a geographic region of interest; (3) forming an informal network of co-investors; (4) establishing a target compound rate of return (or multiple); (5) clarifying procedures for protecting themselves from loss, for example, hedging strategies; and (6) knowing preferred liquidity (exit) alternatives.

Based on research of ICR's investor database, early-stage or high-net-worth high-risk investors also invest in a range of assets, including corporate stock, real estate, cash (e.g., CD and money market accounts), noncorporate business assets, bonds, notes and mortgages, life insurance, and other assets. So while it is true that angels are interested in investing in liquid and relatively liquid assets, they are also interested in investing in private equity, which boasts a range of alternative asset classes, including seed, R&D, start-up, first-stage, expansion stage, mezzanine, bridge, acquisition/mergers, turnaround, special investment situations, and distressed securities (e.g., junk bonds).

Strong evidence suggests that these investors place a small percentage of their money in higher-risk deals—about three to five percent of their equity portfolio. High-caliber money managers confess that they always leave some money for the client to manage, money for clients to invest on their own. It is this "crazy" money that represents their discretionary resource for investments in higher-risk deals. So it is the individual's allocation decision that influences where private equity investment ends up.

As we have stated, angels do possess an investment strategy and—contrary to the erroneous belief of many entrepreneurs—this type of investment is not a crapshoot. The key to understanding angel investment strategy can be found within the concept of allocation decision. Asset allocation, which determines how your portfolio is divided among stocks, bonds, and cash equivalents, each of which differ according to the risks involved and the rewards they offer, is a critical component of angel investment strategy. If the concept of financial planning is essentially analogous to a road map, then asset allocation is the road itself. Angel investors are typically diversifying their equity portfolio by placing a small percentage of the money allocated for equity investments directly into private deals. Based on our research, this ranges from three to five percent.

Alternative investments, which generally have a low correlation to performance of the public stock markets, are extremely useful for high-net-worth investors seeking diversification, performance enhancement, portfolio predictability, and risk reduction. What many entrepreneurs fail to appreciate is that by following the extensive angel investment process model that we have identified and relate in Part 4—the process used by sophisticated angels—many investors are able to manage risk of investment into early-stage companies. Although 33 percent of the time these investors report loss of capital, 66 percent of the time they are getting some or all of their investment back, or earning returns from savings and CD account levels through highly significant multiples of ROI.

To better demonstrate this point, consider the array of hedging strategies that investors use to help manage risk in private deals. Angels hedge their risk using a number of unique risk-management strategies, including co-investment strategies or sharing the risk with other investors even when the investor has the financial ability to fund considerable portions of the investment transaction alone. Hedging strategy also can include the development of a diversified portfolio allocation strategy, whether it's along geographic lines or industry lines, stage of development, or some other criteria inherent in the private equity portfolio to create diversification. In addition, investors manage their investment size and use milestones and phased investment to ensure that the company is meeting its milestones before putting in the investor's full financial capability. The angel investor becomes further actively involved in the venture. He does this in a constructive way by adding value and defining a role in which he can make a contribution, one that allows him to remain in close touch with the venture in a constructive capacity, allowing him or her to monitor the venture to identify any potential problems before they begin to drive the company. Angels are adept at developing deal structures, that is, terms and conditions that help to moderate some of the risk; for example, obtaining a liquidation preference, or insuring through their negotiation of the investment arrangement a multiple on investment before proceeds from the company sale or asset sale or other liquidity event would provide an ROI to earlier-round investors.

Furthermore, angels are careful to not invest in deals without complete and competent business plans that include explanations of business strategy, a clear revenue model, adequate financials, and clear valuation assumptions. Typically, angel investors will have advisers to handle aspects of the investment due diligence process, and sometimes investors will get involved in angel investment groups, formal and informal, to take advantage of the concept that "two heads are better than one," meaning that they will share some of the monetary risk, due diligence exercise, and deal finding with other respected investors. And last, angels will sometimes wait for established lead investors to negotiate the terms of a transaction before considering adding the company to their private portfolio—an approach used not only by passive investors. One need only ask entrepreneurs who have heard from investors that they must "find someone else to be a lead investor; then come back and I'll look at the deal."

It is also important to remember that alternative investments do not track the public market and so can still provide returns regardless of developments within the public market. Individuals have made investments into companies in specific industries that are not doing well in the public stock markets, yet at the micro, or private level, these companies will still be performing profitably and will potentially provide returns to the angel.

Exhibit 6.8 shows the specific elements that influence the decision to invest in a particular venture.

First, the investment in a particular company must match the investment strategy of the individual investor. If the investor desires income, he or she will invest in a subordinated note providing interest or perhaps in preferred stock providing a dividend. If the capital strategy is to generate capital appreciation and capital gains, the investment will be in a common or preferred equity deal, requiring the investor to hold that position for a period of five to eight years, hoping that the stock will increase in value.

EXHIBIT 6.8 The Allocation Decision

- Match investment strategy
- Stage of life
- Risk posture
- Part of business cycle of interest (experience)
- Relative attractiveness of participatory investing
- Net worth, income, liquid financial assets on hand

Another factor in the allocation decision reflects the investor's stage of life. Investors in their early thirties are concerned about buying a house, saving for a child's education, buying a boat, taking a grand vacation, or perhaps buying jewelry or art. These investors, in other words, are less likely to have the discretionary income necessary to make these kinds of investments. However, by the time these investors have reached their late forties to late fifties, the kids are out of school, the house is paid off, and more discretionary income or net worth is available. So more discretionary income or net worth becomes available at a time when their income has increased or has reached its peak. Thus, the stage of life of investors has a significant impact on the allocation decision. Remember, too, that based on one's age, different hold times for investments are palatable.

Additional impact arises from the investor's proclivity for risk. One who can stomach the ambiguity associated with the earlier-stage deals will likely sport an aggressive risk posture, a willingness to invest in an early-stage deal, preseed, seed, or start-up. One who cannot stomach the ambiguity and risk—despite having the money—probably will gravitate to later-stage private equity transactions, such as a leverage buyout of an existing company, one that has a financial history, or to a mezzanine financing with a higher level of confidence in payoff in 18 to 24 months.

Another aspect of the allocation decision of private investments is the investor's experience in various stages of the investment cycle. An investor is like a physician: The doctor who feels engaged in the early stages of life is likely to go into pediatrics, while another physician might opt for taking care of the elderly. In the same way, a private investor may like to associate with early-stage companies, reflecting his or her earlier successful experience, perhaps as president of an early-stage company.

Investors tend to let their background experience guide them in assessing risk. They are inclined to compare their experience in various stages of the company life cycle with potential venture investments, and gravitate to ventures at stages of development they are familiar with. We know other investors who have had great success in turning around old, staid, bureaucratic enterprises. So if we take an early-stage deal to someone who has been president of a large corporation, he or she may not understand or may feel uncomfortable. There simply may be no grasp of the interpersonal relationships, or the political and emotional dynamics, of such an enterprise. Two things have to fit: the stage of the company in the business cycle that the particular investment represents and the experience of the individual investor.

Next in the allocation decision is the relative attractiveness of the participatory investment. As we have indicated, value-added investing means more than supplying capital, particularly for an individual participatory investment that is a time-intensive activity. One of the reasons venture capitalists have moved out of such investments is not only that venture capital funds have become much larger, but that those individuals managing the funds do not have the time to sit on five or ten boards. The private investor is looking for that participatory role most likely to furnish the necessary level of involvement. So the relative attractiveness of this type of time commitment—a value-added commitment beyond the element of money—is a prominent component of the allocation decision.

Last, but centrally important to the allocation decision, are the levels of the investor's net worth, income, and liquid financial assets—the tendons of the entire investment process.

CHAPTER 7

Types of Private Investors

*I should like to have a more perfect knowledge of things, but I do
not want to buy it as dear as it costs.*

—Michel de Montaigne

INTRODUCTION

Every private investor would appreciate having a "more perfect knowledge
of things," but operating, at best, with an imperfect knowledge of the "dear
costs" of things, each has decisions to make—as you are about to discover
from their own words. Taken together they form a highly articulate verbal
community that talks straight, an information-rich, information-sharing network of idiosyncratic individuals.

In his 1997 *Inc.* article, "My Life as an Angel," Norman Brodsky speaks
to what drives these networks of investors: "For me, there's nothing like it—
the business of seeing a business rise up from nothing . . . There's just something unbelievably thrilling about seeing the growth, watching the numbers
go up, getting the business to stand on its own . . . I can't get enough of it."
He continues: "These deals . . . offer me the opportunity to teach other people some of the things I've learned over the years and to share with them the
excitement of bringing a new business into existence."

The variety of individual private investors we enumerate in Exhibit 7.1
forms a nexus, a large group within which we differentiate types. Based on
our experience, and based on countless conversations and interviews with investors, we have selected individuals who we feel capture the essence of types
of angels from among the more than 1,359 listed in ICR's database. From

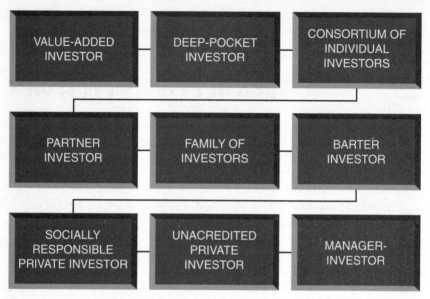

Exhibit 7.1 Typology of Angel Investors
Source: International Capital Resources

these conversations and interviews with private investors have emerged patterns of like-mindedness within similar investment orientations.

To know the types, to glimpse their differing motivations, is to evaluate what investors are looking for and determine whether your time would be wasted or well spent in dealing with certain investor types. Thus, understanding and distinguishing types of investors form the rationale for this chapter.

In assessing investors, entrepreneurs are dealing with singular individuals, not impersonal structures such as banks. Beneath the facade, all banks are the same. Their criteria for granting a loan fit a single mold. Their ratios, calculations, and protocol are stamped out cookie-cutter style. Their loan-to-risk computations are cloned. On the other hand, no monolithic investment criterion dictates when and where private investors are likely to invest, although they share much, as we have noted. But neither are they of infinite variety. Angel investors fall into types, the types we delineate here. So as you listen to the barter-investor, the value-added investor, the deep-pocket investor, and so on, weave these individuals into generic types of the private investors you will be meeting and asking to invest in your vision.

Our first type of investor is the value-added investor.

THE VALUE-ADDED INVESTOR

Value-Added Investor #1

I either jump into the plan or the plan jumps out of my hands.

I've been involved in a broad range of industries over a lot of years. This includes the experience of having worked with a company that, when we started, was doing about half a million in sales and grew to $80 million in sales within two years. We have bought up about 21 companies and gone public and done amazingly well. The common thread that runs through all of my activity is my background in building ventures. The financial investments I've made in companies, for the most part, have ranged from $50,000 to $150,000 per company (Exhibit 7.2).

Location of the company is an issue for me. If I can't drive to the company within an hour of my base, San Francisco, it becomes a real stretch for me. I have invested in out-of-state deals, but I'm not comfortable with them. Furthermore, industry is not as important as the economic opportunity, the point being that I am a generalist and not a technologist. I look at each case on its own merits. I perform the due diligence. I've invested in both loans and equity. I look for an opportunity to advise the companies. That's the reason I do all this, because I like helping companies.

Private investors who spend time with companies are called value-added investors, which is precisely what we are. I'm a very active

EXHIBIT 7.2 Value-Added Investor

- Very experienced investors and former investment bankers and venture capitalists
- Storefront venture capital firms
- Short due diligence cycle, require business plans
- Make multiple investments
- Want to help grow business and have fun doing so
- Lead investor searches out investment opportunities and makes an independent decision to invest and often suggests investments to others
- Very strong network of co-investors whom they leverage and who trust their judgment
- Become extremely active and involved, however, only for short periods; problem solver orientation
- Tend toward industry concentrations
- Invests close to home
- Invests $50,000–$250,000 in either debt or equity

Source: International Capital Resources

investor. For instance, I've just completed a merger for two companies that I've been involved with. I've done all kinds of things with these businesses, which is precisely what I enjoy doing.

I am a follow-on investor. I've been in a number of situations in which there have been deep-pocket investors who put a million dollars or more in companies that I eventually got into as a follow-on investor—a situation I like to see. I'm not saying that a follow-on investor has to have $1 million in the company, but if there is a major investor in the company, it's nice for me to know, as a follow-on investor, that he or she has a lot more invested in the company than I do, that he or she is going to carry the company through the blips. This is exactly what has happened and exactly what has saved some companies that I've been involved in. So being a follow-on investor attracts me.

For me to become involved in companies at the idea stage, I have to see that each company has a good product, a ready market, and a management team with a lot of experience in its field. If the company has some revenue, I'd prefer to see about $1 million in sales. The CEO is also important in a company that I look at.

And, in my mind, the people in the company have to have, at the first cut, the four Ps. They have to be passionate, persistent, pleasant, and penetrable. By passionate I mean they have to love the business they're in. They have to live it seven days a week in their heart and their soul. They have to be persistent in reaching for the appropriate goals, they have to do it with fervor, but they also have to commit to the follow-up issues associated with any task. And I mention that especially in regard to my recent experience with a person of great vision but no follow-up. The people in the company also have to be pleasant to work with. Compatibility is an issue. In fact, treat your investor as your partner. Finally, they have to be penetrable, that is, open to advice—extremely important, especially given my involvement with businesses. Part of this is having a collectively logical mind, that is, the people have to be able to think logically through business issues.

I'm at the point in my investing career where I really discourage plans being sent to me. Initially, I want to look at an executive summary. In terms of a nondisclosure issue, you're probably going to find investors who are willing to sign every nondisclosure statement coming to them, or they won't sign even one because of the liability. You can get around that by giving them the executive summary, which typically doesn't have any proprietary information in it. Then you will see if they're interested and carry on from there. I usually review the executive summary, which gives me a real quick idea of what the business is, then turn to the resumes—because those are the people who are going to make it happen. Then I either jump into the plan or the plan jumps out of my hands.

I want to plug something I call mutual due diligence. As much as an investor is going to do due diligence on your company, you should do due diligence on the investor. And you should think about what kind of investors you want, what they're going to bring to the table. I think there's a whole host of questions you can ask. From my experience, an organization like ICR brings together quality investors. By contrast, you have no idea what you will find out there on the street.

One of the sensible questions for an entrepreneur to ask investors is whether they have ever done this kind of thing before. Have they been involved with a company and with the kind of investment they're about to make with you? Because if they haven't been through the downside of working with a business, I don't think you want to be in the position of a trainer. It takes an awful lot of time out of what could be an awfully good company.

Value-Added Investor #2

What I ask—and I've learned this question painfully—is whether the venture can survive as a business in the short term, say 6 months, a year, or 18 months, whatever it takes to get to a positive cash flow.

I've been on both sides of the table, as a principal, as an investor, both for venture capital firms and for my own account. I've also been on the entrepreneur side of the table raising money. I am an absolute expert in this business, because, after 20-plus years in the business, I've been in more traps and made every mistake you could make as an investor. The trick is not to make them more than once or twice. That's probably why I'm such an expert. This is very much an apprenticeship business. That is, the investor learns by doing.

I focus on a few areas, trying to sift the weak from the strong in investment opportunities. Number one for me is the market. Let me just say up front that the definition of your market is the key. Obviously, as an investor, I want to see that there's a big enough market so that if you have to shift strategy or change course, there's enough room to do it.

Specifically, I'm interested in the appropriate market segment you're doing business in. And if it's the San Francisco Bay Area, fine. Tell us how you're going to capture the San Francisco Bay Area and use that as a model for expansion into other cities. Zero in on your segment and talk about that.

If you've got a product and you want to attract third-party investors, the entrepreneur needs to think about the following: making that product into a business, using the personal skills of your team, creating a distribution network, and multiplying your expertise into similar kinds of products or services. Then mill all that together to make a business that has a chance to grow and to attract third-party capital.

I want a product or a service that offers customers a compelling reason to buy it. That means it needs to be different from whatever else is out there, because you're obviously going to be a small business going against the big guys. But—and this is where I've gotten a lot of arrows in my back—it cannot be so different, so revolutionary, so unique that you have to do a lot of missionary selling to convince people that this is a product to buy. Now, that may be fine for larger institutional investors or venture capital groups that are in seed-development capital. That's what they do. The technology guys and engineers who do due diligence aren't the people who write the checks. The people who write the checks are the purchasing managers, so you need to convince me that the theoretical demand for your product can be converted into dollar orders in the short term.

A second criterion for me is survivability. This, however, is a double-edged sword. When I look at a plan, certainly I want to see a big enough opportunity to make it worth my while, or an opportunity to shift course if necessary. That's great. But what I ask—and I've learned the answer to this question painfully—is whether the venture can survive as a business in the short term, say 6 months, a year, or 18 months, whatever it takes to get to a positive cash flow.

How are you going to do that? How are you going to sell product in the short term to generate cash internally? I think this is absolutely critical. What is your sales strategy? How are you going to get those orders in the door? What is a realistic sell cycle for your product or service? If it looks like it's two months, it's probably four months. I've learned that the hard way. I've been in some deals where the technology worked, the product was great, the people liked it, but the sales cycle turned out to be four or five times as long as we thought and, as a result, we ran out of cash and had to engage in down-and-dirty financing to bring in capital at a much lower valuation level.

Another factor is financing strategy, an aspect that goes with the survivability. As I mentioned, I will look to see whether the company can generate cash in the short term to survive. Also, have you thought about a long-term financing plan? And I know that's a little difficult when you're scratching around trying to figure out where the next dollar of capital is coming from, but it's important to have, just like you have a marketing plan, a sales plan, a manufacturing plan, a plan to bring in capital in various stages, and a strategy to attract the kind of investor who would be ideal at those stages.

Last, what are your plans to fill out the management team? In an early-stage company, obviously the key person is the founder, the CEO. Few early-stage companies can declare, "We have our whole management team in place." Obviously you don't, and we investors understand that. But I'm interested in your thoughts about how you're going to fill those important positions, such as a salesperson, in the early stage, and what your plans are for bringing on those people in a logical progression.

Value-Added Investor #3

I try not to make investments that I don't think the venture community will be subsequently interested in.

As someone who has been making private venture investments now, I guess, for the last seven or eight years, I believe that most investors are not aware of the tremendous concentration of investments in just a few areas. I was at a dinner with some people from professional venture capital firms—two of the larger Silicon Valley venture capital firms—who admitted to me that in the last three years, more than 80 percent of their investments had been made in the following areas: software, networking, multimedia, and the last area was wireless. And so you can look at presentations made today and 90 percent may fall out of those areas. There may be one telecommunications-related activity and the bulk of the investors will be in other perfectly reputable areas, but areas not very accessible to the venture capitalists.

I'm not sure why the industry tends to concentrate like this. I think it tends to want to put a consortium together and work in areas each consortium can then become expert in. As far as my own investing philosophy is concerned, I find it very difficult to fight these trends, so the bulk of the investments I have been making in the last couple of years tend to fall in those same areas. However, it's the exception to the rule that probably makes for the best opportunity, so I think all of us have to be willing to look in other areas.

I make investments in the $50,000 to $250,000 range. I don't make them outside of the local Bay Area. I've had some bad experiences in trying to fly to Boston or commute to Los Angeles to help make investments. I try not to make investments that I don't think the venture community will be subsequently interested in. And I don't make investments outside of what would generally be called the high-tech area.

Formerly, I was a senior executive with a major computer hardware manufacturer, so I'm involved mostly in that industry. Those are the businesses I'm interested in. So I don't want to invest in services, in medical, or in distribution.

Value-Added Investor #4

I like to very quickly get an idea of the product, the market, the competition. Then I go right into the people, because the people are the ones that are going to make it happen.

In being asked what I look for in companies, I always respond that I'm looking for the product and the market opportunity. And once I understand that, it becomes 99 percent management. I've been through enough companies to know that management is the key to making any plan work.

I've had the experience of being part of a start-up company that went public, and I've had the experience of working with a Fortune 100 company, of being responsible for billions of dollars in assets and thousands of people. But the most fun has really been in helping to grow young companies, which I've done all my life.

I'm very involved in these businesses and spend my time on the most important problems or the biggest opportunities. I try to focus my time on the things that make a difference for the company. I do debt and I do equity deals with companies. The average investment that I've made has ranged generally from $50,000 to $150,000 per company.

The industries I've been involved with have been diverse. What drives me is the economic opportunity more than the industry, but I shy away most definitely from anything exotic. I'm involved in due diligence. I've invested in businesses related to the mountain bike industry, the software that helps make the health care system more efficient, and the coffee business. So I diversify and it's a lot of fun. I am a generalist.

For me, the critical ticket for the laundry is the business plan. Ninety percent of the deals that I look at have business plans and, frankly, the flow, the funnel, has been real big over the years. I've gotten to the point where if I just get the executive summary I'm a happy camper. And if it's of interest, I'll talk with the company.

The companies are located in the Bay Area. I like to get there if they need me. Then I look for a return on investment, which, obviously, ranges. Also, there has to be a variety of exit strategies. One recent exit was the acquisition of the company. Acquisitions are very nice.

Gross margins, I have found, are pretty important; the bigger the margins, the more attractive it is—for a simple reason. There are positives and negatives to large gross margins, but I have found, generally, that with the bigger gross margins, there's more forgiveness for problems that a young company has. In fact, it has saved a few of them.

The projected numbers that you have in your business plans definitely are important, but they're not as important to me as the assumptions that underlie them. I will spend time carefully going through those assumptions, trying to comprehend the depth of understanding and the degree to which the company has grasped all the components of its business. I have rarely found projected numbers actually occurring, so I'll spend the time on the assumptions.

When I get a business plan, I'll first take a look at the executive summary. I hope it's not more than a couple of pages. Then I go right to the resumes. In other words, I like to very quickly get an idea of the product, the market, the competition—all the basic things you put in an executive summary. Then I go right into the people, because the people make it happen. If they pass muster, I'll spend the time going through the plan.

Value-added investors, I think, are really important. I will tell you this: I've dealt with an awful lot of companies; the most successful ones have had value-added investors who have brought more than money to the table and they've helped grow the business in ways that money alone can't.

Also, companies need to do their homework in understanding the market dynamics and understanding distribution. Obviously a business plan deals with the marketing issues, the competition, the distribution, the pricing, the market needs, how to sell, and strategy. But when I sit down with the people in the company, I have found, unfortunately too often, that they do not have the necessary depth of understanding of those issues. If a company doesn't understand its market and understand how to access the market, it's going to face serious problems.

A lot of people running these companies are technically oriented; they have a great idea of the product and its applications. But the issues are broader than that. A common issue I see occurring with companies centers on a naughty F-word: focus, focus, focus. The problem is the lack of it. It's easy in the early stages of the business to pursue opportunities as they arrive, and multiple opportunities typically do arise. But it's the highly disciplined businesses that succeed.

In experiences I've had with a few companies I've invested in, I learned a particular lesson. It really saved me; it saved a certain part of my anatomy located just below my waist. There was a lead private investor, a major investor who had invested close to $1 million in the company. I felt secure because I knew that he had deep pockets; he had a vested interest in, and a history with, the company, so I knew if problems arose—and they did; they always do—he would keep that company afloat. The lesson is this: Among your private investors, getting one in particular who can bring added value along with a significant amount of money can mean the difference. I think if you have a compatibility and you know your investor, you're going to bring something to the company that's of real value.

Our second type of investor is the deep-pocket investor.

THE DEEP-POCKET INVESTOR

Deep-Pocket Investor #1

Even if you give up a significant chunk of your company to get the right management in place, you'll be way ahead for having done it.

In my career I've been an accountant, a lawyer, a consultant, a CFO of high-technology start-up companies, and most recently I'm president of a software company. I have been an active individual investor, and over the past 15 years have done 15 investments, roughly one a year, although it's more a matter of accumulating enough money to make the next investment than it is an ability to accommodate them. The rate of investment seems closely related to my earnings from other things. These 15 investments ranged in amount from $10,000 to $90,000. The average is about $50,000 to $100,000 (Exhibit 7.3).

My experience as an entrepreneur puts me squarely in the middle of individual investors. And when you put up private placement out there and you're looking for 10 to 35 people on a regulation D offering, that's the kind of folks you're going to get. Of my 15 investments, five have been winners, four outright losers—"losers" as in all my money is gone—and five have either not had their outcome determined or have more or less broken even. Of the 15, nine have been in start-up or early-stage companies; three have been in venture capital funds—in which my money was pooled with other people's and then professional management hired us out of the funds—and three have been in real estate.

I have divided my primary investment criteria between those that are absolutely essential and those that are merely essential. It's like saying in a business plan that you want to have an analysis of the market and a description of the people and a financial forecast and a description of the assumptions. I want good grammar and correct spelling.

EXHIBIT 7.3   Deep-Pocket Investor

- Built and sold company
- Corporate not technical background
- Emphasis on deal structure to mitigate risk
- Invests only in what he or she knows
- Prefer that investor(s) hold control, e.g., outside board
- People and plan equally important
- Can be lead or independent investor; can search for opportunities, makes independent decision to invest, suggests investments to others, welcomes leads from respected colleagues, but always relies on own judgment, and investigation in deciding to invest
- Geographic preference
- Fun is a factor
- Targeted ROI of 50%/year
- Some involvement to make a contribution
- Open to both debt and equity
- $50,000–$100,000 per investment, 1–3 investments per year

Source: International Capital Resources

If it doesn't have all that stuff, I'm disappointed, though I may still make the investment.

At the top of my list of criteria is a high ROI—at least 50 percent a year—50 percent a year after all of my discounting of time slippage, risk assessment, and everything else. Only in an early-stage deal are those kinds of returns usually offered, which is what drives me to early-stage companies. Sometimes—and I've made this kind of investment a couple of times—you can do a short-term debt instrument that has that rate of return. It happens when somebody has an existing business, an opportunity that requires capital, an opportunity that has the level of risk no bank wants to back. By having something that combines debt and maybe some warrants, or some other equity component as a sweetener, you can get the same 50 percent return and have a short liquidity time— certainly an added attraction.

My second criterion demands exceptional management, especially a solid CEO. Over time I have found that even if the rest of the management team is good, it's really only the CEO that people invest in. And having been a CFO—a somewhat humbling experience—has helped me crystallize the need for a top-notch performer in that position. Generally, an investment becomes a gamble on that individual and, as an investor with some experience, I've decided that, after ROI, there's hardly a more significant consideration in my deciding to invest or not invest. Obviously, if that person changes, the risk of your investment changes a lot, so how committed the management is and how committed the funding sources are become critical. If it's a start-up company, I cannot fund the whole thing out of my own pocket.

One of the common themes among my investment losers is not finding enough financing to take the venture all the way. It wasn't because the idea was all bad. (At least, no one but the people who turned down the investment would say so.) There need to be people with deeper pockets than mine as part of the deal structure, a structure in which my interests are aligned with theirs, so that they don't get a big return if I don't get a big return.

In addition, I prefer that investors as a group have control, certainly control if downside contingency occurs. If the management or founders as a group have control and want to keep control, they'd better have been in business a while and have had some revenue and perhaps even made a profit. If there is a 50-50 split—which is often the case in the early-stage deals between capitalists and workers—I think the capitalists need to have a way of gaining control if milestones are not met.

An essential criterion focuses on local connections. First, all my investments are in the Bay Area; the exception occurs where there is a strong local connection and the company is actually operating somewhere else or considering relocating to that area.

Another criterion of mine in deciding whether to invest is whether the opportunity is available for input to management, typically a board seat. Because of the skill sets I have, I usually can count on people asking for my help to set up accounting systems, or hire lawyers, or write their business plans, or evaluate the deals for them. Thoroughness of the business plan is very meaningful. I run across entrepreneurs—or would-be entrepreneurs—who actually hire other people to write their business plan for them. It's one thing to hire somebody who can do an Excel spreadsheet better than you can, but I have never seen a CEO able to run a company successfully who couldn't describe in writing what the plan was for that company—and do so in a fairly articulate manner.

So I think it is essential for you to write the plan demonstrating an understanding of the market, a careful forecast of the future expressed in numbers, complete with the assumptions for a forecast. Frequently a business plan has page after page of month number 10 as well as month number 24. However, what I'm more interested in is three or four pages of careful assumptions carefully described, plus prepaid expenses based on the industry average, and the amount of capital required in year number 2—coming from a public offering or other investors. Or else we're going to tap you if we can for another round.

What also gets my attention is a business plan that includes in its terms an action plan from someone who demonstrates that over the next 90 to 180 days, from the time the company receives the money, he or she can enumerate what exactly has to be done to make this business go. The more specific those kinds of milestones are, the more comfortable I am in knowing that I can measure progress after I've made the investment and calibrate how I should react; that is, whether I've made a mistake, or whether I should put money in if I'm asked. This is a very good way both to monitor the investment and to assess how management is doing and what you can do to help them.

I favor a short time to liquidity. I don't think of myself as a long-term investor, but I turn out that way in many of these ventures. A fax company that I helped start had a business plan that declared we would go public and have $50 million in sales in five years. It's got about $10 million in sales and probably another three years till liquidity—now that it's been in business six years. That's typical. And I've found that there are good enough opportunities in the public stock market that provide liquidity with moderated risk.

If I'm going to have a long-term, definite ending in a private company, I'd better have some chance of liquidity along the way. I don't necessarily want to pull my money out, but the company needs to have a plan for stages of investor returns. I'd like also, as a secondary criterion, to have the possibility of a very high return. Maybe you think a 50-per-cent-a-year return is high. To me, a very high return means it is an Apple Computer in the making, or a medical device that everybody in the world wants, or a solar energy company, alone among the whole industry, that actually makes something everybody wants.

Also, I look for people who have done it before, hopefully very successfully. This usually means that they are coming out of the same industry, maybe another company, and they're just going into business competing with the former employer. Or in some other way they have been successful entrepreneurs and are working now in something very closely related. And, finally, I look for some downside protection.

I'm quite willing to walk away from investments and lose all my money, but I prefer that there's some kind of second chance at getting part of my money back or parlaying it into something else of value. I think also that the fellow investors need to be able to contribute something besides money. Finally, the process ought to, on a whole, just be fun if it works; otherwise, it becomes too painful to think about.

What most entrepreneurs sell is a story, and what most investors, particularly the more sophisticated investors, want to buy is management. When you're out there selling to people who are investing $15,000,

$20,000 at a crack—your friends and members of your family—the story becomes a question of what they are buying. If you're going to succeed in raising the money for a larger, more sophisticated investment, and if the company, in turn, is going to succeed, you're going to have to show the more sophisticated investors that you've got the management team in place—or know how you're going to get it in place—and also show that the team has formulated a clear plan of action.

Management is the key to being able to deal with unexpected problems certain to arise. So if you are an entrepreneur with a great idea and a great story but you don't have the management expertise, get it. Even if you give up a significant chunk of your company to get the right management in place, you'll be way ahead for having done it. Qualified management is one of the most difficult parts of a business plan to evaluate because resumes can all be made to look great. How do you evaluate what someone can really do? I have found that I need to do a lot more due diligence every time I review a potential investment. Having done it several times, I have been surprised at instances of outright fraud, outright cover-up in which people were not revealing everything.

Personally, I'm a generalist. If it looks like it can make money, I'll take a look at it. For example, a potato chip plant in Colorado already had an empty building where the company was going to set up its plant, and it was already sourcing the chips from a Texas operation. From a look at the business plan, from all the numbers, all it needed was capital to get machinery in there and start producing, instead of buying, the chips. The company was going to be making money in no time. It was in the stores, a really ready-to-go operation. It already had shelf space and name recognition in the area. But it wasn't telling the whole story.

So how do you uncover that? It's a difficult thing from an investor's perspective. You have to be very careful. It's very important for entrepreneurs to reveal everything and to have integrity, or else you are building in your own doom. You're not going to succeed by hiding things. It all comes back to bite you. So make sure you tell a potential investor the bad news first, and if they're still interested after they hear the potential difficulties, you've got someone that's ready to go through the trials and tribulations with you. But if you're giving only this wonderful story about the future, and the investor buys into that, what happens when the first problem comes along? Now you've got problems beyond anything you have anticipated.

I, by the way, have an entrepreneurial background myself; I haven't always been an investor. I remember someone explaining the difference between institutional and private investing, a distinction sometimes difficult for a private investor to remember: The private investor does not have to invest! Sometimes the story is so attractive that you are lured into it and say, "Wow, this is hot; this really has sizzle." But you have to have that management team to keep the bacon frying or the sizzle fizzles.

Perhaps the greatest disservice that's been done to entrepreneurs is the saying that if you build a better mousetrap, the world will beat a path to your door. It's just not true! The shelves are lined with better mousetraps. If you have the right management you can take an inferior product, make it succeed, and make money. So don't buy into a story that just because you've got something unique and better than what's already out there that you're going to succeed. It takes a lot of hard work and correct management decisions.

In terms of my own investments, as I said, I'm a generalist. Generally, $50,000 to $100,000, sometimes a little more per investment. I've been a public investor and actually was a commodity trader for many years, which led me to understand risk and decide that the risk involved in investment in private companies made sense. In fact, it's kind of the same game. You expect to lose. You have to be willing to accept losses; the wins just have to be big enough to compensate for them. So as a commodity trader, I found that if I could be right 30 percent of the time I could make a lot of money, because I cut my losses short and my winnings were big ones.

Deep-Pocket Investor #2

A good CEO without an exit strategy is much better than a poor CEO with an exit strategy. If it's a poor CEO, you know what your exit strategy is; it's called a Chapter 11 or a Chapter 7. So to me the quality of a CEO is the most important thing.

When I look at a business plan, my interest is heavily weighted toward the numbers. I look at projections going out only about three years, because after three years, I've never found a crystal ball that was clear enough to mean anything. The other thing I'd look for in a business plan is a reason to believe the numbers are good. I would expect a write-up saying it's a projection, but why should I believe this projection is solid? I do not want just words; I do not want just numbers. I really think you have to feel ownership of that business plan. You have to believe in it; otherwise, you can't sell it. When you ask for investor capital, you're asking the investor to buy your perception or your business plan.

Companies never go broke if they always have enough cash. Since the only time companies go broke is when they run out of cash, really work on your cash projections, your cash flows. The size of the investment I typically look for is something in the $100,000 to $250,000 class. So I would say I'm a smaller investor.

The enterprise should be projected in the black within 18 to 24 months, or have a reason why it's not profitable within that time frame. If our projections are good only for three years, we had better be in the black 18 to 24 months out.

The president of the company should really consider that his investment in the company is a modest living and his real income should come through stock options. If the president isn't willing to live modestly as he's building the company and figure his payout comes at the end with the stock offering, or stock options, I really question whether this is the person to run the company. I'm not concerned as much with an exit strategy as I am with the quality of the CEO. A good CEO without an exit strategy is much better than a poor CEO with an exit strategy. If it's a poor CEO, you know what your exit strategy is; it's called a Chapter 11 or a Chapter 7. So to me the quality of a CEO is the most important thing.

Also important is that the company be big enough to have an outside control board. I would not be interested in owning control of the company, but the company has to have an outside control board. And I will help in the area of actively recruiting board members, because my firm belief is that if you have a board with experienced businessmen and those members have all run businesses larger than this one, you have increased your chances of success. And getting an outside control board, gathering people who will truly participate, is not that much of a problem, and not that expensive either.

No single customer should represent more than 5 percent of your volume. If you have a customer who represents 20 to 30 percent of your volume, you no longer are making the business decisions; your customers are.

In my investments the majority of the business assets are located within two to three hours of my home. As an investor I want to go out and be able to kick the side of the wall, or kick the desk, and find out where the hell the investment is. I don't want an investment a five-hour plane ride away. You also want to go out and see what other people think of the business, depending on what the business is and depending on whom you'd ask.

Time frame? I'm comfortable with looking at a 10- to 12-year, maybe a 15-year investment, as long as the projections forecast that we can grow by internally generated cash flows. If you're going to show rapid growth, you're going to need additional rounds of investors, and additional rounds of investors may demand more than the first group did. May not, but, in turn, may.

I guess everything boils down to three important things: the quality of the CEO, the feasibility of the projected balance sheet, and the reasonableness of the business plan. The rest becomes second fiddle. If you can get those three things in order, you should be able to get an investment.

Deep-Pocket Investor #3

I'm not going to continue looking at a deal where I don't feel very, very comfortable with the people. That's not only a feeling that they're straight, but also that they're honest. And I gotta like them. Otherwise, I'm not going to invest.

I'll just make one comment up front: I'm a real expert in this business because in the 12 to 14 years that I've been in this aspect of the business, I have personally made every investment mistake you can make. Or I've witnessed the mistakes.

The trick in this business is to learn by doing business and to try not to make the same mistake twice. But oftentimes we get caught up in the entrepreneur's and the founder's enthusiasm. That's as it should be. That's the kind of business this is—more art than science.

My particular background is eclectic: I've been on both the entrepreneur side and the venture capital side. Last year I spent the better part of the year working as the founder of a company and I was humbled by that experience. So I certainly have empathy for people on that side.

One of the things that came out of that experience is a respect for knowing the market. I see a lot of plans stating that the market is $5 million, or it's equal to the gross national product, or it's this or it's that. I would urge you to concentrate on how you're going to get to that market, to zero in on what the served market is. And, like all of these things, there are entries on both sides of the ledger. Certainly there is the focus: You want to have a niche; you want to have a small market; but, at the same time, that market has to be big enough.

Like any business plan, like any good entrepreneur, you can count on shifts in your strategy once you get into the market. So I would urge you to also understand the market and be comfortable with the fact that it's big enough to accommodate the necessary shifts in your strategy. If you're in a very small, very well-defined, limited market, you're not going to have the luxury of shifting your strategy, so you'd better have a concept for a product that is proprietary or has significant barriers to entry.

As an investor in technology, nontechnology, and service companies, and as a board member of seven small companies, I look for what is really different about the concept. Now that difference doesn't necessarily have to be proprietary technology. It can be the different distribution strategy. It can be a different way to service an area that's not now being served well.

I spent most of my life in the corporate rat race, and I left it in my late forties to start my company, not because I had a burning, compelling desire to start a company, but because I'd been running a company in Silicon Valley and, as you sometimes hear, the venture capitalist will terminate a president when the moon gets into a certain position. I fell victim to one of those venture capitalists. I couldn't get a job anywhere else so I started a company.

I had been in the equipment leasing field for a lot of years, so I started in that. I capitalized the company with $1,000 and went after a market that all the big people in the equipment leasing field said was impossible to succeed in, and that was financing start-ups. They thought my concept was that I would take incredible risks and go down the tubes. They were wrong on both counts.

I wasn't taking terrible risks. I wasn't gambling on my ability to discern a good deal from a bad deal. What I was doing was structuring each transaction as a professional financier might structure a real estate transaction. And so I mitigated risk, if you like, with available collateral. I capitalized the company on $1,000 and in the first year, before my own salary, we made about $17,000. So I paid myself a salary of about $15,000—about a third of what I had been making before—so I could show a profit of $2,000. I had this strong compulsion to show a profit.

And 14 years later, our pretax earnings were a million and a half, and I sold it. And, since that time, I've been taking life a little easier, and from time to time, I invest. I have looked at literally thousands of deals because I focused on emerging-growth companies, start-ups in a wide variety of fields, but primarily in high tech (though I had very little high-tech background, it was primarily in electronics, and I never took physics). And I'm still as green in technology as I was when I started. But it isn't a knowledge of technology that helps you determine a good investment.

I don't talk from theory, I talk from practice, practice as an investor, occasionally putting money into deals. There are a lot of similarities between the institutional and the private investor. You know them as well as I do. Don't think you can get by without a good business plan. You can't. It's absolutely essential. It would be like going out in the street without your pants or skirt on. You've got to have a good business plan.

And you have to associate with professional people who will be available as soon as you get into operation: a good CPA, but even before you start, a good corporate lawyer. And you don't need big people. I'm not knocking the big firms by any means, but it's been my experience that when you're very small and not exactly flush with money, the big firm gives you a junior, someone inexperienced. In smaller firms, on the other hand, you get principals, the more experienced people, those with the fire to help you and with a desire to make a name for themselves. When you're dealing with a private investor, you are dealing with principals. So, select your professional advisers with care. They are essential.

I don't put my money into Hollywood, looking to associate with the stars, but I will tell you this: I ran my own business and I function today on the philosophy that I'd spent 25 years in the corporate rat race and liked most people, but, now and again, you come across some real so-and-so's. I vowed to myself to deal only with people I like. I'm not going to continue looking at a deal where I don't feel very, very comfortable with the people. That's not only a feeling that they're straight, but also that they're honest. And I gotta like them. Otherwise, I'm not going to invest.

What are the things that will make you likable? Your commitment, your understanding of what you are doing, your analysis of your risks. This is where most people go wrong. They seem to think that the potential investor doesn't want to hear the bad news. If he hears the bad news, he's going to get scared off. I get scared off when my investee demonstrates that he is or she is oblivious to the risks. So I want someone who has taken a hard look at the risks.

Let me give you an example of some of the more subtle things that I think motivate principals and career people. In the leasing/lending industry, particularly with emerging growth companies, it's commonplace to take additional collateral. I'm sure you know what I mean by that: collateral above that which you are leasing, taking the form of cash, perhaps, or cash equivalent.

Now let's create a hypothetical example. This is a young, high-technology company. They have $4 million of the institutional venture capitalist's money in the bank; they have a series of timed CDs, but are not making a product yet. They're going to use that cash to meet the burn rate until the product comes out the door. They want to lease half a million dollars' worth of equipment. I come along and say, "I want a couple hundred thousand dollars of that money and I'll give you an interest rate on it just like the bank; in fact, I'll give you a quarter of a point more and then I will release that money to you as you meet certain benchmarks." Meanwhile, my competitor—a big guy—comes along and offers the same thing but says, "I don't want the cash; give me an assignment of the CD, or a letter of credit drawn on a credible bank like Citicorp or Bank of America."

Why does he do that? I won't say I wouldn't touch his offer with a ten-foot pole; if I couldn't get anything else, I would take it. But he doesn't want the cash, and the reason he doesn't want the cash is because his legal department has warned him that under certain circumstances in a particular state, in a particular city, there might be trouble. They cite a case in 1973 in which a very aggressive bankruptcy trustee got caught holding a cash deposit that, in fact, was part of the bankruptcy estate. They're worried, of course, about the same thing happening to them. So this competitor says, "I don't want the cash; I want a letter of credit." And I say, "Baloney! Give me the cash."

Cash is king to me. If a bankruptcy trustee attempts to do that to me, I will fight him. He isn't stronger. He's not using the money of the estate to launch this legal attack. We're about evenly matched. This isn't the question of the big guy against the little guy. I'll fight it. Well, I did fight it, a hundred times, and it never bothered me. The difference is in motivation. As far as I'm concerned, it's my money, and if I've got a nice piece of cash from the lessee covering it, it does a lot for me. It helps me sleep at night. It also motivates my lessee, because I've got his cash, cash he'd like to get back one day. But doing it the other way would put my job in jeopardy if anything went wrong. I would have made a big mistake.

Another thing, I find that investing with others is the norm for several reasons. We all attract people because of our interests. If you play the violin, you probably know other violin players. If you fool around in the private investment marketplace, you know other people because, generally speaking, you don't play that game unless you like keeping very close to what's going on in the community.

For instance, I knew nothing whatever about high technology. The only reason I formed a company leasing to high-technology companies was because I happened to be living in Silicon Valley. Had I been living in Oregon or Washington, I'd be in fishing boats and lumber—and bankrupt by now. If you like a particular field, you want to keep talking to people who are active in it.

So, if I go into a deal, I will turn to other people for three very powerful reasons. One of them is that I may turn to someone who is closer to a technology I know little about. I'll turn to somebody who understands that field and, very likely, it'll be someone who, like myself, is investing. This way, I gain knowledge of a technology I'm not familiar with. Second, if I think it's a good deal and I know other people who I think deserve it, I let them take a part of it. And third, I'm probably not going to make a cold investment. I'm probably going to want to get involved in one form or another, maybe not actively, but when I put money into a company, I want to help them. It's not like selling insurance, calling on all your friends. I'm not being critical of that field, but, generally speaking, I've identified with a small company, I like the people, I like what they're doing, I believe in them, I want to help them. I don't demand a board seat unless I have a significant position. So I'm going to turn to other people whom I know, but I'm not going to go hunting for money like an investment banker.

Normally, I do want some involvement. I'm not necessarily going to be attracted unless I feel I can make a contribution somewhere. I'm not looking for operating management responsibility. I'm through with that part of my life, and I like things the way they are now. But if the thing is going downhill, I have to realize I am stronger than the individual running the show; I have to get him out and get myself in—something I don't otherwise want to do.

That's why I will not go some distance away. Like carrying an umbrella, I hope it never rains. If I stay close to home, fewer problems seem to crop up. This means that people are absolutely critical. You've got to have confidence that they can do what they say they will do, and that they have got the sticking power to do what they say they will do.

Deep-Pocket Investor #4

One thing I do not want to hear is that it's going to be a wild ride and a lot of fun. If I want to have a lot of fun, I'll go fly an F-14.

I've been investing since 1988. I've done a wide range of investing in several different types of firms. Overall, my investments probably total about $20 million now, including those of my co-investors. I've invested in insurance, financial services, money management, investment advisory—those kinds of things. I'm pretty diverse. I have no requirements in terms of geography. I've invested in a firm outside the United States, a firm in New York, a firm in Iowa, where I'm from originally.

I really look for innovation and passion—"fire in the belly." But you can get some sense of that, I imagine, in looking at an executive summary or business plan. I like to sit down with the people, look them in the eye, find out their backgrounds, find out what drove them to this investment and basically what their personal commitments are. I think that that's very, very important.

I try to add value whenever I can, particularly if it's needed. I have been doing this a long time and my vision is usually pretty good and I have found that I can help an entrepreneur substantially if he or she remains open to ideas. One thing I do not want to hear is that it's going to be a wild ride and a lot of fun. If I want to have a lot of fun, I'll go fly an F-14.

On the other hand, one thing I do want to hear is that you have an executive summary that tells me what it is you need, what the potential market is, how much you're looking to raise, and what kind of rate of return might be expected with the size of this particular market.

Explain where the technology is coming from, how it's going to be developed. Elaborate on your concept; tell how it is innovative. Explain why your product or service is superior to the techniques currently in place and what the relative cost would be. Tell why it's superior, what the relative cost advantages or disadvantages might be, and just explain a little bit more of what it is. You have to be a little more excited and tell *why*. Why you're at the company, why you believe in this, and why you are spending the amount of energy that you're expending.

The third investor type is the consortium of individual investors.

THE CONSORTIUM OF INDIVIDUAL INVESTORS

Consortium Investor #1

Our group has three investors with quite diverse backgrounds. And because of that, our investment interest is very diverse. One of my colleagues and I most recently founded a multimedia software company in the educational software field. We went through all the trials and tribulations that I'm sure many people have gone through. I started from self-financing through friends to institutional financing and we were fortunate throughout the process.

We finally sold the company to a public software company last year. We learned a lot about what you don't do and what you need to do in order to be successful. One of my co-investors has gone the more traditional institutional investor route in the retailing field and cofounded a company that received a venture backing and then went public last year. He's been very successful. So from that experience of both self-financing and the traditional institutional venture capital funding, I think we've learned the ins and outs of how to get from here to there from the viewpoint of the people seeking money.

So, we're most interested in talking to people. Our interest in funding is in the $50,000 to $500,000 range. We're looking at seed funding to early-stage funding. Retailing is an area we are very interested in, and the software technology area as well because of our backgrounds. And lastly, we are interested in consumer-related investments. So that pretty much hits the entire spectrum (Exhibit 7.4).

Consortium Investor #2

We like to get very close to the entrepreneurs, the people who start the business, the people who have the ideas. We offer them some oversight; we offer them a sounding board, and, of course, we offer them some capital.

I am an individual investor, working with about half a dozen other people, all of whom have started, run, and then sold businesses, but have continuing interest in nurturing small businesses. We're a loose confederation of investors. We don't have a company structure as such. We respond to each opportunity as we see it.

Our focus is on the people involved in starting a business. We like to get very close to the entrepreneurs, the people who start the business, the people who have the ideas. We offer them some oversight; we offer them a sounding board, and, of course, we offer them some capital.

We generally work in technology-based areas, often manufactured products. We don't do a lot of seed ventures but, in fact, we just invested

EXHIBIT 7.4 Consortium of Individual Investors

- Loose confederation of private, individual investors (unrelated, typically 3–6)
- Experience in start-up, running, and selling their businesses
- More passive involvement; seek oversight; sounding board role
- Will invest in technology and product opportunities, as well as start-up companies
- Individuals make their own decisions, may not always invest as a group
- Extensively connected with "deep-pocket"–type of angels with whom they co-invest or to whom they refer deals
- Seek some protectable advantage
- Invest $50,000–$500,000

Source: International Capital Resources

in a small one last year that turned out quite well for us. We didn't carry it to the prototype stage. We managed to sell it to an East Coast company for a fairly substantial return on investment. Normally, we're looking for return in the area of 10, maybe 15 percent. The days of 20 and 25 percent, I think, are behind us.

Consortium Investor #3

As we look at the lower end, at start-ups or seed money, we don't really care if it has the potential of becoming a company. All I really care about is if it has the potential of making money.

My group is a loose confederation of private investors who look at individual deals, make their own decisions, and may or may not end up investing in the particular deal as a group. Basically, I think we classify deals in two categories. We invest in deals less than $250,000. In bigger deals we have a number of well-heeled private investors that we will bring in, simply pass the deals to, or become co-investors with.

A difference exists, I think, in the way we, or I as an individual, will approach some of these opportunities. As we look at the lower end, at startups or seed money, we don't really care if it has the potential of becoming a company. All I really care about is if it has the potential of making money. That simply could mean that it's a product or technology that, unto itself, is not going to turn into a $50- or $100-million-a-year company. But it may turn into a $10 million product line that GE would love to have, or that some international company feels it can manufacture and distribute more efficiently overseas.

I think Silicon Valley is full of opportunities that are masquerading as companies, but are really product opportunities or technology opportunities that need to be developed and then put together with an exit strategy that makes everybody involved a little bit wealthier. The larger deals are company deals. They generally are things to be looked at much farther along the path; they probably have a proven concept, maybe they've done some test marketing, and have most, if not all, of their staff in place.

On the low end, we typically look at technology deals simply because that's our background. On the higher end, because there's generally more information in place, we look at a broader range of ideas. I look at what I call value-oriented opportunities. And, from that perspective, I consider their protectable advantage. Typically, protectable advantage means patent protection, technology protection, a lock on distribution channels, something like that.

It may be a great technological idea or a great technology opportunity, but if nobody cares except the inventor, it's of no value. And if somebody does care, the question is whether they will pay, whether it can be done profitably. And probably one of the more important things to me because I come from a sales and marketing background is how to get to them. How do you distribute whatever you've got? In that respect, when I look at an opportunity, I will look first at the market, at the marketing aspects of it.

Second, I'll look at the technology aspects of it and, third, at the people. When it comes to the decision-making phase, I reverse that process: Who are the individuals involved? What does the technology look like? And, how are they going to package that technology and market it? Beyond that, I look for people who believe in focusing on the customer.

The fourth type of investor is the partner investor.

THE PARTNER INVESTOR

Somebody once defined the survival of the fittest to me as not being the strongest, but finding the niche where you can exist and make things happen. So it's not the "fittest" that counts; it's the "fit."

I've been looking for an investment for eight months. I left my job in January, and I've had this long-term goal to buy into a business. Basically, my career has been sales oriented and general management, which I think is key to being a successful entrepreneur. I operate where the rubber hits the pavement. I dislike meetings and bureaucracy.

But I do like collaboration and teamwork, and I think that to be successful in the kind of environment we're talking about you need to have—and I think I have these elements—a lean, seat-of-the-pants operating style from running small businesses, extensive direct sales and marketing experience, finance and numbers discipline. And I've acquired that from working on an $80 million leverage buyout, and a lot of calluses from fighting for customers in competitive markets and from navigating the corporate jungle. And you have to have a very strong desire to do a deal, and you have to be very focused about it.

I have a collaborator whom I met at an event hosted by ICR, a collaborator who's been at it for 18 months and he's running out of money—and he's got a lot more money than I do. So, it's a tough slog. So you have to be focused. The key part of all this is to generate deal flow. You have to develop as much deal flow as you possibly can, and you have to constantly get feedback from the marketplace and refocus your efforts. That's what I've been doing.

There is no path in this process. It's constant invention, reinvention every day. I have a little model in front of my desk that for me reflects this whole process. I call this model the funnel strategy. Basically, the way to succeed is to employ six ways in closing more sales, or employ six ways in getting more deals going—all of which depends on the size of your funnel. In other words, get more of an effort going; weed out unprofitable prospects. The idea is to fail quickly; get off the stuff that isn't happening immediately because you can burn a tremendous amount of time on wasteful action.

Don't work on the undecided that have little chance of going further. Find better prospects. Increase the speed. I think the key is more throughput. It's all about throughput. It's about replenishing your funnel every week. And don't chase one deal too long; instead, continue to feed the funnel. This is the model I've used to work on deals. I've created deals by answering ads in the paper; I've worked with business brokers; I've networked with people; I've used direct mail, a CD-ROM database, mailed more than 700 letters to targeted businesses located within specific Standard Industrial Classification (SIC) codes, zip codes, and types of businesses.

In fact, out of those 700 letters, I received 40 calls, a 5 percent response rate. I've evaluated more than 100 businesses, evaluating them across a wide range of criteria—from just a quick phone call during which someone runs the gist of the business by me to doing full due diligence. I've made four offers on businesses: One was a manager-investor opportunity, while three were to purchase. I'm in escrow on a deal right now, hoping it will work out.

Since everyone is different, you have to figure out what people want, that is, you have get to people who want to do your kind of deals. It's a waste of time to talk to people who don't. My deal is that I had about $200,000. I also have $140,000 in credit cards that I worked very hard to accumulate over the last few years. Credit cards are being used to finance about 25 percent of the small- to medium-size businesses in the United States today. And if you evaluate what private investors want in terms of return, I want a 30 percent return on the investment from my deal. Credit cards are really the cheapest forms of financing—if you have the guts to do it.

I built up a wish list that I kept on my bulletin board. I'm looking for an international business, a consumer product leading to an ongoing relationship in the business, a business I could bring value to. As an individual investor, I don't have an unlimited supply of money, so critical for me is what value I bring to the party, what value I add to the business.

The business has to be able to respond to aggressive direct sales, respond to strong, capable management. The business has to be local. I want to be able to ride my bicycle to work. I want casual dress. I want it to be part of a "wave" out there, a wave that is home office, aging population, information technology, and so forth. I want it to be fun. I want to be president. I want a good return on investment. I don't want it dominated by few customers or few vendors. I want an exit strategy so I can cash out for cash. In my current deal I got about 70 percent of this stuff. That's the way it goes.

But the really critical piece in terms of keeping the whole thing together is the chemistry and trust among the people involved. Things have to be very good, but things are better if the chemistry is excellent. Everybody has different needs and wants. Understanding this one fact in terms of the whole process, plus being able to deal with rejection, is dead center. Basically, it's not about being the smartest, or having the best product, or looking the best, or even having the most money. It's about getting the right fit.

All those other things help, but somebody once defined the survival of the fittest to me as not being the strongest, but finding the niche where you can exist and make things happen. So it's not the "fittest" that counts; it's the "fit." That's what this process is all about for me.

This type of investing takes persistence; it takes throughput, as much throughput as you can muster and emotionally tolerate. It is draining. You simply cannot do it all by yourself. Firms like ICR can help. You have to delegate. And you have to collaborate. I met someone at an ICR event who has helped me. Now, we meet every three weeks and collaborate on the process and share ideas and share leads (Exhibit 7.5).

The next type of investor is the family of investors.

EXHIBIT 7.5   Partner Investor

- Buyer in disguise
- Very high need for control
- Is trying to build network or has developed some co-investor relationships
- Would prefer acquisition of established company but lacks financial resources
- Lead investor who searches for opportunities, makes independent decision, and suggests investment to co-investor network
- Wants to be president
- Able to invest $250,000–$1,000,000

Source: International Capital Resources

EXHIBIT 7.6   Family of Investors

- Family money is pooled, and a trusted, skilled family member coordinates investment activity
- Very astute investor, MBA minimum, many Ph.D.'s in coordinator role
- Contribute experience, intense involvement for short periods of time
- Group investor likely to invest only if there is group consensus
- Very common among Asian investors in Bay Area
- Invest $100,000–$1,000,000

Source: International Capital Resources

THE FAMILY OF INVESTORS

We believe we can contribute not only the funds but also the experience in management, as well as provide the connections we have in the Far East and in some countries in Europe.

I'm new to the United States. We still have some investments in the Far East—Taiwan, Singapore, and also China. We also have some business connections in Europe. But, basically, we are a family-owned business, a small group. We are interested in information services, computers—both hardware and software—as well as medical industries.

We view investments in amounts ranging from a few hundred thousand dollars to several million dollars for each project. We like to look at the early-stage venture, as early as possible. We believe we can contribute quite a bit of experience, just as we have in the past.

Our company has been in the high-tech business for more than 20 years. We have been handling very complicated processes, such as air traffic control, radar, defense equipment, and small components. So we believe we can contribute not only the funds but also the experience in management, as well as provide the connections we have in the Far East and in some countries in Europe (Exhibit 7.6).

The sixth type of investor is the barter investor.

THE BARTER INVESTOR

We have an active business today that might dovetail with what you do. We have an infrastructure in place. We advertise for customers, we process customer orders, we warehouse, we ship, we build computers, we service computers in the field. We do all sorts of things: bill, invoice, and collect. All of these things we might be able to add to your business.

Do you need the money, or do you need what you're going to use the money to buy? Our company operates in a limited area, looking to make investments and participate in your company. So that sets us apart, narrows the scope, if you will. Our business is to try to dovetail with what's out there, something that could be a good fit for us. My partner and I are knowledgeable in starting up companies. We both have done several.

We have a company that operates and provides business-to-business services throughout California. And what we are looking for is investing in an early-stage idea or business that we can contribute money to. But equally as important to us is the infrastructure of the business. We have thousands of customers, we bill them, we collect, we negotiate bank lines, we do marketing—we do all of these things.

My partner and I are interested in participating in new ideas, in growing a new business. We are interested in the expansion phase of a seed-capital or start-up business, defined by us as a venture with a working prototype ready to roll, what we call a beta test. We are interested in the early stage of testing or initial growth capital. Mezzanine, bridge, or IPO is beyond our scope. So that is not what we are looking for.

We feel a capable management team is necessary, as everybody says, but it doesn't have to be completely formed. Because of our participation, we believe that we can fill some of those holes, give a running start to the company, get it going a little faster than might otherwise be the case.

Quality product or service is of interest to us. Technology advantage is always nice. Proprietary is desirable but not necessary. We like a substantial market potential, a $10 to $20 million revenue target in five years with compatible financial objectives. And this is one of the stumbling blocks that I run into many times with entrepreneurs: The entrepreneur has to agree we are not just building a good lifestyle for that individual. So we have to have an exit strategy within a time frame that we can mutually agree on.

Business categories of interest are communications, the Internet, computer software, and multimedia. Of course, every time I hear of a new business outside these categories, I get interested and I add that to my list. And not so much multimedia CD-ROM games, but multimedia interactive marketing, or some projects we're working with now, such as financial and business services, even light manufacturing or distribution. We're fascinated with the idea of producing a product and distributing it.

Our company is in the computer rental, leasing, and sales business, primarily rental. People always ask what the difference is between rental and leasing. If you think of it as a Hertz rental car kind of thing, as opposed to long-term leasing, that's what it is. Computers cycle in and out of the shop every day. People call and order. We deliver, install, then pick them up when they're through, put them back on the shelf, and rent them to somebody else. The investment of interest to us might have a direct fit with some other business we've had.

We are interested in early-stage companies, ventures in the idea stage, in the process of being organized, a start-up, a venture that has been in business less than two years, that is completing product development, and maybe has some sales. First stage, expansion stage. Everybody has a different definition for these terms, but we're interested in a venture with a working prototype that has been through beta testing and is in need of initial growth capital. Mezzanine, bridge, IPO are beyond our financial capability. We are not interested at that level.

We look for general investment criteria. Of course, first comes a good management team. We invest in key people as much as the product or the technology. That team should have industry experience and be able to execute its business plan. We don't expect you to have all the holes filled, because we are interested in being active investors. We are not passive investors in that sense. So between my partner and me, our backgrounds cover finance, accounting, marketing, and general management, and we are interested in a couple of people with an idea and a good market to pursue. We believe we can fill in some of the holes.

Quality product, service, or technological advantage is important. Of course, the proprietary advantage is desirable but not necessary. Anything very high-tech may be beyond us in terms of our understanding, so we're probably not equipped to evaluate that very well. But applying a technology, a proven technology, to a business is something that we are experienced in.

The product should have substantial market potential, a potential for $10 to $20 million in revenues within three to five years. We say that because of what our experience has been. From a liquidity standpoint, you have to have at least $10 million if you are going to do anything in terms of getting liquidity for your investment after that period of time. Actually, I've rarely seen a business plan that worked out the way I expected within one to two years, but I am looking at an investment growth projection that gives me a feel for the size of the market. Substantiating the size of the market is very important to me. If you can't convince me of that, I don't think you've done enough homework to attract our investment.

We are active managers, so in early-stage deals we're interested in a significant piece of the company for our investment, ranging from 30 to 60 percent of the company. It depends on your stage of development and the capital required. We can provide an incentive for founders. You're going to give us a business plan that says, "Here's what I can do"; and we'll say, "Fine, we'll put some money in," and maybe we have 51 percent at that point. But if you meet the business plan, you earn 20 percent back and dilute us, and so forth.

So we're very flexible in terms of how we go into a venture, but we want a significant equity position in the company. Common stock or convertible preferred, purchase options, licensing agreements, joint ventures—we would consider all of these things. Let me back up a minute on that. We have an active business today that might dovetail with what you do. We have an infrastructure in place. We advertise for customers, we process customer orders, we warehouse, we ship, we build computers, we service computers in the field. We do all sorts of things: bill, invoice, and collect. All of these things we might be able to add to your business, if you think of us as an "incubator" as well.

So, our investment might take two forms: The first is a cash check; the second, or combination of the two, enables us to save you a lot of cash by leveraging off the infrastructure that we already have in our company. And we operate throughout the state of California. Participation in the business, representation on the board, part-time management. My partner and I, or one of us, depending on the needs of a particular investment, would be willing to spend half our time in the early stages of that company.

We are interested in communications, data services, and telecommunications—providing it is not too far out. Also, we're interested in computer software. I would say we're interested in vertical market applications: financial and business services. Our company, even though built on computers, is really a business service; in fact, that's all it is. And light manufacturing or distribution is another interest of ours. In other words, if we can make it, manufacture it, put it in a box, and ship it out repetitively, that's something that's simple enough that we can understand. So that really forms the outline of our investment objectives.

If you want to place us in a potential investment or a company's potential investment, put us in cash terms of up to a quarter of a million dollars. And I would like to think of adding infrastructure equivalent to that amount in terms of saving you cash (Exhibit 7.7).

The seventh type of investor is the socially responsible investor.

EXHIBIT 7.7   Barter Investor

- Provides what you would have used capital to buy in exchange for equity
- Participative—not passive
- Early-stage preference
- Offers capital and infrastructure (an incubator model)
- Management is most important criteria
- Independent investor who relies on own investigation in deciding to invest
- Venture must have capability to grow to $10 million minimum in 3–5 years
- Invests up to $250,000 and frequently supplements with guaranteed line of credit

Source: International Capital Resources

THE SOCIALLY RESPONSIBLE PRIVATE INVESTOR

> *I think that people who come into this kind of business perceive
> needs and have values. Those individuals in the nurture capital
> process are people with a clear sense of values. The companies that
> have integrity, that have a product, that have meaning to them are
> the ones that I think really matter.*

There's a big gap and a lot of misunderstanding about what venture capital is. *Venture capital* serves as the generic term that refers to the full range of direct investments in the private equity class. But, typically, a venture capital firm fills a gap in which you have either a fairly complete management team or a fairly well-developed product.

Many times a management team is missing a number of key elements, or a product has just entered the field. But because of their fiduciary responsibility to investors, the venture capital community can't look at the technology and can't look at the company. In this regard, it resembles a bank. This capital gap between the founders, on the one hand, and the banks and the venture capital community, on the other, has fostered what I call nurture capital. The terminology speaks for itself. You nurture a company, helping it any way you can. It means a lot of hand-holding, a lot of intimate relationship with that particular business.

It seems to me people often cling to the impression that venture capital is interested only in making money. I don't believe that's true at all. I think that people who come into this kind of business perceive needs and have values. Those individuals in the nurture capital process are people with a clear sense of values. The companies that have integrity, that have a product, that have meaning to them, are the ones that I think really matter.

We end up putting a spin on the developments and technologies of the companies that we get involved with; we add a dimension, a spin, just like spin on the bowling ball spreads it wider than it really is, creating a greater impact on the target.

My perception is that in the United States especially, but around the world as well, very little knowledge exists about what is happening in the petroleum field. Our economy runs on oil, and we are about to see a major transformation, such as we saw here in the 1970s—except that this time the entire world will suffer. In the 1970s, United States oil extraction peaked, and, you may recall, a couple of years later major repercussions occurred. But we possessed the unique advantage of still being able to import oil.

The globe will not have that possibility, at least from oil. About five years from now when production peaks, oil expectations will continue to grow. There are many people working on putting plants in China, for example, and in India, building cars and, sadly, fueling expectation that oil will be available. The trouble is there won't be any oil. This event is a mere five years away and when it happens, we're going to have to import oil. The problem is there won't be any oil to import.

The only source of imports we have is the sun, so my perspective is that solar energy applications are a major area of investment interest for me. And we're going to see a major transformation and the potential and the technology in renewable and in energy conservation and, suddenly, the cost of oil is going to be so high that these investments will have potential for the next century as well.

People claim that there's still plenty of oil out there. Sure enough, there is. But the reality is that while we had gushers in the 1950s, oil is going to be harder and harder to get in the years to come, and the yield we derive for the same amount of effort is going to be less and less. So it's going to be less and less exciting to go after oil. Between 1977 and 1991 we discovered in the United States 5 billion barrels of oil. However, we consumed twice the amount we extracted. It doesn't take an Einstein to figure out that this is a losing proposition. If your business plan doesn't take this into consideration, and you plan to be here five years from now, then you have some thinking to do.

And if you are interested in working with me in terms of investment programs, this is really what drives me. I think that the money will flow if the service is there. Making money is not the goal; profits and return become the score that gets chalked up after the goal has been reached (Exhibit 7.8).

The next investor type discussed in this chapter is the unaccredited investor.

EXHIBIT 7.8 Socially Responsible Private Investor

- Nurture capitalist, seeking intensive hand-holding situations
- High need for personal interaction, less able to provide savvy business support
- Seeks to be associated with individuals with "high values"
- Prefers ventures addressing major social issues
- Seeks reasonable ROI while supporting people/ideals consonant with "enlightened" personal values
- Often inherited wealth with extensive investment capability
- Referred investor, relies on recommendations through trusted advisors

Source: International Capital Resources

THE UNACCREDITED PRIVATE INVESTOR

I initially get excited by the concept, but I think ultimately, I invest in a venture because of the entrepreneur rather than the concept.

I spent 24 years with a Fortune 500 chemical corporation, specializing in real estate development, a major business of the firm. I started as a junior accountant of a subsidiary, then left six years ago as vice president in charge of the company's activities. Since then, I have combined investing in a few start-ups with a financial and consulting practice.

I'd rather try to spread my apples around a little bit more, make smaller investments in a bunch of different companies, companies in which I would like to spend some time in an important capacity. I might like a management role, perhaps a board role; I might like to serve as an interim CFO, though only one day or so a week (Exhibit 7.9).

In looking at deals I'm typically going to make an investment in the $10,000 to $25,000 range. I get talked into higher amounts occasionally, but that's where I start out. I don't have to make a deal. People who represent funds have to place a certain amount of money. If I don't invest in a private enterprise, I've got the money in the stock market or in something else. So it's really a question of taking it out of alternative investments.

I typically look for some type of niche, obviously at start-ups. Often I'll go in with a bunch of other investors because that's the thing to do with a large amount of money.

But to me the story is much more important than numbers. The business plan is really important, but numbers usually aren't very reliable no matter how well they're done. So the concept is much more important. People may have an idea of what they want to do with product

EXHIBIT 7.9 Unaccredited Private Investor

- Less experienced, less affluent private investor
- Looking for a role in earlier-stage situations
- Not a patient investor; plans to get money out in 3–5 years
- Must "really get to know" investee
- "Spreads his apples around," making multiple small investments
- Used to invest in real estate, now has a preference for technology
- Invests close to home
- Has to justify investment to spouse
- Typically a referred investor who is primarily influenced by recommendations from a knowledgeable person
- Invests $10,000–$25,000 maximum

Source: International Capital Resources

A and that really makes sense to me. Then they want to continually reinvest and go on. I can understand they want to do that from their perspective. But from my perspective, I would just as soon make the investment in a joint venture, get my money and my return out of it. Maybe during the course of the investment, I'll get sold on continuing in the company, but I don't necessarily structure it that way going in.

I think that in small investments, one of the main things investors have to worry about is being able to justify investments to their spouse. Believe me, the worst thing is to have to explain to your husband or wife why you lost $10,000 to $15,000 in such-and-such a company, the same money you could have used on a luxurious trip to Tahiti, or on a material purchase of some kind. That's probably the toughest sell, the one sell I try to avoid.

I would prefer to be thought of as a friend or member of the family. I want to really get to know the CEO; that's the kind of company I'm going to invest in because I think no matter how you write the documents, what's really important is whether that entrepreneur's going to treat you fairly over a long period of time, whether he or she is intelligent, and will work hard. I initially get excited by the concept, but I think ultimately, I invest in a venture because of the entrepreneur rather than the concept.

One other thing that's important to me in concept is accessible geography. On a business plan, I think it becomes a terribly important sales tool.

The final type of investor—the manager investor—is discussed below.

THE NEWEST BREED OF ANGEL: THE MANAGER INVESTOR

Manager Investor #1

Now, six months ago when I first began investing, I would have characterized myself as a novice. Over the past six-month period, however, I have grown considerably: I would now characterize myself as simply inexperienced.

I am what ICR has categorized as a manager investor. This means that any investment I make is into a company I want to play a role in, a role in the pursuit of that company's business activities. It certainly does not mean that I am interested in control. But it does mean I want to be active; I want to be aware of what is going on. From my standpoint, this becomes a necessity (Exhibit 7.10).

Now, six months ago when I first began investing, I would have characterized myself as a novice. Over the past six-month period, however, I have grown considerably: I would now characterize myself as simply inexperienced. My bet is that there are a number of people like me who haven't had a great deal of experience in investing in start-ups, so I hope it will help you to know how I pursued this area.

Probably you have seen the company profiles that ICR periodically makes available. These have been extremely helpful to me. They offer within a very short period of time a perception of what a company does, what its product is, what its marketplace is. These profiles supply an excellent overview of opportunities, letting a person like me zero in on the 10 percent of the deals that make sense to me (Exhibit 7.11).

EXHIBIT 7.10   Manager Investor

- Affluent, senior-level executive or former business owner reentering workforce and buying a "last job"
- Focused on making one investment
- Less experienced at direct, participatory investing
- Referred investor who asks questions and reads materials but can be primarily influenced by recommendations from a knowledgeable person
- Very long due diligence cycle
- Less tolerance for risk, so seeks more developed ventures
- Seeks high level of involvement for extended period of time
- Invests $100,000–$200,000, staged investment

Source: International Capital Resources

EXHIBIT 7.11   Characteristics of the Manager Investor

- 40s to mid-50s. Mid- to late-career manager or former business owner, seasoned executive, astute business analyst
- Full-time operational involvement; will provide support and industry savvy
- $100,000–$200,000 to invest. Not a deep pocket for subsequent rounds
- Less concerned about control, more concerned about sharing founder's vision; however, does desire at least some influence
- Typically well connected both geographically and in the industry
- Not interested in seed stage, but will consider more developed start-ups
- Prefers business with demonstrated viability, less inclined toward turnarounds; more concerned with the business than with pro forma statements (e.g., what is produced, who the competitors are, debt on balance sheet)
- Will require a business plan
- Will seek to benefit from appreciation on equity, and will seek steep discounts in private negotiations; will aggressively negotiate price; will want potential for above-average returns
- Will seek long-term commitment, "chemistry" with current management and founder, and geographic proximity to home or desired locale

---

I suspect that I've looked at maybe 50 or so of those company profiles. I probably ask for either additional information or an additional conversation with ICR principals, or maybe product information—sometimes even a business plan, if it's available—on maybe 10 of those 50, having eliminated 40 of them. From there I believe I met personally with 6 of the remaining 10, having become sufficiently interested in 3 of the 6 to conduct more than one meeting.

One in particular I have met with numerous times, and, frankly, some have accused me of making a career out of this one potential investment. But I think I'm in the eleventh hour of that one, and it will no doubt be coming to fruition soon. First of all, I try to take a look at the product and make certain that I feel that it's good, something I can identify with.

Second, I consider whether the marketplace for that product is fragmented, or whether it is dominated by a single or several very large companies. And third, I consider whether this company has any kind of an edge, for example, in its technology. I don't mean that it has to be a technology company, but it may use technology in a way that is more advanced than anyone else—anything, in other words, that might give it the edge. And I check to see if the company has patents on the product, another thing that could give it the edge.

This is typically when I have become serious in discussing the company in depth with its management. Now let me give you three examples of prospective ventures, and tell you how I characterize them. There was a software company that had what I consider to be a very good product and a very good market, not dominated by any single seller or manufacturer of a similar software package. There certainly was and is similar software in the market, but no one dominated it.

My concern with this company was that I didn't feel it had an edge. Additionally, even if they had had an edge, I thought it would slip away very quickly. This may be true of all software; I'm not certain. But I've noticed in the case of Lotus, Excel, and Quattro Pro, that by turns one will come out with a new version containing a few features, then another will match those features and raise the ante two or three features more. Someone else will then match those and raise again. It becomes an unending poker game. I didn't believe that this company could maintain an edge under this circumstance, and therefore I tended to eliminate it as an investment.

The second company was a medical transcription business. It had a very good product. Medical transcription, I think, is a classic example of a function that should be outsourced from a hospital. It's specialized. The people are highly paid. They're intermixed presently with other hospital employees who have dissimilar interests and goals; therefore, it's a function that is ripe for outsourcing.

In addition, it's a function that can be turned into a cottage industry quite easily with technology. And this company, through its planned use of technology, seemed to have that ability. Therefore, I considered it a good product with a good market and, potentially, with a solid edge. The eliminator in this case had to do with the business plan. The projections had included revenue from a contract, but when I examined the contract more thoroughly, I discovered that the projected revenue wasn't there, changing the forecast rather significantly. This circumstance made my equity investment seem considerably more risky than had been the case, and made my desired reward much less realistic. That's when the deal no longer made sense for me.

The third company, the one I have made a career on, is a chair manufacturer. This is a chair so advanced that it comes with an operating manual. Therefore, the marketing job for this chair has been difficult. And though the company has been in business for a number of years, it has been unable to get the product off the ground. They've also been cash starved for a number of years. Their brochure looks amateurish. They have an instruction video that is okay. But they don't have the money to advertise. They don't even have a full-time salesperson. Yet, while they've had a lot of things going against them, I continue to view them as having a good market and a product with an edge. The only failing I have discerned is an absence of investment capital, and that's the reason I have spent as much time as I have on this one. In fact, I'm still hopeful of doing something with them.

Resources for Entrepreneurs Raising Capital

Alternative Funding Resources in Accessing Angel Capital

HISTORY OF THE DEVELOPMENT OF ALTERNATIVE FUNDING RESOURCES

In earlier chapters we have emphasized the trend toward alternative financing methods. Clearly, the business angel investor represents one of those alternative financing modes—a substantial resource, which we have documented. Today's alternative funding resources ease the access to capital for inventors, entrepreneurs, and owners of small, rapidly growing businesses. These resources did not, however, materialize out of thin air. Like everything else we know of, they have evolved from their early contours to today's sweep of alternatives, suggesting ever-new directions to come.

In this chapter, we provide a set of invaluable tools for entrepreneurs in their search for capital. Our overview provides a comprehensive historical introduction to alternative funding resources, particularly those useful in identifying angel and early-stage private equity investors. These resources—past and present—have helped entrepreneurs face the challenge. We also will share research on emerging directions as viable sources of investor prospects and capital.

In Chapter 9, the entrepreneur will find an updated, comprehensive directory of alternative capital resources in the United States.

Historically, alternative funding resources were composed of informal groups of friends, colleagues, and co-investors—individuals who invested in a deal in a specific industry, at a particular stage of a company's life cycle. Those individuals either invested alone or formed a small circle of family, friends, and colleagues that pooled its money and shared the mutual responsibility of due diligence. The group also shared the risks inherent in such deals. This informal concept still exists today. It tends to be focused geographically, offering, as always, the benefits of shared responsibilities and shared risk.

Remember that investors have a vested interest in alternative funding sources—not just entrepreneurs. Investors select from an array of tactical options for creating their deal-flow development mix. The default is the serendipitous approach of sitting around hoping a diamond in the rough will drop into their laps. As one investor told us, "Good investments come to those looking for them." The lesson here is for the entrepreneur to select communication channels, to introduce their deals that investors are, in fact, listening to.

As Exhibit 8.1 illustrates, 57 percent of the angels receive their deals from a friend, family member, or co-worker; 31 percent receive referrals from professionals; and only 12 percent receive referrals from nonfamily members, who are representatives of the firm seeking financing by cold calling them. Only one time in ten will someone who does not know you work with you over a cold call. These statistics bear out that cold calling in this business is less efficient. As we have pointed out, you are not selling stock from a brokerage desk, something you can turn around and sell quickly in order to ease the pain of getting burned.

In our study of 60 angel and early-stage investors presented earlier, we asked, "Please indicate your preference with respect to venture opportunities submitted to you for consideration." The results are:

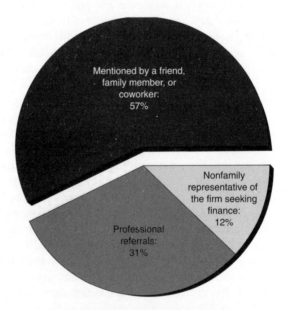

Survey of 600 Investors by ICR, 1998

Figure 8.1   How Angels Find Their Deals
Source: International Capital Resources

Number of Respondents	Categories
18	A large number of referrals, some of which may not fit your stated investment criteria.
42	A smaller number of referrals, most of which fit your stated investment criteria.

Seventy percent of the investors wanted referred ventures to have been prescreened to ensure that their investment parameters were a snug fit. But 30 percent of investors sought more deal flow, even if the ventures they saw did not meet their investment criteria!

This research finding is important because it supports the contention that individual investors and groups of investors face the problem of skimpy deal flow, a scarcity in the number of ventures and transactions that turn up for their consideration.

Exhibit 8.2 further demonstrates the depth of this discontent. A 1996 independent study by Harrison and Mason found that 33 percent of investors were "dissatisfied" and an additional 10 percent were "very dissatisfied" with existing channels of communication available to find out about businesses seeking financing. Such statistics indicate that entrepreneurs would benefit from studying alternative funding resources to determine which might be suitable resources for investor prospects for their particular venture.

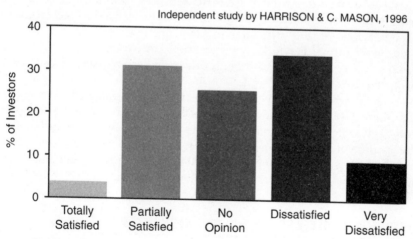

Figure 8.2 Satisfaction of Angel Investors with Existing Channels of Communication and Business Seeking Financing
Source: International Capital Resources

In a small group, each person will have gone about developing his or her own deal flow. Regional focus, the angels' propensity for privacy, the small number of people involved—all these account for the limited number of deals. One of the reasons that these informal groups have traditionally remained small is that, once again, individual investors prize their privacy. As soon as the word gets out that angels are active, they become inundated with deals, few of which meet their investment criteria. Their privacy is suddenly forfeited, which contributes significantly to the difficulty in finding them.

But the intense desire to broaden the scope and quality of the available investment offerings has resulted in increasing formalization of the private equity market. It is true that several secondary elements have contributed to increasing organization, complexity, and formalization in angel groups: for example, the attraction of the venture capital alternative asset class for generating higher portfolio returns; the movement of institutional venture capital to later-stage, larger investments, creating a capital gap that only pooled, angel capital could address; and a large increase in the number of newly affluent, a group that has dramatically changed the face of U.S. wealth, and the trend in this wealth culture toward actively investing more so than the affluent individuals of old. The desire for an increase in deal flow has motivated these organizations and individuals to organize and invest in their communities or in their regions, motivation traditionally reserved by universities, nonprofit organizations, and government agencies in their commitment to regional economic development and job creation.

This interest in community investment and the desire of small, informal networks of investors to increase their deal flow has nurtured growth in more formal mechanisms to facilitate the process of linking ventures with capital, while creating structures to safeguard investors' privacy. And as these more formal networks have been able to cluster separate informal groups of investors, significant pools of capital have blossomed, as we will demonstrate.

Over the previous 17 years, ICR has tested and evaluated every one of the alternative investor development methods described in this chapter. Although some are clearly more effective than others, all have contributed to the creation of a database of 1,359 active, accredited investors, a small sample of which were found to have invested more than $90 million in the past five years.

OVERVIEW OF ALTERNATIVE FUNDING RESOURCES

An overview of the different types of more formal alternative funding resources that have evolved over the past 20 years are listed below:

■ Directories, printed and software-based
■ Incubators
■ Entrepreneurial finance conferences
■ Investor education meetings and conferences
■ Venture forums
■ Venture capital clubs
■ Offline investor networks
■ Online matching and search services
■ Financial intermediaries

The only tools entrepreneurs and inventors used 20 years ago were directories, the granddaddy of which is *Pratt's Guide to Venture Capital*. Then came the upstart, *VanKirk's Venture Capital Directory*, which listed many of the smaller, "storefront" venture capital firms, and more recently *Galante's Venture Capital and Private Equity Directory*. Typically, these resources list from 650 resources (in *Pratt*), up to about 1,600, the majority of which are institutional resources, not private investors. These directories, and others, such as *Private Fortunes* (Gales Research), the *National Venture Capital Association Directory*, and directories published by regional venture capital associations and government economic development agencies, were the only formal tools available to entrepreneurs 20 years ago.

How useful are these directories? The first indication is that many are no longer published. Importantly, the printed directories were riddled with inaccuracies, for example, incorrect addresses or telephone numbers, listing principals no longer with the firm, and wrong or vague investment criteria crippling the directory's usefulness for matching your deal with investor parameters.

And, most importantly, public listings of investors invited tens of thousands of entrepreneurs starving for capital and unschooled in raising private equity to inundate published listings with over-the-transom, uninvited solicitations. Besides being illegal, this strategy has proven to be largely ineffective.

The two original big players in the investor software database field are now out of business. One had concentrated too much on lending sources, inappropriate for early-stage deals. The other merely put into software the information already printed in venture capital directories and available at a fraction of the cost because of public domain. Regardless, these software resources inherited all the problems associated with printed directories. The only searchable software database still accessible is InfonVC (*www.infon.com*). Its list of 1,700 professional venture capital firms and small business investment companies is within reach by purchasing a license.

With the proliferation of desktop computers and advances in development of relational database software, some firms developed these interactive databases. Such software databases permitted users to query the database for certain criteria that describe their deals, such as how much capital they need, their industry, and the location of the venture. Using this relational database software supposedly generated a list of firms that invest in a particular area. But institutional investors and lenders form the primary resources of these databases, since information about the informal investor is largely unavailable in the public domain. Once again, institutional investors must invest; angels do not have to. Thus, these database developers could easily gather data about more traditional, institutional resources and arrange them in a database format. In addition, many financial intermediaries, investment bankers, and consultants misrepresented themselves as "investors" in these databases, further compromising the software's usefulness in fund-raising.

Another trend to address the venture capital gap was the emergence of incubators to assist seed and early-stage start-ups by providing space, business expertise, and "funding." These business accelerators are established by corporations, business development groups, universities, venture funds, consulting groups, and high-net-worth individuals. Currently, 950 incubators operate in the United States, according to the National Business Incubation Association, up from 587 in 1998.

Business incubation is more about business enterprise development than specifically raising capital. Incubators can provide management assistance and provide business and technical support services. But for the most part, incubators have provided access to capital rather than serving as a direct source of capital itself. That incubators help companies improve their chance of surviving is borne out statistically. However, 84 percent of incubators are nonprofit—whose common sponsors are academic institutions, government, and economic development agencies (56 percent)—and, as can be expected, their primary goals are creating jobs, creating a positive climate for entrepreneurs, keeping businesses in their communities for tax purposes, and accelerating local economic growth. And while incubators themselves create jobs and generate annual earnings, the incubators prime motive is not to help the entrepreneurs raise capital.

Many incubators count on capital from venture capital firms for the companies they incubate. People who direct incubators have realized that those early-stage development companies coming to them for guidance also need to raise capital. To get launched, the incubator movement has had to develop connections with capital. Early on, incubator directors realized that to serve their clients, they had to set up liaisons with the financial community to help investment in these companies so that they, in turn, could grow their incubators.

For entrepreneurs fixed on incubator involvement, their best bet is to inquire if angels are participating in the incubator's advisory board. Since incubators provide access to funding, the incubator may be able to facilitate introductions to appropriate investors within its own circle of contacts. Angels do tend to congregate around professionally sponsored incubators in industries of interest to them. It happens to be an efficient and inexpensive way to find deal flow in industries, stages of development, and local or regional areas of interest to the investor.

In our listing of the different, more formal alternative funding resources, we differentiated between entrepreneurial finance conferences and venture forums. Contrary to the belief of many naive, less-experienced entrepreneurs, entrepreneurial finance conferences are typically limited to educational activities as compared with venture forums, whose mission is more focused on introductions between investors and entrepreneurs. These seminars, workshops, and conferences fill the educational gap left by academic entrepreneurship programs and can help with information on preparing and presenting business plans, pro forma financials, and valuation. But their value is very limited in finding investors. It is not constructive for entrepreneurs to look for guidance in raising capital from academics, not-for-profit seminar organizations, government economic development agency bureaucrats, or self-serving consultants using educative strategies for professional service business development.

It is true, as conference promoters will surely tell you, that you will have the opportunity for networking between educational sessions and at mixers sponsored by the event. And a few entrepreneurs have met investors who ultimately invested in their deal in this way. But networking—that ever-present buzzword of the 1980s—was and remains highly overrated. The indirect approach, such as attending entrepreneurial education events, is not the most effective alternative investor development strategy available. If you are interested in such events, we suggest that you consult calendars of business events in your local newspaper or business journal.

The next alternative funding source is a creative strategy used frequently by ICR to locate, identify, meet with, and speak directly to early-stage, private equity investors. Times have changed, and as capital markets have tightened, new strategies become essential to find the available money. Where might we find those investors aggressively making investments in these difficult economic times? This different source of investor prospects that might be appropriate for your deal is unconventional, but effective.

We have identified the premier educational events in the United States attended by early-stage investors, including venture capitalists, institutional limited partners of venture funds, angel private equity investors, family office advisers, money managers, newly affluent active investors, and CFOs of corporate investors. Thousands of currently active investors attend educational events each year for numerous professional development reasons: to improve fund administration; to identify where the returns are in their market; to get tips on raising their own funds; to improve their appreciation of the wealthy investor market; to identify the best practices for accessing private equity deals; to learn how to better structure their deal portfolios; to learn to improve total return on their portfolios; and to examine the latest developments, trends, and strategies for success in the private placement market. This is a mere sampling of the many important topics covered by successful experts, advisers, peers, and other principals in their presentations at these events. If investors are to hunt successfully for the best deals, they need to be armed with the latest, most intelligent information. Entrepreneurs can take advantage of these events to locate, approach, and meet investors from among presenters, as well as from among audiences attendees.

We refer the reader to our directory in Chapter 9 for contact information; however, in summary, only a few organizations have for years successfully hosted the most prestigious, prominent, relevant, and respected events that consistently have attracted hundreds of investors: the International Business Forum has hosted its Venture Capital Investing Conference for 15 years. Here one can meet hundreds of venture capitalists, institutional investors, limited partners, angel investors, and corporate investors. The Institute for International Research presents the Annual Private Placement Industry Conference and Private Equity Markets Summit for private and institutional investors. Asset Alternatives hosts the VentureOne Exchange and Private Equity Limited Partner Summit for venture capitalists and institutional and private investors interested in investing in early-stage ventures. The Strategic Research Institute holds its Annual Venture Capital Conference and Exposition in New York City and also offers its Private Equity Round Up for the private equity industry players.

An "accredited investor," as defined by the SEC set forth in Rule 501 of Regulation D (17 CFR 230.501), includes "Any natural person whose individual net worth, or joint net worth with that person's spouse, exceeds $1,000,000; of any natural person who had an individual income in excess of $200,000 in each of the two most recent years or joint income with that person's spouse in excess of $300,000 in each of those years and has a reasonable expectation of reaching the same income level in the current year." While the entrepreneur can expect the financial cost of attending these events to be dear, the real probability for meeting investors who conform with the rigorous definition of "accredited investor" is high indeed.

One rewarding way to meet investors is through their advisers. Investors can learn the art of early-stage, private equity investing by trial and error—a potentially costly proposition—or, much better, actively learn from other investors and their advisers about how to invest successfully. Like the entrepreneur struggling with how to learn to raise capital, investors must also learn about the art of investing in high-risk/high-return transactions.

The next alternative for building your pool of investor contacts involves attending and presenting at venture forums. The concept of forums operates on the premise that principal players be brought together, using formal mechanisms to link those who need capital with those who have it. Venture forums are sponsored by nonprofit 501(c)3 organizations, universities, incubators, government economic development organizations, angel groups, entrepreneurial and technology organizations, and for-profit groups involved in funding and investment banking, among others.

Many venture forums have closed their doors since the economic downturn beginning in 2000, as a result of state, federal, and academic funding cutbacks and reduced charitable giving to some nonprofits. However, venture forums remain one tool that entrepreneurs should consider and add to their mix of prospecting strategies—and for good reason. An informal study of only 14 venture forums and introductory networks in the United States in operation for 4 to 15 years each indicates that these groups were responsible for $3,593,800,000 in financings. The forums included in this study are listed below, and those still operating can be found in the attached directory, along with many other resources that did not report their results.

Organization	Date Founded (if available)	$ Amount Invested
California Venture Forum	1994	105,000,000
Central Coast Venture Forum	1996	110,000,000
Springboard Venture Forum	2000	1,000,000,000
NYNMA Venture Downtown	1995	1,000,000,000
New Jersey Venture Fair	1997	382,000,000
Arizona Venture Capital Conference	2001	200,000,000
Florida Venture Forum		558,800,000
Southern California Technology Venture Forum		13,000,000
Northwest Entrepreneurs Network Early-Stage Investment Forum		10,000,000
MidAtlantic Venture Forum	1998	2,000,000
Minnesota Seed Capital Network	1999	20,000,000
Technology Capital Market–MIT		100,000,000
Common Angels		25,000,000

Organization	Date Founded (if available)	$ Amount Invested
International Capital Resources (only 60 of 1,359 investors)		91,000,000
Band of Angels		45,000,000

Investors support and attend these events and participate in networks, activities that result in introductions simply because forums offer a time and cost-efficient way to augment deal flow with promising high-growth ventures in need of early-stage equity investment and because these forums offer exposure to a wider range of deals.

While some promoters use the term *venture forum* to describe what are essentially educational events, entrepreneurs should attend only those events whose sole objective is to provide investors and entrepreneurs the opportunity to meet face to face. Although forums may include keynote speeches or perhaps offer a panel discussion by investors, the most productive venture forums for meeting investors are among those that allow entrepreneur presentations of 10 to 30 minutes, similar to an abbreviated investor road show supported by visuals. To have any credibility with investors, the forum must require a rigorous prescreening process implemented by the host organization and its screening executive or committee to ensure top quality deals for investors. A few forums listed in the directory also provide entrepreneurs with advice on their presentations and business plans included as part of their application fee. Some "deal mart" events allow companies that previously failed to be selected as presenters to display information about their venture at a table or an exhibition booth. The most successful forums enable entrepreneurs to meet with investors directly after the presentations or exhibiting, either in break-out rooms or less formally in social gatherings, such as cocktail receptions hosted by sponsors.

Understand that the prospect of meeting face to face, whether you are a presenter, exhibitor, or attendee, is the chief element in selecting which forums to attend. For example, if the forum hosts an investor panel during which an investor discloses investment criteria consistent with the parameters of your deal, you have the opportunity to approach him or her directly during networking breaks to introduce yourself and begin to build a relationship. This is true whether you are a presenter, an exhibitor, or just an attendee in the audience.

The longevity and success of the most respected venture forums illustrate anew government's role as a barometer reflecting, rather than a catalyst driving, change. The government is just beginning to recognize that forums hosted by nonprofit groups facilitate the exchange and flow of capital from both respectable institutional investors and astute private investors. Furthermore, forums allow these investors a glimpse of deals they would otherwise be unaware of, and at the same time offer entrepreneurs a golden opportunity to acquire funds they have searched for fruitlessly on their own.

Sentiment for change in the government's attitude about forums appears everywhere. Eighty-seven percent of the respondents to a poll conducted by California Capital Access Forum agreed that the Commissioner of Corporations should exempt introductions at venture and investor matching events from being considered as public advertising of private placements. One hundred percent felt that the commissioner's office should provide guidance in this matter of advertising, advertising presently prohibited by California Statute 25102(f).

Through such grass roots polling and other rising pressures, both the SEC and state departments of corporations are beginning to recognize that laws enacted to protect unsophisticated investors from unscrupulous individuals inappropriately restrict deals introduced by experienced entrepreneurs (principals in the ventures) to seasoned investors (highly astute financial analysts with industry track records in this type of investing).

Venture capital clubs operate like venture forums. The chief differences are that clubs are smaller, less formal, and meet more often. But screening of ventures is just as rigorous, although fewer companies present at their meetings and the presentations are shorter. Venture capital clubs that had their start in 1974 with the Connecticut Venture Group are a specialized spin-off not unlike the small investment groups that comprised associations such as the American Association of Individual Investors (AAII). These groups brought together a number of novice investors, supplied them with the proper material, and assisted them in building a portfolio. Maybe they pooled their money; maybe they did not. Perhaps they just worked together. They operated much as informal angel networks do today, but used group-think to improve their understanding and appreciation of investing. Figuring prominently in the mix was the camaraderie and preference to co-invest and share due diligence.

But because traditional investment groups emphasized publicly traded stocks, those interested in venture capital did not feel welcome. So there has come the spin-off of the venture capital club movement, numbering about 150 to 200 venture capital clubs across the country, with typically 12 to 80 members. Members tend to be geographically focused, smaller investors, although the clubs typically include a few more affluent, seasoned angel investors who serve as mentors, as well as participants in transactions. Within the angel investor community, we find a bimodal distribution: One segment invests smaller amounts ($10,000 to $50,000); a second segment invests significantly larger amounts ($100,000 to $1,000,000) over the course of a transaction.

Although individuals in a venture capital club could maintain their privacy, the venture capital club publicizes its endeavor, which stimulates deal flow to the club. This allows individuals to share the deal flow, which increased geometrically, but also share the responsibility of due diligence as well as the investment's risks. A complete list of venture capital clubs in your region is available by contacting ICR at *www.icrnet.com*. Also, some of the most prominent venture clubs are listed in the directory in Chapter 9. In venture capital clubs and offline investor networks, the majority of members are accredited investors, and the most prominent organizations require a member to complete a legal form attesting that he or she meets the previously defined "accredited" status. Members pay dues to help defray operating costs associated with administering the organization, promoting its events and conducting meetings.

Some investor groups have become more formalized, and members are expected to meet investment requirements of the group. Perhaps they are expected to invest a minimum amount each year or pledge to invest an amount over time, for example $25,000 to $150,000 over a number of years. Much like ICR's own network of investors, many new members come not from having seen an advertisement but from a referral from existing investors satisfied with their experience and involvement in the group. The club or group typically has a paid manager or director responsible for operations.

Venture capital clubs usually hold monthly meetings, a breakfast or dinner meeting, for example. The programs are similar. There may be a guest speaker, entrepreneur, or investor, followed by presentations by prescreened companies sponsored by a member. The pitch can last for as little as five minutes to as much as 30, depending on how many presenters the group has scheduled. Added to that are questions from the audience.

Some clubs or groups will decide as a group, through voting, for instance, whether to move to the next step with the company by assigning a member to take the lead in due diligence. Depending on the organization, after due diligence is shared at a subsequent meeting, the group may decide to invest or reject, or individuals may pursue or reject the deal independently.

Prescreening of deal flow is a major activity of these groups. A screening committee or senior member may join with analysts to prescreen and review documentation on the ventures submitted for consideration. They assess whether the deal fits their criteria. Regardless, the deal reaps serious consideration, possibly securing a "sponsor" for management that helps the deal along among existing members of the club or group.

We believe that in the next few years entrepreneurs will see the advent of a cohesive infrastructure provided for active investors through regional informal networks, more formal investment clubs with a professional manager, and, for more passive investors, pledge funds, as well as limited partnership funds specifically for angels. By pooling money and sharing risk, the duties involved in the angel process, and the tasks associated with it, more formal angel investment structures can open the door to larger, more developed deals of less risk for investors. By sharing the task with more experienced investors, novice investors can avoid pitfalls, and so create more informed evaluation, as well as help to increase angel investors' co-investment resources and access to portfolio diversification.

For example, a large number of benefits emanate from the angel club concept. We think that these represent something less organized than a fund, a more informal structure that active investor colleagues tell the authors they are looking for. They help reduce some risk, and in many cases do so with less resource obligation. It's a great help in processing deal flow, especially when you start generating high levels of deal flow and it helps to leverage investor's time, energy, and financial cost associated with due diligence. It allows the members to candidly become the sponsors of the deals they like among a peer group, and it allows the highly isolated angel investor who may not live in a major metropolitan area to expand their co-investment circle. It provides a discreet way for mentorship of less experienced investors, and it can, from our experience at ICR, expand due diligence. All these factors combine to reduce the risk of early-stage investing.

By organizing deal flow development mechanisms through the club, the deal flow is increased and, because numerous people are involved in the club, managing the due diligence for the larger deal flow or at least the prescreening process becomes more feasible. Because membership includes angel investors from a range of disciplines and functional types of expertise, the ability of the club improves not only to invest but to help get the companies into shape for future institutional or venture capital rounds.

Our research does suggest that about 65 percent of angel investing is done on a regional basis anyway, and this lends itself to the idea of regional investment clubs. Currently, the regional focus is sometimes refined further to an industry focus, or a stage of development focus. Also some angel clubs have developed an incubator division by packaging the expertise of the angels who provide advice for business, function in an advisory board capacity to presenting companies, and assist companies further in raising capital.

The bottom line for entrepreneurs is the capital. When dealing with clubs or offline investment groups, investors can invest capital in different ways; for example, individuals invest directly into the company; the club could set up a fund or LLC that collects money from members; then a fund/LLC invests in the company, or the organization itself may pool money of members with outside investment partners, and the organization itself invests into the company.

The offline investor network offers a different type of resource. ICR uses a number of proprietary and pioneering techniques to build angel and private equity investor databases, develop deal flow, enhance entrepreneur documentation and presentations, and facilitate bringing ventures and capital together. The firm uses all the mechanisms listed as alternative funding resources in conjunction with its proprietary database of investors to identify a "fit" between a qualified venture and an investor's criteria, and to help bring the parties together and build relationships that lead to financing. The 17-year successful history of the firm is available at *www.icrnet.com*.

Wealth management professionals understand that as the size of the wealth market increases every day, so too do they need to be aware of the new breed of investor and potential client. Affluent investors now expect and demand online access to information, security, and the same high level of client services. The key for these professionals is to ensure that their Internet efforts meet the desires of current clients, as well as attract the newly affluent market. Using online financial services is more common today than five years ago. However, the concerns for privacy protection and confidentiality of information online remain the same.

The next category of alternative investor resources is online matching and search services. The oldest is the MIT Venture Capital Network. Whenever computer technology matches the criteria of an investment with those of the investor, the network sends the investor an executive summary describing the venture. This process preserves confidentiality—the big issue—while creating an added value: Investors receive only those deals that meet their criteria. These networks supply a valuable service, and studies echo the refrain of participating investors: They appreciate the screening and the privacy that these organizations furnish.

Of course, since few charge fees beyond those for the processing of documents, these networks also provide entrepreneurs and investors with an inexpensive mechanism to expose their deals. And to avoid conflict with securities laws, networks charge no finder's fee. Still, they do endure a rigorous qualifying procedure before being granted their nonprofit status.

Investing or finding investors or investments online is different from other alternative resources because most experts agree that angel and venture capital investing is felt to be based on a face-to-face relationship. Since the Internet may be changing these expectations somewhat, entrepreneurs should contemplate the options offered on the Web when they consider the financing tools they might use to gain access to private equity investors. Today's entrepreneurs need to adapt and learn new roles and responsibilities in accessing the newly affluent.

Though predicted in the late 1990s pre–dot-com bubble burst era by business magazine sages and research gurus, the "capital democracy" that was supposed to emerge from the Internet and create an active, efficient capital market linking investors and entrepreneurs in low-cost transactions has not yet materialized. Venture capital is not being raised in large amounts online, nor has angel capital matched online swelled to the optimistic levels predicted at that time.

Our research for the resource directory in Chapter 9 confirms this. We visited more than 2,000 online web sites, compiled as finance resources between 1998 and 2003. These were publicized or described as alternative funding resources that fit our listings presented in this chapter. Of the 2,000 sites, 85 percent were out of business; the domain name was for sale, or the owners had changed their business to something other than facilitating early-stage financing. This is a sobering fact for entrepreneurs assessing various alternative funding routes, paths, and mechanisms, because if they are going to spend time and resources on trying to raise capital, they want to make sure they are using an effective resource.

Private equity investing is not being changed by the Internet, but it can be helped by it. The higher ROI potential and the recent recovery of segments of the venture capital market will continue to fuel interest in private equity investing over the Web. The freedom of viewing deals, easily and quickly, at minimal cost of time and money on well-designed, full-service sites continues to be a draw for some investors, a number that will likely increase. As long as the site addresses the most pressing concern of the wealthy market—privacy and security—then the web sites have a chance. The safety of information available online must not be compromised. Sites must protect the investor's identity, contact information, and choices. In addition, web site managers must absorb relevant SEC and National Association of Securities Dealers (NASD) guidelines. (We refer the reader to our Appendix B for details.)

The concept that entrepreneurs will meet angels through an Internet network does seem to contradict much of what we have emphasized in this book. Investors prize their privacy (we need hardly say it again) and will be reluctant to share on a web site their names, addresses, and the like. To do so would expose them to every crank deal and oddball character in cyberspace. So the way for entrepreneurs to take advantage of these resources is to look for respected sites, sites with a history, sites willing to publish their investment results, provide significant security measures, and, most important, post only prescreened deals that meet their investors' posted criteria. Also, these sites must meet all state and federal legal requirements. Listed in our directory are a number of Internet matching and search services still in operation and that claim to have investors.

Last, but of major focus, our research implies that financial intermediaries are a rich resource for locating private investors for the entrepreneur's venture. Within the alternative capital resource classification of financial intermediaries, we include finders, select access database firms, brokers, and placement agents.

The great English Renaissance figure Francis Bacon bemoaned the truth that "In all things no man can be exquisite." We simply cannot do all things, much less do them well. It is no weakness, then, to admit that you need help in raising capital. Managing your business leaves little time to raise money. When neglected, businesses suffer. Worse, the principal who ignores the company's operating responsibilities while building capital will neglect the unwelcome blips certain to appear on the company's radar screen, problems that can quickly mushroom into dire circumstances.

Financial intermediaries are professional service providers whose sole function is to help the entrepreneur raise money. The competent intermediary becomes your marketing partner and increases your efficiency and effectiveness in raising the capital being sought. Using an intermediary enables you to spend more time on your venture, and less on raising money. In a word, using an intermediary is simply more efficient.

Perhaps you believe you do not need help from an intermediary because you have raised money in the past. But think about how much the market has changed over the past five years: You are competing with tens of thousands of money managers and perhaps hundreds of thousands of deals. Many alternative asset classes besides venture capital and private equity are competing for the same money. Six hundred fifty venture capital funds and 16,000 registered investment advisers are all after the same high-net-worth investors. Moreover, many ventures are vying for the attention of private investors. Thus, while you have been immersed in growing your business, several major changes have occurred: Start-ups need more money; external capital and financing have diminished; and more competition exists for start-up capital.

In some cases, entrepreneurs have only raised money from cofounders, family, and friends. But success at raising cradle equity does not correlate with success at raising capital from unrelated angels or venture capitalists who will subject a proposal to extensive due diligence.

In some cases, entrepreneurs have been away from the fund-raising market for three to five years. Since the dot-com fiasco, the investor roster has changed, as have the amounts investors are willing to part with. It is easy to lose touch with the dynamic angel and private equity market. It is not uncommon to meet an entrepreneur who raised millions in the early to mid 1990s, yet suddenly cannot seem to raise a penny beyond family and friends today. He or she may no longer know today's investors—and much depends on knowing investors well. The competent financial intermediary knows investors well.

Financial intermediaries—whether finder, broker, database manager, or placement agent—have one thing in common: the underlying financial skill derived from investment banking. And the investment banking landscape has changed dramatically during the past five years, when consolidation has reigned. In San Francisco, Hambrecht and Quist, Robertson Stephens, Alex Brown, and Montgomery Securities have closed, with some having merged into larger financial institutions. The industry lost 6,000 jobs from January to June of 2003 alone!

A shift to research has occurred, creating reliable research reports on private equity, something lacking in the post–dot-com bust because the market for investment banking services has contracted severely. The large firms, such as Goldman Sachs, Morgan Stanley, CS First Boston, Merrill Lynch, and J.P. Morgan Chase, issued 264 IPOs at a mean value of only $300 million per deal. The competition among these investment banks is stiff.

While the top-tier firms like those mentioned above and second-tier firms like SG Cowen, along with regional brokerages with large retail departments (e.g., Piper Jaffay) will not be appropriate for early-stage companies seeking angel investors, their plight, and that of boutique investment banks, will have an impact on the accessibility of financial intermediaries who can help the entrepreneur.

The financial intermediary's stock in trade is having a pool of investor prospects with whom they have existing relationships, and knowing about these investors and their preferences and criteria. They can identify who in their database or region is actively investing and what they are looking for in investments. In addition, they are aware of your competition, other deals out there, and the valuation and deal structure terms and conditions being agreed to in completed transactions. Furthermore, they understand what channels of communication are most effective in reaching their contacts, and what is necessary on the entrepreneur's part to get the deal noticed. The competent intermediary adds value by helping him or her determine if his or her deal is even right for the private equity market in the first place. And ensuring that the documentation and offering are compelling and consistent with the investor's expectations.

A financial intermediary helps you accomplish things quickly—a special benefit for start-ups, development firms, or expansion ventures lacking stellar performance records. In their up-to-date databases, intermediaries keep detailed records of those private investors who have responded to introductions; they can link you to qualified investors, casting a wider net for prospective investors, helping you win appointments. The role of the intermediary is, after all, to match legitimate buyers (investors) to legitimate sellers (entrepreneurs) and to introduce entrepreneurs only to investors who have expressed a strong interest in their deal.

Investors and entrepreneurs alike see the competent intermediary as value-added, as a marketing partner, not as a retail salesperson peddling stocks and bonds. The competent intermediary retained at a reasonable price will save you time and improve your chances of success with information and follow-ups of qualified leads. He or she can help you meet your fund-raising goal, thus reducing your risk of falling short. Meanwhile, by spending more time building your company, you can make money for your other investors. Remember, your business is to make money, not raise it.

As competition for the investment dollar of the high-net-worth market increases, how can the intermediary help the entrepreneur to create private offerings that will attract wealthy investors?

What exactly do intermediaries do? During interviews the intermediary assesses the chemistry among the partners. He or she becomes involved in what normally turns into a full-time relationship. The intermediary will help with the business plan and offering memoranda—all amounting to a financing proposal package. The good intermediary will also help prepare sales material and put together a marketing road map. The professional intermediary is a competent, full-time person with whom you will share a positive relationship.

Depending on how much time intermediaries are retained to work the entrepreneur's campaign, they will prospect investors, using a number of channels open to them. They mail, fax, or e-mail information and make telephone calls to selected or interested investors whose criteria fit with the entrepreneur's deal. They will introduce the deal without leading or selling them unless they are a licensed broker-dealer.

While private investors are difficult to reach because of their schedules, the good intermediary knows how and when to contact them. The able intermediary will get through to investors with greater efficiency, getting to prospects the entrepreneur's summary or "elevator pitch." He or she will earn consideration for the entrepreneur's deal because investors appreciate referrals from a respected intermediary.

One caveat, however, is in order to ensure that the entrepreneur holds reasonable expectations: The task of an intermediary in a private placement of an angel investor is to match the investor with the deal, not sell you or your deal. Selling yourself and your deal is your responsibility, not that of the intermediary. The intermediary also helps prepare financial proposals and venture documents and provides feedback, sometimes delivering criticism others would feel uncomfortable mentioning. They can change the way you market yourself. Last, well-organized intermediaries document their activities, providing call reports of contacts, leads qualified, and schedules of presentations. Experienced intermediaries can also coach entrepreneurs in their presentation skills and can alert them to what investors are looking for.

The following list details the services that a good financial intermediary will and will not perform.

A good intermediary:

- Will not represent any deal.
- Will not place the burden of screening on the investor and will prescreen deals to meet investor requirements.
- Will not make an introduction to an entrepreneur without knowing the investor's capability and criteria.
- Will understand a deal before introducing it to investors.
- Will not waste an investor's time with inappropriate or poorly prepared deals.
- Will assist entrepreneurs and investors with the increasing administrative workload associated with introducing investors in private placements.
- Will not "sell" a deal to investors, or undersell an introduction.
- Will create multiple opportunities for entrepreneurs to tell their story.
- Will follow up introductions, but only when there is reason for doing so.
- Will not use pressure in introductory activities.

Financial intermediaries help entrepreneurs raise money and place highly illiquid securities. The intermediary will provide prospects, and the intermediary will supply counsel on other programs to expand the investor pool from beyond their contacts as well, for example, venture clubs, forums, and so on. Intermediaries will work on smaller deals unattractive to larger investment banks, retail brokers, and boutique investment groups. They work exclusively on private placements and have a cultivated database of investors they can bring to the table to consider qualified deals. They are experienced in and knowledgeable about the private equity market and will be the entrepreneur's guide through the capital-raising minefield. Last, they possess an innate aptitude for fund-raising, a quality lacking in many more technical entrepreneurs.

The question remains: How do you find a competent, trustworthy intermediary? Intermediaries abound. But the entrepreneur must select one who can get the job done. Most seem charming, articulate, persuasive, and assertive. But to find the best, look below the surface. Ask your attorney, your accountant, and advisers whom they respect and why. But also gain firsthand knowledge of those you consider: Read their books; attend their speeches; visit their offices; speak to their partners and associates. Speak to them yourself. Ask whom they represent, how they work with clients, what they charge, and what results they have achieved.

Finally, ensure that your company fits the intermediary's profile. Also ensure that no conflict exists between your venture and any other of the intermediary's current or prospective clients. Then talk with some of the intermediary clients, both entrepreneurs and investors. Last, select the most qualified intermediary based on price. A good intermediary will help you raise money and finish the job quickly.

The time and the money saved by a skillful financial intermediary will more than cover the cost of their fees.

CHAPTER 9

Directory of Alternative Funding Resources

In this chapter, we have compiled a comprehensive directory of alternative funding sources. Inventors, entrepreneurs, and small business owners looking for early-stage or expansion capital can use resources listed below to grow their pool of angel, venture capital, and corporate investor prospects. The categories presented include the following:

- Directories, printed and software-based
- Incubators
- Entrepreneurial finance conferences
- Investor education meetings and conferences
- Venture forums
- Venture capital clubs
- Offline investor networks
- Online matching and search services
- Financial intermediaries

DIRECTORIES, PRINTED AND SOFTWARE-BASED

Galante's Venture Capital and Private Equity Directory. Published by Asset Alternatives, 170 Linden Street, Second Floor, Wellesley, MA 02482 (781) 304-1400. This directory contains almost 1,760 profiles of venture capital and other private equity firms. The directory is also available on CD-ROM in a searchable software database.

Corporate Finance Sourcebook. Published by National Register Publishers at *www.nationalregisterpub.com*. This directory lists 1,600 investment sources and 1,800 professional service firms. A handy resource for entrepreneurs seeking financial intermediaries to assist them in raising capital.

INFONVC. A searchable software database, accessible by purchasing a license. The software lists 1,700 venture capital firms and SBICs. Available at *www.infon.com.*

INCUBATORS

National Business Incubation Association (NBIA). A complete list of incubators in your region is available from NBIA. Contact: *www.NBIA.org.*

ENTREPRENEURIAL FINANCE CONFERENCES

ICR's Angel Financing Conference. The premier entrepreneurial finance educational event in the United States. This is not a networking event or forum; it is an intensive educational workshop on understanding what investors want, how to present and structure your business plan and investor presentation, how to target the angel market, and how to work with investors you have been introduced to through alternative funding resources. More than 50,000 entrepreneurs have attended this event since 1989. The presenters have been sponsored by more than 200 major entrepreneurial organizations. Contact: International Capital Resources, 388 Market Street, Suite 500, San Francisco, CA 94111. (415) 296-2519. *www.icrnet.com.*

INVESTOR EDUCATION MEETINGS AND CONFERENCES

International Business Forum (IBF). Produces a number of conferences, including Venture Capital Investing, Corporate Venturing and Strategic Investing, and Early-Stage Venture Investing. Contact: IBF, 575 Broadway, Massapequa, Long Island, NY 11758. (516) 765-9005.

Institute for International Research (IIR). Produces such conferences as Private Placements Industry Conference, Private Investment Strategies Summit, and the Family Office Forum. Contact: IIR 708 Third Ave., Fourth Floor, New York, NY 10017. (888) 670-8200.

Strategic Research Institute (SRI). Produces such conferences as Investing in Early-Stage Deals, The Private Equity Roundup, and The Venture Capital Conference and Exposition. Contact: SRI, 236 W. 27th Street, Eighth Floor, New York, NY 10001. (646) 336-7030.

VENTURE FORUMS

Council for Entrepreneurial Development (CED). CED encourages and assists entrepreneurial development in North Carolina. Members include entrepreneurs, investors, financiers, service professionals, public policy makers, and university faculty who focus on the needs of Triangle area growth companies. CED provides a forum where members share their expertise to create a supportive environment for growth companies in North Carolina. CED also produces an Annual Venture Conference during which a number of presenting companies have been successful at meeting investors and raising capital. Contact: CED, P.O. Box 13353, Research Triangle Park, NC 27709. (919) 549-7500 (ext. 117). fax: (919) 549-7405. *www.ced.nc.org.*

North Florida Venture Capital Network (NFVCN). Managed by Enterprise North Florida Corporation, the not-for-profit NFVCN is designed for private investors, angels, and institutional investment companies seeking information on companies in need of financing. It is likewise designed for business and investment service providers and not-for-profit entrepreneurial support organizations throughout northern Florida. Contact: NFVCN, 4905 Belfort Road, Suite 110, Jacksonville, FL 32256.

Oklahoma Investment Forum (OIF). The Southwest Capital Conference by OIF showcases approximately 30 high-growth regional companies and hosts an Innovation Expo that provides a look at new products, technology, and ideas being developed in Oklahoma. Attendees include venture capitalists and private equity investors from around the country interested in early-stage companies. Contact: Oklahoma Investment Forum, 415 South Boston, Suite 800, Tulsa, OK 74103. (918) 584-8884.

Mid-Atlantic Venture Conference. Provides a forum for entrepreneurs to present to potential investors and produces a Private Equity Investment Conference that highlights a variety of young investment opportunities from the Mid-Atlantic region. Industry focus is on IT, nanotechnology, telecom, and biotech. Hosted by the Greater Philadelphia Venture Group. Angels and venture capitalists attend. Contact: Mid-Atlantic Venture Conference, Eastern Technology Council, 435 Devon Park Drive, Bldg. 600, Suite 613, Wayne, PA 19087. (610) 975-9430. *www.mavc.org.*

Private Investors Network (PIN). PIN, an angel network whose parent organization is the Mid-Atlantic Venture Association, brings together accredited investors and growth companies in Maryland, Virginia, and the District of Columbia. Contact: Private Investors Network, The Baltimore-Washington Venture Group c/o Dingman Center for Entrepreneurship, The

Maryland Business School, University of Maryland, College Park, MD 20742. (301) 405-2144. fax: (301) 314-9152.

CT Venture Group. The largest venture forum in the Northeast. In its eleventh year, considered a major venue for accessing capital. The Crossroads Venture Fair assists the development of high-growth enterprises by promoting capital formation in Connecticut. Contact: *www.cvg.org.*

Private Investors Forum. Provides a forum for entrepreneurs to present business plans to investors for the purpose of obtaining financing. Sophisticated institutional and private investors who invest in small, privately held, early-stage companies attend. Members make their own decisions; this group is not an investment pool. Investors negotiate their own terms directly with the company. Contact: *www.AngelVentureFair.com.*

Southern California Technology Venture Forum. Offers premier companies an unparalleled opportunity to position themselves competitively in the search for private investment. Sponsored by Ernst & Young LLP; Southern California Edison Investor Forums; Troop, Stuber, Pasich, Reddick & Tobey; Jones Day, and Wedbush Morgan Securities. Contact: Southern California Technology Venture Forum, 515 South Flower Street, 32nd Floor, Los Angeles, CA 90071. (213) 236-4845

California Venture Forum. California Venture Forum showcases and matches start-up and early-stage companies with an audience of potential venture capitalists and private investors. The forum is sponsored by Southern California Edison among others. Contact: Tech Coast SBDC, 2 Park Plaza, Suite 100, Irvine, CA 92614. (949) 476-2242.

Central Coast Venture Forum. An all-day forum for linking venture investors and growth companies seeking capital in Santa Barbara, Ventura, San Luis Obispo, and Northern Los Angeles counties. Showcases the region's fastest growing entrepreneurial, early-stage ventures and emerging growth companies. Angels and venture capitalists attend. Sponsored by the Central Coast Venture Forum (CCVF). Contact: CCVF, 402 E. Gutierre Street, Santa Barbara, CA 93101. (805) 879-5202.

Arizona Venture Capital Conference. An annual program that brings together the region's leading investors and venture capitalists with emerging-growth businesses seeking funding. Focuses on companies from the Southwest, sponsored by the Greater Phoenix Chamber of Commerce. Forty percent of presenting companies have raised some funding. Contact: Arizona Venture Capital Conference, Greater Phoenix Chamber of Commerce, 201 North Central Ave., Suite 2700, Phoenix, AZ 85073. (602) 254-5521.

Emerging Technology Business Showcase. This forum for technology-based businesses in Florida attracts companies with the potential for $10 million to $15 million in minimum sales seeking capital funding to introduce investors seeking investment in technology-based businesses. Rigorous screening by a selection committee. Contact: Enterprise Development Corporation of South Florida, 3416 S. University, Deerfield Beach, FL 33328. (954) 577-8722.

The Springboard Venture Capital Forum Series. Springboard Enterprises' venture capital forums are intended to increase access of women-led firms to investment opportunities and to assist women entrepreneurs in navigating the equity markets. The forums provide women entrepreneurs with a platform for greater visibility and strategic connections to investment and business development experts in the community. Seven forums have been held in major markets since early 2000. Contact: Springboard Enterprises, c/o GWV at Mt. Vernon College/Somers, 2100 Foxhall Road N.W., Washington, DC 20007. (202) 242-6282.

Investment in Innovation. This two-day event highlights emerging technologies being developed by more than 50 small, mostly privately held medical technology companies seeking partnering and/or investment. The meeting will draw an attendance of up to 300 or more senior executives from the investment community and major medical technology, biopharmaceutical, biotech, and other companies. Contact: Med Tech Insight, 21071 Cedar Lane, Mission Viejo, CA 92691. (714) 969-7648.

Venturenet. This venture capital forum presents approximately 20 Internet and software companies, and offers an equivalent number of nonpresenting companies featured in their entrepreneurial exhibit area. Extensive prescreening to select presenting companies by a committee of bankers, attorneys, accountants, angel investors, and venture capitalists, among others. Contact: Software Council of Southern California, 2461 W. 208th Street, Suite 202, Torrance, CA 90501. (301) 328-0043.

Florida Venture Forum. This forum assists entrepreneurs in identifying sources of capital. While its roots were in education, it is now in its 14th year and has attracted more than $558 million in investment for later-stage Florida companies. Contact: *www.flvencap.org.*

Early-Stage Investment Forum. Presented by the Northwest Entrepreneurs Network. An event for early-stage start-ups to present business plans to prospective angel investors and venture capitalists. Deals are subject to conscientious prescreening. Approximately 15 companies each present for 15 minutes. Exhibit space is also available. Contact: Northwest Entrepreneurs Network, P.O. Box 40128, Bellevue, WA 98015. (425) 564-5701.

Great Midwest Venture Capital Conference. A 13-year-old forum for introduction of early-stage companies to an audience of high-risk, private, and institutional investors. Aggressive prescreening. Approximately 26 companies will each present for up to 12 minutes. Contact: Indiana Business Modernization & Technology Corporation, 10 West Market Street, Suite 450, Indianapolis, IN 46204. (317) 635-3058. *www.gmvcc.com.*

Angel Oregon and Venture Oregon. This annual conference and forum host speakers, panels, and invite prescreened companies to present to an audience of investors and service providers. Approximately 350 attend. Contact: Oregon Entrepreneurs Forum, 309 SW Sixth Ave., Suite 212, Portland, OR 97204. (503) 222-2270.

Annual Investment Conference. In its 10th year, this forum is hosted by the Massachusetts Software Council. The objective is to provide presenting companies access to capital. About 200 technology angel and venture capitalist investors attend this annual event. Contact: Massachusetts Software Council, One Exeter Plaza, Boston, MA 02116. (617) 437-0600 (Ext. 14).

University of Upstate New York Venture Forum. Exclusively to spotlight university spin-off ventures in various high technology disciplines. Investors attending include angels, venture capitalists, and corporate technology partners. Contact: (716) 636-3651. *www.resuny.org.*

Long Island Capital Alliance. Focused on bringing together entrepreneurs, investors, and service providers for community benefit. Provides the Long Island/New York Metro Capital Forum. In its ninth year, up to 20 companies will present to an audience of capital providers. About 500 attendees. Contact: *www.Licapital.org/CapitalForum.*

VENTURE CAPITAL CLUBS

A complete listing of venture clubs in your region is available at *www.icr-net.com,* or call (415) 296-2519.

Houston Angel Network (HAN). An investment group that conducts monthly meetings. Provides presentation opportunities to Houston area early-stage companies. Founded in 1999, HAN focuses on IT, life sciences, space sciences, and energy. The angel network hosts the meetings for investors to view presentations by prescreened applicant companies. Contact: Houston Angel Network, 410 Pierce Street, Houston, TX 77002. (832) 476-9291.

New Jersey Entrepreneurial Network. Holds a monthly "elevator pitch" meeting. Some educational focus, but emphasis is on brief elevator pitch style introductions by companies followed by networking. Investors and service providers attend. Contact: *www.njen.com.*

Tech Coast Venture Network. Brings together entrepreneurs, capital sources, and service providers at its meetings and conferences. Focus is on the Orange County/Southern California business community. Contact: Tech Coast Venture Network, 1405 Warner Ave., Tustin, CA 92780. (714) 258-8347.

128VC Group. A venture capital club with monthly meetings. The group offers a networking venue of individual investors and professional venture capitalists interested in emerging technologies and markets. Presenting companies introduce themselves to the group and explain their goals. Contact: *www.128VCG.com.*

Venture Association New Jersey (VANJ). Hosts periodic monthly elevator pitch meetings with entrepreneurs presenting briefly to investors and service providers. Also offers educational events and Annual Entrepreneur Expo, offering exhibit space to entrepreneurs. Contact: VANJ, P.O. Box 1982, Morristown, NJ 07962. (973) 631-5680.

Ohio Venture Association (OVA). Hosts its five-minute forum monthly. Business owners present brief descriptions of venture opportunity for the purpose of helping raise capital. Focus is on new ventures seeking early-stage investors. Prescreened ventures present business plans that must conform to OVA guidelines. Contact: Ohio Venture Association, 1120 Chester Ave., Suite 470, Cleveland, OH 44114. (216) 566-8884.

Gathering of Angels. A group holding monthly meetings of private, high-net-worth investors, venture capitalists, and service providers from the New Mexico region. Its mission is to provide seed-level financing to start-ups and early-stage firms, and to help with growth financing. Each month four presentations are made by companies prescreened by the executive director and steering/review committee. Contact: *www.gatheringofangels.com.*

Rockies Venture Club (RVC). A nonprofit organization serving as a catalyst to entrepreneurs in the Mountain Region. Entrepreneurs seeking capital funding from this area are invited to the RVC monthly meetings. The club presents a series of five-minute presentations followed by dinner and networking. Angels and venture capitalists in attendance. Contact: Rockies Venture Club, 1805 S. Bellaire, Suite 480, Denver, CO 80222. (303) 758-3885.

Minnesota Seed Capital Network. Introduces private investors to high-tech, early-stage firms trying to raise capital in the $250,000 to $5,000,000 range. Entrepreneurs who present are prescreened by a steering committee that selects or rejects them. Committee includes investors, academics, executives, attorneys, accountants, and public relations professionals. Claims 47 companies have raised capital. Contact: Minnesota Project Innovation, 100 Mill Place, 111 Third Ave. S., Minneapolis, MN 55401. (612) 338-3280.

Common Angels. A group of 50 Boston area private investors. All have founded and/or run high-tech companies. They work with and invest in start-ups to help build successful IT, software, and Internet companies. Claims to have financed 22 companies. Contact: *www.commonangels.com.*

Band of Angels. A formal group of 100 former and current high-tech executives who provide counsel and investment capital to start-up companies, bridge capital, and follow-on financing rounds through their Band of Angels Fund, L.P. Contact: *www.bandangels.com.*

OFFLINE INVESTOR NETWORKS

International Capital Resources. A uniquely positioned angel and early-stage investing company. Since 1989 the company has built a prequalified database of 1,359 accredited investors. A recent study of 60 of these investors reports investments exceeding $90,000,000 into 46 companies over the previous 5 years. The company works with entrepreneurial clients to build a pool of investors for current and future financing rounds using a number of proprietary investor development programs pioneered by the founder.

ONLINE MATCHING AND SEARCH SERVICES

www.cfol.com. Focuses on entrepreneurs and angel investors. Commercial Finance Online (CFOL) boasts the largest business finance search engine in the world. CFOL assists with new referral partner development through a variety of searches, partnering sites, web pages, and links to help fund your business.

www.dealflow.com. DealFlow is strictly an information service, not a venture capital firm or a broker-dealer. It offers a free listing to an entrepreneur or a venture in need of capital and the expertise of private investors; it also offers a free search of ventures by private investors or venture capitalists. In DealFlow, an entrepreneur can search by keyword to find investors interested in particular products and markets before submitting his or her name to the list. Meanwhile, private investors can download venture listings immediately. In addition, DealFlow contains a Strategic Partner database.

www.venturescape.com. For entrepreneurs with promising start-ups, Venturescape is a portal to venture capitalists and institutional investors. The visitor can search for venture capital sources on the Venturescape database and route their business plan to selected venture capital firms through the site.

www.businessfinance.com. For more developed small businesses, business-finance offers operating companies the capability to search for more traditional growth financing, such as loans, equipment lease financing, and factoring.

www.angeldeals.com. An outgrowth from the Venturepreneurs Network, Angeldeals serves the Northeastern United States. Originally conceived to assist in funding early-stage deals, Angeldeals is now an online resource network for entrepreneurs seeking funding, consultants seeking clients, and people seeking jobs. The site claims an online mechanism to connect entrepreneurs with private investors and venture capitalists.

www.vfinance.com. vfinance offers an online search service for venture capitalists and angels. Visitors can post their business plan, and the site publishes venture capital data. The site claims to attract deal flow for investor-client consideration, and therefore provides some level of brokerage services.

www.mincorp.org. The Minnesota Investment Network started in 1998 after being capitalized by Minnesota Technology Inc. MINCORP is a community development venture capital fund. Its goal is to provide equity capital to Minnesota companies while focusing on growth companies that have the potential to both grow revenues and ROI and create jobs in the region.

www.localfund.com. Localfund functions much like a portal and offers access to regional capital sources through its central database site. Localfund has affiliate groups located across the United States that host networks in their respective geographic regions.

www.tcnmit.com. Technology Capital Network is a not-for-profit service organization that connects start-ups and high-growth companies to potential investors through a confidential web-based listing service. TCN claims accredited investors with special interest in early-stage companies. This organization is subscription based, and is not a broker or investment adviser.

www.venturevest.com. VentureVest Capital Corporation offers a matching service called VentureVest Angel Network that claims to bring together angel investors from the Rockies and Southwest with emerging companies seeking additional capital to achieve corporate goals.

www.capmatch.com. Capmatch is an online matching service for entrepreneurs and angel investors. Investors can search for investment opportunities and browse short entrepreneur-prepared elevator pitch summaries. Investors contact entrepreneurs if they are interested.

www.capitalsearch.net. The Capital Solutions Network through the Venture Cast program offers a web-marketing application to showcase ventures to investors via the Internet and e-mail. Capital Search claims to be a resource for entrepreneurs and investors to joint venture on projects of mutual interest.

www.privateequity.com. PrivateEquity is a portal offering a wide range of links that provide resources for companies raising capital. The resource types included are capital, service providers, search firms, investment bankers, and education resources.

www.businesspartners.net. Business Partners is a nationwide Internet-based listing service connecting potential partners, angel investors, investment bankers, and venture capital firms with start-ups, businesses, and entrepreneurs. Its service to its members include, among other things, a full listing search, private and federal grant searches, business incubator searches, business partnering, business buyers and sellers, and business consultants.

www.ventureseek.com. Venture Seek currently has ten investors on its site. This resource is for entrepreneurs seeking capital and funding for start-ups and growth companies. The site claims a secure and easy-to-use online application for entrepreneurs to showcase ventures to potential investors, venture capitalists, and angels. The visitor creates a listing providing a brief overview of investment parameters. Investors' profiles are also provided with an anonymous code number to determine their investment criteria before listing your venture.

www.acenet.csusb.edu. ACENET is currently undergoing a restructuring. The SBA, in concert with securities regulatory agencies and with guidance from investment organizations, created ACENET. ACENET claims to be a service that posts the securities offerings of small, growing companies that can be viewed anonymously by accredited investors, especially those interested in woman- or minority-owned companies. In 2000, the SBA approved the privatization of ACENET Network operators, and ACENET became an independent not-for-profit.

FINANCIAL INTERMEDIARIES

Refer to the Corporate Finance Sourcebook listing in this chapter under the heading "directories," or browse *www.icrnet.com.*

CHAPTER 10

Building Your Own Database of Angel Investors

INTRODUCTION

New technology comes bundled with steep learning curves. As one story goes, during the 12th century reign of Henry II, forks made their first appearance in England, much to the bewilderment of all the nobles at court. Unsure of what forks were and how to use them, those gathered at dinner that first night pondered the matter a good while, then finally figured it out—or so they thought. No longer hesitant, England's nobility vigorously proceeded to poke each other in the eyes.

So we have in extremis the consequences of unleashing the latest technology on the uninitiated. To be sure, setting up a highly sophisticated computer program is far less painful than the jab of a fork in the eye; still, the irritation and torment of the former can be sizable. For many, there remains hardly anything more mystifying than using a computerized relational database. Even with the help of experts, pitfalls await. In particular, entrepreneurs going it alone need to understand what they are in for. What skills will they need to master to build a database? What technical expertise will ensure that information so painstakingly gained is not lost—information gathered from an alternative funding network, an individual search effort, or a financial intermediary?

But first, the question: What is a relational database? A relational database consists of data from which relationships among various pieces of information can be established, allowing the user of the database to look for specific fields, either individually or in combination. These fields—names, addresses, investment criteria, and so on—make up individual records; multiple records make up a database file. A relational database connects these fields—pieces of data—from the various records to target particular markets the user wishes to reach. The user might want to assemble all individuals within a specific income level living in a particular zip code area. In a relational database, the end user can pluck any combination of fields from any combination of records, enabling him or her to relate only the desired information.

Relational databases replace old-fashioned databases, those composed of so-called flat files, tediously rigid sets of information. Similar to relational databases, traditional databases offer only whole records, but the various fields within those records cannot be isolated and then joined with matching fields from other records in the database. The whole record is pulled, or nothing is pulled at all. The telephone book is a nonrelational database. In using it, the address cannot be pulled separately from the name and then related electronically to its counterpart in other areas of the telephone book. This example illustrates the value of a relational database.

The strengths of a relational database, as we have indicated, lie in the ease of accessing data. A relational database allows the user to better target a specific audience. The user can pick out with a keystroke or two only those fields desired. People can be selected by preferred investment size or by last name. In a relational database, all information is incorporated within one big file and all fields or records can be related within that file, indexed, or grouped in any number of ways, depending again on the objective of the search.

HURDLES

Database expert Don Siebert, who built ICR's relational database, warns of the problems even experienced database managers face in establishing a database for the end user. Setting up fields in each record is only the first among the tasks awaiting someone about to embark on the murky electronics of database development. There is no margin for error. Even very sophisticated relational database programs are unforgiving. For example, a field containing "Smith, Jr." can precipitate problems. No comma is allowed, for example, in a program that uses the comma to delimit fields (i.e., to tell the database program where one field ends and the next field begins); thus, the comma cannot be used as it is used in normal punctuation. Even where there is no information in a particular field, the comma must still appear so that the program can determine that a field is blank. The program looks at a comma and reads a new field. Otherwise, all fields move forward: A city appears in a state field, a state field appears in a zip code field, and so on. Missing commas furnish scrambled information. Missing only one such technicality makes the entire database useless.

Another hurdle to leap may involve the database application itself. Siebert spent 100 to 150 hours becoming familiar with Access, one of the better-known computer-generated relational database programs, a program that sports "Wizards," a feature that purports to help the user set up the database more easily. The Wizards are supposed to lead the user through the steps necessary to create a query. (A query enables the user to search repeatedly for designated categories of information among all the records.) By setting up queries, the user can search the database, automatically accessing the desired information. And if the same set of information is likely to be required often, template queries can be established within the program. The user normally would not want all the fields of all the records for every mailing but may consistently want the same fields from different records for separate mailings. Also, there are additional types of queries, such as ICR's ability to copy records from one table to another table, a feature essential for exporting information to its mailing, fax, and e-mail distribution lists. Fine and necessary though they are, queries take some study.

Using one of these more sophisticated packages can become extremely difficult. Without computer experience and database experience, an individual can get swamped quickly. Often the user has to reach beyond the manuals provided in the database package. Even finding the right third-party manual is a challenge. Each of the best-selling database application programs has generated dozens of manuals written to explain what is often impossible to decipher in the database company's user manual. The best way to shop for third-party manuals is to enter a bookstore with a few questions in mind. If you find the answer in one of the choices on the bookshelves—and understand what it says—odds are you have a decent book to work with. The quest for clarity has spawned an entire industry of third-party manuals, most notably the "For Dummies" series.

Too often, however, third-party books themselves offer little relief. Many are written by techies or programmers in a language that does not translate well into layperson's terms—repeating one of the problems the user faced in the first place. In addition, the reader may have to catch on to proprietary terminology: One company's nomenclature may not match another's, so the same thing is called by two different names. It becomes the reader's task to match the different terminology.

Once a person has selected a program, he or she still faces the formidable task of designing a database that fits specific needs. These programs supply designs that may turn out to be either too generic or, in some cases, too narrow. It is left to the user to map out a working design. And for the novice, trying to map a snug fit gets tough.

Cardinal rule number one, claims Siebert, is having patience and foresight: patience in setting up a database, foresight in knowing what you want your end result to be. "You have to know precisely what you want to do with your database," he cautions. "Having to redesign fields within the structure of a database creates even greater problems than creating the original design. You really have to give your design some forethought—setting up fields, setting up how things relate. And then you have to take a step back."

The better-known programs provide ways to change things, such as a field name. But if a user follows the program's method of changing the field name, all references to it must also change. When a field name changes, nothing refers to that field anymore, so all queries and all tables must reflect that change. If a user just dives in, he or she will get only so far, and then . . . trouble. Thus, only a full understanding of the program's potential precludes a setup that needs revamping.

This problem arises in particular in a business setting. "When I first sat down with the people at ICR," recalls Siebert, "and we talked about what they wanted, they didn't realize everything they could get out of it. They wanted to change their emphasis halfway through the project. Fair enough. It was just a matter of not knowing fully what a relational database can do. When I installed the program, they began to appreciate its potential. I was able to go back and make it do what they wanted it to do. Now they're really set. Any competent mail house or professional using it to manage a telephone campaign is going to be able to take their disk and give them just what they want. The point is that you can't be afraid to try things, whether it's filtering for a particular piece of information or whatever. You have to be able to just go for it. But you can go for it only when you understand fully what the program can do."

For example, with its custom-made program, ICR can designate in what order the cursor will move, allowing the user to avoid stepping through the fields according to the program's original design. This enables the user to jump from selected field to selected field because certain fields are used more than others. The cursor can jump in the order selected by the user. It is possible, of course, to buy a preset package, basically a sales-contact kit, but it is likely not to fit well. The whole purpose of a relational database is to make sure it fits the user's needs. Otherwise, why bother?

Another cardinal rule is understanding that a relational database is designed to save time, not cost time. If you have the time and the inclination, you can do it yourself. If you do not, either suffer through with a packaged program or hire someone who can design it specifically for your needs. After all, people rooted to the database are supposed to be in the field collecting names or contacting people in the database for introductions, research, or whatever. The big weakness in setting up a relational database is that unless you know what you are doing—that is, in designing anything beyond a basic contact list—a database really is simply not worth your time. People trying to get the attention of private investors had better have more than a list for putting on labels and sending out Christmas cards. So stick with your forte. Stick with what you are supposed to be doing. Remember why you are in business.

Finally, a person setting up things on his or her own may not only invite problems but become overwhelmed. Nowadays the user has to be familiar with variations in hardware, the computer's operating system, and the fine points of the application program. He or she has to know which is doing what—for example, which functions Windows is handling and which functions are performed by the database application. Exhibit 10.1 pinpoints what is involved in the setup of a computerized relational database.

DATA ENTRY

One such overwhelming task is data entry, the ongoing, accurate collection of information. Again, everything has to be just so—using only the standard abbreviations for states, for example. In gathering data entry information, the source must be readable; names from napkins dampened at lunch by the bottom of a wet glass are of little use. With legible sources of information, the user can hire data entry personnel. Without readable sources, the user loses valuable time—time that could be used in getting on with the real task of furthering the capital-raising process.

However, "garbage in, garbage out" is the watchword in data entry. With each inaccurate entry—the wrong state, the wrong name, inaccurate investment criteria, or simply spelling something incorrectly—the database's effectiveness is diminished. Without absolute accuracy in the information entered into the database, all is for naught.

It is also important to understand that if you go it alone, data entry is a never-ending, time-consuming process. Keeping a database updated is easiest when maintenance is done regularly, even daily, even if it means updating file information from someone immediately following a telephone conversation. Getting the information at that time eliminates having to have other

EXHIBIT 10.1   Setup of a Computerized Relational Database

Managing the database development budget
Networking considerations
    Installing a backup system
        Data entry
        —Initial input, maintenance, and updates
        Decide on export formats
        Create relational queries and templates
        Design database to fit specific criteria
        —Fields, records, files
        Select your database application

Source: International Capital Resources

people do it, or having to write the information in longhand and then entering it into the database. It should become a daily routine, but it takes time, discipline, accuracy, and patience. Waiting, say, until the end of the month makes for a weekend-consuming task.

The question arises about when a company keeping track of such information should switch to a computerized system. The answer, we suggest, comes when the company is spending more time doing things manually than it is in making contacts to sell its offering—the real reasons this endeavor was started in the first place. Another signal comes when the company has had to hire people to manually keep up with the influx of information.

BACKUP

Another cautionary note seems worth sounding: the possibility of losing an entire database of information. It happens, although rarely. A database needs to be backed up, a feat accomplished with relatively little effort. If the system does crash, eliminating everything, the information can always be restored from the backup.

For safety's sake, the user can simply copy the entire file over to another area of the hard disk, although this is not the best way to back up such valuable information. If the disk crashes, the user loses both the backup and the master file. The safest way is to copy the data onto floppy disks or tape, storing these copies off-site. Fire, a natural disaster of some sort, and even a break-in are all good reasons to keep copies of a back-up disk or tape at home. Even if someone burglarizes the office and makes off with the computer, the backup tape is safe. A computer can be replaced by the insurance company, plugged in, and the information restored by tape. Barely skipping a beat, the company's capital-raising campaign is back in operation.

COST

Finally, in going it alone, one has to consider the expense of setting up a relational database. First comes the expense of the software, the application program itself, costing a few hundred dollars. Cost continues to decrease for database software and Pentium-based computer hardware. Additional hardware—a good printer is necessary—would add several hundred dollars. Still, with any word processing, a printer becomes essential. A basic printer entails minimal cost and is fast enough for a small operation.

But those are just opening costs.

Another expense involves training, depending on how computer literate the user is to begin with. Windows is very user friendly; going from square one should not take too much time. The tasks are repetitive, which speeds the learning curve.

Help from a consultant, however, is a different matter; at an average rate of $100 an hour, the user had better be able to catch on quickly The same rate usually applies for a phone call to a consultant sitting at home or for an on-site visit.

For the database to be up and running and the project customized, 15 hours seems reasonable. There is hardly any point in slaving over something that does not quite work for you. It makes little sense to spend time and money, only to come up with something that could have been pulled off the shelf.

The most expensive component, however, will be data entry, that ongoing, tiresome task we discussed at length earlier. Data entry is not a one time expense. In time, it could very well dwarf all other expenses combined. When support is necessary, a temporary employment agency can supply a competent data-entry person for $16 per hour.

Earlier we presented different ways of securing financial resources: by renting them, that is, renting the names from other databases; by growing them, that is, getting the names of people you know, then asking them for the names of people they know; or by buying them, that is, using an alternative financial resource to obtain new investors for your venture. In this chapter we have plotted the task the individual faces in attempting to engineer a proprietary relational database, specifically for meeting the venture's financial goals. Most likely, entrepreneurs successful at raising capital from private investors use all three strategies to some degree.

PART Four

Understanding the Angel Investment Process

CHAPTER 11

The Venture Investing Process

INTRODUCTION

Private equity investing is a process that falls victim to popular myths that venture investment returns are the result of luck, managerial experience, landmark technology, or inside information; but make no mistake, successful angels and venture capitalists have an underlying process that winners follow. The elements of the process are not only intertwined but also recursive. That is, the aspects of this investment process, though discrete (as described in this chapter) nevertheless weave themselves around each other. A sequence is perceivable, though, again, intertwined. In a word, paradoxically, everything happens at once over an extended period.

Entrepreneurs raising capital must recognize that this investment process is used by investors to better manage the risk inherent in early-stage, private equity investing. While on the surface it may appear that the successful investor has nonchalantly hit a home run, what is neither seen nor appreciated is the amount of time, effort, and, of course, financial and emotional resources that have been poured into each of these aspects of the investment process. The investors do so to protect themselves as best they can from the pitfalls associated with long-term, highly illiquid investments requiring active involvement to build a sustainable company that consequently ensures a payoff for the investors.

To navigate this investment process, the entrepreneurs will be called upon display interpersonal skills and diplomatic and political dexterity. Understanding their role during each activity will help them to achieve their financial goal.

The phases of the investment process that we will discuss here include deal generation or creating and identifying a flow of attractive investment opportunities; navigating due diligence through screening, investigating, evaluating, and analyzing the venture's merits; ascribing value to the venture to determine equity share for investors; structuring the deal and terms of investment; monitoring the investment and defining participation and assistance levels postinvestment, and identifying and managing exit to harvest returns.

Underscoring the investment process are risk management and hedging strategies unique to the early-stage, private equity transaction. We will also discuss how entrepreneurs can expect investors to assess the risk in their deal and the tools investors will use to reduce that risk, whenever possible.

GENERATING DEAL FLOW

Historically, private equity investors, particularly angels, found their deals using such informal means as referral from family and personal contacts (e.g., friends, associates, and so on) or referrals from professional service providers (e.g., attorney, accountant, or investment advisers); or they may have received an unsolicited contact from a nonfamily representative of a company seeking financing. If this were true today, and these channels were the only means available, entrepreneurs would be limited to investor development approaches, such as networking with friends, family, associates, and colleagues of wealthy individuals; and cultivating referral sources among advisers to the wealthy, such as financial advisers, investment bankers, doctors, securities attorneys, accountants, tax advisers, certified appraisers, entrepreneurial finance consultants, commercial bankers, and preferred SBA lenders. In addition, entrepreneurs would rely on cold calling leads they generate as investment prospects to pitch their deal, an approach our research suggests may be successful less than 10 percent of the time. And desperate entrepreneurs also might be tempted to place classified advertisements soliciting capital, an error that could lead to sanctions and penalties.

However, based on our research, we find that investors today are shifting from informal to more formal deal flow development. And the reason for this is clear. In our earlier chapter titled "A Strategy That Works," we refer to the concept of the funnel, suggesting that entrepreneurs need a pool of investor prospects, perhaps three to four times as many potential investors believed to be necessary in order to complete their financing round. Similarly, investors need to generate significant deal flow, more so than is possible through informal means, to discover the few promising ventures that merit capital investment. Herein lies the opportunity for entrepreneurs seeking investors—each of whom cherishes privacy—to understand the channels used by investors to find their deals, and understand pathways best designed to identify and locate those qualified investors ready to invest.

The more formal strategies that investors use to generate deal flow we discussed earlier. These include listing in directories, printed and software-based; participating in venture forums; joining venture capital clubs; participating in online and offline investor networks; participating in an advisory capacity for incubators; and becoming involved in public relations–based approaches, for example, publishing articles on angel investing, contributing to research studies, and offering interviews for business articles on venture capital.

A review of the major directories, such as *Pratt's* and *Galante's*, will surface institutional and a few smaller groups of private investors, for example "store-front" venture capital firms. Also, investors join associations and then become listed in regional association directories, like the one from The New England Venture Capital Association.

Most directories are available in software form, easing the search for investors whose investment criteria fit the entrepreneurs' deals.

Venture forums provide entrepreneurs the opportunity to meet investors, whether they present their company, exhibit, or just attend in the audience, taking advantage of networking opportunities offered by the organizers. Even if companies are not selected to present, investors are sometimes involved in screening committee roles and are accessible that way.

Venture capital clubs host monthly meetings. While some are closed to members only, others open their doors to nonpresenting entrepreneurs. Since these meetings usually center around breakfast, lunch, or dinner, opportunities arise to strike up conversations and initiate relationships with regularly participating active investors. Of course, this same strategy can be used at investment conferences that private and institutional investors might attend for professional development reasons to hone their skills, an important quality of many sophisticated investors. (The great Spanish cellist Pablo Casals was once asked why he continued to practice hour after hour, day after day, even after he had long been acknowledged as the world's greatest. His answer: "So I can get better."). Certain perceptive investors feel likewise; they too want to "get better" at what they do.

Becoming active in online and offline investor networks means listing your deal to gain exposure. Most online matching services are passive; that is, they list your deal, leaving it up to the investor to contact you. Such is not the case with offline networks, which conduct searches to find investors who fit your deal parameters and actively contact them for you in order to determine their level of interest in the deal.

A number of investors have elected to volunteer for advisory boards of incubators. This is an efficient way for investors to find early-stage deals in industries of interest and geographically close to home, an effort to minimize travel. The incubator provides extensive resources that to some degree reduce risks in company development. This fact is borne out in research showing that incubated companies have better survival rates than nonincubated ventures. The investor may get involved as a mentor, adviser, or board member. Incubator directors recognize the importance of capital for companies under their wings, and when they think they feel they have found a fit, will make the proper introductions.

On occasion, we have located investors for our research and for ICR's database through articles published by the investors, or locate them after having heard them interviewed, or noticed their being mentioned in an article or research study on angel or venture investing. Whether having published an article or speaking at a meeting, a number of investors realize that deal flow benefits sometimes outweighs their need for privacy, and they will put themselves out there. An online search done periodically for recently published articles and books on angel capital, venture capital, and early-stage or private equity investing offer the best method of finding article-based leads.

Last, but important, is an entrepreneur's source of investors, ironically, collected from other entrepreneurs. Why would other entrepreneurs pass along an investor referral to you? Simple. It may be that the investor is no longer willing to put any more money into that other entrepreneur's deal; or the investor may have rejected the deal but, in doing so, disclosed investment parameters closer to your deal than their own.

DUE DILIGENCE

As a direct result of losses endured in the private, IPO, and public market following the dot-com and technology bubble burst, investors have become more skeptical of entrepreneurs' enthusiastic claims. An important implication is that investors have returned to basics, and due diligence again forms a vital aspect of the investment-mating process. Detailed investigation has returned front and center—elaborate and painstakingly thorough due diligence means entrepreneurs can expect full legal and financial audits, assessment of market potential, background and reference checks on founders and entrepreneurs involved, interviews with former superiors, peers, subordinates, and associates, in-person meetings between the parties for a thorough review of the business plan, and research with customers, suppliers, competitors, and technology experts.

This stage of the venture process determines the company's strengths and weaknesses by assessing its realistic future profit potential, and its potential of providing returns to the investors. Investors look into due diligence to identify the risks in the venture and the deal.

Private investors investing in early-stage, direct investments are investing into private transactions not subject to the same level of rigorous disclosure with which public companies are obligated to conform. Since entrepreneurs are not required to provide this same level of disclosure, investors have learned the hard way since 1999–2000 that they must assume full responsibility to inform themselves about all aspects of the investment. Investors are now going to extreme lengths in their preinvestment investigation and analysis of venture attributes to make more informed investment decisions.

The depth of that due diligence will vary by investor or investment group and by the specific venture opportunity. But typically the due diligence phase will be headed by an individual if you are working with a group. As you can see from the due diligence checklist below, responding to questions from these many categories can consume time:

- Management team skills and background
- Reference check
- Industry sector research
- Customer/supplier/distributor interviews
- Product realization and tests
- Market growth potential and competition
- Technical expert questions on technology
- Valuation
- Financial history and projections
- Business strategy and concept
- Intellectual property and protection
- Supporting documents

Due diligence comes down to the investor asking questions—many, many questions. Good ones. Due diligence becomes the entrepreneur's "final exam" that the venture passes (by raising the money)—or not. Entrepreneurs need to be prepared to answer these many questions and need to appreciate that others will be asked many questions as well—for example, questions about fellow founders, all the management team, past employers, the venture's potential customers, suppliers and distributors, and experts. In research we reported earlier, the majority of investors surveyed stated that they had used technical advisers in making past investments and planned to again use technical experts.

To some degree, the questions entrepreneurs can expect to face are those normally answered in creating a thorough business plan. Since questions form the cornerstone of the due diligence process, we have collected over the years questions asked of entrepreneurs by investors working on the process. We have organized these questions in a separate due diligence chapter to help the entrepreneur prepare for the more rigorous levels of investigation we anticipate for them. By preparing, entrepreneurs may be able to shorten the time involved in the due diligence phase, thereby reducing some of the costs in scrambling to find answers later, that is, at a time when such scrambling could sink this already weighty process. So we urge entrepreneurs to project a positive attitude to promote the venture's strengths and competitive advantage; and we caution them to be candid about risk factors and weaknesses, particularly weaknesses in the management team, technology, or market. In fact, the entrepreneur should preclude the investor's detection of such risks and weaknesses by being ready with proposals to remedy them. It is preferable by far to be straightforward on such issues; being so accrues to your credibility in light of lately more skeptical investors.

BUSINESS VALUATION

Business valuation techniques constitute an indispensable and integral phase of the venture investing process. Investors have always sought comparables for valuation. For example, in one of our previous books, we suggested that the best test of the practicality of a deal's pricing is whether it can attract and be sold to another private investor at the same price, although not necessarily at the highest price—in other words, sold at the same valuation to the investor.

While the value of an illiquid company may be more a function of finding an investor than of financial formulae and calculations, investors, sensitive after being hurt by overinflated valuations negotiated in the boom times, are prone to use various business valuation models, including among others cost approaches (cost to recreate) and income approaches (capitalization of income and discounted future cash flow analysis).

Regardless, value is generally agreed to be about finding the present value of future cash flows, in which cash flows could be proceeds from the sale of stock or interest and dividend payments.

Most investors use a combination of these approaches to ascribe value to the early-stage, nonoperating company without revenues. Understanding the salient drivers in valuing a company will help entrepreneurs make their ventures more valuable in the perception of investors. Valuation is so important, as well as technically complex, that we have dedicated an entire chapter to adequately address the subject.

In this section, we want to convey to entrepreneurs that valuation is not a precise form of financial analysis, but is more akin to an art form, or at times, horse trading. Such subjective factors as experience and cohesiveness of the management team, investor familiarity with the industry of the venture, perceived competitive advantage or lead to market, whether "missionary" selling will be required to introduce the product, likelihood of the need for follow-on financing, the extent to which the deal had been "shopped," and how persuasive and committed the entrepreneur is perceived as being are qualitative elements that can conspire to influence the most elaborate quantitative financial valuation techniques. Entrepreneurs would do well to pay heed to these subjective elements, as well as to their elegant financial arguments of value.

Potential risks and rewards vary substantially during the different development stages of a new venture. Despite every entrepreneur's confidence in his or her "sure thing," more new ventures fail than succeed. Investors need a few big winners to offset the losers. Depending on the risks, compound rates of return from 20 percent to 25 percent or more are not unreasonable expectations for investors to take the risk and loss of use of their capital. So in our chapter on valuation, we will also present information on investors' expected rates of return, and implications for entrepreneurs' discussion of exit plans.

Also, since value is in the future, any calculations are fraught with the complications influenced by incomplete information, rapidly changing environmental factors, unproven management, untested technology, and undeveloped markets. So determining value in the early-stage deal is subjective precisely because so much depends on something that has not yet happened. Last, the negotiation skills, styles, and techniques used by investors and entrepreneurs themselves to resolve their valuation differences can become essentials that influence the valuation outcome.

The private equity players who threw caution to the wind in 1999–2000 are more realistic today. Premoney, seed-stage values of completed transactions in the past year (2003–2004) have a median value of $3 million. First rounds have a median premoney value of $9 million. Quite a drop from the historic highs just before the dot-com bust. Gone are the astounding multiples at which many Internet start-ups with no earnings or immediate potential for revenues had been valued. Investors have regained their gravity, and entrepreneurs seeking capital need to pay attention to having reasonable expectations and be cognizant of the potential for down rounds.

Although the number of down rounds decreased in 2002–2003, this was due more to investors shifting to later-stage investments rather than to their reducing aggressive negotiation over value. In down rounds, preexisting investors are forced to address a steep decrease in valuation. This situation, if not fully managed, can create considerable legal issues and liability for the board and other inside stockholders. Remember that majority stockholders have a fiduciary duty to minority shareholders, among others, and directors can be held personally liable for breach of fiduciary duty. So it becomes critical in facing down rounds to demonstrate alternatives before resorting to the financing at that value. There must be complete disclosure, approved by shareholders, perhaps an outside fairness opinion, and directors and officers (D&O) insurance and indemnification.

In conclusion, valuing the early-stage company inevitably means that the investor must take an equity ownership position that will produce an expected annualized rate of return over a reasonable period commensurate with this investor's tolerance for risk. Valuation, therefore, does crucially depend on the creation or expansion of a sustainable, going concern into a marketable commodity through an event that provides liquidity for the investors.

To the extent that entrepreneurs have mitigated risk through product development, marketing, sales, customer endorsement, and development of an effective, cohesive management team, the entrepreneur will see his or her valuation increase. Because of these characteristics about venture value, entrepreneurs will appreciate the investor perspective with which they must deal: investors must be convinced of the merits of the venture before discussing valuation; investors believe that demand for capital exceeds supply and will embrace this leverage in any negotiation; skeptical investors will always discount entrepreneurs' projections (give them a "haircut"); investors will build their own cash flow models from the entrepreneur's data, paying particular attention to potential for dilution for unforeseen follow-on financings; and last, investors in today's market will be skeptical of entrepreneurs' claim of IPO's as their primary exit plans. Even in boom times—now long gone—fewer than ten percent of venture-funded deals provided liquidity via IPO!

NEGOTIATING AND STRUCTURING THE DEAL

Venture investor Anthony Perkins is quoted as saying, "If there is any guide to structuring investments, it is to isolate whatever the biggest risk is in a deal, and structure the initial investment so the money is used to eliminate that risk." In the new capital-raising reality facing entrepreneurs today and for the immediate future, be confident that investors have altered their investment approach from the boom times of 1999–2000. Whether in response to investment losses incurred, or for other reasons mentioned, investors now place a premium on risk management, hedging strategies to minimize the downside, and co-investment strategies to share the risk. As investors pay more attention to due diligence, aggressive valuation negotiations to establish pricing and stricter deal terms have become the norm. Certainly, for early-stage companies seeking private equity financing, terms, or the key covenants in investment contracts, have changed.

For example, 75 percent of deals, according to the Strategic Research Institute, are done at "down" valuation. Consequently, transactions that will meet with the motivations and goals of each party require innovative structures and time lines to avert overdilution of employees and founders. With capital uncertain or unavailable for many young technology companies, and valuations in a continuous state of flux, there is considerable stress on investors and entrepreneurs to emphasize negotiation of price and deal structure.

With regard to structuring transactions, the biggest change now facing entrepreneurs is that deal terms are more investor friendly than was the case five years ago. Deal terms that originated before the dot-com era have gained momentum since the post-2000 meltdown of Nasdaq. PricewaterhouseCoopers takes this view: "It is fair to say that entrepreneurs don't have a lot of leverage today; terms are structured to ensure greater payoff to 'investors' as compared to entrepreneurs and founders." At bottom, then, it is a case of supply and demand.

RISK AS A DRIVING FORCE BEHIND DEAL STRUCTURE

All investments, by definition, have risks. Early-stage, private equity investing carries very high risk. In direct investing, entrepreneurs must empathize with the investor, understanding that ultimately there invariably comes the intricate decision about how to manage that inherent risk. Common sense tells us—as does our experience—that investors will do a number of obvious things to try to reduce risk, for example, be highly selective and thoroughly analyze every deal before they invest; diversify their private equity portfolio by private equity class, region, technology, industry, or stage of development; structure transactions with any collateral available; stage follow-up capital infusions based on management performance and accomplishment of predetermined milestones; negotiate steep discounts as a premium for investing early; never investing at the first price/valuation suggested by the entrepreneur; and search early for co-investors who will confirm the investor's judgment and be willing to invest a like amount at the agreed valuation—in effect confirming the deal is worthwhile before they invest in it.

Risk can vary significantly, depending on different dimensions of an investment—for example, the category of the private equity class and the company's stage of development. The private equity class of investments has broadened to encompass a range of different transactions: preseed, seed, start-up, growth, mezzanine, leveraged buyout, buyout, spinout, post-venture, turnaround, special investment situations, and distressed security investing. The life cycle of potential portfolio companies evolves from start-up to expansion to mezzanine. Of course, risk stands significantly higher in the earlier stages of the development of the venture, a stage in which founders attempt to comprehend the concept, the company's reason for existence. At this stage, management capability remains limited as they struggle to clarify strategic advantage, develop a business plan, and commence to prove practicability.

In addition to considering the stage-of-development risks inherent in early-stage transactions, investors will typically analyze five other risks. First, management risk does not center on the more obvious question of qualification of the individuals; this aspect of due diligence is taken for granted. The real management risk is whether the principals involved can perform as a team and carry the venture through to a liquidity event, or to exit.

Another risk involves the product. If we are dealing with a start-up or early-stage company, with the product in development, the investors are being asked to put up money before a prototype has been developed. Whether the product can be made to work becomes a critical risk.

A third risk of these types of ventures centers on the market. Will the market accept the product? Such a consideration involves the push-pull of market forces. Having to push a product onto the market makes missionary selling necessary—an expensive proposition tied to considerable risk. However, a product being pulled by market demand means less risk.

Operations, another area of risk, depends on a company's ability to meet its sales projections. Can the company produce with quality the projected volume to meet customer expectations, keep them happy, and maintain their loyalty (and the company's reputation)?

Still another risk associated with early-stage ventures is financial risk, an assessment of how much money will be needed beyond the investor's investment. If a venture needs $10 million in the next round, and the investor's contribution is only $50,000, a major financial risk looms. There is that chance that the entrepreneur will not be able to raise such a sum in the current market, unless the venture is stellar. So financial risk has to do with raising money for the balance of the present round and future rounds necessary to move the company into becoming a profitable venture.

The last type of risk is a business strategy risk, the assessment of the potential that the company's targeted market could change during the venture's beginning. Can anything occur that might have an impact on the acceptance of the company and its strategy in the market?

For many private equity investors, the "venture" in venture capital has been a misnomer. Venture capitalists in many instances have avoided investing in start-ups because they believed that the risk/reward ratio was unattractive compared with the opportunities to enact mezzanine transactions with shorter time horizons. This perception has spread, attracting a disproportionate amount of money over the past several years to the later-stage segment of the financial spectrum. Inevitably, the market has responded at the seed end of the spectrum with lower entry level pricing and an improving risk/reward ratio.

DEFINITION OF NEGOTIATION

Negotiating is a process by which the investors, entrepreneurs, and their advisers reach an interdependent mutual decision that the transaction is a good deal. This involves clarifying and agreeing on what the investor and entrepreneur will give to and receive from each other in completing the transaction. It is not win-lose; instead, each person attempts to understand and consider the other's concerns. While it is generally believed that "those with the gold, rule," entrepreneurs who overly concede accrue resentment and anger that surface later, confounding relationships with investors. As the nineteenth century English writer Samuel Butler put it, " It is not he who gains the exact point in dispute who scores most in controversy, but he who has shown the most forbearance and better temper." Entrepreneurs must make their negotiation objectives a fair deal, and be willing to give the investor some protection if the entrepreneur fails to meet milestones.

Negotiating begins after due diligence, and only when the investor has decided to go forward. At this stage, the entrepreneur needs to negotiate the structure of the deal and work through development of an agreed-upon preliminary understanding into legal documents. The parties will have to decide on an array of issues. Commonly, such negotiations are between the lead investor and the entrepreneur. Remember, investors will be motivated to secure terms and conditions to protect their financial downside by negotiating an agreement that allows investors some degree of influence and control in decision making. Following are negotiating guidelines for entrepreneurs:

- Be clear and accurate.
- Take your time.
- Bring in an attorney only after you have reached some level of verbal agreement with the lead investor.
- Negotiate for yourself; do not delegate to a third party.
- Since angels don't have to invest, if they reject your offer, try to understand the terms and conditions under which they *would* invest.
- Avoid feelings of personal rejection; focus instead on issues.
- Constantly requalify the investor prospect to ensure they are "real" investors.

ELEMENTS IN STRUCTURING THE PRIVATE PLACEMENT

Based on research by ICR of more of more than 3,000 companies and 480 completed deals, 65 percent of transactions concluded at the seed, R&D, and start-up stages used the private placement as the transaction structure. It is no accident that the transaction most commonly used by angels is the private placement, which typically involves cash for equity, and is flexible because it encompasses all types of offerings not publicly sold. The private placement is the issuance of treasury securities to a small number of sophisticated private or institutional investors. The common exempt offering involves such financing considerations as debt, equity (usually preferred stock), or some type of investment unit (preferred stock or debt issued with warrants).

Angel investors use four categories of securities: common stock; preferred stock; convertible preferred stock; and, of course, convertible longer-term debt and convertible notes. Warrants are also used with both equity and debt notes.

The most common investment security in private placements is preferred stock that converts at the option of the holder into common stock. This feature will allow the holder to share in the success should the company be sold, merged with another company in a stock swap, go public, or exit through some other liquidity event. Preferred stock also customarily has a liquidation and dividend preference over common stock, "full-ratcheted" or weighted-average antidilution protection, certain voting rights, and, possibly, a redemption feature that becomes effective after a specified number of years.

In almost all cases, the only way investors in these types of transactions can benefit from the risk that they have assumed is to share in the upside potential if the venture proves to be successful. And the only way they can do that is through equity. This reliance on preferred stock provides other, less obvious benefits to investors. For example, it provides leverage to influence management when things go askew; also, preferred stock requires the entrepreneur to remain in contact with the investor. This provision creates warning mechanisms that permit the investor to change management or set time frames and conditions for making changes when they become necessary.

Preferred stock can also provide some income through dividends, although this is not a circumstance typically arising in early-stage ventures. However, preferred stock is redeemable by the corporation, which may set up a sinking fund and establish compulsory payment.

Sometimes companies will issue warrants that can be used to acquire a greater percentage of the company based on its actual results. For example, investors who disagree with the premoney valuation proposed by the entrepreneur can be offered warrants to purchase additional shares of the company as a hedge. The warrants become exercisable if the company fails to perform according to plan or an agreed-upon set of milestones. They can also be structured to be exercisable to varying degrees, based on performance criteria.

The exercise price of the warrant is another variable. It could be priced at the initial closing purchase price, be priced at fair market valued at the time of exercise, be floating until set based on performance against milestones, or be nominal. Again, the goal of the investor will be to structure the warrant so that the return on the shares originally purchased, together with the warrant shares, result in the targeted internal rate of return.

Entrepreneurs will discover that some investors prefer to "lead" the round, drafting terms of the deal and negotiating terms with the company and other investors. Other investors may hold a more co-investment strategy orientation, and be willing to co-invest on terms originated by lead investors. A variety of motivations lead investors to become more active or passive. We refer readers to *The Angel Investor's Handbook* for a more comprehensive discussion of active versus passive private investors.

OVERVIEW OF DEAL TERMS AND PROVISIONS

Entrepreneurs have burned up so much of investors' money that they have to expect more demanding deal terms. Over a three-year period, a 1.5 multiple amounts to a 15 percent annualized return—a total that in the minds of venture investors, who have left trillions of dollars on the table, will not cut it. As a result, investors may seek more demanding provisions in hopes of improving returns; but in the early rounds of deals, such terms—regardless of how onerous—most likely will never come into play. This is because it would be more prudent to just shut down a "washout" company and take the write off than it would be to execute protections that in the end would provide no monetary benefit.

For purposes of our discussion, we focus on terms most likely to appear in earlier-stage term sheets or agreements, with the assumption that punitive provisions are recognized as not contributing to building great companies; nor do such provisions foster good relations and long-term alliance between entrepreneurial managers and investors. However, given current economic conditions and recent downturns in the capital markets and investment banking/brokerage prosecutions, the new-found emphasis on such terms is unlikely to go away any time soon.

Entrepreneurs should be familiar with the many possible deal terms that can be drafted into placement memoranda, subscription agreement, term sheet, stock purchase agreement, shareholders agreement, or ancillary legal agreements that can be drafted following negotiations. Some of the terms, such as valuation, security, rights and provisions, we've briefly touched on. Most angels have a set of standard terms as a starting point for their investments. More experienced entrepreneurs and founders will also be familiar with these terms. Regardless, all terms should be understandable and acceptable to subsequent investors, and must accommodate the many potential "hedging" strategies, such as staged investment, mentioned earlier.

Once the amount of investment is determined, the security to be used is considered. We have already spoken of common stock, preferred stock, convertible preferred stock, and convertible notes. The security that best provides upside capital appreciation and downside protection from the investor perspective is convertible preferred. Convertible debt is much less attractive, since it carries a negative impact on the balance sheet, and few start-ups can afford to also pay interest. Preferred stock carries preferences, potential for dividends (rare in start-ups), liquidation preference, voting rights, convertibility elements, and redemption rights. Preferred shareholders will have a priority claim over common shareholders to assets if the company fails, equivalent to the investor's original purchase price of the security plus any accrued dividends. Preferred shareholders vote with common shareholders and are entitled typically to one vote for each common share into which preferred shares may be converted. They may also have special voting rights, for example, to elect the majority of the board upon any breach of the terms in the preferred stock purchase agreements. Preferred stock is normally convertible into common stock at the holder's discretion, except when automatic conversion obligations are agreed to.

Convertibility will occur at a specific price per share or at attainment of a specific goal. The convertibility ratio is commonly expressed by a formula based on the original purchase price, adjusted for stock splits, dividends, and sales of common stock at prices lower than those paid by preferred shareholders.

Redemption terms or rights offer the investor means by which they can recover their investment. Redemption can be optimal or mandatory after a specific period of time. A stepped-up redemption price is sometimes built into the agreement to provide investors with a certain return on investment. In mandatory redemption, a preferred stockholder may be forced to exercise conversion or lose the upside potential of his or her investment. In our experience, the majority of done-deal term sheets provided for mandatory redemption or redemption at the option of the venture investor.

Vesting is a term relating to investor demands that shares be issued to the management team members over time, or, if founders shares have already been issued, that the company have the right to repurchase shares if an executive leaves the company. Obviously, entrepreneurs prefer to purchase shares up front and be 100 percent vested without the company having repurchase rights. Negotiating a compromise is paramount, so that partial vesting occurs at the time that capital infusion occurs, followed by full vesting over time, while vested shares would be subject to repurchase by the company if the entrepreneur leaves the company.

Investors will negotiate dilution terms as well. Because companies require multiple rounds of financing, investors are justifiably concerned about their equity position being diluted relative to the entrepreneur's share. Dilution provisions are designed to prevent dilution. Antidilution adjustments, for example, can affect the number of common shares issued when an investor's preferred stock is converted.

Full ratchet antidilution protection, which lowers the conversion price to the price at which any new stock is sold, no matter the number of shares, obviously favors the investor. Weighted-average antidilution provisions adjust the conversion value by applying a weighted average of the purchase price of outstanding stock and newly issued stock. Because of the longer "earn back" period—an average of eight years, based on our research—there is a greater pressure for investors to negotiate antidilution terms. Remember Murphy's Law? In a recent study of 80 venture financings, 36 percent of terms provided for ratchet antidilution, and 64 percent for weighted-average antidilution.

In research of recent financings conducted by ICR, 90 percent of the time liquidation preference was negotiated beyond family and friends and cradle equity transactions. The majority of these financing were at 1.5 times to 3 times multiples, and the majority of these provided for participation. About 25 percent of the time, our review of deals disclosed that price protection provisions were subject to "pay-to-play" terms. This provision makes the continuation of protection for the investor contingent on the investor's purchasing at least its pro rata share of any future issuance priced below the conversion price. Pay-to-play provisions usually also provide for conversion of nonparticipating investors' preferred stock into common stock.

As angels continue to protect their downside, they also seek terms regarding representation on the board of directors. Remember, investors view themselves as owners. By specifying the percentage of directors to be elected by each class of stock, investors can address their fear about dilution of representation rights that subsequent offerings might cause.

"Drag-along" provisions are more common today than they were five years ago, as investors include terms requiring a company to vote as told. Drag-along voting rights, particularly when a big liquidation preference is present, and there is investor concern that management might not approve the deal because of their share, are now finding their way into term sheets and purchase agreements.

We also see to a lesser extent terms relating to employee stock purchase, for example, allocation of shares available for employee incentives, co-sale "take-me-alongs" relating to right of first refusal, and management "carve outs" or bonus plans upon sale that guarantees that the first $1 million or more of the sale goes to common holders in addition to anything they might receive because of the stock that they hold.

Last, entrepreneurs must be ready in the current litigious climate to provide D&O insurance, ensuring indemnification of investors with board seats, an expense rarely contemplated in forecasts.

OVERSEEING AND ADVISING POSTINVESTMENT

Investors use the early phases of the venture investment process to manage risk before investing. To manage risk after the investment is made, however, investors implement monitoring strategies to track the performance of the venture. Monitoring strategies are designed to identify problems before they require drastic action to rectify them. Based on our research at ICR, angel investors experience a total loss of their investment 11 percent of the time; 24 percent of the time they experience partial loss; one third of the time, early-stage investors lose investment capital—quite a motivation to monitor postinvestment venture performance.

Monitoring early-stage investments is a form of control mechanism. Think of the instrument panel a pilot uses to monitor a flight, particularly a flight imperiled by low visibility. Like pilots in fog, investors find themselves flying in bad weather because projections fuel most of what has lifted their investments off the ground. Little is based on historical financial fact or current reality. Fueling an investment's gas tank are conjectures based on assumptions.

Given these circumstances, investors need to create their own instrument panel. By doing so, they put in place an early warning system capable of alerting them to dangers so they can take corrective action. Investors, then, have to know how to set up an instrument panel whose dials they can read. This ability to read the panel means that investors establish their own instruments—ones appropriate to the venture, ones they are familiar with.

"We believe," declared the late President Ronald Reagan, "that no power of government is as formidable a force for good as the creativity and entrepreneurial drive of the American people." Angel investors in particular share Reagan's vision, one that elevated the entrepreneur. Likewise, instead of overly focusing on onerous covenants in legal investment agreements, most early-stage investors, once having made a decision to invest, choose to trust management. So the absence of legal contract terms and provisions serves only to increase the importance of monitoring mechanisms to fill the void.

Conversely, some investors aware of the need for monitoring, if not control, because of past investment losses, will have negotiated deal structures mandating monitoring functions, for example, board of directors service, or staging of investment based on management's achieving predetermined milestones. These terms are designed by investors to help reduce risk, and increase investor control, and allow the investor to monitor, if not influence, management decision making.

Instruments that entrepreneurs can expect investors to use to monitor the venture's performance fall into two categories: passive and active monitoring and evaluation methods. Hands-off monitoring involves periodic review of financial performance information, for example, tracking monthly or quarterly financial statements using a strict reporting schedule and requirements. There would be daily or weekly contact with management through in-person meetings or telephone conferences during which the parties discuss performance against planned milestones. Investors will also maintain vigilance related to investment terms and conditions negotiated earlier and structured into investment agreements.

Investors will track how management is using capital invested, and the rate at which funds are being "burned." Investors will try to detect problems by scanning costs, sales, earnings, profits, contract close rates, orders, product development schedules, hiring, conformance to budget, and so on. Such monitoring could lead investors to take action or suggest plan or strategy revisions.

Individually and collectively, these monitoring devices amount to being able to help when help is needed, instead of waiting past the time when adversity can be reversed.

Perhaps the best example of passive involvement is participation by investors in the board of directors or advisory board if concerns arise about D&O exposure. The primary function of early-stage company boards is to monitor and evaluate the performance of management and suggest actions necessary to correct situations for the good of the company and its owners.

Involvement by the board is a monitoring strategy that allows investors to exercise some degree of influence on decisions and pass along successful managerial and extensive experience and knowledge to less experienced entrepreneurs. Boards permit investors a nonexecutive role to function as a sounding board as well as to add value.

Active monitoring and advisory functions also allow investors to add value, but are characterized by a more hands-on approach to provide follow-on support and to influence management decision making. Rarely are entrepreneurial management teams complete, with all the necessary functional skills present in the team. Based on our research at ICR, 25 percent of the time, angel investors step in personally to fill those gaps lacking in the management team. More specifically, in our study of 60 early-stage ICR investors, investors reported that they were qualified and willing to provide management assistance in the following areas: 48 percent in marketing and sales; 28 percent in production; 13 percent in R&D; 23 percent in personnel; 63 percent in general management; 15 percent in financial planning; and 5 percent in engineering.

As one investor put it, "What also gets my attention is . . . an action plan from someone who demonstrates that over the next 90 to 180 days, from the time the company receives the money, he or she can enumerate what exactly has to be done to make this business go. The more specific those kinds of milestones are, the more comfortable I am in knowing that I can measure progress after I've made the investment and calibrate how I should react— that is, whether I've made a mistake, or whether I should invest additional capital if I'm asked. This is a very good way both to monitor the investment and to assess how management is doing and what you can do to help them."

HARVESTING RETURNS: REALISTIC EXIT STRATEGIES

While venture and angel capital had been described as "patient money," we have never, after 15 years of experience of working with early-stage investors, heard an investor declare, "I wish I had spent less time thinking about exit and liquidity before I invested." An exit route is the means by which an investor leaves an investment and through which he or she is able to realize returns.

Alternative exit strategies include IPO, sale of investor's stock back to the founders, leveraged buyout and recapitalization of the company, sale of the company, merger or acquisition with a publicly traded company in exchange for liquid or tradable stock, or transfer of stock to other investors.

Not all companies are IPO candidates. And given the sluggish nature of the IPO market, entrepreneurs would be better served to not overemphasize IPO as their primary strategy for exit, particularly to angel investors. With 22,000,000 private companies in the United States and just 30,000 public companies, fewer than one tenth of one percent are traded on the major stock exchanges. The IPO as a liquidity vehicle for venture-backed companies—though beginning in 2004 to show signs of life—has dried up, and is a mere shadow of the $69 billion, 546 IPOs investors funded in 1999. This fact, combined with rigorous listing requirements, high fixed costs of the IPO, complex regulatory requirements (e.g., Sarbanes-Oxley), and the requirements that the company has grown large enough to float its stock on a major exchange, all contribute to conspire against the daunting prospect of exiting by an IPO.

Today, thousands of companies are turning to merger, acquisition, and corporate buyout to provide exit and liquidity. Merger can involve the investee company being combined with a larger corporation or being acquired by the same and receiving cash and marketable securities for the sale. When strong strategic benefits are present, trade sales or sales of one company to another are possible transactions, for instance, synergistic products or technology. Buy back is an exit route in which the investor cashes out by selling securities back to the founders, typically when the terms of the sale are tied to operating performance and cash flow of the company. The leveraged buyout is a buy back using debt. The prearranged take out can be an exit for private investors in marginally performing companies. This method has the investor tendering to the company a percentage of the company shares, shares held at a price that relates to a predetermined multiple of earnings or cash flow. The entrepreneurs can have a call that would be exercised at some multiple value after they have successfully achieved a pre-agreed on level of earnings or cash flows. Another liquidity route is the secondary sale, or the sale of some or all shares to a third party.

Returns to investors take the form of long-term capital gains realized after an extended period during which an investment provides little or no liquidity or marketability. The method and timing of liquidation expectations are important variables in a venture capital investment decision. Shared exit expectations are particularly critical for ventures with limited prospects for a public offering or acquisition by a larger firm within the typical five- to ten-year exit horizons of venture investors. It is important to make clear early the investor's interest in achieving liquidity at the highest price within a specified time frame, for example, seven years. This interest in achieving liquidity needs to be more than a verbal agreement; terms should be clearly specified in writing and on solid legal ground. In developing a strong set of terms and conditions during negotiations, do not underestimate the importance of auditing, monitoring, and engaging good legal counsel.

Many angels and high-net-worth, early-stage investors, it is true, are motivated by nonfinancial returns. Such altruistic driving forces include creating jobs in regions of high unemployment, investing in socially useful technology in medicine or nonpolluting energy, financing ventures created by women and minority entrepreneurs, and the personal sense of accomplishment that building a sustainable company engenders. However, another, more primal, drive operates in today's economy, a reason why institutions entrust $200 million to $400 million with a small handful of venture capitalist money manager-investors, a reason they invest $7 million to $10 million per deal into 30 to 40 companies within three to five years. The reason is simple: 15 to 20 of those company investments, particularly earlier-stage, will provide five times returns in seven years and, at exit, the investors plan to own 25 percent of the company. Since in today's market, exit is more likely to be merger, acquisition, or sale, the current range of transaction prices of $100 million to $300 million starts to give the reader a sense of the capital appreciation possible, and why this type of investing remains a part of institutional portfolios.

Angels and other investors will want to clarify exit routes early in the discussions with entrepreneurs. While they will focus on helping the company succeed, they want to be able to get their investment back and earn a return for the loss of use of capital. So entrepreneurs need to identify alternative, plausible exit routes early in the negotiations.

What, then, are reasonable early-stage investor's expectations for financial returns?

Invariably the questions will arise for the investor: "How much can I make?" and "How much can I lose?" Remember, for investors to realize attractive rates of return, they may be more interested in avoiding a bad investment than in hitting a home run, the former often carrying a bigger wallop than the latter. Investors attempt to avoid the bad ones by using the venture investment process we described in this chapter. Investors also possess expectations about rates of return that they and their colleagues believe to be reasonable and realistic. Returns on investment are the result of various combinations of good judgment, skill, and luck (although we should remember that the harder we work, the luckier we seem to get).

Private equity five-year returns for 1,600 U.S. venture capital and private equity funds range from 54 percent for early-stage and seed-stage venture capital funds to 7.6 percent for later-stage venture capital funds. The 20-year private equity performance of early-stage/seed venture capital funds remains steady since the early 1990s at 19 to 20 percent. Important to comprehending ROI for venture investors is the time that investors hold the investment before they exit to harvest returns. For example, a three-times return on investment earned in three years yields a 44 percent ROI, whereas a three-times return on investment in five years drops the yield to 38 percent ROI.

Exhibit 11.1 shows how one venture capital fund fared in its investments.

By contrast, consider the targeted rates of return in Exhibit 11.2. While investors may target aggressive annualized multiples, actual results often fall short of the investment plan objectives.

In ICR's 1999–2000 study of 1,200 angel investors queried on internal rates of return, we found that over a mean hold term of eight years, 39 percent reported all or partial loss of investment; 19 percent reported break even or nominal returns; 30 percent reported cumulative returns of 50 percent or

EXHIBIT 11.1   Professional Venture Capital Returns* on Investment

Total loss	11.5%
Partial loss	23%
Break even	30%
2–5 times investment	19.8%
5–10 times investment	8.9%
10 or more times investment	6.8%

*Cash on cash + capital gains.

EXHIBIT 11.2   Annualized Targeted Rates of Return

Description	Internal Rate of Return*
Seed/start-up	60%–100%
Development+	50%–60%
Management team revenues/expansion	40%–50%
Profitable/cash poor	30%–40%
Rapid growth	25%–35%
Bridge to cash out	20%+

*Before applying subjective factors.

more per year; and 12 percent reported returns exceeding 100 percent. These returns were all cash-on-cash, plus capital gains. Most investors interviewed for our study stated that they aimed for a minimum of 30 percent internal rate of return for investments in start-ups, establishing reasonable return expectations. Angels are also acutely aware of entrepreneurs' tendency to underestimate the time to liquidity, which holds significant implications as we have presented for rate of return.

CHAPTER 12

Preparing for Due Diligence

INTRODUCTION

Over the years, ICR has collected questions asked of entrepreneurial clients who have gone through due diligence with investors accessed through the firm. We have organized the many questions compiled in this chapter through their research using a framework developed by venture capitalist Justin Camp. Entrepreneurs can use this framework and the questions compiled by ICR and us to help prepare themselves for the inevitable due diligence audit.

The early-stage venture capital due diligence framework presented here was used in two of the Wharton School graduate-level MBA courses. For a complete presentation of this research, we refer the reader to another Wiley Finance book by Mr. Camp titled *Venture Capital Due Diligence*. A complete citation can be found in the Suggested Reading List (Appendix C).

An investor relies on solid judgment in evaluating a deal on its own merits. To do so mandates a comprehensive investigation and analysis. Due diligence is no more than the caution any prudent person would exercise with his or her own money. Nothing takes the place of a full venture audit, an in-depth investigation spanning prescreening, assessment of management, examination of the business opportunity, scrutinizing intangible aspects of the situation, and diagnosis of the legal and financial aspects of the deal. The investor is judging the workability of the early-stage investment. To do so entails interviews and meetings, document reviews, and extensive research and analysis. Experts will be used to facilitate background checks and provide technical expertise beyond that of the investor. Especially when the investor is considering a venture outside of his or her experience, practicing due diligence and using outside advisers will take on even more importance.

In this chapter we have organized the essential queries that entrepreneurs will need to be prepared to answer. We also provide suggestions on documentation the entrepreneur must have on hand during the investigation.

PRESCREENING

Because investors must go through "mounds of manure to find a jewel," they tend to prescreen for red flags to weed out ventures that do not justify in-depth due diligence.

The quality of the business plan suggests the quality of the venture, the deal itself, and the people who wrote it. At ICR, fewer than two percent of business plans received are given serious evaluation. The rest simply don't merit in-depth analysis. The business plan presentation is vital to getting an in-person meeting with investors. We refer you to Appendix A on drafting an investor-oriented business plan to better appreciate what investors typically look for in venture documentation, organization, content, and presentation.

The source of the deal is another prescreening aspect. Was it referred by a trusted colleague or intermediary, or was it sent over the transom via the Internet by someone unknown to the investor or a circle of contacts?

Who are the company's advisers? Who were the attorney, accountant, business consultant, investment banker, or intermediary assisting the company with capitalization strategy? The quality of advisers associated with the firm is an indicator of the good judgment of management.

Is the investor familiar with any of the other angel or venture capitalists, family, friends, or cofounders who have invested in the deal? Investors add relevant value through their experience and knowledge over and above the capital they invest. The extent to which the current investor pool offers resources to grow the company makes the venture more attractive to other investors.

One prescreening question we ask at ICR is whether current customers or companies involved in beta tests will provide endorsement of the company, its management, or its technology. Relationships with customers or potential customers suggest the potential for the company and its product to succeed in the marketplace.

Sophisticated early-stage, private equity investors commonly have an investment plan and a portfolio allocation strategy. They will ask themselves whether the venture fits with their investment strategy, for example, industries or technologies that they know and understand. They will also consider if the company's stage of development is compatible with their risk tolerance and portfolio diversification strategy. There are varied levels of risk associated with seed, start-up and expansion stage business. Compatibility with investors' tolerance for risk is a paramount condition in order to invest.

Investors have maximum limits. They are not confused about how much they can invest per deal. In ICR's study of 60 investors from its database, the maximum amount investors would consider investing ranged from $25,000 to more than $1 million. There needs to be compatibility between the investor's preferred investment amount and the minimum investment acceptable to the entrepreneur.

We also reported in ICR's study that 23 percent of respondents preferred proximate location (within 300 miles) to where they lived. Is the company located geographically in an area of interest to the investors, they would ask. Not all investors are open to ventures out of state. Whether because of the difficulty of travel or because of their inability to monitor the investment adequately, investors designated geographic proximity as an essential consideration.

Chemistry between the investor and entrepreneur is essential to any favorable decision to invest. Angel investors in particular invest in entrepreneurs who positively enhance the investors' images of themselves. We invest time and money in those persons who uplift us, those who make us feel better about ourselves. These are long-term commitments, perhaps eight to ten years until liquidity—longer than most of today's marriages. Chemistry among the parties is a mandatory element for success, not just sale of the security.

Last, investors today are concerned about exit: Is the company's proposed exit route believable to the investor, and do the time horizons and return multiples fit with their investment strategy? Whether IPO, acquisition, sale or merger, or building a sustainable company to operate for cash, positioning the investor for dividends or buy back, the liquidity event needs to fit with the investor's strategy and expectations.

MANAGEMENT

People get funded, not plans! The "A" manager with a "B" plan is always preferable to a "B" manager with an "A" plan. High-quality people are the primary criterion for investing in a deal. To assess management team quality and its capability, investors will question the quality of management and, if they are present, the members of the management team. Quality is explored through questions about the individual entrepreneurs, for example. Investors will ferret out the truth about each team member through reference and background checks to verify the integrity, academic credentials, and people skills, as well as through checks on civil, criminal, credit, and, yes, even driving records. Investors question management's skills, correcting the inevitable miscalculations and other mistakes as the company grows. Entrepreneurial fervor, confidence, vision, and ability to solve problems are areas investors look at keenly.

The past judgment of managers based on their business experience is questioned. The management team is examined as well in terms of their diversity, skills, completeness of functional expertise, willingness to accept help, and commitment to the venture long term. The board of directors, advisers, and investors are also assessed, along with management; for example, board diversity and skills, ability to spend time, investors' experience, contact networks, and skill at counseling managers. Based on our research, investors have attempted to assess these characteristics of management with such questions as those listed below:

1. Who are the managers of the company? Who holds the major authority? Who is the key decision maker?
2. What are the major achievements of the CEO? How successful were his or her previous ventures?
3. Is the CEO personally familiar with the specifics of the company's operations?
4. How has the CEO dealt with major problems the company has faced before?
5. What are the CEO's financial goals in being involved in the company?
6. What is the management team's background? Do the team members' past industry experiences dovetail with their current job responsibilities? What are the members' reputations in the industry?
7. Have team members been involved in any other start-ups or public companies? Has any member of the management team previously made money for investors?
8. What is the relationship between the management and the board of directors?
9. Who sits on the board of directors? What is his or her experience and qualifications? Has he or she managed more developed, successful companies?
10. What is the total compensation of all officers in the company? Their salary, commission, bonuses, loans, expense reimbursements, profit sharing, etc.? What was their compensation in their previous positions?
11. What is each manager's stock ownership, and how much, if any, of his or her own capital has been invested in the company? What is the CEO's ownership following financing? What is the ownership of outside directors?
12. Have members of management worked together before, or are they related? Do they exude a palpable team spirit?
13. Are there any vacancies in the management structure, or is any member of the management temporarily filling a position until a permanent professional is located? What is the plan to recruit and fill positions?
14. If the CEO were not available, is there a suitable replacement on the team?

15. Has any member of the management team sued or been sued within the past five years?
16. Has any member of the management team ever been convicted of a felony?
17. Are there any civil or criminal charges pending against any member of the management team?
18. Has any member of the management team ever been terminated from a management position? Has any member left the company? Why?
19. Has any member of the management team personally filed for bankruptcy or been involved in a state receivership within the past five years?
20. Has any member of the management team ever been the officer of a company that has filed for bankruptcy?
21. Has any member of the management team been disciplined by a regulatory agency or professional association within the past five years?
22. Obtain personal and health data on all of the key managers. Are management personnel in good health? Has any member of the management team disclosed any serious difficulties in his or her private life (divorce, psychological breakdowns, alcohol or drug problems)?
23. Is any member of the management team not expendable? If yes, why? What will happen if he or she becomes unavailable?
24. Have there been any SEC problems or violations in the past 10 years for any manager, officer, or director? Has the management team signed employment contracts? Do these include noncompete clauses?
25. Have there been any problems within management, and if so, have those problems been resolved? Have there been any changes in the management team within the past two years? How do they communicate now?

BUSINESS OPPORTUNITY

This section of the due diligence framework assesses the business opportunity. The audit questions relate to the product or service and underlying technology, market and competition, distribution, and the business model (i.e., how the company will make money), and will include questions about the industry, innovation in terms of R&D, and aspects of production.

Whether the venture's technology is revolutionary, creating a new market segment, or evolutionary focused on exploiting a narrow market segment, these questions will apply in due diligence. This part of the evaluation gets to the heart of the business model: examining product/service design, whether it works, and if the product or service is something the customer wants. Investors may bring in experts to assess the technology and stage of development. Feasibility is analyzed by talking with customers, distributors, and others. Questions try to clarify the size of the market, growth rates, and reasonable penetration goals. Competitors, proprietary advantage, intellectual property, and positioning strategy round out aspects of the business that investors will ask questions about. Investors will collect information to estimate gross profit margins and look for recurring revenue streams in the business. The sample of questions asked of entrepreneurs in the past about the business opportunity are listed below.

Industry

1. What industry (or industries) is the company involved in? How many companies are in the industry? How is the industry structured (product, price, geography)?
2. Are any large players accounting for a significant share of the business in the industry? Describe the market share.
3. How would you define the competitive structure of the industry (fragmented, oligopoly, monopoly, etc.)? Which way are mergers and acquisitions heading (vertical or horizontal)?
4. What is the failure rate of companies in the industry?
5. What has been the annual industrial sales growth rate, and what is it expected to be over the next five years?
6. What has been the annual earnings growth of the industry? What are the projections for the next five years?
7. Is the industry subject to cycles? How volatile are industrial sales and earnings during economic cycles? Indicate the best and the worst possible scenarios.
8. What are the significant barriers to entry into the industry?
9. What is the success rate for new entrants into the industry? Do any company patents suggest the company's industry will succeed?
10. What is the history of the industry? Have any recent events had an impact on it?
11. What government agencies regulate the industry, and does the company expect any future changes in the degree of regulation?
12. To what extent is the industry unionized, and what has been the impact of recent labor contracts in the industry?
13. Identify the key elements influencing future industry growth, for example, market growth changes, economic trends, consolidations and economies of scale, price differences, interest rates, government regulation, environmental issues, technological innovation and product development, and foreign competition. How might these factors influence projections for the company?

Products or Services

1. What is the current product line? Describe each. How reliable are the products? Are samples available?
2. Which product is the most profitable for the company?
3. How does the product work? What problem does the product solve? Does it solve a "real" problem or fulfill a "real" need?
4. What is proprietary about the product?
5. Has all R&D been completed on the products? What is the timetable for new product introductions?
6. How is the product priced? Who establishes the price and the price structure? What are the past and present price trends in the industry?
7. What is the estimated remaining life span of each of the company's products.
8. If applicable, what is the current status of the patent for the process or product? Is a copy available?
9. When were the products introduced? At what point are they in their life cycle? Are changes in the products planned?
10. Can the product be massed produced, or does it require customizing?
11. Estimate revenues and the market share for all products over the next 12 months.
12. What are the margins for each product, and how will they change as the market share increases?
13. What are the customer service requirements for each product? Describe any customer service operations. Are any customer services contracted out to third parties?
14. What is the company's warranty policy? What is the current and projected warranty expense?

Market, Sales, and Distribution

1. What is the dollar size of the market by product? What is the annual market growth rate by product? What are the projections for three years? What are the data sources?
2. What is the company's marketing strategy? What are the annual advertising expenditures, current and projected? What is the company's selling proposition?
3. What are the central objectives in marketing? How will the strategy be implemented (e.g., is there an array of promotional activities planned)?
4. How does the company's marketing strategy compare with competitor's information? What market research has the company conducted? Are copies available?

5. How do sales breakdowns/projections by product compare with industry data?
6. Who are the company's customers? What do they buy? How big is the average order? Is there any backlog of orders, purchase orders, or letters of intent? Are customers fiscally sound? To what extent are customers repeat purchasers? How do customers perceive product quality? Is the company dependent on a few key customers?
7. How does the company find customers? What is the time and cost to close sales? Does this fit with projections? Is intensive personal selling required?
8. What are the key variables in the buying decisions? What are the price, quality, terms, etc.? Can customers shift from a competitor to the company, or is it difficult to change?
9. What are the sales performances of key salespersons to date? Are their sales currently covering the costs of marketing and sales functions? How are they compensated? How is their performance evaluated?
10. Has their performance been compared with sales projections?
11. Does the company participate at trade shows or conventions?
12. Does the company advertise? What is the average cost? Are there standing orders? What are the advertising expenditures for the past two years, and what are the projections for the next three years?
13. What is the cost of product packaging, and what image does this packaging convey to the customer?
14. Is a sales force currently in place? Is their experience relevant?
15. What types of warranties, guarantees, or service contracts are offered to customers?
16. If there is a customer problem, how is it handled?
17. Has the company established any distribution, joint venture, or technology transfer agreements?
18. How many distributors does the company use? How does the company select them? What is the rate sales volume? Does any single distributor account for a large amount of the company's sales? What are the remuneration arrangements with distributors? What are the credit terms? Are copies available of distributor marketing agreements?

Competition

1. Ranked by sales, who are the company's largest competitors?
2. Are they fiscally sound, well capitalized, and profitable? What are the present and future respective market shares?
3. What is their focus: Are they expanding niches in the industry? Are they expanding into new markets or diversifying into other industries?

4. How does the company differentiate its product from the competition? What is unique about the product?

5. What are the barriers to entry in the company's industry? Is it easy or difficult to enter this business?

6. How does the company compare to the competitors in terms of product, price, market share, functional expertise, capital resources, and management?

7. Has the number of competitors increased or decreased in the past two years, and do you expect this to change? Are there new entrants expected?

8. How do competitors usually deal with small competitors (push them out of the market, buy them out)? What is there competitive strategy?

9. At what sales level do you believe the company is a competitive threat to other companies, and how much market share does that translate into?

10. How does the company plan to combat the competition, and vise versa? For example, compare product features and price points to those of competitors.

11. Has the company identified any of its competitors in the international marketplace? If so, who are the three largest, and what are their geographic market shares?

12. What research has been conducted on competitive products? Is documentation available on competitors?

13. What competition might the company face from products from other industries that may be substituted for its own?

Research and Development

1. Who are the key engineers and R&D managers and personnel? What is their technical background?

2. What have been the costs and benefits of the major R&D programs completed during the company's history?

3. What are the current R&D programs and projected costs and time until completion? What are the expected outcomes? How were these programs selected? Why?

4. What new R&D projects are planned following financing? What are the costs and anticipated benefits? How is R&D monitored?

5. How does the company's expenditure (or projections) for R&D compare to industry standards?

6. What is the company's strategy to ensure protection of its proprietary technological development, etc.? What about its patents, confidentiality agreements, and so on?

7. What is the condition of the R&D facilities and equipment?
8. Has R&D generated reports for management? Are copies available?

Production

1. Are there any pending issues related to the Equal Employment Opportunity Commission or Occupational Safety and Health Administration?
2. What type of production process is used (e.g., continuous or batch)? What are the major operations? What are the sequence, relative cost, and space requirements for each? What is the extent of automation?
3. What is the length of the production cycle and cost of the setup? Identify the key components in the production process.
4. What is the level of technological complexity of the elements used in the production process? Any downtime problems?
5. Is the process labor intensive? What could be automated? What would be the cost of automation?
6. What backup systems have been created to deal with possible production problems?
7. Is the company vulnerable in any way to current or projected energy availability from suppliers for its production fuels or for transportation of its product to customers? What means of transportation are used to ship the finished product to market?
8. What kind of scrap or waste is generated by the production process? Are there potential issues with disposal, including environmental pollution? If necessary, check with the appropriate agencies for air, water, waste, and land issues.
9. What production stoppage has management encountered? Are there any alternative sources of production if there is an interruption in the current assembly line?
10. What are the optimum inventory levels for the finished product and for raw materials? Is the current level of inventory at the optimum level?
11. Is any part of the production process subcontracted out? Who are the subcontractors?
12. Compare the data from the above inquiries with available industry data.

INTANGIBLES

In this section of the early-stage venture capital due diligence framework by Camp, he assembles concepts not quantitative in nature, but, in fact, the more subjective perceptions of investors. These concepts include focus, momentum, "buzz," "gut" feelings, and factors that do not readily fit in other categories, for example, whether the deal is perceived as having been "overshopped."

Focus—or lack thereof—is about the entrepreneur trying to be all things to all markets. Our experience is that some entrepreneurs, driven by their own creative juices, tend to diverge from the laser point focus needed early in venture development instead of converging on an innovative solution for a relevant problem in a targeted market. This leads to a waste of resources and less impact on prospective investors.

Momentum has to do with the perception that the company has hit milestones and the belief that this implies the likelihood of its making the next goal or objective. For angels this is manifest in seeing the company as more developed or "real," that is, carrying less risk.

"Buzz" relates to how aware people "in the know" are of the venture or its technology. Successful public relations seems more important to venture capitalists than to angels, perhaps reflecting the angel penchant for privacy, or perhaps the concern about legal aspects of promoting the private placement.

"Gut feelings" is perhaps the most underrated investment criterion in private placements. While the due diligence audit suggests a natural approach to decision making, in fact, there exists a dimension involved in selecting these types of investments that is more "right brain" or intuitive. It is not only a decision based on what is said and on the data collected and analyzed, but what is unspoken, nonverbal information gleaned by astute, highly experienced investors who themselves have been entrepreneurs. Their antennae are sensitive to what is conveyed wordlessly, yet is apparently—to them—accessible. These perceptions get processed along with logical analysis in making the final investment decision.

Last, investors can draw conclusions about the quality of the deal if the deal has been in the financing market for an extended time and was rejected or only partially funded by other investors. The greatest risk to entrepreneurs in misusing the strategies proposed in *Angel Capital* is to overshop a deal by taking it to many inappropriate alternative financing resources. By committing this error, the entrepreneur will soon learn the hard way how small the early-stage financing community is in their region. If a deal comes around to investors a second time and is not funded or is underfunded, this circumstance sends a strong message that other investors have concluded that the deal lacks merit, that it does not deserve serious consideration.

LEGAL DUE DILIGENCE

The early-stage venture capital due diligence framework organizes queries about the selection of the business entity, intellectual property, past and pending litigation, and transaction issues related to the offer to sell securities—specifically, according to Camp, legal terms, conditions, and provisions that can have an impact on the investors return on investments. Having legal counsel is obviously necessary for the entrepreneur at this point to understand such provisions as the security to offer, conversion rights and terms, carve-outs, pay-to-play, dividend preferences, warrants, voting rights, repurchase/vesting, and staged capital commitments. These provisions could be included in various legal documents associated with the private placement, for example, the private placement memorandum, subscription agreement, terms sheet, stock purchase agreement, shareholders' agreement, and ancillary agreements, such as employee confidentiality agreements. During this phase of due diligence, investors strive to explore and discover whether any hidden or potential legal problems are lurking in the deal.

We are not lawyers, so the information in this section is not to be construed as legal advice. The purpose is to sensitize the entrepreneur to terms likely to crop up during negotiations with investors, terms about which the entrepreneur may want to seek legal advice. But the main reason is to preclude the entrepreneur's using clauses that investors find unattractive.

Questions about the form of the organization have to do with whether the venture is a corporation or an LLC. LLCs combine the advantage of corporate limited liability with one-level taxation of a partnership and has essentially replaced the S corporation. The C corporation permits free and ready transferability of ownership by sale of stock, without affecting the continuing existence of the business or title to its assets. Investors prefer C corporations because of their flexibility of financing through the sale of various types of securities to many investors.

Corporation structure is also preferred for an array of tax benefits that accrue to the investor and the corporation itself. If stocks are held for five years, there are capital gains tax savings, and gains can also be deferred through re-investing. The benefits to the corporation can help it to conserve capital, something very attractive to the investor. Other questions may relate to where the corporation was formed and whether any required government filings were appropriately made.

Any questions related to intellectual property protection examine whether there are any patents, copyrights, trademarks, or trade secret rights, and whether there will be any impact of these assets on the venture's potential. Concerns arise that perhaps third parties will claim intellectual property, so this possible dilemma is also researched. Patents give exclusive use rights to holders for extended periods, a protection many investors value. Such value of the patents themselves may be scrutinized by the investors' legal counsel. Also subject to examination will be any agreements to protect the integrity of confidential information. Copyrights, trade secrets protection, licenses, invention assignment agreements, and other agreements are scrutinized during this portion of due diligence.

The framework organizes questions about the transaction into this phase of due diligence. In our discussion of negotiating and structuring the deal, we have already introduced rights and terms, antidilution protection, carve-outs, pay-to-play, warrants, board voting rights, repurchase/vesting terms and staged capital commitments, right of first refusal, and redemption rights. Entrepreneurs and investors in successful deals tend to work together in customizing this array of terms to best fit with their respective needs and expectations.

Investors want to know the type of security, for example, convertible preferred or preferred with warrants. Convertibility provides investors with protection and priority early in the investment, and the ability to participate in liquidity events later as well. Investors want to understand or clarify the terms of conversion, for example, ratio of conversion or timing of conversion and whether conversion is automatic or voluntary at investor discretion.

Antidilution protection protects investors' share of ownership in the company when it changes the structure of common stock or capital structure, for example, with a stock split. Antidilution protection ensures that preferred stock holders, for instance, retain the same ownership share of the company after any structural change as they held before the change. Investors will ask questions about the type of antidilution protection that is available and how it will work, because such provisions can become complicated. Also subjects for investor queries are questions about carve-outs, defined as exceptions for certain stock issues that do not trigger antidilution provisions, and pay-to-play provisions that require investors to participate in down rounds to ensure the continuity of antidilution protection.

When a particular early round has very high levels of risk, investors may ask about warrants. Warrants provide holders a right to purchase additional stock at a fixed or predetermined price for a set period. Investors may ask about availability and terms associated with warrants.

Investors are concerned about control. One investor told us, "The only time I've lost my investment happened when I had no control in the situation." Investors making significant investments will want to know about representation on the board and whether voting rights are obtainable.

To influence management, investors ask about equity incentives. These are the purchase rights to buy back stock of exiting managers and employees, and vesting of stock to managers over time instead of issuing stock all at once. Investors also negotiate another control by staged capital closings. By investing needed capital over time and only after management accomplishes planned milestones, investors can control performance to plan and budget, and so perhaps reduce some risk in the deal.

The final set of questions in the framework's legal due diligence pertains to exit and liquidity. Investors become involved in early-stage, private equity financings because they believe that ultimately there will be a way of getting out, and in so doing they will realize appreciation on their investment and loss of use of capital for years.

Questions about registration rights focus on the investors' right to participate in liquidity events and to register their securities for public sale, for example, an IPO. Also investors might want to demand registration rights that give investors the right to mandate the company to register their shares. Piggyback registration questions will query the rights for investors' shares to be included in any new shares issued by the company. Questions about drag-along rights center on provisions providing investors to force the sale of the entire company if investors find a buyer or merger candidate and negotiate an acceptable deal. Anti-lockout terms have to do with the investors' rights to be bought out if such actions are acceptable to management. Tag-along rights ensure that investors participate with entrepreneurs, if they decide to sell out to a third party.

In addition to the questions explained above, our research among entrepreneurs had identified the added due diligence queries investors have used to assess investment parameters:

1. What is the company's fund-raising strategy?
2. What is the total amount needed in this round, and what percentage of that money is expected to be venture capital?
3. What will be accounted for in the use of proceeds once financing is complete?
4. What is the funding schedule (how much and when)?
5. How much has been raised to date?
6. What are the terms and conditions of the private placement?
7. What will the total dilution be at the end of funding?
8. Is all equity diluted equally?
9. List all categories of investment made by the company (common or preferred stock, convertible, debt, etc.).
10. What is the timetable for a public offering?
11. How much time is spent by management promoting the company's stock?
12. Is management experienced in raising capital?
13. Does the company have an investor/public relations firm? If so, what are the terms of its contract?
14. What is the budget for promotional (funding) activities?
15. Who is the securities attorney?
16. Has the company granted director status to investor groups?

FINANCIAL DUE DILIGENCE

The final section of the Camp framework focuses attention on financial analysis. Investors will carefully analyze financial projections or pro forma financial statements, since start-ups do not have historical financial data. This is a way for investors to think through financial implications of management decisions made in preparing the business plan.

Investors will ask questions about burn rate (the amount of capital used by the company per month to implement its plan), current and future financing risk, and valuation. However, the primary focus here is on financial forecasts or pro forma financial statement analysis. In the next chapter, we will address valuation; in this section, we concentrate on analysis of financial projections.

Can management reach the forecast objectives? Projections are structured around the objectives developed by the management team during the planning process. The marketing, sales, and operations strategies and plans indicate the financial requirements. The industry trend analyses imply specific assumptions about likely future conditions. Investors will evaluate projections and the assumptions behind projections. Especially when projections were prepared using spreadsheet software by the entrepreneurs themselves, expect close examination.

The range of pro forma financial statements that investors will request and analyze include budgets, cash flow data, income projections, pro forma balance sheet and income statements, break-even analysis projecting when the company will begin profitability, and cash flow break-even analysis specifying when the company can stop raising money. Cash flow statements project the cycle of turning sales into cash that pay the cost of doing business and to turn a profit. Cash flow analysis also reflects credit and collection policies and projected financing activity. Cash flow analysis tells the investors when cash will be needed.

The remainder of financial statements analyzed will be the income statement projecting revenues, expenses, and earnings over three to five years. The balance sheet shows assets and liabilities and equity of the company on a given date.

Questions About Projections

- How did management arrive at its financial projections? Develop a list of key assumptions used by management to prepare the financial projections.
- If a company is actually generating revenues, has it met projections to date?

- How might ratio analysis be used with the projections?
- Should projections be discounted? What impact does such discounting have on the company's valuation and the amount of equity appropriate for the investor?
- Are the projected revenues accurate? What are the costs to attain revenues? What are the projected profits?
- What is the estimated return based on discounted projections?
- What is the past record of actual cost against projected cost?
- What are the company's expected financial needs? Investors want to know funding requirements: how much? when needed? type of funding appropriate? equity offered capital? Not only will investors ask how much funding is sought, but how it will be used.

Questions About Capital Requirements

- What is the company's capitalization strategy? Long term, short term, or both?
- How much more capital, based on the company's proposed funding schedule, needs to be raised before the company can finance operations and growth from income and from the use of traditional credit-type financing?
- At what point will the company be able to internally finance future growth?
- What is the total amount of capital needed for this round?
- What will be the total dilution at the end of the funding schedule? Is all equity diluted equally? What securities is the company using or offering?
- Is there a timetable for IPO or exit?
- Does the company need approval of any entity other than the board of directors for this financing?

The balance sheet illustrates the financial condition of the company by showing what it owns and what it owes at the report date. The balance sheet lists the assets required to support the operation of the business. The liability section shows how these assets are to be financed.

The assets section of the balance sheet includes information on current assets, property plant and equipment, other assets, and intangibles. Current assets include all cash of the company. Current assets also include marketable securities at lower cost or market value, accounts receivable less doubtful accounts, notes receivable collectible within one year, inventories, prepaid expenses, and any other current assets. Property, plant, and equipment can provide information on land, buildings, machines, leasehold improvements, furniture, and vehicles, less any accumulated depreciation. Depreciation relates to tangible assets, such as a building, car, and so on.

Other assets, such as intangibles, will provide balance sheet information on goodwill, patents, franchises, trademarks, copyrights, and licenses, less any amortization. Amortization is a way of reflecting periodic changes to income to recognize the distribution of the cost of the company's intangible assets over the estimated useful lives of those assets.

Questions on Assets in the Pro Forma Balance Sheet

Cash

- How many depository accounts? Identify all cash accounts.
- Average balance per account during the past year?
- Have all bank accounts been reconciled?

Receivables

- What percentage of the company's sales are on a credit basis?
- What are the terms?
- What credit checks does management perform before extending credit?
- Are credit reports updated?
- What percentage are delinquent? How long before delinquent accounts are collected? Is there an allowance for an account that may be difficult to fully collect?
- Does payee recognize receivables as being due?
- How and when are receivables recognized?
- What percentage of sales are cash versus credit customers?
- What are the credit terms?
- Who makes the decision about extending credit?
- Does the company have any allowance for bad debts?

Inventory

- What inventory valuation method is used (cost or market value)?
- When was the physical inventory last reconciled (present market value)? Was a year-end physical inventory taken?
- What is the turnover rate?
- What condition is the inventory in? Is any of it obsolete?
- Are inventory controls in place? What is the policy or procedure to minimize the amount of money tied up in inventory?

Fixed Assets

- Description, cost, and current value of each fixed asset? What is the replacement value for plant and equipment, and how does this compare with the book value or the liquidity value?

■ Are depreciation methods used consistently?
■ What percentage of the company's assets are leased? What are the terms? How does the value of capital leases compare with the fair market value?
■ Who approves capital expenditures?
■ Are any assets pledged as collateral or subject to liens?

Other Assets

■ Is management expensing R&D, or is it capitalized as an asset and expensed over a defined period?
■ Is management invested in marketable securities? Which securities and why?
■ Are there any deferred costs or intangible assets? How are these valued?
■ Is there a pension plan? Are there any funding requirements?
■ Are there any reserve accounts to cover bad receivables or warranty claims?

The balance sheet liabilities section covers current liabilities and long-term liabilities. Current liabilities are those that will be due within a year and include accounts payable, notes payable, and accrued expenses; for example, salary, interest, professional fees, insurance expense, warranty and taxes, income taxes payable, and revolving lines of credit. Look at any large accounts payable. Consider taxes in some detail. For example, take the time to understand what the company's applicable federal, state, and local income taxes and excises taxes are and any special industry tax considerations, such as depletion allowances (and write-offs). It's important to understand in reviewing the income tax payable whether the company is current on all of the taxes it owes and whether it has filed all tax returns, whether it has ever been audited, and whether it is in compliance with sales and payroll taxes.

Long-term liabilities—those due beyond a year—include items such as deferred income taxes because of accelerated write-offs, long-term notes, and debentures.

Questions About Liabilities

■ How much debt has the company incurred? How many loans does it have outstanding? Request legal loan documents. What is its debt service schedule and payment history?
■ What collateral has been offered up for loans?
■ Have there been any personal guarantees or corporate guarantees for loans?

■ With what companies does the firm have payables due? Is any one company owed more than 10 percent of the payables? How old are outstanding payables?

■ Obtain a complete list of loans and notes payable and details on each. Gather information on payment histories and any defaults, and on any guarantees for loans.

■ Are there any off-balance-sheet financings? What are their terms and conditions?

■ Any unrecorded liabilities or product liability claims?

■ Are there any accrued liabilities outstanding?

Shareholders' equity is the total equity interest all shareholders have in the company. It is the amount shareholders would split up if the company were liquidated at balance sheet value. In the balance sheet, the shareholders' equity section involves a detailed description of all capital stock, whether those stocks are preferred or common, and any additional paid-in capital. Paid-in capital is any amount paid for stock over the stated value or the par value per share of that stock. Also included in the shareholders' equity discussion is information on any retained earnings of the company. Investors may also ask about capitalization history.

Questions on Shareholders' Equity

■ A chronological list of all past financings.

■ A discussion of why the company raised money and at what valuation.

■ Evaluation of whether loans are all paid to date.

■ Evaluation of whether dividends have been provided as promised.

■ The state of investor relations.

■ Description of any personal guarantees, assets, or collateral that have been pledged by the company.

■ Managers trying to pay off company debt or alleviate any personal debt through the financing.

■ The person (or persons)—if anyone—who will have liquidation preference over the investor's investment.

■ The company's present capitalization.

■ Data on all shareholder equity and classes of stock used by the company, including the type of stock, number of shares authorized and outstanding, any voting rights, dividends, warrants and options outstanding, the owners' names, prices offered, and any special terms. Determine whether any of the following items are also included: stock option plans, restrictions on stock, preemptive rights, rights of first refusal, convertible instruments, and agreements for further issuance of stock.

An income statement is a record of the revenues and expenses for a given accounting period. An accounting period is usually one year. The forecasted income statement matches amounts the company expects to receive from selling goods and services and other income against cost and outlays incurred to operate the company. The income statement is also called a profit-and-loss statement or—when there is a loss for the period—a statement of operations. The accuracy of a pro forma income statement is directly related to the assumptions used in creating the sales plan.

Questions for the Income Statement

Sales

- How are sales or revenues or losses recognized?
- Are sales front loaded; that is, recognized before being collected in full?
- To what extent are future revenues dependent on R&D projects in process?
- At what rate are revenues projected to increase annually for the next three years? How does this compare with industry estimates?
- Are forecasts based on historical results, trends, or any industry analysis?
- How were projections developed? Should they be discounted? Have projections been achieved in the past?
- What method was used to forecast growth: trend projections, market studies, management's best guess?

Costs

- How does the company recognize costs of production? Recognize overhead? For example, is it using standard costs that it corrects for rework?
- How are costs budgeted, monitored, and controlled?
- What are the critical costs to keep under control?

Earnings

- Is management contemplating any potential future earnings adjustments, such as salary adjustments, different tax provisions, and so on?
- Has management provided realistic best-case and worst-case circumstances for projecting earnings?
- When potential increases in costs are incorporated into the projections, is gross profit percentage maintained in the projections?

For both new and existing businesses, the cash flow forecast is the most important projection because it details the amount and timing of expected cash inflow and outflows; that is, it incorporates sources of cash and uses of cash in any given time frame to determine the cash outlay and the net cash available. In effect, the statement of cash flows examines changes in cash resulting from all business activities. Generally, the cash flow in the start-up years of a business will not sufficiently finance the operational needs. Cash inflows often do not match the outflows on a short-term basis. The cash flow forecast will indicate these conditions and enable the investor to evaluate management's plan for cash needs.

Given a level of projected sales and capital expenditures over a specific period, the cash flow forecast will highlight the need for additional financing and indicate peak requirements for working capital.

Questions for the Cash Flow Statement

■ How many depository accounts are there? What are the balances in those accounts? How much cash does the company have?
■ How much cash flow does the company handle monthly?
■ Does the company have multiple collection points?
■ How many disbursement accounts does the company have? Who authorizes payments? Who is in control of disbursements?
■ At what point in time will cash flows become positive?
■ What is the monthly cash burn rate, and how will this forecast fluctuate pre- and postfinancing?
■ At what rate are earnings projected to increase over the next three to five years?
■ Is the company taking advantage of discounts for early payment when available?
■ Is the company maintaining the minimum cash balance required in its operating accounts?

Why does the company need capital now? How will the company use the funds currently being raised? These questions are answered in the use-of-proceeds statement. Normally, the uses of proceeds cover such capital expenditures as purchase of property, leasehold improvements, purchase of equipment and furniture, and other types of capital expenditures. In addition, in a use-of-proceeds listing, working capital commonly will be required for such activities as purchase of inventory, staff expansion, new product line introduction, additional marketing activities, and other business expansion activities. In some instances, debt retirement or establishment of cash reserves will be the focus of the use-of-proceeds section.

Questions for the Use of Proceeds

- If the company has raised money in the past, how did it use past funds?
- Why does the company need money now? Specifically, how will it use the money? Spell out each item that the company plans to spend money on.
- Are there any broker fees that portions of the proceeds will go to pay?

Investors will most likely ask for a list of assumptions used by management in preparing all pro forma financial statements. How were assumptions developed? Are the details believable?

Questions on Financial Assumptions

- What are the chances of the company's achieving projections?
- What major problems did you identify in the projections, and what are management's plans to overcome them?
- Can the problems be realistically solved within your time frame to achieve returns?
- If the company fails to achieve financial objectives and must be liquidated, what is your downside recoverability?
- Based on further financial requirements for the company that have been identified, are you prepared to reinvest in the future?

In addition to financial statements, entrepreneurs can expect requests for lists of investors, advisers, directors, and other resources for reference checks. A list based on our experience of requested references and other materials is provided below. In addition, miscellaneous documents investors might request include a capitalization table disclosing pre- and postfinancing ownership, organization chart, resumes of key management with references, certificate of incorporation, business licenses, list of officers and directors, employment contracts, noncompete agreements, list of suppliers, and leases. If an operating company, investors may ask to see tax returns for all years filed, materials of any past or present lawsuits, insurance policies for key personnel, patents, trademarks, copyrights, details on outstanding stock, R&D reports, incentive plans, any SEC filings, list of depository accounts, and credit reports.

LISTS FOR REFERENCE CHECKS

Be prepared to supply names and contact information for the following:

- Institutional investors and lenders
- Any investment banking firm involved in the transaction
- Law firm and corporate legal counsel
- Names of the accounting firm(s) for the past three years
- Bank(s), banker, and any private credit source
- Board of directors, officers, and advisory board
- Broker dealers or underwriters involved in the transaction
- Private and corporate investors and any other stockholders in the company
- Finders or financial intermediaries assisting the company
- Consultants, past and present, who advised or analyzed the company
- Appraisers involved in valuation of the company
- Key customers
- Landlord
- Public relations, marketing, promotion, or advertising firm retained by the company
- Institutional industry analyst following the industry and venture capital firms investing in this industry
- Key competitors
- Top three publicly traded companies in the industry.

CHAPTER 13

Valuation of the Early-Stage Company

INTRODUCTION

If any term receives reverential treatment in the business of financing a venture, it is surely *valuation*. And such distinction is well earned. Valuation haunts every aspect of a venture; in its very scope, valuation becomes the entire process writ small. No deal gets very far without it; no deal can be torpedoed more quickly if it is off the mark. The best test of a deal's practicability and pricing is whether it can attract, and be sold to, another private investor at the same price—in other words, its valuation. However, investors typically will rely on their own judgment in evaluating a deal.

John Cadle, a valuation expert, has sage advice about valuing a venture. To begin with, explains Cadle, unlike buying an existing business with lots of assets—an event possessing formulated definitions of what value is—for the early-stage company, no recognized definition of valuation exists. Cadle warns entrepreneurs to realize that in an early-stage venture, the value is in the future. Therefore, definitions are limited. Determining value in early-stage investing is highly subjective, because such determination depends on something that has not yet happened.

So our bias is that valuation is more art than science, a tricky business based on judgment and assumption. Valuation at best is imprecise, an estimate or extrapolation with no hard-and-fast rules for the entrepreneur to follow. Methods of calculating value are customized, not standardized. Once the investor decides his or her interest in investing, valuation begins.

Thus, into the valuation mix go many subjective elements: the experience and cohesion of the management team; the size and growth rate of the market; whether the business is in manufacturing, service, or retail; whether the product or service has a competitive edge; whether the venture is a product or business; the degree of market development (missionary selling) required; the likelihood of additional financing, planned or not; whether the exit strategy is realistic; whether the deal has been overshopped; and how persuasive and committed the founders and management team are.

With so subjective a mix, valuation is best deferred until later on in the process, after you have that investor believing firmly in you as an entrepreneur, after he or she is sold on the dream. It is a big mistake, cautions Cadle, to bring up valuation too early; better that valuation be considered later on in the relationship.

PRICING AS GOOD JUDGMENT, NOT FORMULAE

One element that characterizes all early-stage ventures is their illiquidity. As we mentioned, one test of a deal's practicality and pricing is whether it can attract and be sold to another private investor at the same price, although not necessarily the highest price—in other words, sold at the same valuation to another investor. In addition, investors could do worse than to seek opinions from their network of co-investors to obtain the bids of other respected, experienced investors. Estimates from others that reasonably approximate an investor's own appraisal can increase confidence in valuation assessment. Ironically, the value of an illiquid company may be as much a function of finding an investor as that of financial formulae and calculations.

To repeat, investors rely on their own judgment in valuing a deal, a judgment mandating considerable investigation and analysis. Some factors have an obvious effect on value (i.e., low risk means higher value); computing value is a complex affair fraught with problems. Valuation is not a precise form of financial analysis; it is more akin to an art form or, at times, even horse trading. In valuation, subjective factors we mentioned can simply eclipse objective factors. The mass of intangibles is often overwhelming and weighs heavily on investors, causing two sophisticated investors to reach two different estimates of value. For example, to the extent that investors are familiar with the business, they might give the entrepreneur a higher valuation because they perceive their risk as being lower, whereas the investor who is investing in a business about which he or she knows nothing will not. Since value is in the future, definitions are limited. Limited too are calculations influenced by incomplete information, rapidly changing environmental factors, unproven management, untested technology, and undeveloped markets. Determining value in early-stage investing is highly subjective because so much depends on something that has not yet happened. In addition, the negotiation skills of the investors and entrepreneurs themselves can become variables influencing the valuation outcome.

In the wake of stock market fluctuations, the spotlight now falls more than ever on the vagaries of valuation. In 1999 to 2000, public market companies with little-established earnings had been trading at 1,200 times earnings, and 5 percent of the entire stock market contributed 70 percent of the wealth by the end of 2000. It seemed that even public equity players threw caution to the wind. Public enthusiasm pushed valuations very high by historic standards, especially since a number of start-ups had been more successful than anticipated.

The astounding multiples at which many Internet start-ups with no earnings or immediate potential for earnings had been valued at the time has served only to reemphasize the use of traditional valuation models to estimate early-stage technology company value. Investors are relying on common sense for guidance, using comparative analysis of similar firms to ascertain proper funding levels, valuation, and equity share. If the venture fails, any valuation is irrelevant. In private investing, survival is everything. As we have reiterated, smart investors are risk averse, regardless of what entrepreneurs believe! The foremost thing they want to know is not what their return on investment will be in five years but whether the company will survive at all. Entrepreneurs can talk glory, but if the company cannot survive the first 18 months, negotiations about value become immaterial. So first the entrepreneur has to convince an investor that the company will survive.

Finally, we want to reiterate a point we made in the negotiation section, one especially important when the investor invests a larger percentage of the total financing round and plans to be more active in the company after investment. Entrepreneurs may come across investors who choose to be an aggressive negotiator, that is, don the guise of the stereotypical Wall Street investment negotiator and beat the entrepreneur down to get the best possible deal, squeezing everything possible out of him or her. Keep in mind that the chemistry between the entrepreneur and investor must be there in order to make the early-stage investment work. An investment relationship suffers from inherent fragility because it's so risky. Most knowledgeable investors appreciate that it's folly then for an investor to try to squeeze every last dime out of the entrepreneur, first because valuation is so subjective, and second because such behavior destroys the chemistry essential to a healthy working relationship. For those who fail to understand that entrepreneurs will remember bad treatment at this stage: the entrepreneur must have the courage to walk away. These partnerships require the investor and entrepreneur to work together for a long, long time. And no investment transaction can long endure a backlog of resentment by either party.

RISK

In valuation, then, everything centers on the degree of risk. When investors look at an investment prospect, they hope to determine the amount of work the entrepreneur has already done in developing a product, developing the market, or selling the product—all things that reduce risk in the deal. Again, such determination remains subjective.

Furthermore, risk is layered in terms of the stages of the deal. Obviously, if only a concept exists, if we have no more than an idea, we place ourselves at great risk. In fact, the investor may feel that despite the talent and trustworthiness of the entrepreneur, the risk simply remains too great.

On the other hand, if the entrepreneur is already selling a product, and the market has already validated its willingness to buy it, the risk is substantially less. The valuation depends largely on how investors perceive the risk. Different investors will perceive risks differently. Investors will not measure risk in the same way or to the same degree. Investors want answers to some specific questions: How much risk remains in the deal? How far along is the entrepreneur in the process? Has validation through other investors occurred? Is the market already buying these products or services?

Investors struggle with these questions as they try to value the company to determine whether they will obtain enough ownership percentage to justify the risk of investment and lose the use of capital for an extended time.

Thus, as an entrepreneur you must defend your valuation in terms of risk/reward. You have to understand the process that the investor is going to go through. You should have in mind a range of valuations. Valuation, after all, is a negotiation, probably one of the more subjective negotiations an entrepreneur will endure because of so many nonfinancial factors—nothing pat, nothing to map the area. No set value at one percent of revenue, or one times revenue, or a price-earnings multiple. In valuation, where there is no earnings, there cannot be any price.

The question becomes one of why an investor should invest in you. What makes you a decent soul? What is right about the deal? How might it be structured to lower the perceived risk?

But before all other considerations comes the importance for the entrepreneur in selling the dream to the investor, best accomplished by bringing that investor into your vision of the future early on. Make sure that you and the investor have the appropriate chemistry, a vital aspect of any venture.

The part such chemistry plays in valuation is hard to overestimate. Because these types of investment are such precarious things, because so much operates beyond our control, good chemistry among the active parties is paramount. Compatible chemistry with sophisticated investors who understand the risks is far more important than a high initial valuation.

And without investors who understand the risk, who understand that private investing is a long-term process, who are willing to sail with you for the long run, frankly, a high initial valuation is a shallow, short-term victory, often a negative rather than a positive. Entrepreneurs should trade a lower initial valuation for helpful, smart partners with the right chemistry and the willingness to stand by them.

Valuation, after all, boils down to what percentage of ownership of the business the entrepreneur is giving to the investor in order to get the capital needed to grow the business. In effect, the entrepreneur is bringing in a partner, somebody the entrepreneur will virtually be living with. Valuation is not a sale, after which the buyer strolls away. This is partnership—a partnership built on compatibility. Moreover, the smart entrepreneur will be hoping to get more from that partner than just money. In fact, the chances are better than not that the entrepreneur will be returning to that same partner for additional infusions of capital. So valuation is far more complex and selective than simply selling a business to the highest bidder and then cartwheeling away.

Valuation, then, can certainly occur prematurely. It can dampen a relationship like nothing else. It can badly influence a deal, especially if it occurs before the entrepreneur sells the dream. Make no mistake; early valuation has killed many early-stage deals.

Valuation is not guided by something as unchanging as a euclidian formula. The best that valuation can offer are rules of thumb. And again, all investors may view such "rules" differently. How investors perceive risk, or stage of the venture, relates to value. In other words, the higher the risk investors perceive, the higher the return they will require; the higher the return they require, the lower the valuation is likely to be. The farther along you are, the less risk investors perceive. Put another way, investors are willing to pay more for what you already have.

NEGOTIATING VALUATION

The pricing of venture investments is part art, part science, and part old-fashioned Yankee horse trading. Old-fashioned Yankee horse trading, of course, means negotiating. And few things, it seems, escape negotiation. "Every desire that demands satisfaction—and every need to be met—is at least potentially an occasion for people to initiate the negotiation process," noted Gerard I. Nierenberg 30 years ago in *The Art of Negotiating.*

Negotiating means dickering over *fair market value,* a term defined by the American Society of Appraisers as "the price at which a property would change hands between a willing buyer and willing seller when neither is acting under compulsion and both have equal access to all relevant information about the business." However, in early-stage companies, as we have said, value lies in the future, infusing valuation with its subjectivity. Such subjectivity renders established definitions useless. Cadle offers, instead, this expanded, real-world definition of value for the small early-stage business: that "point at which an investor's fear (risk profile) is in equilibrium with his greed (return requirements)."

Valuation is part of negotiation. In fact, valuation provides the basis for negotiation.

As we have said, in the valuation negotiations, the parties are trying to come up with percentage ownership between the investor and entrepreneur. The objective of the negotiation is to bridge the gap between an entrepreneur's high expectations and an investor's valuation model. The entrepreneur seeks to relinquish the least amount of equity possible in order to obtain the capital necessary to grow the company. Meanwhile, the investor pushes for lower valuation to own more of the company so that at exit, when multiples on investment are realized, capital appreciation will have justified the risk.

So it is in the interest of both parties to use multiple valuation methods in trying to arrive at a mutual value. Since early-stage investors are risk averse, they appreciate the risks involved in early-stage investing and intend to manage those risks through due diligence, valuation, negotiation, and close monitoring of the venture after they invest. Additional valuation tools successful investors use include correlating desired return with time to liquidity, discounting projections, establishing realistic desired multiples for cash-out in advance, and correcting equity share with dilution factors. For the entrepreneur, the amount of money raised is a function of the value assigned by the investor and the result of successful negotiations. It will not pay the entrepreneur to be unreasonable, even when the market value attained was less than expected.

In the real world, then, an equity ownership position should produce an expected annualized rate of return over a reasonable time period proportional to the investor's tolerance for risk. Valuation in this context does not depend on hard assets, prior sweat equity, intellectual property, book value, or similar items. These factors enter into the equation only to the extent that they can generate future value. Valuation depends on the creation or expansion of a going concern into a marketable commodity through an event that provides liquidity for the investor, such as by acquisition or IPO. Valuation also depends on the amount of risk that has already been mitigated by the company in product development, marketing, customer franchise, and cohesion of the management team.

In sum, entrepreneurs need to alert themselves to certain existing conditions. Leverage in establishing value normally operates in favor of the investor for the following reasons: approach to value is primarily subjective, not objective; there exists a limited, inefficient market; the seller (entrepreneur) needs capital while the buyer (investor) does not have to invest; and the investor may not believe he or she has all the relevant information about the business.

SWEAT EQUITY

Valuation is an emotional issue with entrepreneurs because their egos are involved. They want value for their sweat equity, the time and effort they have previously invested in the venture. Understandably, entrepreneurs want the highest value for the hard work they have already invested. Most angel investors appreciate that sweat equity enters into the negotiation, because it is a way that entrepreneurs show investors how dedicated they have been. Investors, of course, want somebody who is willing to do anything to achieve a projection. *Perceived* sweat equity is important in the investor's evaluation of the entrepreneur.

But attributing monetary value to that sweat equity in a valuation calculation is difficult, if not impossible. Sweat equity gets translated into specific value in this way: If the investor is comfortable with the management, the investor will decrease the estimated risk of this deal, resulting in a higher valuation. This move by the investor results, in turn, in more equity for the entrepreneur. For example, the entrepreneur might want to be back-paid, saying, "I could have gone to company X and earned half a million dollars a year. I've been doing this for five years now, and I've only been paying myself $50,000 a year, so I want to be back-paid for the $450,000 per year I gave up. In other words, I want $2 million." This proposal is ludicrous. Successful investors are more sophisticated than that. They simply don't play that game anymore.

The investor appreciates that entrepreneurs have chosen years of sweat equity instead of a salary, that they may have mortgaged their home, and so forth. But smart angel investors judge that sweat equity only on what they will realize from this point on. The arrow points to the right, not backward to the left. What is on the investor's mind is how far along the entrepreneur is in the process and what the investor can get in the future for his or her investment.

So sweat equity carries different emotional messages to entrepreneurs than it does to investors, a difference that entrepreneurs especially need to understand. Your facts and the investor's facts may differ markedly. Failing to get inside the investor's perspective on this issue can quickly derail the valuation process. These are different perceptions, different starting points. The task falls, of course, on the entrepreneur because it is the entrepreneur who must try on the investor's shoes, not the other way around.

For a time, during the dot-com boom, the early-stage, private equity investment culture changed from when sweat equity meant working in the garage and taking salary cuts in exchange for equity to entrepreneurs working in palatial buildings and taking handsome salaries as the angel investors continue to pump in money. If improved rates of return are to be achieved by investors, the equation had to change. The fact is an entrepreneur may be able to find some investors who are unsophisticated and thereby gain an unrealistically high valuation. But an initial ego gratification of an exorbitant valuation on sweat equity belies the essentials of a long-term partnership, a mutually respectful and beneficial partnership built with investors who understand the business and the process, partners who will be there to smooth the inevitable bumps in the road.

THE "LIVING DEAD"

So if the entrepreneur is concentrating on sweat equity, what is the investor mulling over? We have an idea of what sweat equity means to the entrepreneur. But in valuation, different starting points are generated by the cavity between the entrepreneur's sweat equity and the investor's fear of gaining membership among the "living dead." Who are the living dead and what does the term mean to investors?

If you have a business and an investor invests in you, he or she becomes your partner. You are your own boss, having a wonderful time manufacturing your widgets—as any entrepreneur would. Things are fine with you. But if the investor can never obtain liquidity from the investment, a problem emerges. The business is doing well, and you are enjoying what you are doing because it is what you enjoy doing for a living. But to the investor, the investment is a failure because he or she cannot get money out at an appropriate multiple of the investment. The investor needs a liquidity event. As John Cadle explains, "If I'm looking at a deal, and I think I can get liquid in two years, I'll probably accept a lower rate of return, rather than accept a long-range development project that is not going to be liquid for seven years."

Liquidity can be achieved through a number of different mechanisms— for example, through a sale back to the entrepreneur, a merger, an acquisition by a public company, trading of illiquid stock for publicly traded securities, the sale of the company to other entrepreneurs, or an IPO. The investor has to keep in mind that very few of all venture-backed companies in the past several years have reached liquidity through IPO. Either the entrepreneur has to buy the investor out or some other situation has to occur that turns the investment into a return for the investor. In other words, the investor has to get money out of the investment sometime. If none of these alternatives works, we have an investor who has become a member of the living dead.

And while IPO is only one way—and not the typical way—to obtain liquidity, people are often fooled by the publicity generated by an IPO. The fact is that many more businesses are merged or acquired than experience an initial public offering. Perhaps this is the reason entrepreneurs often fail to realize how important it is to impress in advance on the investor what liquidity options are available out of an investment.

No investor wants to suffer in financial purgatory by being left in a venture without liquidity. For many investors, being a member of the living dead has been a dreadful financial experience—hanging in limbo, not wanting to slip backward, but unable to move forward. The money is in, but the investor has no way to get it out.

STRATEGIES FOR CIRCUMVENTING NEGOTIATION ROADBLOCKS

One way to address valuation issues and mitigate investor risk is to use the conversion ratios that we discussed earlier. One method is through the conversion feature of the preferred stock. Commonly, preferred stock will initially convert on a one-to-one basis at the time it is issued. In the event of antidilution protection on a down round, the conversion ratio will automatically adjust so that each share of preferred stock will convert into more than one share of common stock. This mechanism offsets the lower-priced issuance by increasing the preferred holder's ownership percentage in the company.

The same mechanism can be used to address a valuation issue. Suppose an entrepreneur believes his company should be valued at $10 million while an investor thinks it is worth only $7 million. With a $1 million investment at a $10 million premoney valuation, the investor would end up owning 9.1 percent of the company; at a $7 million premoney valuation, the investor would own 12.5 percent of the company. The investor states that he or she would agree to the $10 million valuation if the company were able to recruit a certain CEO within three months.

For example, the entrepreneur could sell the investor a 12.5 percent stake on a postinvestment basis but provide that the conversion ratio of the preferred stock be adjusted to result in a lower number of common share equivalents if the CEO joins within the specified time frame. Variations such as this one abound. The conversion ratio might have three different possible settling points based on the reaching of various milestones. Or the ratio might not be set at all until some future point when milestones can be measured.

Another way to resolve a valuation disagreement is to provide for multiple closings of the investment. An investor may be willing to risk a portion of the amount requested of him up front, but may be unwilling to put in the whole amount at the proposed valuation.

For example, the investment agreement could provide for an initial clos- ing of 50 percent of the total amount to be invested. The agreement could then provide for an additional closing of the remaining 50 percent to occur before a specified date, based on the company's achievements of milestones. These milestones would be negotiated between the parties and would consti- tute the thresholds that the investor feels are required to merit each remain- ing portion of the investment.

Depending on the stage of the company, the milestones might relate to stages of product development, the hiring of a CEO, the issuance of a patent or copyright, new customer contracts, revenue levels, or, for more developed companies, levels of operating income. In Internet companies, milestones often relate to the beta stage of a web site, a targeted number of subscribers to a service, or a deal with a portal company or other strategic partner.

Critical to this multiple closings strategy, of course, are the understand- able, simple milestones that people can agree on. Fuzzy milestones (e.g., per- haps different interpretations of a cash flow formula) later become serious hindrances to the company's progress. In structuring a deal in this way, the entrepreneur is declaring that if he or she fails to perform, the investor has the option—but not the obligation—to put in further money, perhaps nego- tiating a lower valuation.

FUNDAMENTALS OF VALUING START-UP VENTURES

In early-stage companies, as we have said, value lies in the future. Such un- certainty renders less useful the established valuation formulae, which de- pend on more precise data and calculations. Valuation expert John Cadle offers instead an expanded real-world definition of value for the early-stage private business: "That point at which an investor's fear (risk profile) is in equilibrium with his greed (return requirements)." Ultimately this is accom- plished by coming up with an agreed on percentage ownership between the investor and the entrepreneur.

In the real world, then, an equity ownership position should produce an expected annualized rate of return over a reasonable time proportional to the investor's tolerance for risk. Valuation in this context does not depend on hard assets, prior sweat equity, intellectual property, book value, asset re- placement, or similar items. These considerations enter into the equation only to the extent that they can generate future value or for comparative pur- poses. Valuation depends on the creation or expansion of a going concern into a marketable commodity through an event that provides liquidity for the investor, such as by acquisition or IPO. Valuation also depends on the amount of risk that has already been mitigated by the company in product development, marketing, customer franchise, and cohesion of the management team.

MACROECONOMIC FORCES IN VALUATION

Valuations and multiples or ratios in the public stock market, supply of capital and level of capital demand, current and projected interest rates set by the Federal Reserve are all examples of macroeconomic factors that might determine an investor's valuation. Meanwhile, more subjective determinants, that is, individual investor requirements, can significantly influence the valuation calculation, a calculation that might include the risk profile of the investor, the risk associated with various company characteristics (e.g., stage of development, management experience, and time to liquidity), the level of investor involvement, and the dilution.

For current or potential angel investors, a number of macroeconomic determinants can influence their valuation of a company. The following checklist may help in weighing some of those factors:

- The stock market. While the stock market obviously determines the value of a publicly held company, it also affects privately held companies. The higher and more buoyant the stock market, especially IPOs, the greater the impact on early-stage company valuations. Internet companies serve as prime examples. The problem in the late 1990s was the absolute explosion in IPOs, primarily Internet companies. That explosion was compounded by the compression of time. In the late 1980s and early 1990s, the standard waiting period from seed stage to either an acquisition or an IPO was three to five years, usually closer to five than to three. In the case of Internet companies, market watchers in the late 1990s viewed one or two years as a long time.

  Today presents a different set of circumstances. The tech stock meltdown, the dot-com bust, and the moribund stock market all conspired to reduce valuations. While many public stocks are still considered overvalued, the impact on the private equity market is more insidious. Without access to the IPO market, a huge overhang of venture-backed early-stage and first-stage companies (estimated at 7,000 companies) await liquidity events. This backlog could take years to provide exit, unless they are written off. The primary impact has been downward pressure on early-stage, private company valuations in private placement offerings.

- Money supply and capital demand. The money supply for early-stage companies has suffered contraction. Many venture capital firms are husbanding capital to finance portfolio companies, more developed investee companies that may be unable to raise capital or find an exit. It is estimated that as many as 50 percent of early-stage venture capital funds may no longer exist in five years. Corporate and institutional investors have all but disappeared from the early-stage market. And angels who suffered losses in both their public and private portfolios to the tune of trillions are investing less often and making smaller investments. Most important, increased caution is manifest in longer due diligence cycles and increasing negotiation pressure on valuation and deal terms, causing increased expense, longer time frames to raise capital, and increased equity distributions to investors. All this is happening as entrepreneurs find themselves competing with more and more developed companies for a smaller pot of gold.

■ Interest rates. By June 2004, the Federal Reserve had lowered interest rates a dozen times to their lowest level in 20 years. Interest rates at the time of publication are showing signs of upward pressure with slight trends in inflation. However, the Fed had kept rates at historic lows for two years and the rates appear relatively stable. A lower interest rate theoretically will lower the "hurdle" rate for equity returns in general, and the returns for venture capitalists and angel investors in particular. When interest rates go down—that is, when the risk-free rate decreases—investors anticipated lower rates of return for the use of their capital; the result is that valuations on early-stage deals have stabilized at the lows attained in 2002 and 2003, and, in fact, have shown some improvement. In effect, valuations of private companies are inversely correlated to interest rate trends on investment instruments such as Treasury bonds. When an investor can only earn a few percent on lower-risk or risk-free investments, not even keeping up with inflation, there is a pressure to invest a portion of discretionary net worth/capital into higher-risk/high-return private deals. And entrepreneurs are now starting to see angels reenter this market.

RISK PROFILE OF THE INVESTOR

Different types of investors have different risk profiles. Things will be different among private investors, newly affluent investors just entering the market, and professional investors. And things will also be different within each group. Moreover, these risk profiles are often hardwired, or tough to readjust.

Angel investors' orientation to risk is not monolithic. So valuation of the same venture can vary significantly depending on which individual investor is evaluating the deal. If he is an institutional venture capital investor with a billion-dollar portfolio and he is investing $1 million in a company, he is probably willing to take more of a valuation risk. If he is an angel investor, and this investment is one of only three, and he is investing 50 percent of his available capital in the deal, this calculation will be affected by the investor's risk profile—and thus have an impact on the valuation.

The only way to mollify the investor's perception of risk is to work on the subjective factors that will make him feel more comfortable with the deal. In other words, as the entrepreneur, you must convince the investor that you are the world's greatest manager, convince him of the vision, sell the dream. Rather than sell investors on the subjective elements of the venture, some entrepreneurs mistakenly try to convince investors that they don't understand their own risk profiles.

COMPANY-SPECIFIC RISK

Stage of development, experience of management, time to liquidity, and projected return multiples are just a few of the elements at the company level that can have an impact on valuation. For example, early-stage companies, unproven management, longer time to liquidity, and returns not significantly above those available in the public market will all serve to reduce an investor's valuation of a venture.

The stage of a company's development is a measure of investment risk and is an important aspect in valuing a company. In fact, the stage of development may be more important in describing the risk than the current round of the investment. The success of investments in start-up companies is subject to the whims of the capital markets, because these companies have to raise money frequently, and if market conditions are unfavorable, severe dilution can result. On the other hand, later-stage companies are subject to the whims of the new issue window.

Potential risks and rewards vary substantially during the different stages of development in a new venture. Despite every entrepreneur's confidence in this "sure thing," more new ventures fail than succeed. However, investors need only a few big winners to offset the losers. Depending on the risks involved, compound rates of return from 25 percent to 50 percent per year or more constitute targeted expectations. There is a direct relationship between stage of development, as defined earlier, and market value, as calculated by the angel investor. This gets translated into variation in expected rates of return—for example, 60 to 100 percent rates of return for seed or start-up companies, and 20 percent rates of return for bridge or mezzanine financings.

The pricing curve shown below (Exhibit 13.1) captures this relationship

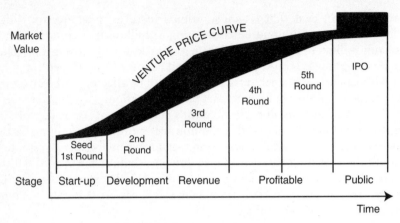

Figure 13.1   Venture Price Curve

and to some extent explains the angel's penchant for earlier-stage deals. If the angel investor gets into the deal on a start-up basis, he or she will pay a lower price (lower valuation) and correspondingly take on a lot of risk, but with the potential for higher returns to compensate that risk. Development- and revenue-stage companies have many of the same risks as a start-up; that is, the investor does not know if the companies possess all of the ingredients necessary for success. Yet, as the chart illustrates, the valuations are significantly higher than the start-up, with less potential for high returns because of higher valuation.

The reason for this perhaps is clearer in the stylized graph (Exhibit 13.2). The stage of development—start-up, development, revenue, profitable, or public—has a direct correlation with market value. Consequently, the targeted rates of return of early-stage, private equity investors will correspond—for example, 60 percent to 100 percent for seed or start-up, versus 20 percent for a bridge to cash out.

Using projected revenues, profits, and growth rates, entrepreneurs and investors should arrive at a shared vision of the venture's value for the three to five years that follow financing. A business plan built on realistic assumptions is an entrepreneur's best friend at this point in the pricing process and negotiation. At least four basic principles are involved in arriving at a pricing decision: (1) the division of equity determined by future value and equity required to compensate investors at competitive rates; (2) the greater the expected worth of the venture at some future time, the lower the share of equity required to purchase any given amount of capital; (3) the longer the track record of a new venture, the lower the investment risk, and therefore the lower the share of equity required to purchase any given amount of cap-

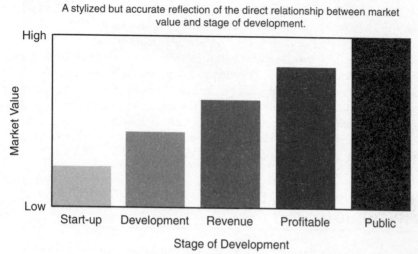

A stylized but accurate reflection of the direct relationship between market value and stage of development.

Figure 13.2   Valuing the Venture over Time

ital; and (4) the shorter the waiting period to liquidation, the lower the risk, and thus the lower the share of equity required to purchase any given amount of capital.

In addition, remember that investors will most likely seek opinions from their network of co-investors in order to obtain the bids of other respected, experienced investors. Estimates from others that reasonably approximate an investor's own appraisal can increase confidence in a valuation assessment.

INVESTOR INVOLVEMENT

Especially relevant to the angel investor is the degree of involvement in the company that the investor will take after he or she invests. It's natural for former entrepreneurs, now angels, to become active in a company in which they invest; for example, as director or consultant, or even in an operational management role. If the investor can have some degree of influence or control (*control* being the operative word here) over the direction of the company, most would be inclined to give that company a higher valuation, because they are involved. Conversely, if the investor is a minority shareholder, that is, a passive investor vulnerable to the whims of the entrepreneur and especially other investors (who may come aboard in future financings and gain control of the deal), he or she will most likely place a lower value on the company.

The level of involvement by the investor will dictate the degree to which that investor will perceive that such involvement lessens the risk in the deal. No involvement other than reviewing periodic reports and attending meetings (i.e., a passive involvement) will probably not be seen as lessening risk. Providing advice or counsel as needed and requested will not have an impact on risk. However, representation on the board of directors, working full- or even part-time with the company and, in some cases, joining the founders' team as a member will most likely be perceived as reducing risk, if the investor is experienced and knowledgeable in the industry and possesses the necessary functional skills needed by the company.

CORRELATING RATE OF RETURN WITH TIME TO LIQUIDITY

Once the investor has looked over the deal and feels comfortable with the risk, he or she is in a position to develop an expected or desired range of returns. Next, based on due diligence and deal structure negotiations, the investor can estimate the amount of time to liquidity. In the case of the early-stage company without cash flow, earnings will likely come at some future date.

Investors correlate time to liquidity and expected rate of return, so that the longer the period of time until liquidity, the more the investor expects as a return. The higher expectation helps justify to investors their increased investment risk and the loss of access to his capital. But seed, R&D, and start-up companies rarely, if ever, have cash flow or earnings, so calculations are used to deduce valuation, which will necessarily involve projections and estimates, reasonable targets, and realistically attainable targets. This is especially the case since technology companies derive their voracious appetite for capital from the same growth rate that lets them offer high potential investment returns. So early-stage technology companies are loath to pay dividends or interest during the term of the investor's hold. Instead, these companies will reinvest any cash surplus into their own high growth. Again, liquidity, return on capital, or investor profit is dependent on an uncertain future.

MULTIPLES

Another consideration that enters into the investors' valuation calculation is the multiple that future buyers will be willing to pay. Investors will rely on estimates of future net earnings and comparable cash flow multiples in calculating valuation. In addition, investors will attempt to be realistic in their targeted level of returns.

The investor will try to get a feel for what the market will bear, regardless of the liquidity mechanism. For example, the investor might say, "If I invest for X years, I'll need to make Y times my investment." What all markets pay can be measured as a multiple of the original investment. Of course, we are talking about the probable price here, not the highest price. Identifying other companies in the same industry with comparable market value is not an exact science.

To begin this comparative analysis, the investor will, we hope, use reports that explain valuations in completed mergers and acquisitions. IPO data are also readily available in the public domain to help calibrate market value conditions. These reports indicate what multiple of earnings, cash flow, or sales is typical in valuations of other private and comparable firms in the industry. While this approach may seem to be based more on intuition than on objectivity, it can provide the investor with benchmarks and guidelines on current market value. The key is using comparable companies!

In ICR's own research, we see investors targeting multiples of five to ten in seed-stage, three to six in start-up, and two to four in development-stage companies. In contrast, institutional investors are targeting multiples of ten for start-ups, four to eight in the development-stage, and three to five in profitable-company investments. It is important to note here that the angel and institutional investors are not evaluating the projected performance of an investment using ROI. Instead, they measure how many multiples they can make on their money over what period.

One calculation used by investors is the premoney comparables method. The investor observes other private equity or venture capital transactions to find out what other premoney valuations are currently being given by investors to companies with similar characteristics to the venture investment they are considering. In other words, how are these deals priced? The investor might use public stock multiples, price-earnings (P/E) ratios, and/or merger and acquisition sales values. This helps the investor develop an assortment of acceptable values for negotiation purposes. The investor can then estimate the required current equity ownership percentage by dividing the investment amount by the premoney valuation plus the investment amount.

Rates of return on early-stage venture investments are time sensitive. Sophisticated investors spend time and energy considering liquidity—that is, how they are going to get out—before they invest. Exhibit 13.3 shows what happens to ROI over different time periods for a given multiple on an investment.

You can see from Exhibit 13.4 how important it is to the early-stage in-

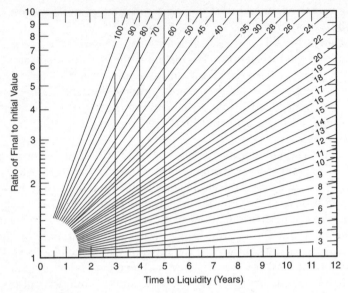

Figure 13.3   Correlating Rate of Return with Time to Liquidity

vestor to achieve liquidity as soon as possible and realize the gains. ROI associated with higher multiples typically requiring longer hold times clearly do not justify the risk exposure of longer-term investments.

DISCOUNTING PROJECTIONS

As a group, entrepreneurs rarely achieve projected sales as soon as expected, and they incur more costs than anticipated. Therefore, they usually need more capital sooner than they anticipated. Start-up companies ordinarily require several rounds of funding before they become financially mature enough to qualify for sale, merger, acquisition, or IPO. This entrepreneurial planning failure boils down to dilution for the angel and a negative impact on returns. One technique the investor uses to ensure his percentage ownership when he analyzes projections for valuation is to give them a "haircut."

In other words, successful angel investors are skeptical and always discount projections and develop their own cash flow models when they consider an investment proposal, paying particular attention to the possibility of unforeseen additional financing needs. The principals of early-stage enterprises rarely forecast cash requirements accurately, not because they are bad managers, but because the situation is fraught with circumstances beyond their control. When entrepreneurs say $1 million absolutely will do the job,

Internal Rate of Return on a Multiple of Original
Investment Realized Over an Assumed Time Period

Years	Multiple				
	2	3	4	5	6
2	41	73	100	124	145
3	26	44	59	71	82
4	19	32	41	50	57
5	15	25	32	38	43
6	12	20	26	31	35

Figure 13.4 Correlation of Multiple over Hold Time

sophisticated investors are thinking otherwise—and with good reason. The sophisticated investor's mental cash register is clicking away as it adds numbers to the entrepreneur's modest valuation appraisal.

Angels discount the optimistic entrepreneur's projections by 25 percent to 33 percent or more when they calculate venture valuation, and the entrepreneurs have been willing to give away more equity to get the investor's capital. Present-value formulae, which we will present shortly, for calculating value incorporate a discount rate, using interest rates combined with a risk allowance to discount cash flows. Entrepreneurs need to remember that investors will not forget that they have substantial leverage in valuation negotiations, especially for smaller deals in today's market that do not meet the criteria of institutional venture capitalists. Whereas a venture capitalist or angel might use a risk premium of 39 percent for an early-stage equity deal, an institutional investor scheming a traditional debt private placement might limit the discount to 18 percent.

VALUATION METHODOLOGY USED IN EARLY-STAGE, PRIVATE EQUITY TRANSACTIONS

While a number of different financial calculation methods are available, not all are applicable to early-stage ventures, and their applicability varies.

Asset-based valuation rarely applies since most early-stage companies have few tangible assets. Some analysts suggest replacement value may be substituted; however, you just end up with the sum of replacement costs of what assets are tangible. This is more a reflection of the cost of buying assets, not a fair market value estimate.

More commonly, investors use the approach involving market multiples discussed briefly in the previous section. This calculation entails obtaining the observed market value of a comparable company relative to earnings. Herein lies the rub: What constitutes "comparable"? Some analysts use similar industry, products, customers, ownership structure, or other factors. Investors are also aware that entrepreneurs have many ways available to influence pro forma earnings forecasts (e.g., EBITDA) and still be within the guidelines of generally accepted accounting principles (GAAP). EBITDA is often used in earnings-based valuation calculations.

The discounted cash flow method of valuation is a derivation of the free cash flows valuation method. Free cash flow valuation defines the value of the company as the present value of the expected future cash flows in excess of those needed to operate the company. The company's value is a function of the present value of its free cash flow discounted with the company's cost of capital, plus the value of the company's nonoperating assets (e.g., any investments insecurities). The discount rate is a measure of the company's cost of capital.

The venture capital method of discounted cash flow is a concept based on estimates and assumptions. Also, the calculations of net present value can be effected in the venture capital method by qualitative, nonnumerical factors. The venture capital method is just another version of the discounted cash flows valuation calculation, basically adapting the method to make it more appropriate for start-up and early-stage ventures.

Central to the venture capital method is determining the future potential of the venture. This is called the terminal value, the projected net earnings in the terminal year or year of projected exit, multiplied by an appropriate multiple of earnings. For instance, the multiple might be the P/E ratio of a comparable company, appropriate for a company that has successfully achieved the projected forecasts. The P/E ratio becomes the current market price of a public company's publicly traded stock divided by current annual earnings per share amount.

Terminal value can be expressed as:

$$TV = PNI \text{ at } TY \times PER$$

where TV = terminal value
PNI = projected net income from projections for year of exit
PER = price-earnings ratio of comparable company
TY = terminal year—future year when investor's shares are sold

As the reader can see, terminal value is measured as a ratio of financial performance for a comparable company. The P/E ratio is applied to net earnings to estimate a future value at the terminal year, usually estimated at three to five years out. Also, it is apparent that forecasts and assumptions will drive the accuracy of the calculation.

For investors attempting to determine how much of the company they need to receive for their capital to attain their targeted return, the investors need to now calculate the present value of the company. Whereas terminal value reflects potential, present value equals the terminal value of the future company minus the capital to get the company to that stage. Calculating present value becomes a way to quantify risk to the investor, the time the investor puts into the company, the loss of the use of capital during the term of the hold, and to some extent to compensate the investor for losses in other deals. To capture this, the investor uses a discount rate obtaining present value of future income streams. We have witnessed discount rates ranging from 20 percent to 70 percent.

To calculate present value, the investor discounts the terminal value calculated above. The discount terminal value is a function of the investor's required rate of return. Converting terminal value to present value necessarily involves the investor in determining his or her target ROI, for example, a five times return in three years yields a 70 percent ROI, whereas a ten times return in five years yields a 58 percent ROI.

As we mentioned earlier, investors give projections a haircut. High-risk, illiquid companies, requiring involvement for an average of up to eight years, plus time, energy, and entrepreneurial optimism—all are reasons why investors indulge in this precaution.

Present value (PV) can be expressed as:

$$PV = \frac{TV}{(1 + ROI)^Y}$$

where TV = terminal value or annual net earnings projected for the terminal year multiplied by the P/E ratio of a comparable company

ROI = required or targeted rate of return

Y = number of years to exit

Once terminal value and discounted or present value has been computed, a calculation can be made to determine the required ownership percentage of equity the investors will need to reach their investment return objective. The minimum equity stake that investors will request can be expressed as:

$$\frac{A}{PV} = E$$

where A   = investment amount
       E   = minimum percentage share of company equity required
       PV = present value

We point out "minimum" equity stake required because most investors will further correct this third calculation to compensate for potential dilution from future financing rounds, both expected and unforeseen. We will discuss dilution factors in the next section. As you can see from these formulae, the higher the ROI that the investor expects and demands, the lower the company valuation will be. However, the high discount rate becomes the primary means to compensate the investor for the loss of the use of his or her capital, risk, or entrepreneurial errors, and still allow him or her a reasonable return.

DILUTION

The next element that the prospective angel investor will consider during valuation—in addition to desired returns and time to liquidity, discounting of projections, and clarifying multiples—is an assessment of how much additional capital a company will need to get to the point that the envisioned liquidity event can or will occur. More often than not investors are skeptical about an entrepreneur's claims of what it will take to get to break even and to the point that operations and growth can be funded from internal cash flows and traditional credit lines. So the prudent investor will create a dilution factor to compute into the valuation process.

While dilution may not be at the forefront of every valuation calculation, many angel investors have learned from painful experience that entrepreneurs rarely, if ever, perceive that the company will need a lot more capital than anyone had estimated. Just a little calculation will help investors understand that for their investment to obtain their targeted and justified rate of return, they need X percent of the company. If the entrepreneur has miscalculated, and significantly more money is needed than has been projected, investors will suffer significant dilution and fail to make their targeted rate of return. That is why dilution is rarely separated from negotiation of deal structure by investors to protect the individual investor's share, should more money be needed later.

Less experienced angel investors commit a relatively common oversight in their failure to recognize the difference between premoney and postmoney valuations. Valuation of the company is called "premoney" because the value was established before taking into account new investment. In other words, the value is based on a view of the current climate for the company in a specific industry or based on current revenue and some multiple of projected revenue for the year. For instance, if a company has a premoney valuation of $10 million, the angel investing $1 million would purchase 10 percent of the shares of the company outstanding before it issues shares to the investor. When the $1 million investment is added to the $10 million premoney valuation, on a postmoney basis, the investor will hold approximately 9 percent of the outstanding shares of the company, with a postmoney valuation of $11 million.

Though no statistically valid research is currently available, our anecdotal research gleaned in speaking with almost 4,000 entrepreneurial companies suggests that 90 percent of the deals worked out will need more money than originally projected. The result is dilution, best explained this way: If a deal calls for $1 million, 12 months later it will need more money. An investor with a 40 percent ownership for the first million dollars is faced with three options, if, say, another $500,000 is necessary. The investor can put in $500,000, or he can put in a portion of it, or he can choose not to put in any more money at all, in which case, to survive, the company has to raise the $500,000 from somewhere else.

With all three options, the investor suffers dilution. He has to put more money in to maintain his 40 percent ownership, or his stake will shrink. Come liquidity, how much of the company will the investor own? The answer is that the investor will own less than when he started out. This illustrates the dilemma a company creates when it needs additional money. This scenario dramatizes dilution—something else that investors seriously ponder during the valuation process.

How can the investor arrive at a dilution factor? As an example, let's say that the investor and entrepreneur agree that the company can achieve $2 million in earnings in three years. They also agree that in three years buyers can be found who will pay 20 times earnings for the company. Therefore, based on these assumptions, in three years the company would be worth $40 million (that is, $20 \times \$2$ million = $40 million). Let's also assume that the investor has offered to invest $1 million, and he has decided to seek a 30 percent return compounded annually over the time period. What percentage of equity in the company does the investor require in order to obtain the targeted ROI? Using his handy calculator, he determines that the present value of the company is $18,206,645—$40 million/$(1 + 0.30)^3$—and that the $1 million investment requires a 5.5% equity stake in the company ($1 million/$18,206,645).

However, the investor not only needs 5.5 percent equity in the company today, he needs 5.5 percent in equity three years from now as well to ensure the return. Here the dilution factor comes into play. If the investor is uncomfortable with management's forecasts and determines that more capital may be needed than is projected, he can incorporate a dilution factor into the equity share calculation.

Let's assume that the investor estimates 20 percent more capital will be required than management projects. To protect himself, the investor must increase his equity ownership percentage to ensure that in three years he will attain the targeted return. The investor must therefore correct the 5.5 percent equity percentage figure to account for the increased capital that will be required. This is accomplished as follows: 5.5 percent = 80 percent X (where X = equity share, corrected for dilution). The 80 percent figure is derived by subtracting the 20 percent additional capital required from the original 100 percent of value. Therefore, the investor will seek a 6.9 percent equity share (5.5 percent/0.8 = 6.875) to ensure his 30 percent return in three years. The dilution factor accounts for unanticipated needed capital.

TRUISMS IN THE VALUATION PROCESS

Entrepreneurs must grasp some truisms regarding their position with investors. Be convinced of the merits of the opportunity before discussing valuation. Also recognize that demand for capital greatly exceeds supply; embrace this leverage in favor of investors during valuation negotiations. Furthermore, understand that investors always discount projections, so run your own cash flow forecasts, paying particular attention to unforeseen follow-up financing requirements. And remember, in the past five years, fewer than two percent of venture-backed exit transactions have been through IPOs.

It is worth taking a closer look at some of these truisms.

First, prospective investors will not necessarily share the entrepreneurs' level of enthusiasm for the project. Investors must be thoroughly convinced of the merits of the opportunity before any discussion of valuation or terms. Entrepreneurs have to understand that sophisticated investors are besieged with projects. Investors could look at business plans seven days a week. A project may soak up 100 percent of an entrepreneur's life, but it constitutes only one more business plan on an already prodigious stack of business plans as far as the investor is concerned. So entrepreneurs have to adjust their mind-sets; they have to concentrate on selling the investor on why this venture is a great deal. Also, entrepreneurs sometimes become upset because an investor fails to jump at a project; they fail to realize that the investor may have invested in three similar projects, each of which turned sour. As we mentioned earlier, for most early-stage enterprises, the demand for equity capital largely exceeds supply. Consequently, investors have substantial leverage in valuation negotiations.

Second, entrepreneurs must allow for the high degree to which investors are risk-averse. Some entrepreneurs think that venture capitalists love risk. But investors who do are not investors for long. No investor, especially no professional venture capitalist or sophisticated angel investor, is in the business of jauntily taking a flyer. No investor is interested in floating out there on gossamer wings. To the wise investor, a venture must be built on tresses and struts. The way investors stay alive is by minimizing their mistakes. So entrepreneurs, along with everyone else, need to cast off the misconception that early-stage investors love taking risks. Investors try to manage risk against return. But the popular notion of investors lovingly embracing risk is hogwash.

A third truism is that investors will always discount projections in reviewing a proposal. The management principals of early-stage enterprises rarely forecast cash requirements accurately, not because they are bad managers, but because the situation is fraught with circumstances beyond their control. As we have suggested, nearly all new deals need more money than their management team had thought. Such discrepancies between hope and reality are woven into the fabric of building dreams. The fictional Willie Loman, Arthur Miller's failed salesman in *Death of a Salesman,* is eulogized this way by Charley, his sympathetic next-door neighbor: "A man has got to dream, boy; it comes with the territory." But Willie failed to realize that some dreams must come to earth. Unforeseen follow-on financings are a fact of life in early-stage investing. Follow-on financing weighs heavily in the valuation process. When entrepreneurs say $1 million and no more will do the job, sophisticated investors are thinking otherwise—and with good reason.

Another truism: Acquisition or buyout is the predominant method for achieving liquidity for small company shareholders. We have already pointed out that the primary method of achieving liquidity is not IPO—far from it. But the misconception remains. Too often, entrepreneurs and their business plans say they will take their company public in five years. Given the current IPO market and its prospects for recovery, odds are that such an event will not occur. So entrepreneurs need to consider how that investor is going to achieve liquidity.

Axiomatic is the truism that any valuation becomes irrelevant if the venture does not survive. Survival, survival, survival—in private investing the word rings like a Buddhist mantra. As we have reiterated, smart investors are risk-averse. The foremost thing they want to know is not what their ROI will be in five years, but whether the company will survive at all. Entrepreneurs can talk glory, displaying the infamous hockey stick projection extending through the next five years, but if they cannot survive the first 18 months, further talk becomes immaterial. So before investors even look at anything else, the entrepreneur has to convince them that the company will survive.

CAVEATS FOR THE ENTREPRENEUR

There is, however, a caveat attached to selling investors on the survival of your company. It is this: Watch the fine line between a straightforward sales job and overselling, because you are not walking away from this transaction. You are going to be partners with this individual. The critical thing in obtaining the fairest price for both of you is to emphasize your strong areas—without hoopla, without hype. Then you must justify, not hide, the weak areas of the venture. Concede—to yourself as well as to others—that every deal has weak areas; otherwise, it would not become a high-return opportunity.

Many entrepreneurs do not want to confess weaknesses. They will claim that everything is great. "There is no competition; people are grabbing this thing off the shelves." This attitude is not only unrealistic; it is unfair, not only to the investor, but to the entrepreneur as well. You are dealing with smart people who want you for a partner. They understand conditions that surround the process; they understand that the opportunity presents itself because there are holes in the deal, and because unknowns lurk everywhere.

So talk about the holes; talk about the unknowns. Do it up front. Maybe your investor can see something he or she can help you with. But if you gloss over them rather than reveal them, the investor will question your ability—if not your integrity—and whether your feet hover anywhere near the ground. Of course, such common sense should pervade the whole process, not just valuation.

Part of having your feet on the ground involves a realistic view of the market size and growth rate, two things entrepreneurs seem to have, understandably, an inveterate desire to inflate. With no intention of fooling anyone, they talk about huge markets, entering the worldwide telephone business, perhaps, instead of focusing on the narrow market they will serve. Entrepreneurs must realize the market segment they are after.

Because many entrepreneurs have heard that investors want to invest only in areas containing huge markets, many entrepreneurs express themselves globally, or in billions of dollars. But the global nature of the venture depends on the deal. Recall the diversity among investors. Not all investors—perhaps very few—are globally motivated. Again, when talking about your project, be realistic. To the sensible investor, realistic assessment has a circumference narrower than the globe yet worth more than a billion fantasy dollars.

Other, but no less important, subjective factors enter into the valuation mix—the sales cycle, for example. It always takes longer than you think to bring a product to market. You may have great customer market research that proclaims how much people are going to love the product, but nobody has written a check yet. Distributors may rave, but no one is talking floor space.

So you have to understand what point of the cycle your product is in, an understanding that results in having to walk a fine line: You do not want to be too early and have to spend all your money educating the market on why it needs your product. Nor can you afford to be too late, behind everybody else. This is why you have to understand the length of time the sell cycle for the product is going to take. Entrepreneurs can become dazzled by their vision, overlooking this aspect of the process.

Another pitfall awaits even the best product. In three years, the company may be producing the world's greatest product, but not selling it. If educating the marketplace and educating prospective competitors soak up too much time and energy, the venture will die. This scenario captures a company exhausting its capital in educating the market without being able to sell the product. Three years later that company is out of business. Survivability dries up, vividly clarifying the critical nature of the sell cycle.

Although no hard figures have been tracked, a reasonable guess would suggest that 90 percent of the deals worked out will need more money than had been originally thought. Then what you have is dilution. The investor is diluted when he or she has to put more money in to maintain their percentage ownership. Come liquidity, how much of the company will the investor own? The answer is that the investor will own less than when he or she started out. This illustrates the problem created by needing more money than was originally thought. This constitutes dilution, something investors seriously consider in the valuation process.

All these considerations influence perceived risk. So to the extent that you can convince an investor that less risk is involved in the deal, he or she will raise the valuation. To the degree the investor cannot be convinced of low risk, one of two things will happen: The investor will walk away because of too much risk for the desired rate of return, or the investor will write a check but the valuation will sink because the need for a higher rate of return rises.

How to Write and Present an Investor-Oriented Business Plan

Charles Roedel
Roedel and Company
San Jose, CA
(408) 265-5235

THE TARGET AUDIENCE

Presenting your business to investors is essential in building business success. Your business plan must offer a desirable opportunity that encourages the investor to take the next step—just based on written pages. When you have the opportunity to make a presentation on your business, you are the focus of attention and your presentation material provides images to enhance understanding. In both cases, you must understand your audience and provide the right information in a manner that will help investors develop a reasonable understanding of your business.

Investors present an experienced audience with a vast array of skills. You must carefully consider how your information will be received and plan accordingly. Our observations spanning many years provide the following insights.

Investors:

- Are very intelligent.
- Are entrepreneurs themselves.
- Have worked many long hours building a young company, just like you.
- Have struggled with too many action items and no resources.
- Have mortgaged their home and possessions to make ends meet.

■ Have painfully experienced the time and effort necessary to develop their product or service.
■ Have painfully experienced the time and effort necessary to win early customers.
■ Have painfully experienced the time and effort necessary to ramp sales.
■ May not be experts in your particular field and are not looking to become experts.

The business plan must focus on why your solution provides a very desirable customer benefit.

■ Understand that an entrepreneur must begin with a laser focus on your core business.
■ Have learned that creating and executing against a well-devised business plan is key to success.

Investors are looking for a business plan that:

■ Presents the opportunity in an honest, believable manner.
■ Doesn't talk down to the reader.
■ Covers the appropriate information with a minimum of fluff.
■ Provides an executive summary that provides a crisp overview.
■ States points using clear statements with minimum embellishment.
■ Presents specific information in an organized manner without repetition.
■ Is presented in a readable, eye-pleasing way.

Considerations to optimize the acceptance of your plan:

■ Place your logo on title page and use a tiny version on each page.
■ Your title page should include company name, date, address, plus contact name, title, phone, fax, e-mail, and web site.
■ Provide a disclaimer paragraph on the title page.
■ Provide a footnote to show that the business plan is proprietary and confidential and note DO NOT DUPLICATE on each page.
■ Use a table of contents with section numbers and page numbers.
■ Consider dividing the executive summary into two columns: left column entitled "Overview" and the right column entitled "Details."
■ If appropriate, show a picture of the product in the executive summary.
■ If you are offering more than one product/service, or more than one marketing approach, or more that one business model, carefully distinguish each and maintain differentiation throughout the document. Business plans that try to combine different approaches in broad generalizations often result in confusion and loss of credibility.

- Use graphics, such as market segment pie charts, to attract attention.
- As appropriate, use photos of your team, products, and facilities, as dividers between chapters.
- Use tables, charts, and bulleted lists to present information in an easy-to-read form.
- Tables should have clearly defined titles, legends, label rows, and columns so that information in the table is understandable without the need for support text.
- Provide footnote sources for references such as market survey reports.
- Consider using an expanded timeline chart that combines time frame and assumptions for different elements, e.g., development, marketing, operations, and financial.
- Providing thumbnail photos of officers adds a personal touch.
- Present financials using standard practice formats. Trying to invent new ways to present financials will become a diversion for the investor.
- Be consistent. If a numerical example is presented in two different portions of the document, be sure they match.
- Details on product technology can often be discussed in a white paper placed in the appendix rather than in the plan body.
- Use a binding method that makes page turning easy.
- Use a standard text format. Some plans have been created in a landscape presentation format, but the result doesn't provide the investor the stand-alone, explanatory text with expected detail information. Save the presentation format for your live presentation to investors.

Rewrite a business plan that:

- Starts by presenting grandiose statements without defining the real business.
- Overwhelms the reader with so many pages it looks like an unabridged textbook.
- Presents information in a disorganized or incoherent manner.
- Presents information based on "current status," which is already several months old.
- Provides the same topic in multiple sections with contradictory information.
- Uses improper grammar or misspelled words.
- Presents a title page that is missing contact information and business plan version date.

As your team works to create business plans and presentations, be aware of these points and strive to provide information in a manner consistent with the Private Investor Criteria in Chapter 6.

INTRODUCTION TO THE BUSINESS PLAN

This question-and-answer format is designed to guide you in the development of your business plan.

The probing questions will assist you in collecting the information you will need to make informed business planning decisions. This is a comprehensive workbook and, as such, explores all aspects of different types of businesses. Answer the questions appropriate to your company or venture. As you proceed, the questions will stimulate your thinking about your business, providing you with new insights into the planning process.

Remember that the business plan is not only a compilation of answers to a series of questions but a written reflection on the conclusions that you draw from going through the questioning, research, analysis, and answering process.

WHAT DOES YOUR BUSINESS PLAN NEED TO CONTAIN?

The process outlined here is based on more than 15 years of experience; on more than 200 major planning-related assignments for start-ups, small businesses, and large companies; on interviews with investors and lenders; and on review of hundreds of successful and unsuccessful business plans. We advise you to include the following sections in your business plan:

CREATING A BUSINESS PLAN

 I. Executive summary
 II. Mission or charter
 III. Description of the business
 IV. Ownership structure and equity
 V. Description of product/service
 VI. The market
 VII. Description of industry and trends
 VIII. Marketing strategy
 IX. Marketing plan
 X. Sales plan
 XI. Operations, research and development strategies, and plans
 XII. Management, organization, personnel, and information systems
 XIII. Objectives and milestones
 XIV. Financial projections
 XV. Supporting documents

I. Executive Summary

Your objectives in this section are to create a readable, credible, brief overview of your business plan. A second, equally important, objective is to demonstrate appreciation of investor or lender needs. From a funding acquisition perspective, the executive summary may be the most important tool for introducing your offering to lenders and investors. A final objective of the executive summary is to motivate and entice the reader to review the document in its entirety.

Although mentioned first and placed at the front of your plan or under separate cover, the executive summary is best written last, since it serves as a concise overview of the business plan and highlights the key points from every section of your completed plan. In a few precise, clear sentences, the executive summary crystallizes the hours of labor you have spent in researching and writing each section. A maximum of one or two pages is recommended.

Your objective in writing the executive summary is to get the reader's attention and to stimulate his or her interest.

Suggested key points with criteria weighting:

- The company (10% weight)
  - Define business purpose.
  - Provide summary of your company's history and current status.
  - State overall corporate strategy and objectives.
- The products or services (20% weight)
  - Describe important features and benefits—relate to market needs and to the competition.
  - Describe existing products and status of new projects.
  - Discuss pricing and margins for both your products and your competitors' products.
  - Explain proprietary position—trademarks, patents, trade secrets, and special production/process.
  - Articulate any relevant regulatory or environmental issues.
- The market and marketing strategy (30% weight)
  - Market analysis—size, anticipated growth, key changes, trends.
  - Market strategy—How are you going to reach the market? What gives you a special advantage?
  - Product/service—What makes you different? What gives you a special advantage?
  - Evaluate competition—Who are they? How much of the market do they control? What are their advantages/disadvantages?
  - Discuss the issues of circumstances that "drive" or create the market—What compels people to buy?

■ Management (30% weight)
  ○ Give brief background of key individuals—specifically, why they add value to the company, and their past successes and achievements.
  ○ History of working together as a team.
  ○ Identification of immediate and future personnel needs and initial organizational structure.
■ Financial summary (10% weight)
  ○ Provide revenues, income, and expenses projected over three- to five-year period. Justify your financial assumptions. Include any past financial history.
  ○ Define funding requirements—How much is needed at each stage of development within the next five years?
  ○ Describe the history of previous investments.
  ○ Indicate an exit strategy (i.e., mergers, acquisitions, or IPOs). Compare with similar businesses and their results.

II. Mission or Charter

The mission statement says—in a few words, a graphic, or an image—what your business should be about. The statement defines the thrust of your business.

Exercise in preparation for writing your mission statement:

What do you want to accomplish from your business? Think about why you are in business.

What is important to you about your business? What excites you about it?

Explain how the short-term and long-term personal goals of the owner(s) harmonize with the business requirements and objectives.

List the benefits to the community; for example, retaining or creating jobs, building rehabilitation, meeting the community's needs, increasing the community's tax base.

III. Description of the Business

Your objectives in this section are to display your knowledge of your business and to provide the historical background leading up to your current situation and request for funding.

Describe the historical development of your business.

Describe the general nature of the business that you are in:

_____ Manufacturing

_____ Retail

_____ Services

_____ Wholesale

How do you generate revenues and make a profit?

What is unique about your business?

Is the company's development stage in start-up or is it a continuing business?

List the major expenses in your business.

Work into your description of the business the following information: Name of the business. Year founded. Name of founder. Location of the business. Number of employees. Features of the area (accessibility to customers). Description of facilities (size, zoning, age, and condition). Lease. Legal form of organization. Major equipment involved in your business. If current business is different from past business or firm is considering expansion, explain. Briefly summarize any future plans—both short-range and long-range—for expansion or relocation.

IV. Ownership Structure and Equity

What legal form does this ownership take?

_____ Sole proprietorship

_____ Partnership

_____ Corporation (date, state of incorporation, type)

_____ LLC

Explain any significant ownership changes that have occurred, subsidiaries, and degree of ownership, if applicable.

List the names of principal owners and roles they played in the firm's foundation.

Give the percentage of interest of principal owners or managers in the business. Present sources of funds.

Give the expected sources of future funds.

List the principal shareholders and note the stock that each principal holds.

Disclose the borrowings of the business.

If you are a start-up, be sure to consider the following:

How will ownership/equity be distributed?

Briefly give the background on the founders, active investors, key employees, directors, and consultants.

If the business is a corporation, give the classes of stock, shares authorized, shares issued and outstanding.

If the business is a partnership, give the respective partners' interests.

V. Description of the Product/Service

The key to writing about your product or service is to focus on its benefits and how you will meet a need. Include printed materials that provide detailed descriptions of features and how a service works in the Supporting Documents section—for example, drawings, photos, brochures, services flowcharts, patents, trademarks, engineering studies, or proprietary features. Whenever possible, provide factual documentation supporting your belief that the market will buy your product—for example, sales performance, letters of commitment to purchase, or purchase orders.

Some questions to prepare you for writing the product/service description section are:

What problem does your product or service solve?

What results can customers expect? Are they visible? Valuable? Measurable?

What does your product do or your service deliver to the customer?

Is the product or service in a developmental stage?

How was the product developed?

If you purchase the products that your company sells, describe materials and supply sources, availability, and product cost. Also describe your purchasing department.

Are you dependent on one supplier for materials? If overseas sources or vendors are subject to shortages, what is your backup?

What makes your product/service different? How is your solution different from or better than the solution offered by competitors?

How complex is your product/service to use? Is training needed to use it?

What risks, if any, are inherent in its use?

Are there government regulations relevant to the use of your product or service?

Will customers need to change the way they do things in order to use it?

What is the cost of and profit on each product/service line and the break-even point?

How will funding affect product/service lines?

Describe your research on future products.

VI. The Market

Who are your customers? (It is essential to your success and credibility with the readers of your plan that you demonstrate knowledge of who your customers are or will be.)

The following questions will help you begin an evaluation and profile of your target markets:

What is the geographic scope of your market: local, regional, national, or international? Current versus potential customers?

What are your targeted markets? Are they individuals or other businesses? How many potential customers are there in each target market segment?

What is the size of your market? What are the trends in your market?

Give a general description of your customers. Use demographics when possible to describe the following: age, gender, income. If your customers are companies, are they merchandisers? Service organizations? Manufacturers? Original equipment manufacturers (OEMs)? Government? Contractors? Industrial distributors?

What is the average purchase amount of your product(s)/service(s)?

How do you know that potential customers need your product or service? What evidence do you have of customer acceptance?

Is the target market aware of its need for the product/service? Explain.

How many competitors are there in your target market? Give name, location, and size. Who are the emerging competitors?

What is your competitors' market share distribution? Is there a single competitor or multiple competitors? Who are the most powerful competitors and who are your future competitors?

What percentage of the total market do you think that you can currently capture as customers? In one, two, three, or five years? How did you determine this figure?

What impact will funding or lack of funding have on these projections? What is the time frame?

What could prevent you from achieving your goals? Is the market aware of you? What is your image in the marketplace?

What is the major advantage of your company over the competition? What is your competitive edge—for example, barriers to competition or entry, stable customer base, or proprietary technology? What are the strengths and weaknesses of competitors? (Barriers to entry include patents, high start-up costs, substantial expertise required, and market saturation.)

Why do customers buy your product/service over your competitors'? Is it price? Quality? How will you exploit this advantage?

Who is involved in the decision to buy your product/service?

How do you—or will you—find out what your customers want?

_____ Customer surveys

_____ Outside market research

_____ Secondary research

_____ Trade association data

_____ Focus groups

_____ Suppliers/Distributors

_____ Trade literature

_____ Published market data

_____ Inquiries by prospects

_____ Pre-sales

_____ Orders

What do customers expect regarding customer service?

Is demand for the product/service changing? Explain.

How did you determine your price, by cost-plus-margin or market price?

How do your competitors price?

Will your price give the competitors some advantage? Explain.

Will the market pay your price? How do you know?

VII. Description of Industry and Trends

In this section you will describe both the industry of which your business is a part and significant current or emerging trends.

The trends you need to examine could be economic, regulatory, sociological, and technological trends that have, or may have, implications for your business's growth and/or survival. Any trend with a probability of occurring and having a positive or negative impact on any aspect of the business is to be considered and described in this section.

The forces considered at this stage in the writing of the plan are those that are out of your control but can significantly have an impact on your business. (This section may be difficult for some people because the task concerns thinking through hypothetical scenarios and developing possible alternative responses to events that have not occurred and for which there may be no precedent. However, this is the time to consider these possibilities—not later, when an opportunity has been missed or when you find yourself in an adverse situation.)

What is the size of the industry? What are its growth trends? What is the maturity of the industry?

What is the competitive nature of the industry? Are there barriers to entry and growth?

What effect might emerging trends have? Do they represent opportunities or threats (e.g., vulnerability to economic factors)? What effect will seasonal factors have?

Describe the overall financial position and performance of your industry.

What are the economic trends that could have an impact on demand for your product and to which you need to adapt—for example, continued recession, worsening recession, more rapid recovery from recession than originally anticipated? Inflation? Labor costs?

What are the sociological changes to which you need to adapt (e.g., changing demographics of the population)?

Are there any trends in the customer market that could have an impact on sales projections, or in the labor market that could impact cost projections?

What are the new and emerging technological developments in your industry with implications for your growth or survival?

Are there any regulatory trends with implications for your business? What about new or impending legislation?

List your key assumptions about the economic, regulatory, sociological, and technological trends that may have an impact on the environment within which you operate or plan to operate or expand. Also consider supply and distribution factors and any other relevant financial considerations.

VIII. Marketing Strategy

In this section you explain your marketing strategy. The first step in developing your strategy statement is to give thought to the driving force behind your long-term marketing goals.

Driving Force: The Principal Behind Strategy

What is the driving force behind your business or dream? Are you driven by the products or services you offer? Do you have strong relationships with specific markets served?

Is your primary focus return or profit? Other?

Describe in detail the driving force behind your business.

Defining Your Strategy

To begin the process of defining your strategy, answer the following questions:

What is the thrust or focus for future business development? What will be the scope of products/services that you will offer?

What is the future emphasis or priority and mix of products/services that fall within that scope?

What are the key capabilities required to make this vision happen (functional, human, and physical resources)?

What does the vision imply for growth and return expectations?

Strengths and Limitations Assessment

What has made you successful?

What has held you back?

What are your company's strengths? What are you best at? What is your unique advantage? What value do you add?

What are your company's weaknesses?

What are some key assumptions about the competition?

Strategic Issues Analysis

Based on your answers to all of the above questions, list the issues that you have identified that might affect your business's growth.

Now list your offensive strategy for leveraging your strengths into opportunities.

Now list issues you identified that will affect your business's survival.

Where are you vulnerable?

Based on these survival issues, list defensive strategies to protect yourself from threats that result from your business's weaknesses.

Now build a strategy statement that incorporates the best mix of strategies appropriate to your situation.

IX. Marketing Plan

To whom are you going to sell and how are you going to get them to buy? This section answers these important questions and displays to your audience that you know how to reach your customers. Show the reader your road map for successfully achieving sales projections. Your objective in this section is to be comprehensive, specific, and realistic.

The comprehensive Marketing Plan section will thoroughly explain the scope of your marketing activities quarter by quarter for the period encompassed by your business plan, including market research, positioning, pricing, collateral materials, marketing support systems, communications and distribution channels, merchandising, and sales.

The positioning paragraphs must cover your market research and competitive analysis and include answers to the following questions:

What are the weaknesses of your competitors?

How profitable are they?

Differentiate your company from competitors among the following factors: market share, price, profits, quality, R&D, reputation, and sales and service.

How will you win customers away from competitors while building your own base clientele?

Given these data, how can you differentiate your appeal to potential customers and position product/service in your marketing communications?

Presentation on pricing considerations needs to include answers to the following questions:

What is your mark-up goal?

What is your cost per unit?

What is your selling price?

What is your pricing rationale and how does it compare with your competitors'?

Paragraphs about how you will communicate with your target markets need to answer these questions:

How will you reach prospects to communicate that you exist and have something to sell?

Describe your web site and how it fits into your marketing plan. What is the main purpose of your web site? Is the web site logically organized and easy to follow? Does it have an attractive "look and feel"? Do all the pages present a professional uniform appearance? Does your site provide comprehensive information about your product or service? Are visitors able to download information about your products or services? Does your site provide customer communication that makes it easy for them to communicate with your company? Is your site able to accept online orders?

Where will you advertise: Print? Display? Electronic? Direct? Other?

What types of internal merchandising and visual displays do you plan?

What about your public relations: Press releases? Seminars? Speeches? Associations? Articles? Other?

Any promotions anticipated?

How will you implement referral development: Customers? Employees? Friends/family? Suppliers? Others?

What methods of distribution will you use? How will you get the product/service to the customer? What will your distribution costs be? Will you use a direct sales force? Mail order? Are there other distribution channels you can access?

X. Sales Plan

In this section you begin to build support for the sales projections. Your plan must satisfactorily resolve the basic sales issue of how to achieve the most cost-effective sales.

Respond to the following questions before you prepare your sales plan:

Will you employ salespeople?

If yes, how many?

How will salespeople be selected?

Based on realistic projections of sales per salesperson, how many salespeople will you need to achieve your sales goals?

What supervision and training will salespeople require?

What are the responsibilities of the salespeople? What commissions and incentives will you provide?

What type and number of sales support staff will be needed?

What will be your credit policy?

What are your sales forecasts? What have been the historical sales trends in your company or industry in the past three years?

How would funding affect sales forecasts?

What do you project to be the cost of sales?

What is the basis for your cost of sales projection?

What percentage of sales is cost of sales?

What do you estimate the total sales expenses to be per month? Per quarter? Per year?

How much does the business need to sell to break even?

What trends highlighted earlier could seriously change your projections?

How will you convert contacts into sales?

How will competitors respond to your sales tactics? What will be your response?

What percentage of sales do you expect returned?

If you are a larger organization, diagram the sales organization.

XI. Operations, Research and Development Strategies, and Plans

Service Firms

Describe the methods of providing services.

Provide an outline and schedule of all business activities.

Describe your hours and days of operation.

Include work flow diagrams if the service is complex.

What equipment and suppliers are needed? What is the relationship of price, delivery, credit, and quality?

Indicate how you will keep costs down.

Manufacturing Companies

Describe the manufacturing plan, plant, and facility requirements.

How will products be physically produced, packaged, and delivered, including any special machinery that might be necessary?

What are your quality and cost control procedures?

Concisely describe your production strategies. Use these statements to answer the following questions:

What processes or technologies will be used to produce or deliver the product?

Describe your production schedule, equipment, and technology to be used.

What product costs are required in order to achieve sales goals (e.g., variable labor requirements)? Include wages and fringe benefits.

Describe quality control and productivity rates.

What is the manufacturing budget for the period covered by pro forma projections?

Indicate capacity utilization.

In order to meet growth goals, what will be your future staffing? What are your supply and distribution requirements?

Are there any safety, health, or environmental concerns?

What will be your future inventory storage and maintenance?

What will be your future equipment and facilities requirements?

What impact would funding have on this plan?

Describe concisely your R&D strategy and plan. What are the R&D objectives within the time frame of the business plan? Have scheduled objectives been accomplished?

Are there any planned enhancements of current products?

Have results of past research and development activity justified investment?

What product development efforts are currently in process or planned?

How appropriate are these in light of current marketplace developments?

Include a progress report on past and current R&D; for example, has it brought products to market in a timely manner?

Include a department budget for a time frame of the business plan.

Describe staffing, equipment, and facilities.

General

Are there any other lawsuits, not previously mentioned, in which the company is a party?

Who is the corporate legal council?

What type of insurance is needed for this business? (Please disclose a summary of all insurance coverage.)

Who are the company's insurers?

Does the company have all necessary licenses, and building and operating permits?

Does the company have all essential contracts and joint venture agreements fully executed?

Is the company currently, or in the past, in arrears regarding federal, state, or local franchise and income taxes? Payroll taxes? Real estate taxes? Personal property taxes? Sales taxes?

Have there ever been inquiries or reviews by a taxing authority?

Disclose all real estate currently owned, leased, or otherwise used by the company.

Is there any other topical area regarding the company, not covered by this section, that you feel would be important for the investor to consider during the evaluation process?

XII. Management, Organization, Personnel, and Information Systems

In this section your objective is to show how the ability and track record of your company's management forms the key to its success. To do this you must objectively evaluate your management and board of directors (if appropriate) to determine the strength and capability of your business and to let the audience know the result of this evaluation.

Who is involved in the business? Include resumes for the founder, owner, key managers, and specially trained technical staff in the Supporting Documents section. These will include name, position, background information on performance, key accomplishments, history of positions held and length of time with the company, industry recognition, specialized skills, education, age, and community involvement.

How would you evaluate each of the key management and board personnel?

Describe the respective duties and qualifications of key employees, including years of experience in the assigned position.

How do key managers' skills complement the president's skills?

What roles do the key managers play in daily operations?

Who wrote the business plan? Did you use consultants or specialists? If so, list the consultants' names.

Are there any skills missing that are necessary for the firms success?

What are the limitations of management?

List the names and addresses of all professional resources available to the business, including:

Accountant: _____

Insurance broker: _____

Attorney: _____

CPA: _____

Bankers: _____

Securities or investment banking firm (if appropriate): _____

Do you have written job descriptions for key management personnel? If yes, include a summary in this section. If no, write job descriptions.

Outline the succession plan in case of the loss of key personnel.

Explain remuneration for management. What is it about your remuneration plan that will attract and keep quality talent? Salaries? Benefits packages? Incentives? Promotion opportunities? Organization? Other?

If you are a corporation, who is on the board of directors?

Do you have an advisory board? If yes, what are the members' credentials?

Where is the location of the headquarters of the business?

Include a current organization chart for your business and anticipated organization chart if changes are imminent, or if you are a start-up.

Describe each division or department and its function and personnel.

Do any employees require special training, education, or experience?

Does the company provide any special training or educational programs?

Describe current staffing levels and the expected turnover in the business.

How competitive are the company's compensation and benefits programs?

Provide breakdowns on skill levels, hours worked, wage rates, whether unionized, and so on.

Describe recruitment strategy and major competitors for the local workforce. How successful have you been?

If you use independent contractors, explain. Show that you conform to IRS requirements.

Project personnel needs in order to accomplish business plan goals (e.g., management to be added).

Describe your compensation package, including salary, insurance, advancement opportunities, and profit sharing.

Include personnel policies as a separate document available on request.

If unionized, describe your relationships with unions. When do contracts come up for negotiation, and are there any likely union drives?

Management Information Systems

What method do you have for getting important information to help you manage your business?

What are your methods of record keeping?

What regular and timely reports do you generate that tell you how well you and the company are doing relative to the business plan objectives? Daily? Weekly? Monthly?

What computer hardware and applications are you using or going to obtain in order to generate these crucial reports?

XIII. Objectives and Milestones

The purpose of this section is to get you to write down your goals for the business.
     The following objective-setting procedure has been used by hundreds of companies. It is brilliantly simple and will lead you to clear statements of objectives and the important steps you must start taking now to achieve your dream tomorrow.

Objectives

1. Clearly state where you want to be at the end of the period covered by this plan.

2. Identify the primary roadblocks to successfully achieving your vision.

3. Identify the internal strengths and resources needed to achieve success.

4. Identify internal weaknesses that must be overcome in order to achieve success, for example, facilities limitations, location relative to customers, and so on.

5. Put in priority the primary advantages and disadvantages identified above.

6. What external events or situations may impact your ability to achieve your objective, for example, legislation, regulation, economy, and so on?

7. If you are an existing company (not a start-up), what will be your ability to achieve goals without any changes—for example, sales, income, margins, working capital, liquidity, and so on?

8. What are the most serious challenges or problems you are currently facing? What benefit would be realized if these problems were solved?

9. Based on the assessment provided in answering questions 1 through 8, list three to six objectives you want to achieve (long-term and short-term).

   1. _____   4. _____

   2. _____   5. _____

   3. _____   6. _____

10. Now, for each objective, list the three most important tasks that must be accomplished in order to achieve the objective.

11. List any operational changes that must occur in order for these tasks to be accomplished.

12. What internal or external resources must be secured to accomplish these tasks?

13. What will each objective require in terms of personnel and costs?

14. List the risks associated with tasks to accomplish your objectives.

What action can be taken to minimize or avoid these risks?

15. Which objectives and tasks leverage your strengths? Which are unaffected or limit the vulnerability caused by your weaknesses?

16. Are there any objectives or tasks that you lack the resources to accomplish?

17. Develop a chart that lists the following: the objectives you have chosen, the most important steps to accomplish for their realization, the dates for accomplishment, the milestone measures you will use to evaluate performance, who will be responsible, any status reports on your progress to communicate to all involved, and any contingency plans.

XIV. Financial Projections

Financial management can be the determining factor in the survivability as well as the success of your business. It is important to make careful financial projections as a way of both planning and controlling the business. While accounting is essentially a record of historical performance of the business, financial projections, or the creation of pro forma financial statements and budgets, helps you to think through the financial implications of the decisions made during the preparation of your business plan.

In previous sections of the business plan, you have analyzed the market and set objectives. In this section you will put into financial terms the strategies detailed in the business plan. You document the past in financial terms (if applicable), take a forward look, and complete the final task in writing the business plan, that is, forecast likely conditions and project allocation of resources to support future operations.

Will You Be Able to Reach Your Objectives?

Your projections are to be structured around the objectives developed by the management team during the planning process. The marketing, sales, and operations strategies and plans spell out the financial requirements. The industry and trend analyses imply specific assumptions about likely future conditions.

The key in preparing this section is to be realistic. Critically evaluate the potential for profitability of your venture. You have to believe in the accuracy and attainability of your projections and, equally important, convince others that the financial projections are realizable. If you have been in business, then you will have past financial data to guide your projections. If this is a start-up, you will need to be creative in seeking out comparative ventures, be detailed in capturing projected cost data, and be realistic in sales projections. Be reasonable. If your projections for market share, profit, growth rate, sales performance, and/or operating margins significantly deviate from industry standards, you will surely face an uphill battle building trust with funding resources.

Be prepared to defend both your projections and the assumptions behind the projections. Be consistent about assumptions. Start with all your key assumptions regarding wages, benefits, pricing, production costs, sales, volume, market projections, and inflation, and support them as clearly as possible. If you made an assumption in the operating budgets, be sure the pro forma statements reflect it. Document and footnote all assumptions on the pro forma statements.

Interrelationships of Financial Projections

We recommend that you include pro forma financial statements, cash budgets, and operating budgets. Begin by projecting separate sets of departmental budgets based on current and desired funding. Then develop cash flow, income projections, and, lastly, your pro forma balance sheet.

Also, consider developing the projections on a monthly basis for the first year, quarterly for years two and three, and annually for years four and five—if you forecast that far into the future. It is critical that you include footnotes describing significant assumptions used in preparing any financial statement projection. Worksheets to guide the preparation of your projections are included at the end of this section.

Begin your financial projections with the operating budgets. These projections detail forecasted department revenue and expense patterns. For example, pro forma sales projections and pro forma departmental expense budgets can be consolidated into a forecasted operating budget for the sales department. The sales forecast projects when sales will occur, the volume of sales, and, thus, your gross revenue. (Refer to Worksheet #1 and Worksheet #2 for sample schedules.)

Next, develop cash budgets or cash flow statements using Worksheet #3. Cash flow statements are detailed projections of the cycle of turning sales into cash that, in turn, pays the cost of doing business and, you hope, returns a profit. The cash flow statement describes cash in and cash out and when. A cash flow analysis and projection will reflect your company's credit and collection policies, trade credit, and other financing activities, and purchase and disposal of fixed assets. This projection informs you when cash will be needed before a cash crisis occurs.

Last, prepare the pro forma financial statements, which include your assumptions about future performance and funding requirements, that is, income or profit and loss statement, and balance sheet. The pro forma income statement projects the company's revenues, expenses, and earnings over a specific period of time. When you subtract your expenses from your income, you will have your net profit or loss for the period. Use Worksheet #4 as a sample income statement to guide your projections. The balance sheet shows the assets and liabilities of the company on a given date. When you subtract liabilities from assets and owners' equity, the difference is the company's net worth. Worksheet #5 will guide your preparation of a pro forma balance sheet. Also, include historical income statements and balance sheets, if they are appropriate.

Demonstrate that you understand break-even point. Describe the level of sales volume required to break even and candidly discuss the likelihood of earning at least that much. The break-even point is that level of sales that covers the fixed and variable costs of providing your product or service. You will need to know your fixed costs (rent, utilities, insurance, etc.), those that remain constant regardless of sales. You will also need to know your variable costs (cost of goods, sales commissions, etc.), those that will increase with sales. Explain why you are confident in meeting or exceeding the break-even point.

Comment on how you will adjust to situations differing from stated expectations.

If you are an existing business, include income statements, balance sheets, and cash flow statements for the past three years.

What Are Your Financial Needs?

The purpose of these financial documents is to help you assess future performance and funding requirements. After completing the projections and statements mentioned above, you will be able to state (1) the amount of funds needed over the course of time covered by the business plan, (2) when funding will be needed, (3) the types of funding most appropriate (e.g., debt or equity based), and (4) what you are willing to give up to get the funding. In the case of a loan (e.g., loan amount, collateral, interest rate, and repayment schedule) or in the case of equity financing, state the percentage of the company to be given up, proposed return on investment, and the anticipated method for taking out the investor (buy-back, public offer, or sale). You also will be on firm ground when describing how the funding will be used and be able to prepare a uses of funds statement.

Funds Sought and Exit Strategy

Indicate how much money you are seeking, how many investors you plan to have, how the funds raised will be used, and how investors or lenders will get their money out. (Use Worksheet #6 to guide your preparation of a "Sources and Use of Funds Statement.") Attach a risk disclosure document that includes an evaluation of potential risks inherent in your enterprise; assess risks and describe steps to minimize risks.

XV. Supporting Documents

Once you have completed the main body of the business plan, consider the additional records that should be included pertaining to your business. These supporting documents are records that back up the statements and decisions in the body of the plan. Include resumes, financial statements, credit reports, copies of leases, contracts and letters of commitment to purchase, legal documents, maps of location, descriptive materials about your products or services, collateral sales and marketing materials, reference lists, glossary of terms, and any other miscellaneous documents best assembled with the plan.

WORKSHEET #1

PRO FORMA SALES PROJECTION

ABC COMPANY, INC. PRO FORMA SALES PROJECTIONS

FOR THE YEAR ENDED 20XX

Product Line(s)
Product(s)

YEAR	Jan	Feb	Mar	Apr	May	Jun	Jul	Aug	Sep	Oct	Nov	Dec
PRODUCT LINE A												
1. Product 1												
Shipments (Units)												
x Avg Price/Unit												
Gross Sales												
2. Product 2												
3. Product 3												
n. Product N												
PRODUCT LINE A												
GROSS SALES												
PRODUCT LINE B												
PRODUCT LINE C												
PRODUCT LINE N												
TOTAL GROSS SALES												

WORKSHEET #2

QUARTERLY SALES BUDGET

ABC CORPORATION QUARTERLY SALES BUDGET

FOR THE YEAR ENDED 20XX

TOTAL	1 st Quarter	2nd Quarter	3rd Quarter	4th Quarter
Basic data: Unit sales (number of units): Product A				
Product B				
Product C				
Price level (per unit): Product A				
Product B				
Product C				
Number of salespersons:				
Operating budget ($000): Sales revenue				
Less: returns, allowances				
Net sales				
Cost of goods sold				
Margin before delivery				
Delivery expense				
Gross margin				
Selling expense (controllable): Salesperson's compensation				
Travel and entertainment				
Sales support costs				
TOTAL SELLING EXPENSES				
Gross contribution				
Departmental period costs				
Net contribution				
Corporate support (transferred): Staff support				
Advertising				
General overhead				
TOTAL CORPORATE SUPPORT				
Profit contribution (before taxes)				

WORKSHEET #3

PRO FORMA CASH FLOW STATEMENT
ABC CORPORATION PRO FORMA CASH FLOW STATEMENT
FOR THE YEAR ENDED 20XX

	1st Quarter	2nd Quarter	3rd Quarter	4th Quarter	YEAR	Assumption
Sources (uses) of cash						
Net earnings (loss)						
Depreciation and amortization						
Cash provided by operations dividends						
Cash provided by (used for) changes in: Accounts receivable						
Inventory						
Other current assets						
Accounts payable						
Income tax						
Accrued compensation						
Dividends payable						
Other current liabilities						
Other assets						
Net cash provided by (used for) operating activity						
Investment transactions						
Furniture and equipment						
Land						
Building and improvement						
Net cash from investment transactions						
Financing transactions						
Short-term debt						
Long-term debt						
Other noncurrent liabilities						
Sale of common stock						
Net cash from financing transactions						
Net increase (decrease) in cash						
Cash: Beginning of period						
Cash: End of period						

WORKSHEET #4

PRO FORMA INCOME STATEMENT
ABC CORPORATION PRO FORMA INCOME STATEMENt

	Current Year	Year 1	Year 2	Year 3	TOTAL	Assumptions
Net sales						
Cost of sales (schedule will vary based on type of business)						
Gross margin						
Operating expenses						
Depreciation and amortization						
Selling, general, and administrative expenses						
Operating income (loss)						
Other income (expense)						
Dividends and interest income						
Interest expense						
Earnings (before income taxes)						
Income taxes						
Net earnings						
Common shares outstanding						
Earning per common share						

WORKSHEET #5

PRO FORMA BALANCE SHEET
ABC CORPORATION PRO FORMA BALANCE SHEET AS OF
PAGE 1 OF 2

	Current Year	Year 1	Year 2	Year 3	TOTAL	Assumptions
ASSETS						
Current assets:						
Cash						
Marketable securities						
Accounts receivable						
Inventories						
Prepaid expenses						
TOTAL CURRENT ASSETS						
Property, Plant, and Equipment						
Land						
Buildings						
Machinery						
Leasehold improvements						
Furniture, fixtures, etc.						
TOTAL PROPERTY, PLANT, AND EQUIPMENT						
Less accumulated depreciation						
Net property, plant, and equipment						
Intangibles (goodwill, patents) less amortization						
TOTAL ASSETS						

PRO FORMA BALANCE SHEET
ABC CORPORATION PRO FORMA BALANCE SHEET AS OF
PAGE 2 OF 2

	Current Year	Year 1	Year 2	Year 3	TOTAL	Assumptions
LIABILITIES						
Current liabilities:						
Accounts payable						
Notes payable						
Accrued expenses						
Income taxes payable						
Dividends payable						
Other liabilities						
TOTAL CURRENT LIABILITIES						
Long-term liabilities						
Deferred income taxes						
Securities payable (year)						
Other long-term debt						
TOTAL LIABILITIES						
SHAREHOLDERS' EQUITY						
Preferred stock						
Common stock						
Additional paid-in capital						
Retained earnings						
TOTAL SHAREHOLDERS' EQUITY						
TOTAL LIABILITIES AND SHAREHOLDERS' EQUITY						

WORKSHEET #6

SOURCES AND USES of FUNDS

Complete the following form to describe how much money you are seeking and how you will use the funds raised. Be as specific as possible.

Number of funding rounds expected for full financing:

Total dollar amount being sought in this round: $

Sources of funds

Equity financing:

Preferred stock:

Common stock:

Debt financing:

Mortgage loans:

Other long-term loans:

Short-term loans:

Convertible debt:

Investment from principals:

Uses of funds

Capital expenditures:

Purchase of property:

 Leasehold improvements:

Purchase of equipment/furniture:

Other:

Working capital:
Purchase of inventory:
Staff expansion:
New product line introduction:
Additional marketing activities:
Other business expansion activities:
Other:

Debt retirement:
Cash reserve:

PREPARATION AND DELIVERY OF YOUR PRESENTATION

Preparing an Effective Presentation

An effective presentation depends on your ability to communicate with the investor by understanding their objectives and providing a presentation that helps them to see the opportunity for your business. The recommended approach includes the following elements.

Define your Goal

- Ask yourself, "What is the purpose of my presentation? Am I trying to inform? Motivate? Entertain?"
- Then ask, "What do I want people to know at the end of my presentation? What do I want them to think? What do I want them to do?"
- Write out the answers to those questions and structure your presentation around them.

Know your Audience

- A presentation has three important elements: you, the talk, and the audience. The audience is the most important.
- So who is the investor? What are their concerns? Interests? How much do they know about the subject matter?
- And, most importantly, why should the audience listen to you? What's in it for them?
- The more you know about the investor, the more you'll be able to direct your presentation to meet their needs and wants.

Focus

- Determine your core message, the main point you want the investor to "get." Develop at least three different ways to say it. Also identify up to three sub-points.
- State the main point and sub-points in your introduction. "My main point is that anyone can make a great presentation by paying close attention to three elements: content, delivery, and visual aids."
- Notice how short and to the point this statement is. Your audience should not have to guess your main point. Make it clear from the outset.

Outline your Presentation

- In preparing your presentation, start by focusing on your goal (i.e., what you want the audience to know, think, and do).

■ You don't need to do a formal outline but do write out the basic structure. The adage "tell them what you're going to tell them, tell them, and then tell them what you've told them" works well. Give people an overview of what you're going to present, make the presentation, and summarize.

■ Do not write out the presentation. Outline it and talk from the outline.

Have a Good Introduction

■ An effective introduction gets the investor's attention and identifies the topic.

■ Stories or questions are often good ways to start.

■ After the attention-getter, state your main message and sub-messages, and explain how the presentation will benefit the investor.

Keep the Audience's Attention

■ It is essential to hold the investor's attention during the bulk of the presentation.

■ That's challenging. Supposedly the average person thinks at the rate of 800 words per minute, and the average presenter speaks at the rate of 150 words per minute. That leaves lots of time for the mind to wander.

■ To keep your investor's attention, disrupt the flow every 10 to 15 minutes. How? You could:
  ○ Change the media (e.g., show a short video).
  ○ Invite participation.
  ○ Draw a simple diagram on the whiteboard.
  ○ Turn off the slides.
  ○ Tell a brief story.
  ○ Give an example.

Have a Good Closing

■ In closing, summarize your main points and, if appropriate, issue a "call to action."

■ Also consider the "big finish." This oft-ignored tool is much more effective than simply saying, "Thank you." The big finish is the wrap-up story or point you make after the Q&A is finished.

Prepare Visuals

Although there are other software products that can be used to create your presentation, PowerPoint provides an advantage because investors can easily view a copy of your presentation after the meeting. Print extra copies of the slides and hand out to meeting participants before you begin. If you should encounter problems with your computer or the digital projector, you can quickly proceed using the handouts. Some experts prefer only using handouts to keep the investor's attention on you rather than the screen.

Color presentations are more persuasive than black and white. However, visuals for their own sake are meaningless. Have a purpose for the visuals and remember that they are tools. PowerPoint does not give the presentation. You do.

In preparing visuals, include only a few talking points per slide. A good guideline is no more than 20 words or six lines. Better yet, use a diagram or other visual. And do not fill every square inch of the slide. Less is more.

Use a clear, easy-to-read typeface such as Tahoma or Arial. Make your typeface at least 18 points. Use the same size font for items of equal importance and vary the size for items of lesser importance.

Put your name, company, and contact information on the last slide. Keep that slide up while you take questions.

When you are basically finished, have someone review the presentation. It's amazing how many typos or inconsistencies can crop up during the process.

Outline Suggestions

Your outline will vary depending on the company stage of development; however, the following suggestions provide a starting point:

- One sentence description of the company, the problem it addresses, and the solution it provides. Is this the next big thing?
- Market opportunity. Size, growth rate, demographics, leading companies. What is the vision? What are the trends? What new opportunities are emerging? What are the urgent unsolved problems? What solutions would transform the industry? Is the market ready?
- Business model. What are the specific markets and target customers? What products and services will be offered? What is the pricing model? How will we reach the target customer (distribution and marketing)? Who are the competitors and what are the company's unique, sustainable advantages? What is the financial engine (revenue sources, cost structure) that drives the business? Is the overall business model viable, sustainable, and (eventually) profitable?
- Operating/development plan and key milestones. What is the company's current status? What are the major components of the operating/development plan over the next year? What performance measures are in place to manage the business? What are the key milestones that validate

the business and cause exponential growth in market share, profitability, and shareholder value (and are they achievable)?

■ Management, advisers, and partners. Who are they? What role do they play? What are their qualifications and track record? What additional players are ready to join, are in negotiations, or are targeted? Can this team execute the plan?

■ Financial forecast and funding plan. Three-year forecast of revenues; gross margin; earnings before interest, taxes, depreciation, and amortization (EBITDA); and cash flow. Major assumptions. Funding requirements and plan. Use of proceeds. Can this company reach critical mass quickly?

■ Investment opportunity. What is the company offering? What does the company need besides money? What is the profile of the ideal investor? Who are the comparable companies and what ROI did they produce for investors? What are the possible exit strategies and can they be achieved at a high ROI within a reasonable time? Why should I invest in this deal?

As you create your presentation, be aware that your slides are visuals to enhance your key points—almost like a billboard. It is up to you to present the business and to enhance the investor's understanding of the business opportunity.

Legal Primer on Securities Law Issues for Nonlawyers

(Emphasis on Small Business and California)

William D. Evers, Esq.
Attorney at Law
1700 California St.
Suite 470
San Francisco, CA 94109
(415) 202-0906

Note: This is a brief summary and is not to be relied on for legal advice. The subject of securities laws is arcane, and decisions as to how to proceed are factually based. The author assumes no responsibility for action undertaken pursuant to this primer.

CONTENTS

FOREWORD

This primer is intended to assist our clients in thinking through what route to follow when embarking on a program to finance their business. It is not a complete guide, but we hope it will be of some help. It should not be considered legal advice.

1. OVERVIEW

There is a jumble of terms, rules, and regulations in the securities regulatory area. This primer concentrates on a portion of the spectrum—the offering of equity (stock) by small and emerging companies.

There are three primary federal statutes: the Securities Act of 1933 (the '33 Act), the Securities Exchange Act of 1934 (the '34 Act), and the Investment Company Act of 1940 (the '40 Act).

The SEC administers these laws at the federal level and issues rules, regulations, and orders pursuant to the terms of these laws.

The states also have jurisdiction. It's as if there were 50 countries to be dealt with. A minority of the states use full disclosure (also used by the SEC) and the rest use merit review (used by California). New York has a unique antifraud approach. Clearing with the states is called "blue skying." The higher up the scale one goes in being a reporting company (to the SEC), being listed on an exchange, and having substantial assets, the easier it is to be qualified to sell securities in the states. Small business, lacking these attributes, has an expensive and difficult time getting qualified.

1.1 Federal Acts

1.1.1 General—Full Disclosure

The SEC administers the '33 Act based on the policy of requiring full disclosure. The idea is, "Let the facts be told, precisely and accurately, and then, caveat emptor—let the buyers beware." The SEC usually reviews the filing of an application very thoroughly. Regulation A and SB-2 offerings are reviewed in Washington. The initial response is usually received in one month. One then responds to the SEC comments and gets the second round of comments in two to three weeks. Each response cycle is usually shorter than the initial response time. Finally, if and when the SEC finds that their comments have been responded to adequately, the SEC will declare the filing effective. Only when a filing is effective can the actual sale of securities begin.

1.1.2 Securities Act of 1933

The '33 Act deals with the offer, sale, and issuance of securities. Transactions that involve more than one state are under the SEC's jurisdiction: Both public and private transactions are covered.

Under the '33 Act, all companies wishing to sell their stock or other securities must go through a registration process unless the transaction is one that by law or regulation is exempt from registration. Section 3(b) of the '33 Act allows the SEC to exempt from registration small offerings under $5 million. Thus, we have the SCOR for up to $1 million under Rule 504 and Reg. A offerings for up to $5 million. Section 4(2) of the '33 Act covers those offerings not involving a public offering and provides the authority for Rule 506 of Reg. D (see below). Section 4(6) of the '33 Act exempts from registration up to $5 million of sales to certain high-income or high-net-worth individuals or institutions ("Accredited Investors"). All these sections are in the '33 Act.

1.1.3 Securities Exchange Act of 1934

As its name implies, this act deals with trading and regulation of the exchanges. The primary method of regulating broker-dealers is through a self-regulating organization (SRO), the National Association of Securities Dealers (NASD).

The impact of this act on issuers (companies selling securities) relates to the reporting requirements and to trading in the company's securities.

When one files for registration of a public offering, as in an SB-2 filing (but not in a Reg. A offering, which, though public, is anomalously an exemption from registration), one becomes a reporting company. Reporting companies are required to file annual, quarterly, and other periodic reports (on Forms 10-K, 10-Q, and 8-K) with the SEC, submit shareholder proxy statements to the SEC, and follow various other reporting requirements, including being subject to the rather draconian provisions of the Sarbanes-Oxley Act.

Companies also can become reporting companies voluntarily by filing with the SEC. A company must become a reporting company if it has at least 500 shareholders and $10 million in assets.

A small company can have a broker-dealer file information akin to that in a prospectus by complying with the requirements of Rule 15(c)(2)(11) under the '34 Act. This then allows the company to have a market maker and to be posted on the Bulletin Board maintained by the NASD. Bulletin Board stocks are limited to reporting companies only. This has knocked off about half of the stocks previously on the Bulletin Board. Presumably the possible knock-offs have either become reporting companies or have migrated to the "Pink Sheets." Any stock that is traded and has a market maker can be listed on the Pink Sheets, maintained by the National Quotation Bureau.

1.1.4 Investment Company Act of 1940

The '40 Act controls mutual funds and numerous other activities including investment advisers (advising as to funds over $25 million).

This act comes into play when a fund has over 100 investors. It is very restrictive and is the reason venture capitalists have fewer than 100 partners. Quite simply, it inhibits our country from having any "peoples" or "public" venture capital activity. A pity, in that the venture capitalists are no longer very venturesome and do not offer finance in the "chasm" or "gap" area of $250,000 to $5 million.

1.2 Federal Rules and Regulations—Exemptions from Registration

The SEC has promulgated certain key rules and regulations that define those offerings that are exempt from the SEC's registration process. The most widely known areas follows.

1.2.1 Regulation D

Reg. D contains Rules 501 through 508. Rules 504 and 505 are based on Section 3(b) of the '33 Act; Rule 506 is based on Section 4(2) of that act.

1.2.2 Regulation A: Public, Limit $5 Million

Regulation A allows for a public offering as an "exemption from registration" in the form of an Application for Exemption for offers and sales of securities up to $5 million [under Section 3(b) of the '33 Act]. There is an anomaly involved: Even though not registered, the securities are not "restricted" and can be traded (with the same possible limitations as in a SCOR offering, see below). Using a Reg. A does not cause the issuer to be a reporting company, an important distinction from the use of an SB-2, especially since the enactment of the Sarbanes-Oxley Act. Reg. A should grow in popularity because of this exemption from Sarbanes-Oxley.

1.2.3 Rule 504, SCOR: Public or Private, Limit $1 million

This is a safe harbor for public (or private) offerings not exceeding $1 million. The federal government asserts no jurisdiction in a 504 offering. It is under Section 3(b) of the '33 Act (small offerings). This means that if a company follows the requirements of Rule 504, its public or private offering

(Rule 504 and SCOR) will be exempt from the registration requirements of the SEC.

Rule 504 provides the basis for SCOR offerings (see below). All Rule 504 small public offerings, including SCOR, must be cleared with the state regulators. Stock issued pursuant to Rule 504 is not "restricted"; however, in California it frequently is not freely tradable through brokers.

Rule 504 is not usually used for a private offering because one frequently can offer in only one state or use Rule 506. In California, one would probably use Section 25102(f) of the California Corporations Code, which provides for any number of accredited investors and allows up to 35 nonaccredited investors. If the offering is in more than one state, Rule 504 could be utilized with blue skying in each state. Remember that Rule 504 is nothing more than the SEC not asserting any regulatory jurisdiction. At the present time, stock issued pursuant to a 504 offering (public or private) that has registered in at least one state is not, under federal rules, "restricted" except as to "affiliates" (officer, director, and control persons). However, a state may impose restrictions. In California, under Section 25102(f), the stock is technically not restricted, though the investor must vouch that the stock is not being purchased with a view toward further distribution and the stock is usually not tradable through a broker, unless on an unsolicited basis.

Rule 506 requires that a more relatively complex offering document (same as in a Reg. A offering) be given if stock is going to be sold to nonaccredited investors, whereas Rule 504 does not require that any specific form of offering document be used; however, each state may require a disclosure document, especially in the case of a public 504 (SCOR) offering. Regardless of whether a rule requires use of an offering document, proper disclosure of material information is absolutely necessary to be able to avoid and/or defend securities fraud claims from investors.

1.2.4 Rule 505: Private Limit $5 Million

This rule comes under Section 3(b) of the '33 Act (small offerings) and provides a "safe harbor" for private offerings up to $5 million. It is contrasted to Regulation A [also under Section 3(b)] which provides for a public offering up to $5 million. Up to 35 nonaccredited investors are allowed. No general solicitation or advertising is allowed. Strictly prescribed information is required to be given to the nonaccredited investors, including audited financials (offerings of $5 million). Stock issued pursuant to Rule 505 is "restricted."

This rule is seldom used as the requirements for nonaccredited investors are stiff, and, if going for a private placement, one would use Rule 506 (unlimited amount) with its preemption of state review (see below).

1.2.5 Rule 506: Unlimited Private, Preemption

A new opening was created by the National Securities Markets Improvement Act of 1996 in which Congress preempted from the states the authority to review securities exempted from registration by Rule 506, a rule adopted under Section 4(2) of the '33 Act (not involving a public offering). The states cannot review a Rule 506 offering; if to accredited investors only, no prescribed disclosure document is required. However, one would use a private placement memorandum (PPM) to avoid fraud charges. If nonaccredited investors (up to 35) are involved, a prescribed disclosure document is required. The "joker" is that Congress allowed the states to require a notice filing and to assess filing fees just as if no preemption exists. Nonetheless, this is an attractive alternative for those who can find accredited investors. No advertising is permitted. The rule also allows a public offering to follow immediately after the termination of the Rule 506 offering. Stock issued pursuant to Rule 506 is "restricted."

1.2.6 Regulation S

Regulation S provides an exemption from registration of securities that are sold outside the United States by companies meeting certain criteria. Reg. S can be used for overseas sales, either public or private, and either in conjunction with or separate from a U.S. offering. The securities, generally, must not be sold to U.S. persons for one year (equity securities) or 40 days (debt securities). Note, also, that resale into the United States, if done quickly, must be done pursuant to an exemption from registration.

There was considerable abuse of Regulation S as a means of avoiding the SEC's registration requirements. As a result, the SEC has increased the period during which the equity securities may not be sold to U.S. persons from 40 days to one year.

1.3 The States

The states all regulate the offer and sale of securities. Clearing with the states is known as blue skying. As noted above, some states use full disclosure (similar to the SEC) and some use merit review (such as California); however, in administration of the laws, the shades of difference tend to blend. Merit review requires a finding by the state that the offering is "fair, just, and equitable" to the purchaser. This test is frequently met by the administrators declaring the offering is fair, just, and equitable only if offered to persons of a certain level of wealth and/or sophistication. This is known as "suitability" and is used extensively in California under a "limited" (as compared to an "open") public offering permit.

The states belong to the North American Securities Administrators Association (NASAA), an organization that attempts to coordinate state regulation so as to lessen the burden on small issuers. The irony is that most listed (on stock exchanges) companies only need notify the state to be cleared. It is the small issuer that faces the task of clearing in each jurisdiction in which offers (see "The Internet" below) and sales are to be made.

Certain states are cooperating on a regional basis for review. The New England and certain western states are examples. Generally, California is not participating. However, most states, including California, are now (as of June 2004) participating in "coordinated equity review" wherein a state is chosen (by the other participating states) to assign one full disclosure state and one merit review state to review for the states in which offerings are to be made. This process is limited to SB-1 and SB-2 offerings (and S-1's). Unfortunately, this route has lost its appeal due to the fact that each state involved in the applied for clearance tends to put in its favorite restriction, and the result is an unwieldy and restrictive permit. It is usually better to qualify individually in the most promising states.

New York state is unique in that it has an antifraud statute (the Martin Act) administered by the New York Attorney General.

Washington, DC, is even more unique in that it has no securities regulation scheme.

1.4 California Laws

1.4.1 General: Merit Review, Suitability

As noted above, California is a merit review state using "suitability" in public offerings. In a private offering (no advertising, no general solicitation), one is allowed to sell to any number of accredited (California uses the term *excluded*, which includes accredited) investors and up to 35 nonaccredited ones. Only a one-page filing is required in the private offering [see "25102(f)" below].

1.4.2 Section 25113(b)(i)*: Qualification. Public

This is the general qualification section for a public offering; usable if one cannot use SCOR, for example, a foreign (Nevada or other state) corporation not qualifying under Section 25115.

---

*All sections refer to the Corporations Code of California.

1.4.3 Section 25113(b)(ii): Qualification, Public

Provides for California corporations and foreign (out-of-state) corporations that meet certain tests to use the special rule of SCOR offerings.

1.4.4 Section 25102(f): Private, No Review

This is the great escape valve allowing one to raise any amount from excluded investors and not more than 35 nonexcluded on a private basis (no ads, no general solicitation). There is no state review of the offering materials. There are limitations on who can buy securities in an offering under Section 25102(f). Purchasers must have a preexisting business relationship with the company or have demonstrated investor sophistication. The stock is not "restricted"; however, finding buyers without the intervention of brokers (who usually are not able to handle) is most difficult.

1.4.5 Section 25102(n): Private with Announcement

This section allows one to advertise in a private placement with sale to "qualified investors" only. The ad, a "general announcement," is strictly prescribed. It is in the form of a "tombstone ad." Many states are now adopting similar laws. The California act is very complex and, because of this, is the subject of a separate paper. So far, Section 25102(n) has not proven to be very useful, despite early high hopes.

1.5 Accredited and Excluded Investors

"Accredited investor" is defined in Rule 501(a) of Reg. D. There are several categories, the most important of which is a "natural person" with a single income of $200,000 (or joint income with that person's spouse of $300,000) in the past two years and reasonable expectation of that rate of income continuing for the current year, or having $1 million of net worth, including home equity.

California uses the term *excluded* to indicate exclusion from the count of 35 nonexcluded that are allowed under Section 25102(f). Thus, in a private offering, one can have any number of "excluded" investors because they are excluded from the count. There are many categories of "excluded." The primary ones are:

1. Partner, officer, director of the issuer together with their relatives sharing a residence.
2. Owners of more than 50 percent of the shares of the issuer.
3. Promoter.

4. A purchaser who purchases $150,000 of the offering, has enough sophistication (or has an investment adviser with enough sophistication) to protect his or her interests, and whose investment does not exceed 10 percent of his or her net worth.

5. An individual who alone has an income exceeding $200,000 or, with spouse, has income exceeding $300,000 in the two most recent years and expects continuation of this income, or has a net worth exceeding $1 million. Home equity is included, so the definition is the same as the federal for "accredited."

2. PRIVATE OFFERINGS—THE FIRST STEP

2.1 Introduction

Normally, one raises the first funds on a private basis, especially if the need is modest, say, under $1.5 million. The cost is considerably less and the time involved is frequently less, depending on one's ability to raise funds from wealthy sources. These are two basic criteria: amount and contacts. This section reviews various approaches.

2.2 Multistate: Section 4(2) and Rule 506

If one knows wealthy sources in more than one state, there are two primary routes to follow: the safe harbor of Rule 506 or simply Section 4(2) of the '33 Act (not involving a public offering).

If Section 4(2) is used, each state must be "blue skied." There are different requirements as to nonaccredited investors (California 35, Nevada 25, etc.). If only accredited investors are approached, some states require only a simple form and a fee.

Rule 506 has an obvious advantage; it preempts the states except as to fees and a simple filing. One is sure that all one has to do for each state is pay the filing fee and file a Form D report (a few pages showing sales in that state). The disadvantage is that, if nonaccredited investors are involved, the disclosure document is rather elaborate (like an offering circular in a Reg. A offering).

The legal costs of a Rule 506 offering only to accredited investors can be as low as $6,000 (excluding filing fees) if the business plan has good disclosure in which case a "wrap-around" can be used: wrapping the legal requirements around the business plan to provide disclosure sufficient to protect against successful fraud claims in the future.

If nonaccredited investors are approached, the cost rises substantially to around $20,000 to $50,000 because the work is similar to a Reg. A offering, with the exception of not having federal review of the document.

2.3 California: Section 25102(f)

In the event one offers securities only in California, Section 25102(f) stands alone. It permits a private placement of any amount of money to be raised from "excluded" or "accredited" investors and up to 35 nonexcluded investors. The stock would not be "restricted" in the federal sense (no Rule 144) but would be limited in trading (see Section 6 below). If more than one state is involved, either Rule 504 of Reg. D or Section 4(2) must be utilized and each state "blue skied." Section 25102(f) would still be used in California.

Note that if Rule 506 is used, one wouldn't use Section 25102(f) because the state is preempted. When using Section 25102(f), there is no required disclosure document other than that necessary to avoid fraud charges: the classic use of a PPM and a one page reporting form must be filed with the commissioner with a modest (maximum $300) fee.

2.4 Mixture: 25102(n)

This Section allows a modest form of advertising (a "general announcement") for a private placement in California only. It is an innovative step in the right direction. Sales can be made to "qualified" investors only. It has not been very successful in attracting "angel" money. This is an extremely complicated code section.

NASAA and the SEC are pushing all states to adopt laws similar to Section 25102(n) in order to allow advertising (the general announcement is like a tombstone ad) for accredited ("qualified") investors. Many other states have adopted "n"-like statutes with its use restricted to sales to accredited investors, rather than the California "qualified" allowance.

3. PUBLIC OFFERINGS

3.1 Rule 504: $1 Million Maximum

Rule 504 is discussed above. It is a federal safe harbor for public and private offerings up to $1 million. Nothing is filed with the SEC other than a Reg. D form (a simple form showing sales). Rule 504 is much misunderstood: It is simply no federal jurisdiction. Note that the SEC is proposing to declare securities issued pursuant to Rule 504 to be "restricted" under Rule 144.

3.2 SCOR Offerings

SCOR represents an abdication by the SEC [pursuant to section 3(b) of the '33 Act and Rule 504], to the states of jurisdiction over public or private offerings of $1 million or less. California and the 49 other states have SCOR statutes for public offerings. The Form U-7 adopted by NASAA is the required disclosure document. The "new" form has 124 questions, whereas the "old" form has 50 questions. In both instances, all questions must be answered. The states vary as to which form to use. California has accepted both. The U-7 form is not investor friendly. Its emphasis is "legal" rather than financial. Note that it was written by lawyers, not MBAs. This is a public offering, and advertising (approved) is permitted.

In addition, the federal rule provides that securities sold pursuant to SCOR are not "restricted." They may be traded. However, this is a serious trap because some states, particularly California, may well place restrictions on transfers (see Section 6.2 "Non-issuer Secondary Trading" below), and finding a "market" (buyers and sellers) may be difficult, if not almost impossible. There is a move to have Internet markets established so that sellers and buyers can "meet on the Internet." Companies may establish their "matching" service for owners of the company's stock; that is, matching buyers and sellers.

In California, filing with the Commissioner of Corporations is required; there is "merit review." Process time varies from two weeks to six months depending on the reviewer and the quality of the applicant and the application.

3.2.1 California SCOR: Public Offering

Used up to $1 million. Suitability is usually imposed and so is a required minimum amount before funds can be used. Price of stock must be $2 or more. Use of U-7 as a part of the application and as the disclosure document is mandatory. Audited financials are usually required if over $500,000 is being sold. "Reviewed" financials are allowed of up to $500,000. A majority of the board must sign off on the application.

SCOR is used for direct public offerings (DPOs) in many cases. The success rate of DPOs is limited. Only a minority of offerors have been able to raise the minimum requirement for funds. However, issuers with an "affinity group" have met with the most success, for example, catalog companies.

Stock issued pursuant to the SCOR offering is technically tradable, but see Section 6.2 "Non-Issuer Secondary Trading" below.

The state filing fee is $2,500 (up to $3,500 if review has complications). SCOR is not available to out-of-state corporations (unless subject to state jurisdiction under Section 2115 of the Corporations Code), blind pools, oil and gas companies, investment companies, and companies reporting to the SEC. Out-of-state corporations can use Corporate Code Section 25113(b)(1), which adheres to the same requirements and benefits that SCOR provides.

Legal fees in a SCOR offering can vary from a low of $10,000 to up to $30,000 or more in a complex application. Average is probably around $15,000 to $20,000. Again, the legal fees depend on the quality of the client's answers to the 50 or 124 questions in the Form U-7. There is no review by the SEC, but California and the other states do review.

3.3 Small Business Rules: Suitability

In the public offering arena, the California Small Business Suitability Rules are important because they give a break to small businesses. By Rule 260.001(i). the commissioner defines a "small business issuer" as an entity having annual revenues of less than $12.5 million and is a California corporation or a foreign (from another state) corporation subject to certain tests of "doing business" (average property factor, payroll factor, and sales factor of 25 percent in California, with payroll having to be 50 percent Californian, and have at least 25 percent of its shareholders in California).

If the entity is a small business and the sale of securities is $5 million or less, and the offering price is at least $2 per share, the suitability standards, subject to certain other criteria, for the investors are:

$50,000 income
$75,000 net worth (excluding home, auto and furnishings) or
$150,000 net worth (same exclusions)

provided that $2,500 of stock can be sold to any investor. This rule and its $2,500 loophole are not available to companies reporting to the SEC (10Ks,10Qs, etc.).

The $2,500 exemption is important to SCOR offerings in particular. The average purchase in a SCOR offering is around $1,600, so the exemption fits.

3.4 Regulation A: Public, $5 Million Maximum

The Disclosure Document is either a U-7 or a conventional offering circular. The latter is similar to a full prospectus. Some clients prefer the offering circular, even though it is usually a bit more expensive (legal), as it is a decidedly better selling document than the U-7.

Regulation A itself (the federal rule) does not require audited financials. California requires audited financials for an offering without "suitability" standards, known as an "open permit." In some instances, as long as there is sufficiently high suitability, audited financials are not required. Audited financials are strongly recommended for two reasons: better reception by the regulators and better reception by investors. Filing with the SEC is now done in Washington. Paper filing is still permitted.

SEC filing fees for Reg. A offerings have been eliminated by Congress. California has a maximum fee of $2,500. Most states handle Reg. A offerings by coordination, that is, if OK with the feds, OK with the state. California's commissioner can handle by coordination but is not required to do so and usually does not.

A Reg. A, due to the very heavy SEC review and the required precision of offering detail for full disclosure, involves legal fees of $35,000 to $75,000. Expect as much as twice that from large firms. This does not include filing fees and blue sky clearing. Blue sky work done by lawyers usually runs about $2,500 per state (includes filing fees).

Regulation A should return to "fashion" because using it does not result in being a reporting company subject to the rather onerous provisions of the Sarbanes-Oxley Act.

3.5 SB-2: Public, No Maximum

SB-2 is the federal form for public offerings and sales of securities of any amount. It is available to companies that have no more than $25 million in sales or $25 million in publicly held stock float. It is reviewed in Washington and must be filed electronically (EDGAR). The filing fee is rather modest and is scaled on the basis of the amount of the offering.

This is a full-blown registration and involves a detailed prospectus. The issuer becomes a "reporting company" by use of the SB-2 qualification. For this reason, many issuers will not use this route because they wish to avoid being subject to the Sarbanes-Oxley Act.

A registration using SB-2 usually involves an underwriter or investment banker because DPOs over $5 million are not easy to make successful. Because an underwriter has counsel (whose fees are paid by the issuing corporation), legal fees for the issuer range from $50,000 to $125,000, and the underwriter's counsel fees are about the same. It is clear then that, in the event there is no underwriter, an SB-2 makes sense only when the issuer wishes to be a reporting company or is assured of being able to raise the targeted amount of money.

Clearance in California and any state in which offers/sales are made is also required. (As noted, this is blue skying.) This stock is registered and therefore not "restricted."

3.6 S-1: Public, No Maximum

This is the granddaddy of all offerings. It is expensive and is usually used by listed companies or by emerging Silicon Valley IPO companies. Three years of audited financials are required.

4. DISCLOSURE DOCUMENTS

The disclosure document in a private placement is normally called a PPM. The PPMs usually are not subject to review by the regulators. The offering document in a Reg. A offering is called an offering circular. This is reviewed by the SEC in Washington, DC. Most states accept the SEC review, but California normally does its own review. An SB-2 (or S-1) uses a prospectus, which is also reviewed by the SEC in Washington and is reviewed by some states as well, particularly California.

5. INTEGRATION RULES: TIMING

5.1 Problem

This is a complex area. Integration is a curse on small business because it can delay sequential offerings. The problem is best explained by an example: One has a private placement under California Section 25102(f) followed by another private placement. Unless great care is taken to meet the five tests (see below), the two private placements could be integrated, causing the offerings to lose their exempt status because more than 35 nonexcluded investors were involved. This would then require offers of recision to be made to all the private investors.

The safe harbor period under Reg. D is six months between offerings. California more or less follows this rule.

Regulation A, pursuant to Rule 251(c), can be used without the six-month period and also can be followed by a registered offering within six months.

A Section 4(2) and a Rule 506 offering (private) may be followed immediately by a public offering or an intrastate offering [Section 3(a)(11)] within the six-month period [Rule 502(a)]. This is a most important exception.

Suffice it to say that "integration" is a thorny and dangerous area. See the rules below.

5.2 Five Tests

When no specific rule applies, such as Rule 506, there are five tests for integration [Rule 502(a)]. The federal and California rules are similar. The five tests are:

1. Is the new issue part of a single plan of financing?
2. How much time has passed since the offering?
3. Is it the same type of security (common, preferred, notes)?
4. Is the sale for the same general purpose (use of proceeds)?
5. Is the same type of consideration given? Cash or property?

No particular weight is given to any one of the tests by the federal regulators; however, the courts appear to give the difference in security type the most weight.

5.3 Safe Harbor: Regulation D

Regulation D [Rule 502(a)] provides a safe harbor of six months between issues. A Reg. A offering can follow another offering without a time span; however, the amount of $5 million is reduced by any offerings in the prior year [Rule 251(c)].

Rule 506 allows for a public offering right after the termination of a private or public offering. The prior offering under 506 must cease upon filing with the SEC of an application for a public permit.

5.4 California Rules

In the main, California follows the federal rules. The two factors given the most weight are (1) part of a single plan of financing and (2) proceeds used for the same general purpose.

The safe harbor in California is similar to the federal rule (Reg. D) of six months after completion or before start of an offering [Rule 260.102.12(b)].

6. RESTRICTED SECURITIES AND TRADING

6.1 Rule 144

Rule 144 applies to resales by shareholders of stock required by means not involving a registration. The idea is to prevent issuers from selling stock on an exempt basis to a purchaser who then distributes the stock to others. This is held to be an underwriting unless Rule 144 is followed.

The rule prescribes holding periods for stock and makes a distinction between "affiliates" (those who, directly or indirectly, control, or are controlled by, the issuer) and noncontrol persons.

To use the rule, the issuer must either be a reporting company (10Ks, 10Qs, etc.) that is current in its filings or a company that makes publicly available the information required by Rule 15c2-11 (Exchange Act rules). This information covers the basic identity of the issuer, its products, management, financials, and so on.

The rule, if followed, provides a safe harbor for the selling shareholders; that is, the seller will not be an underwriter illegally selling securities.

The holding period under Rule 144, shortened in 1996, is now:

For nonaffiliates:

(A) One year from acquisition from the issuer and/or affiliate one may "dribble" each three months the greater of: up to 1 percent of the amount of stock of the issuer as shown in its most recently published balance sheet; or the average weekly reported volume of trading in the security on all national exchanges and Nasdaq during the two calendar weeks preceding the sale.

(B) After two years one may sell without restriction [Rule 144(k)].

For affiliates:

Same rule as A above; B does not hold.

Rule 144 is very complex—whole volumes are written about it. There are rules and rulings as to the measure of the time period, "tacking" the holding periods, affiliates, and so on. One should not act without consulting an attorney experienced in this field.

6.2 Nonissuer "Secondary" Trading (by a Shareholder Not the Issuer)

A common assumption is that shares issued in a public offering (whether done via SCOR or Reg. A) will be freely tradeable under state and federal law. Although shares issued in these types of offerings are not "restricted" securities under federal law, blue sky laws of various states (most notably California) can limit the ability of shareholders to resell their shares.

When the California Department of Corporations imposes suitability requirements on the investors who buy shares in an offering, the Department almost invariably adds a restriction on the use of broker-dealers for secondary trading of those shares. Essentially, broker-dealers are not allowed to solicit customers to purchase these shares. Instead, these shares may be transferred only under certain limited circumstances, such as:

1. In a private sale to another person.
2. By a broker-dealer in an unsolicited transaction (where the purchaser initiates the contact, not vice versa).
3. Sales taking place in another state where the trade is permitted.

Under recent amendments to federal and California securities laws, many of these restrictions have been eliminated for reporting companies. However, because many companies that sell stock pursuant to public offerings under SCOR or Reg. A are not generally reporting companies (in fact, they cannot be reporting companies if they use SCOR or Reg. A), these restrictions will continue to apply for those companies.

In some cases, the Department of Corporations may place additional limitations on the transfer of shares issued in public offerings as well. Thus, in California, one must not assume that shares issued in a SCOR or Reg. A offering will be freely tradable through the use of broker-dealers; oftentimes they are not.

7. THE INTERNET

7.1 In General

Surprisingly, the regulators, federal and state, do not oppose (they actually encourage) the use of the Internet as a vehicle for the sale of securities.

The reason for their enthusiasm is rather obvious: It is easy to monitor the Internet, certainly easier than the telephone or the mails. This is enforcement made easy. In addition, the regulators appreciate that for the first time there is an inexpensive vehicle that can be used by small and emerging companies to raise capital. The capital "gap" between $250,000 and $5 million may be bridged for the first time by the use of the Internet.

The use of the Internet for selling securities is a cutting-edge issue. Those involved, both private and government, are feeling their way. Direct public offerings (without an underwriter) on the Internet promise to be a very good source of financing for small business.

A brief rundown on how it works would be:

1. The electronic prospectus (U-7, Reg. A Offering Circular, SB-2 Prospectus) must provide the same information as a written prospectus. The "electronic prospectus" is really an ordinary disclosure document usually sent by e-mail to the potential purchaser.
2. If there is a suitability issue, the issuer must question (Offeree Questionnaire) the potential investor to establish suitability prior to accepting any funds.
3. Electronic means (e-mail) may be used to transfer documents. (This saves considerable funds due to lower printing costs.)
4. The issuer must have qualified or have an exemption in the jurisdiction in which the purchaser resides.

In California the Internet can be used in a private placement, subject to strict rules. [See California's Section 25102(n) analysis.] In most states, if the Internet is used, a private placement is not possible.

7.2 The Offer

Traditionally, one was not allowed to offer (let alone sell) in a jurisdiction without qualification or exemption. The Internet, of course, does not respect state or country lines; this means an offer in one state becomes a universal offer. To cope with this, the states are either ignoring the issue or considering the issue or adopting laws and regulations that permit offers without qualification as long as the offer is accompanied by "disclaimer" language that states, in effect, "This is not an offer in any jurisdiction where it has not been qualified. No sale may be made within any state unless pursuant to qualification or an exemption from Qualification." California has accepted the concept of allowing Internet offers that contain the legend or disclaimer just noted.

7.3 Suitability

In the event suitability is imposed by the commissioner, the offeror must obtain a completed offeree questionnaire establishing the investor's suitability prior to accepting any investment funds. Again, this may be done using e-mail to send the questionnaire.

7.4 The Sale

A sale may not be made without qualifying or being exempt in the jurisdiction where the sale is being made.

The Internet, in effect, allows one to "test the waters" by seeing how many inquiries one gets from the Internet exposure. If 50 inquiries come from Texas, one had better qualify to sell in Texas.

Of interest, the purchaser may use a credit card to pay for the his or her security.

8. FEDERAL/STATE

Subject to its abdication in SCOR offerings, the federal government has jurisdiction if any offers (usually ignored) or sales are made in more than one state. The use of the Internet is an example of ignoring offers because one simply says, "This is not an offer in any state where not qualified," and the "offer" becomes a "nonoffer."

For small offerings one usually uses the private placement exemption provided by Section 25102(f) and offers in California (or one's resident state) only.

If more than one state and over $1 million, the federal government asserts jurisdiction. So does each state. One must blue sky (clear) both private and public offerings in each state. A new program, Coordinated Equity Review, promoted by NASAA, involves two lead states handling the clearance for all states. One state coordinates the merit review states and the other state coordinates the full disclosure states.

California has joined. Such review is limited to SB-2 offerings and above. The process eliminates "suitability" in California. Blue skying is laborious and expensive. Caveat: The Coordinated Equity Review process has evolved into an undesirable route because it has resulted in too many restrictions being tagged on by each of the involved states, some of which the issuer may not even wish to be qualified in. Better to blue sky (qualify) only in those key states that appear the most promising for fund raising.

9. THE '40 ACT

The Investment Company Act of 1940 controls mutual funds. If a fund has over 100 owners, it comes under the '40 Act.

The '40 Act is infamous as being extremely restrictive and is one of the primary reasons venture capital is confined to relatively few very wealthy individuals and institutions: a "cartel of capital." The venture capital firms wish to avoid the '40 Act and thus have few investors.

SBICs with more than 100 owners come under the '40 Act. That is the primary reason there are very few (less than ten) publicly owned SBICs in the United States.

Congress, in its last session, passed laws providing for two types of closed-end and single state funds that are exempt from the '40 Act.

The first category is that of economic, business, and industrial development companies. They must be regulated under state law. Eighty percent of the funds must come from persons residing in the state, and only accredited investors may invest (unless the SEC changes the rules, which Congress said it could). Until September 19, 1998, California had a regulatory law that was extremely burdensome. Thanks to the efforts of attorney Lee Petillon with the backing of the California Capital Access Forum, a new law (SB2189) was enacted, which provides a more usable regulatory scheme in

California. This new law should result in California spawning many new business development companies. It is hoped other states will also encourage such activity.

The second category that is exempt from the '40 Act is simply Congress authorizing the SEC to exempt by rule or order closed-end funds that are intrastate in their source of funds with a maximum of $10 million or "such other amount as the SEC may prescribe by rule, regulation or order." There are no prescribed standards as to investors or type of investments. One applies to the SEC for an exemption. This is a promising opening for raising funds to finance small business. It should catch on.

Venture capital funds have successfully dodged the Federal Investment Advisors Act; it appears they do not fall under the state's rules regarding investment advisers. The "blind pool" prohibition rule applies only to public offerings and to Section 25102(n) solicitations.

10. THE USUAL

Usually, in California, a start-up or growing company will utilize Section 25102(f) to raise seed money privately. This is followed by a SCOR or Reg. A offering, keeping the integration rules in mind.

As an alternative, if the entrepreneurs know a number of accredited investors (angels) or are seeking venture capital financing, Rule 506 works well, and it avoids the blue sky issue (other than state fees and a Reg. D filing). Also, Rule 506 avoids the integration problem of a possible six-month wait.

The next stage is either a Reg. A (public up to $5 million) or an SB-2; the latter results in the issuer becoming a reporting company (10Ks, 10Qs, and now Sarbanes-Oxley Act compliance—very expensive).

The question of establishing markets for the stock deserves a separate primer. Suffice it to say there is much misunderstanding regarding market makers, what they do, when, and why. Responsible liquidity does not happen overnight unless there is an investment banker (underwriter) managing the effort.

11. SALES—"AGENTS" (CALIFORNIA)

A question frequently asked is: Who can sell our offering?

If private: Officers and directors can all sell as long as they are not compensated in relation to the sales of securities. Third parties may sell only if they are not compensated.

If public: Unless a licensed broker dealer, an officer or director may sell if not separately compensated for the sale. If separate compensation (officer or director) or third-party "agent," must have a $10,000 bond or post assets with the Commissioner of Corporations. An "agent" is described in Section 25003 of the Corporations Code; the bond requirement is in Section 25216 (Rules Section 260.216.15).

Suggested Reading List

Alarid, W. (1991). Money Sources. Santa Maria, CA: Puma Publishing.

Amis, D. (2001). Winning Angels. New York, NY: Prentice-Hall.

Anderson, J. (2000). Cybervaluation. Washington, DC: Bond & Pecaro.

Benjamin, G. & Margulis, J. (1996). Finding Your Wings: How to Locate Private Investors to Fund Your Venture. New York, NY: John Wiley & Sons.

Benjamin, G. & Margulis, J. (2000). Angel Financing: How to Find and Invest in Private Equity. New York, NY: John Wiley & Sons.

Benjamin, G. & Margulis, J. (2001). Angel Investor's Handbook. How to Profit from Early-Stage Investing. Princeton, NJ: Bloomberg Press.

Bergan, H. (1992). Where the Money Is. Alexandria, VA: BioGuide Press.

Blum, L. (1995). Free Money. New York, NY: John Wiley & Sons.

Broce, T. (1979). Fund Raising. Norman, OK: University of Oklahoma Press.

Burlingame, D. (1991). Taking Fund Raising Seriously. San Francisco, CA: Jossey-Bass.

Camp, J. (2002). Venture Capital Due Diligence. New York, NY: John Wiley & Sons.

Chimerine, L., et al. (1987). Handbook for Raising Capital. Homewood, IL: Business One Irwin.

Coveney, P. (1998). Business Angels. New York, NY: John Wiley & Sons.

Evanson, D. (1998). Where to Go When the Bank Says No. Princeton, NJ: Bloomberg Press.

Field, D. (1991). Take Your Company Public. New York, NY: New York Institute of Finance.

Fisher, D. (1989). Investing in Venture Capital. Charlottesville, VA: Institute of Chartered Financial Analysts.

Henderson, J. (1988). Obtaining Venture Financing. Lexington, MA: Lexington Books.

Gladstone, D. (1988). Venture Capital Investing. Upper Saddle River, NJ: Prentice Hall.

Gupta, U. (2000). Done Deals. Boston, MA: Harvard Business School Press.

Helfert, E. (1991). Techniques of Financial Analysis. Homewood, IL: Business One Irwin.

Hill, B. (2001). Inside Secrets to Venture Capital. New York, NY: John Wiley & Sons.

Hill, B. (2002). Attracting Capital From Angels. New York, NY: John Wiley & Sons.

Holben, C. (1996). California Small Business Access to Equity Capital. Sacramento, CA: Trade and Commerce Agency Report.

Howe, F. (1991). The Board Member's Guide to Fund Raising. San Francisco, CA: Jossey-Bass.

Keely, R. et al. (1998). Business Angels. Boulder, CO: Colorado Capital Alliance.

Kozmetsky, G. (1985). Financing and Managing Fast-Growth Companies. Lexington, MA: Lexington Books.

Kramer, M. (2001). Financing and Building an E-Commerce Venture. Paramus, NJ: Prentice Hall.

Lindsey, J. (1989). Start-Up Money. New York, NY: John Wiley & Sons.

Lindsey, J. (1990) The Entrepreneur's Guide to Capital. Chicago, IL: Probus Publishing.

Lipper, A. (1996). Guide for Venture Investing Angels. Columbia, MO: Missouri Innovation Center.

Lister, K. et al. (1995). Finding Money. New York, NY: John Wiley & Sons.

Long, M. (1998). Raising Capital in the New Economy. San Diego, CA: ProMotion Publishing.

Long, M. (1998). Unlimited Capital. San Diego, CA: ProMotion Publishing.

May, J. (2001). Every Business Needs an Angel. New York, NY: Crown Business.

Merrill, R. (1993). The New Venture Handbook. New York, NY: American Management Association.

Miller, E. et al. (1991). Attracting the Affluent. Naperville, IL: Financial Source Books.

Nicholas, T. (1991). 43 Proven Ways to Raise Capital for Your Small Business. Wilmington, DE: Enterprise Publishing.

Nichols, J. (1994). Pinpointing Affluence. Chicago, IL: Precept Press.

O'Hara, P. (1990). The Total Business Plan. New York, NY: John Wiley & Sons.

Rappaport, S. (1990). The Affluent Investor. New York, NY: New York Institute of Finance.

Reynolds, P. et al. (2002). The Entrepreneur Next Door. Kansas City, MO: Kauffman Foundation.

Rupert, R. (1993). The New Era of Investment Banking. Chicago, IL: Probus Publishing.

Silver, A.D. (1994). The Venture Capital Sourcebook. Chicago, IL: Probus Publishing.

Smith, B. (1984). Raising Seed Money for Your Own Business. Brattleboro, VT: Lewis Publishing.

Soja, T.A. & Reyes M. (1990). Investment Benchmarks. Needham, MA: Venture Economics.

Spencer, M. (1999). Money Hunt. New York, NY: Harper Business.

Stanley, T. (1988). Marketing to the Affluent. Homewood, IL: Business One Irwin.

Stanley, T. (1993). Networking with the Affluent and Their Advisors. Homewood, IL: Business One Irwin.

Thomsett, M. (1990). The Ultimate Guide to Raising Money for Growing Companies. Homewood, IL: Dow-Jones Irwin.

Tuller, L. (1991). When the Bank Says No! New York, NY: Liberty Hall Press.

Tuller, L. (1994). The Complete Handbook of Raising Capital. New York, NY: McGraw-Hill.

Van Osnabrugge, M. et al. (2000). Angel Investing. San Francisco, CA: Jossey-Bass.

Vinturella, J. et al. (2004). Raising Entrepreneurial Capital. Boston, MA: Elsevier.

Webster, M. (1999). Raising Venture Capital for the 21st Century. Bryn Mawr, PA: Buy Books on Web.

Wetzel, W. (1981). Informal Risk Capital in New England. Durham, NH: University of New Hampshire.

Wright, S. (1993). Raising Money in Less Than 30 Days. New York, NY: Citadel Press.

Glossary

Accounts payable   The amount of money owed by a business or service to its creditors.

Accounts receivable   The amount of credit a business or service has extended to its customers.

Accumulated amortization   Accumulated write-off of an intangible asset, such as goodwill or a covenant not to compete.

Antidilution   The action investors must take—having to put in additional money—to maintain the percentage of ownership they had when they first invested in the deal.

Acquisition   Occurs when one company takes a controlling interest in another company.

Angel investor   Although the term is of fairly recent vintage, historically, the concept involves wealthy civic-minded individuals who contributed in various ways to the *polis*; today, wealthy individuals who invest in seed or early-stage companies.

Automatic conversion   Accomplished at the time of underwriting rather than at the time of an IPO; occurs when an investor's priority shares are immediately converted to ordinary shares.

Barter   In lieu of cash payments, products or services themselves are exchanged.

Blue sky   State laws that control sales of investment securities.

Board   A corporation's board of directors; persons who for the good of a corporation's shareholders follow—or refuse to follow—the recommendations of management.

Board rights   Allow an investor to become a member of a company's board of directors.

Boilerplate   Standard wording in standard paragraphs contained in business documents.

Break even   The point at which money earned from a business equals the money invested.

Bridge financing   A venture that requires short-term capital to reach stability and the next round of funding.

Burn rate   The rate at which cash is flowing out of the business on a monthly basis.

Business angel   Private individuals who often add more than money—their knowledge and experience—to companies they invest in.

Buyback   The exit route whereby the investor expects to cash out by selling securities back to the founders.

Buyout   Investors, management, employees, or any other company personnel buy shares in the company in order to buy or retain ownership.

Capital gains   The profit derived from selling a capital asset.

Capital loss   The loss incurred from selling a capital asset.

Cash flow   The money that comes in and goes out of a business; determines the continued survival of a company; tied closely to cash management.

Collateral   Assets used to guarantee payment to a creditor for money lent.

Common stock   Refers to a class of stock issued most often, secondary to preferred stock.

Consortium   An association of companies for a like purpose.

Controllability   A specific individual who owns enough equity in a company to control the decisions of the management.

Convertible   Bonds that can be exchanged for stock at some previously set rate; convertibles can be a source of cash for a company under financial pressure.

Current ratio   Current assets divided by current liabilities—appears on a balance sheet; specifies a company's liquidity, that is, its ability to meet its short-term obligations; often helps determine credit rating.

Deal flow   The number of transactions an investor is able to peruse that may be worth further consideration.

Debenture   A corporate bond not backed by a specific asset but by the issuer's credit.

Debt to equity ratio   Long-term liabilities divided by net worth—measures debt financing to equity financing, that is, the degree to which a company is leveraged.

Default   Failure of a borrower to repay a lender in full; when a provision in a written agreement with an investor is violated by an entrepreneur.

Dilution   Occurs when additional stock is issued, thereby reducing the percentage of ownership of those who already own stock.

Discount rate   Face value—discount charge; what banks and other lending institutions charge for money loaned.

Downside   Equates with the amount of risk taken by an investor in an enterprise.

Due diligence   The *sine qua non* by the investor of the entrepreneur and by the entrepreneur of the investor on every aspect of the other party's history, character, and dealings past and present—and of the soundness of the pending deal. Due diligence has no substitute.

EBIT   Earnings before interest and taxes, what the company has earned before having to pay interest and taxes.

Entrepreneur   Dreamer extraordinaire who initiates the risk in time and money of bringing to profitable fruition his product or service.

Equity   The amount of equity is the amount of ownership someone has in a company.

Exit   The strategy by which investors realize the returns or otherwise free themselves from involvement in a transaction.

Fully diluted ownership   When a company issues all of its shares, their dilutive impact can be measured.

Gross margin percentage   Gross profit divided by sales.

Gross margin ratio   Gross profit divided by net sales—assesses the efficiency in cost and pricing strategy.

Holding period   How long an investor's investment remains illiquid.

Hurdle   In the investor's judgment, the point at which anticipated compensation exceeds risk in an investment.

Income statement   Also known as a profit and loss statement, a report that summarizes a company's income and costs for a specific time period.

Initial public offering (IPO)   A company's attempt to sustain growth by raising money on an exchange, such as the New York Stock Exchange.

Intellectual property   The ideas on which a company has been built, and upon which it becomes discernible from other companies. Such property receives only limited protection from patents, trademarks, and the like.

Internal rate of return (IRR)   Also called the "time-adjusted rate of return" and the "dollar-weighted rate of return"; the rate of interest that equates the value of cash inflows with the value of cash outflows.

Inventory turnover   Costs of sales divided by average inventory—specifies the company's average inventory cycle, that is, how many times a company's inventory is sold and replenished within a set time.

Investee firm   The firm into which investors have invested their money and the added value of their knowledge, expertise, and experience.

Investment   The purchase of shares of stocks, bonds, and so on, with the expectation of income or capital gains.

Junior securities   Upon liquidation, a firm's investors holding junior securities will not have their claims considered until after the claims of those holding senior securities have been met.

Lead investor   The one investor who takes the lead in inducting other investors into a venture.

Leveraged buyout (LBO)   One kind of transaction in the range of private equity class of investments. A group of investors—usually including management—acquires the stock/assets of the company largely through debt financing.

Liquidation   Going out of business; when creditors (this event would include shareholders) take over the assets of a company.

Liquidation preferences   Allows investors on their own to liquidate the company.

Liquidity   Determined by a company's ability to convert its assets to cash.

Living dead   Financial purgatory, when an investor is stuck in a venture with little or no liquidity.

Merger   Joining of at least two companies.

Mezzanine   A venture that has increasing sales volume and is breaking even or is profitable; additional funds are to be used for further expansion, marketing, or working capital.

Multipliers   Increases the assets in dollars an entity supports with capital in dollars.

Net present value   The expected value of a future cash flow discounted to present time using a discount factor proportionate with the risk of the venture's projections.

Options   Seen as a hedge by some and a risk by others, the right given to the investor to buy or sell stock in the future at a preset price.

Payback period   How many years it takes for an investor to recoup an initial capital investment.

Piggyback   Occurs when more than one lender is involved in the same loan.

Postmoney valuation   Measured by the valuation of a company after the investment has been made.

Preferred stock   A class of stocks that takes precedence over common stock in matters of payment of dividends or in liquidation.

Premoney valuation   The valuation of a company before investments in it have been made.

Prepaid expenses   The money that covers expenses incurred in advance, that is, before they are used; involves rent, for example, or insurance.

Price-earnings (P/E) ratio (or multiple)   The relationship between the current market share price of a stock to its earnings; used to determine a share's fair price.

Pricing   The cost a company sets for the customer or client for its product or service.

Private placement   The investment in companies not traded on public exchanges.

Profit margin percentage   Measures the percentage of sales dollars that results in net income.

Public offering The extremely complicated act (having to run the labyrinth of SEC regulations) of "going public"; usually used to sustain a company's expansion.

Rate of return After adjustment for inflation, the return realized annually on an investment.

Receivables turnover Year-end accounts receivable credit sales divided, in turn, by the number of days in the year; used to measure collection problems.

Redeemable shares Shares that a company can repurchase in the future for an agreed-upon price.

Representations What the entrepreneur vouches to an investor is true about the venture.

Restricted stock Stocks that an investor can purchase directly from a company.

Return on equity ratio Net income divided by total shareholder equity; used to measure the company's and the management's effectiveness.

Return on investment (ROI) The amount of return plus the time an investor deems acceptable in realizing that return on the investment; evaluates the efficiency of the company.

Screening The process by which investors weed out the deals that fail to meet their criteria as they look for those they consider worthy of further investigation.

Second-round financing The round of financing that follows the initial or start-up round.

Seed stage A venture at great risk because it is in the idea stage or just in the process of being organized.

Staging Rather than having an investor hand over the entire investment in the beginning, he or she invests in increments as specified milestones are met by the entrepreneur.

Start-up stage A venture at high risk because it is just completing product development and initial marketing, and has been in business less than two years.

Structure The way in which a company will accomplish its financing.

Structure planning The act of defining what the entrepreneurs and investors want to accomplish by the most efficient and profitable means.

Sweat equity The time and effort entrepreneurs have previously invested in building a venture.

Syndication A major hedging strategy by which individual investors act jointly to form a group and pool the money they invest in a deal, thereby ameliorating financial risk.

Third-round financing   Follows the second-round of financing for a start-up.

Treasury stock   Repurchased stock previously owned by shareholders and now held in the company's treasury.

Turnaround   A venture that is in need of capital to effect a change from unprofitability to profitability.

Upside   The potential and often anticipated amount of money investors think they can make on a particular deal.

Valuation   An investor's assessment of the viability and financeability of a venture.

Venture capital   The money raised from investors for equity in early-stage, as-yet-unproven enterprises.

Warrants   A "right" owned by an investor; a guarantee bought by investors when they think a stock will rise; allow investors to buy stock during a fixed period at a fixed price.

Warranty   A guarantee, implied or stated in writing, that what an entrepreneur tells an investor about a product or service is true.

Working capital   Current assets minus current liabilities equals working capital—an accounting term; the net assets that are used to continue the company's operations.

Workout   A company's rather urgent need for getting itself out of financial difficulty through an additional round of financing, reorganization, or possibly both.

About the Authors

Gerald A. Benjamin, M.S., Senior Managing Partner of International Capital Resources (ICR), is recognized by entrepreneurs, investors, and financial intermediaries as one of the nation's leading authorities on the business angel capital market. He published the first angel investor magazine in 1992, and spearheaded the venture conference movement in California, founding the Northern California Venture Forum in 1989. With his co-author Joel Margulis, he has published seven books on angel capital, including *Finding Your Wings: How to Locate Private Investors to Fund Your Venture*; *Angel Financing: How to Find and Invest in Private Equity*; *The Angel Investor's Handbook: How to Profit from Early-Stage Investing* (United States and India); *Raising Finance* (United Kingdom); *Angel Finance* (Japan); and *Angel Finance* (China). More than 50,000 entrepreneurs and investors have attended Mr. Benjamin's seminar "Angel Financing: How to Raise Private Equity for the Early-Stage Venture," which has been sponsored by more than 200 prominent entrepreneurial and investor organizations in the United States. He has developed one of the largest databases of high-net-worth, early-stage, private equity or business angel investors in North America, with over 1,359 accredited investors participating. His research on the investment orientation, preferences, and habits of North American investors has been recognized in such publications as *The Wall Street Journal, Time, Barrons, Investors Business Daily, Individual Investor, Venture Capital Journal, Financial Times of London, Medical Economics, San Jose Mercury News, Investment Advisor Journal,* and *Inc. Magazine*. Before founding ICR, Mr. Benjamin served as an entrepreneurial finance and private investment banking advisor to more than 400 companies in the United States, Canada, Mexico, South America, Europe, and the Middle East. He received his M.S. and B.A. degrees in business from the University of San Francisco.

Joel Margulis has a B.A. in history and M.A. in English from the University of Missouri, Columbia. He is the author and co-author of a number of books covering a range of subjects. He teaches in the English Department at San Francisco State University and lives in Mill Valley, California.

Index